The Political Theology of Schelling

New Perspectives in Ontology
Series Editors: Peter Gratton and Sean J. McGrath, Memorial University of Newfoundland, Canada

Publishes the best new work on the nature of being

After the fundamental modesty of much post-Heideggerian Continental philosophy, the time is now for a renaissance in ontology after the rise of the new realisms and new materialisms. This new series aims to be an interdisciplinary forum for this work, challenging old divisions while borrowing from the ontological frameworks of post-humanism, ecological studies, critical animal studies, and other post-constructivist areas of endeavour. While often working within the Continental tradition, the books in this series will move beyond the stale hermeneutics and phenomenologies of the past, with authors boldly reopening the oldest questions of existence through a contemporary lens.

Editorial Advisory Board
Thomas J. J. Altizer, State University of New York at Stony Brook
Maurizio Farraris, University of Turin
Paul Franks, Yale University
Iain Hamilton Grant, University of the West of England
Garth Green, McGill University
Adrian Johnston, University of New Mexico
Catherine Malabou, Kingston University
Jeff Malpas, University of Tasmania
Marie-Eve Morin, University of Alberta
Jeffrey Reid, University of Ottawa
Susan Ruddick, University of Toronto
Michael Schulz, University of Bonn
Hasana Sharp, McGill University
Alison Stone, Lancaster University
Peter Trawny, University of Wuppertal
Uwe Voigt, University of Augsburg
Jason Wirth, Seattle University
Günter Zöller, University of Munich

Books available
The Political Theology of Schelling by Saitya Brata Das

Forthcoming books
Without Hope: An Ontology of Nihilism by Paul J. Ennis
The Ecstasy of Reason: The Political Theology of the Later Schelling by Sean J. McGrath

The Political Theology of Schelling

SAITYA BRATA DAS

EDINBURGH
University Press

Edinburgh University Press is one of the leading university presses in the UK. We publish academic books and journals in our selected subject areas across the humanities and social sciences, combining cutting-edge scholarship with high editorial and production values to produce academic works of lasting importance. For more information visit our website: edinburghuniversitypress.com

© Saitya Brata Das, 2016

Edinburgh University Press Ltd
The Tun – Holyrood Road
12(2f) Jackson's Entry
Edinburgh EH8 8PJ

Typeset in 11/13 Adobe Garamond by
Servis Filmsetting Ltd, Stockport, Cheshire

A CIP record for this book is available from the British Library

ISBN 978 1 4744 1690 0 (hardback)
ISBN 978 1 4744 1691 7 (webready PDF)
ISBN 978 1 4744 1692 4 (epub)

The right of Saitya Brata Das to be identified as the author of this work has been asserted in accordance with the Copyright, Designs and Patents Act 1988, and the Copyright and Related Rights Regulations 2003 (SI No. 2498).

Contents

Acknowledgements	vi
Preface: The Exit and the Event *by Gérard Bensussan*	vii
Introduction	1
1 Actuality Without Potentiality	41
2 The Rhythm of History	90
3 The Beatific Life	132
4 The Irreducible Remainder	158
5 The Non-Sovereign Exception	182
6 The Tragic Dissonance	211
Bibliography	245
Names Index	250
Subject Index	252

Acknowledgements

I must seize this occasion to express my gratitude to Gérard Bensussan who first introduced me to Schelling. This work is a humble attempt to fulfil the promise made to him some ten years back. The manuscript greatly benefited from conversations with Sean McGrath, Jason Wirth, Clayton Crockett and Emmanuel Cattin. I specially thank Sean for taking an interest in the publication of this work. Kyla Bruff and Sharad Bhaviskar each independently translated the French text of the Preface into English. A grant from my University, under the UPE-II scheme, helped me in collecting research materials for the book. The editorial team at the Edinburgh University Press – Carol Macdonald, Ersev Ersoy, Tim Clark, Rebecca Mackenzie and James Dale – made the publication of the book an unforgettable experience for me.

I don't know how best to thank Sarita and Mrinmay, who have to put up with my countless sleepless nights and who have taught me, no less than Schelling, the mystery of love.

Versions of Chapters 1, 2 and 3 have been published earlier. I would like to thank the journals for permitting me to reproduce the articles here:

1. 'The Irreducible Remainder', published as 'The Irreducible Remainder: Towards the Idea of a Finite Politics' in *Journal for Cultural Research* 16:4 (2012), pp. 418–42.
2. 'The Non-Sovereign Exception', published as 'Schelling: Religion and Politics' in *Politics and Religion* (Delhi: Aakar Books, 2014), pp. 54–96.
3. 'The Tragic Dissonance', published as 'The Tragic Dissonance' in *Analecta Hermeneutica* 5 (International Institute for Hermeneutics, 2013).

Preface:
The Exit and the Event

The work of Satya Das inscribes itself in a profound trend in contemporary Schelling studies. It effectively demonstrates, in its own way, a necessary and sustained attention dedicated to that which, in the history of 'metaphysics' (understood in a broad sense, and not simply according to the Heideggerian tradition), Schelling has created, opened, underlined and inaugurated in an inchoate manner, and to that which, unevenly and differentially, entire currents of contemporary philosophy – including even its most prestigious names – have received, continued, and taken up anew, more or less faithfully, after him. The considerations and content of this 'Protean Schelling', as denoted by the author, and his 'posterity' were examined during the 2013 Strasbourg colloquium.

Inscribed in that which I just called a singular 'attention' devoted to a certain Schellingian heritage, Das' book particularly concentrates on bringing into focus a particular line of heirs, from Kierkegaard to Heidegger, passing notably through Bloch, Rosenzweig and even Benjamin.

As such, this work focuses in a pronounced manner on what is identified in Schelling's work as a fundamental, living *eschatological tension*. It analyses instantiations and figures of this tension in the structural opening of the world to an irrevocable *exteriority* without sublation, to an irreducible and immemorial transcendence through which history and politics can be grasped in their very finitude – and where Schelling sees, not without paradox, a more arduous, and in any case, a more enigmatic problem other than that of the Absolute. This political eschatology, which entails the movement of Schellingian positive philosophy itself, leads, and this is the central thesis of this book, to a work of defection, destruction or deconstruction, according to the author's word, of any political theology founded on sovereignty. It is precisely the question of history and of the structures of historicity that is taken up by Schelling's late philosophy, and perhaps even by the entirety of his thought, indeed since its beginnings, after the secularised theodicy proposed by the Hegelian ontology of history.

The deconstructive eschatology that this work outlines and analyses in Schellingian philosophy, and its opening in the domain of the 'political theology' of history (which would be that of the author of the *Investigations into the Essence of Human Freedom*), is developed, it seems to me, around the two central themes put forth here: the event and the exit.

The event in Schelling is said to be 'actuality without potentiality', which is the title of the second chapter of this book. The proposed reading here consists in observing within it the double, or the other side, of an 'exception without sovereignty', by which it is very well understood how eschatology – which must be distinguished from messianism – arises from the exteriority where 'political theology' (outlined by Das) happens, and which is also the promise of a 'beatified life' for which the *Clara* dialogue opens the horizon.

The exit of philosophy, outside of itself and by itself in a certain way, on which I myself have written – by effectively embarking on a departure from Marx towards a continent other than that of speculative German Idealism – is descriptively taken up by Das in its impetus and dynamic to show that it corresponds, all things being equal, as we say, to Schellingian 'eschatology' in so far as it takes place in a destructive or deconstructive gesture: that of the *ecstasy* in the late philosophy: *ecstasy* as *exodus*. If one were to maintain the comparison with the Marxist gesture, it would be necessary – as should be done and which Das indeed does well at the end of his book – to show the *tragic* overcharge of *the exit* as *the event* in Schelling. There is no hesitation here in taking recourse to the notion of the *caesura* of the Speculative of the late Lacoue-Labarthe, once my colleague here in Strasbourg. Das' demonstration transforms it into a singular usage that allows him – and this is a fruitful hypothesis – to make the caesura itself the hallmark of Schellingian thought, notably, but not exclusively, the complex and difficult caesura proposed in Schelling's late philosophy between negative philosophy and positive philosophy.

By impressively weaving these interdependent and inter-implicated figures of the exit and the event in such a manner, by deploying the most undulating and subtle harmonies, Das' analysis demonstrates very opportunely, if indeed there is still a need to do so, that reading Schelling today can provide a decisive key to the intelligibility of many of the major currents of twentieth-century philosophy – and furthermore that it is absolutely impossible to ignore, regardless of the different envisaged modalities of reading put forth, the key proposed here, along with others. Schelling is indeed, as the author says, 'our real contemporary'.

Gérard Bensussan, Strasbourg, July 2015
Translated by Kyla Bruff

For my beloved father

> The opposite is itself precisely what is nearest. Deserts, mountains, distant lands, and seas can separate us from a friend in this life; the distance between this life and the other is no greater than that between night and day or vice versa. A heartfelt thought, together with our complete withdrawal from anything external, transfers us into that other world, and perhaps this other world becomes all the more hidden from us, the nearer to us it is.
>
> Schelling, *Clara*

Introduction

Epochal closure of metaphysics

Let us begin with the following hypothesis: in the epochal condition of modernity, the discourse of Occidental metaphysics names being as *potentiality* and grasps this potentiality of being as Subject. In itself, it is barely a new thesis – the thesis that the principle (*arché*) of the Subject is the legitimising principle of the *hegemonikon* called 'modernity'. In his posthumously published book *Broken Hegemonies* (2003), written with such elegance and sophistication combined with a rare originality, Reiner Schürmann draws our attention to the tragic denial that gives rise to hegemonies, showing us how each hegemony, founded upon such an *arché*, is destined to its possible destitution when the *arché* is deprived of its power to elicit from us 'normative obligations'. Hegemony expires when its principle of ground becomes impoverished. The legitimising principle of a hegemonic epoch, so it appears, acts like a 'foundation' or 'ground' – the 'why' – of every hegemonic regime and determines each mode of being in the context of constituted phenomenality. Deconstruction at the epochal closure of metaphysics amounts to making manifest the fragility, the precariousness or the destitution of the ultimate *arché* of hegemonies and to showing, beneath the tragic denial, the irreducible *differend* that calls forth incommensurable traits to their *belonging*-together, to the event of their disjointure without subsuming them, by a dialectical cunning of Reason within an overarching totality.[1]

Deconstruction in this phenomenological mode (a phenomenological deconstruction) manifests itself here less as method than as tragic task, which is that of manifesting the *differend* that lies as the 'undertow' of each hegemonic regime, as that which would destitute each hegemonic regime in turn from within. And a peculiar phenomenology it is, which is neither a phenomenology with noetic-noematic coincidence nor one of grasping a phenomenon within the context of constituted phenomenality. It is rather a phenomenology that manifests the limit of the constituted order and that – in order to display the *para-doxa*, the tragic that eludes (precisely at the instance it is repressed) the maximising thrust of language – opens up, once again and infinitely, the possibility of the 'singularity to come'. Schürmann names these two incommensurable traits in their tragic *belonging*-together as natality and mortality, as the undeniable law of the universal and the withdrawal to the other, as traits that singularise us by de-phenomenalising the constituted order of signification: their *differend* renders inoperative the dialectical operation of converting difference into antagonism and then of further subsuming the antagonistic forces into the principle of identity (where identity is thought metaphysically, namely, as belonging-*together*). The thought here is one of broken hegemonies, hegemonies rendered into a fragile operation destined to its own worklessness and deprived of its ultimate principle of ground. If a hegemony (any *hegemonikon*), as constituted order of signification, is constituted by this 'nomothetic operation' (by subsuming singularity into the particular and further subsuming the particular under the law of *Koinon*), such hegemony withers away when the tragic (the disparate in their *belonging*-together) peers through 'the maximising thrust of the universal' and undoes the order of constituted phenomenality. Such phenomenology is, thus, a tragic phenomenology: a true phenomenology is not the nomothetic operation of subsuming singularity into the constituted order of signification, but requires being faithful to *the event of phenomenality* itself, which demands that we leave the phenomenon to itself so that it comes to itself. Such tragic thinking is thinking of singularity; it is the most ordinary thinking that is at once most painful to think, close to us in the way that death is to life in their very incommensurability; its task is to venture thinking the withering away of hegemonies and of our tragic existence in the absence of *arché*, released from the ban of the law which the constituted order violently imposes upon existence. Schürmann names such tragic thinking 'anarchic', a name bearing the risk of covering up what is new in it. He takes this risk which implies a task: a unique task, singular to the instance when the question is that of thinking a new beginning at this epochal closure of metaphysics.

Let us return to the hypothesis with which we begun: in the epochal condition of modernity, the Occidental metaphysics names the potentiality of being as Subject. We rightly suspect another hypothesis already presupposed here, namely that Occidental metaphysics understands being as potentiality and that this is yet to be shown, explained and demonstrated.

Being is understood in its infinite capacity *to be* (being understood in the infinitude of its verbality: 'to be'). The *hegemonikon* of modernity has in its fold its legitimising *arché* ('principle', but also 'beginning' or 'origin') in this self-understanding of being as potentiality: being grasped as potentiality, being grasping itself as potentiality, is the potentiality for self-presence. Being presents itself as potentiality; or, it is the potentiality of being to present itself as presence. Being, grasping itself in the immanence of its self-presence, *phenomenalises* itself as this presence and in its presence. On its fundamental ground, the task of phenomenology – according to the view presented above – is ontological at the same time: its task is to subsume phenomena within the constituted order of signification whose validity or legitimacy lies in an ultimate *arché*, in the law of all laws that does not need any other condition for its existence.

For some time now, we have been speaking of this phenomenality of being of presence, of the self-presentation of being, as a 'metaphysics of presence'. The potentiality, the capacity or the power of being (the capacity to be), lies in the immanence of its self-presence; from the ground of its presence (or, from the self-presence of its ground), being would assert its sovereignty, its sheer capacity to be. From this understanding of *being as potentiality* there can then be deduced a plethora of its attributes and predicates: being is 'existence'; it is an 'actuality' (an act, an acting) or a 'reality' (that has its ontological ground in itself). The actuality of existence would then be derived from the potentiality of being, for actuality would be no more than its potentiality: actuality would rather be thought as the privation of potentiality or as its attenuated variation. The source of the sovereignty of being would, then, lie in this infinite 'capacity to be', in this virile possibility to be which is its own, its very own possibility for self-presence. In its epochal condition that is modernity, metaphysics calls this being as potentiality by the name 'Subject'. The Subject, being as potentiality, is the ultimate *arché* of the modern *hegemonikon*; understood thus, it serves as the principle of legitimacy of the hegemonic discourse of modernity. This comes to pass in its most extreme possibility in Hegel's onto-theological constitution of metaphysics (Heidegger 2002). In its extreme realisation of its possibilities, Occidental metaphysics calls the potentiality of being by the name of 'actuality', precisely thereby excluding *actuality* in its very inclusion; in the very grasping of actuality, in the violence of its grasp (for there is always violence in 'grasping'), in the name of potentiality, actuality remains unthinkable in metaphysics.

Our thoughtful consideration of the mortality (or 'destitution') of the principle (*arché*) of ground, on which hegemonies erect their edifice, is opened in the space exposed by Martin Heidegger's deconstruction of the metaphysics of presence. In so many different ways, Reiner Schürmann too expresses his indebtedness to the Heideggerian deconstruction of metaphysics, which is not the simple destitution of a specific *hegemonikon*, but a *diremption* of *hegemonikon* as such. Heidegger's *step back* from the onto-theological constitution of metaphysics is a gesture of thinking being as event, which is a double bind (*Ereignis* and *Enteignis:* the event of appropriation and the event of dispropriation) that in its abyss (*Abgrund*) opens up the question of origin (*Ürsprung*) again. This is possible when an epoch of metaphysics becomes visible as *epochal*, that is 'regional, dated, finite and finished' in both senses of the word: complete as well as terminated' (Schürmann 1986: 5). Heidegger's abandonment (*Gelassenheit*), following Meister Eckhart's *Gelazenheit*, is the gesture of withdrawal from the metaphysical determination of being as potentiality; it is a withdrawal from metaphysics at the instance when metaphysics manifests itself as *epochal* in all its technological domination and in its disposal of all beings to calculability and to sovereign mastery. When the principle (*arché*) withers away, a new inauguration is in sight. For Heidegger, such inauguration is announced and *beckoned* toward in poeticising and thinking, in two different ways in their neighbourhoods, outside of metaphysics. Abandonment is the unthought of metaphysics: being abandoned by metaphysics, and abandoning metaphysics to its own provenance, mortals are kept open to the other beginning *to come* out of the extremity of the future; in other words, abandonment opens us to the event of the pure future *to come*.

This eschatological event of the holy (*das Heilige*) cannot be determined onto-theologically, that is, on the basis of being as potentiality. Exposed open to the event of *eschaton*, being no longer manifests itself as potentiality. This non-being-able-to-be or this non-potency is not the result of the processual movement of potentiality, and, thus, is never dependent on potentiality; it is the beginning or origin (*Ürsprung*) *to come* out of the future where the beginning and end come to a 'monstrous coupling' (Hölderlin 1988b) out of an essential (dis)jointure of the event. At the epochal closure of metaphysics, thinking and poeticising *abandon* the metaphysical *En-Framing* (*Gestell*) of which technological domination is only the most extreme manifestation (Heidegger 1977). Out of this abandonment, the possibility of thinking 'constellation' arises anew, no longer in terms of belonging-*together* (metaphysics) but as *belonging*-together (the unthought of the event). In abandonment (*Gelassenheit*) the ultimate *arché* of the modern hegemony – the sovereignty of the Subject – is abandoned, without any restitution of a new principle in turn: now it is a question of no hegemony at all, an *anarché* without the law. In abandonment, the potentialities of being as presence expire. Deprived of its legitimising principle, the unthought of metaphysics – that is, *actuality without potentiality* – manifests itself as an excess out of the emptying out (*kenosis*) of being's potentialities, which is not a result arising from potentiality but is an immemorial origin, an actuality before any memory and before any memorial, the event that is the future anterior.

It is in this space opened up by the deconstruction of metaphysics – metaphysics that understands being in its potentiality for presence – that the exigency of thinking *actuality without potentiality* may at all be possible. The following pages attempt to test two hypotheses in their innermost proximity: 1) that in the works of the nineteenth-century philosopher Schelling, such an attempt to think *actuality without potentiality* announces itself in a singular manner, in a style that has remained unique for the time to come. Schelling thereby finds himself at the limit of metaphysics that opens indefinitely to an excess that can't be included within the fold of metaphysics; this limit, in turn, cannot be understood to be a mere exhaustion of the utmost possibilities of Occidental metaphysics. It thereby hints at another beginning that will break away from the long Occidental history of the thought of being as potentiality. 2) Such an attempt to think *actuality without potentiality* enables Schelling to conceive of a political eschatology that puts into question the attempt of any sovereignty in the worldly order to claim ultimate 'normative obligation' from us.

For Schelling, as much as for Heidegger and many others to come, this thinking of *actuality without potentiality* is the event of the future anterior, which he develops with increasing intensity from his incomplete magnum opus *The Ages of the World* (*Die Weltalter*) onwards. There, thinking, finite in its freedom (because of its source in a freedom that is groundless) opens to the *taking place* of the event of immemorial origin that is un-thinkable within the metaphysical discourse of potentialities. This immemorial freedom, groundlessly opening existence *to take place*, does not serve as the principle (*arché*) of ground for worldly hegemonies; it is rather the pre-supposition, an immemorial outside which is repressed, whose tragic intensity of *differend* is denied each time a worldly *hegemonikon* seeks legitimacy by an appeal to a theological foundation. It is this denial of *differend* (the *belonging*-together of disparate and incommensurable traits of being – which Schürmann names as 'tragic denial') which is the fundamental operative labour of dialectical thought: who else but Hegel could give such speculative rigour to such tragic denial (which, as we can see, is also the denial of the tragic)? The concept (*Begriff*) – the grasping (*greifen*) of phenomena – is the speculative labour of subsuming phenomena in the context of constituted phenomenality and names constituted phenomenon as 'actuality'. Here the conceptual language, out of its essential ground, functions as the language of potentiality: the power of the concept lies in grasping the phenomenon in the context of constituted phenomenality. The speculative dialectical thought understands this dialectically as the opposition between the universal and particular, but in this *op-posing* there lies already an unforeseeable violence, a metaphysical violence: it has already denied, without acknowledging this *a priori* denial, the other of the universal which is not the dialectical other but the other *other*, that is, an irreducible singularity bearing the name that weakens the maximising thrust of the concept, namely *actuality without potentiality*. The *actuality without potentiality* – this Schellingian thought par excellence – is what singularises us, makes history futural or eschatological, *temporalises* the phenomenon by withdrawing it from the context of constituted phenomenality.

As such, the *actuality without potentiality* cannot even be understood as an ontological principle that would serve, in an *a priori* manner, as the legitimising foundation of a hegemonic order. Beneath the blazing light of the law (of the concept, of the universal world history, of the state or the church, of the *polis* or of ethnic, autochthonic, autarchic community, of any identity tied up with the nomos of the worldly), the *singularising* actuality of the night (or the night of actuality) withdraws the stake of our existence from our 'normative obligations' and from our allegiances to worldly *nomos*. It thereby *sets us* free by *setting us apart* from the normative foundation of the worldly order and *sets us open* to the immeasurable generosity of an exuberant excess that *ex-sists* without law, without potentiality, without even 'being'. It is absolutely transcendent to all potentiality; an immeasurable excess over being, it is the un-pre-thinkable (*Die Unvordenkliche*) beyond-being (*Überseyn*), outside the logic of subject-object co-relation and free from the servile function as grounding. It is not Being that grounds beings – in a universal and permanent manner, that is, onto–theologically (Heidegger 2002). As such, it escapes all acts of subjectification and objectification and their co-relation on the onto-theological ground (*Grund*) of Being. The *disparate* of actuality and potentiality or singularity and universality de-legitimises all *arché*; this is in so far as *actuality* itself is not, strictly speaking, a 'principle'; it is the de-legitimation of principle as such. The excess of actuality over any potentiality *shows* itself at the instance when the dialectical movement of world-historical Reason arrives at a sudden halt; at this instance, the destitution and emptying out (*kenosis*) of worldly predicates becomes more visible than ever before. This paradox could not be grasped in the dialectical logic of subsumption under the power of the concept: here the negativity of non-actuality does not get converted into the fullness (*pleroma*) of the positive through a process of double cancellation (as in Hegel). It is rather the task of thinking the actuality of the positive that has never been included within the immanent movement of dialectical self-cancellation. The dialectical-speculative movement of thought is the enemy of thinking *actuality without potenti-*

ality: the excess of actuality, its immeasurable generosity, is such that it *always already* destitutes the constituted order of signification, an excess that is also an infinite abandonment (hence the paradox), an abandonment from which the infinitude of a task is inseparable. Here, then, there is no question of a subject-object co-relation nor of a subject-predicate *adaequatio*; it is rather a question of the 'monstrosity of copulation' (as in Hölderlin) out of an essential (dis)jointure; of an epochal dissonance out of which the *historical* erupts for the first time as *historical*. While initiating the dialectical method of double cancellation in its modern form – which is later perfected by Hegel – Schelling, therefore, has to abandon the dialectical strategy altogether and instead elaborate, as early as *The Ages of the World*, a non-dialectical style of narrative thinking.

At the heart of the issue lies this question: how to think the beginning or origin on the basis of the non-potentiality of being, a beginning that is not a result of being's *capacity to be*, a beginning that is not under the jurisdiction of the sovereignty of the Subject? At stake also, we can now see, is the question of the *historical*, for where the question of beginning or origin arises, the question of the *historical* announces itself like a lightning flash. Such questions present themselves as a task for thinking when the regime of metaphysics is abandoned to its own provenance, leaving metaphysics to itself. At the heart of this aban*don*ment lies an essential *don*ation: abandonment not only leaves behind the regime of potentialities, it also thereby *lets* being be; *gives* being to itself. Heidegger, more than anyone else in the last century, speaks to us out of this essential gift (donation) that is proper to the event. Hence the event is *the event of appropriation* (*Er-eignis*), whose enigma lies in its trait of expropriation as its undertone (*Enteignis*: the event of dispropriation). Out of an essential *don*ation in this aban*don*ment, the new inauguration comes to us from the extremity of the future, from an *eschaton* always already given in a promise immemorial. Neither Schelling nor Heidegger trace it back *apophantically* to its origin as presence. The beginning, without potentiality, is never a presence that we can hope to recover through an *apophantic* tracing back. That is why it *ex-sists* without memory and without memorial. This beginning is without *arché*; it is an an-archic origin (*Ursprung*) that *leaps forth* to that which sends us destiny in advance. Therefore it *frees* us toward that which is *to advent* without destiny. The beginning, thoughtfully considered, does not determine us in the way that destiny determines us through its iron laws of necessity; it rather *frees* us *toward* what is *to come* out of a groundless *eschaton*. *Eschaton* is without destiny. Fateless, the event cannot have the mythic foundation to legitimate itself, as the *arché* has for a hegemonic regime in an epochal condition. Here Schelling (like Heidegger) grasps the *eschaton* as freedom outside metaphysics. The *eschaton* is the holy (*das Heilige*).[2]

To abandon also means 'to exit'. If philosophy can be understood as having this profound connection with metaphysics, then it would open us to the exit *of* and *from* philosophy as metaphysics (Bensussan 2007). Eschatology, opening to the advent of the holy without destiny, is an *exit* from metaphysics (from the self-grasping of Being as ground of beings, from being its infinite *capacity to be*). There, then, *ex-sists that which is* otherwise than potentiality: *eschaton* is the *setting apart* and a *departing from* the potentiality of being. At the epochal closure of metaphysics, that which is *otherwise* than potentiality manifests itself for the first time, though it is presupposed already as *what has-been* (*Gewesen*). This manifestation introduces a rupture (so clearly visible in the late Schelling's works) into the univocity of being, into the univocity of the philosophical discourse (as 'metaphysics') according to which there can be only *one* philosophy. If the claim of univocity constitutes essentially the meaning of the system, and if philosophy claims to have the meaning of none other than what we understand as system, then the caesura or interruption that announces itself here would open philosophy to its possible exit. When an ultimate *arché* ('the sovereign referent' in Schürmann's words) no longer anchors the potentialities of the world, the univocity of metaphysics is fractured without repair; the heart of metaphysics is wounded by this irreducible caesura between *actuality without potentiality* and the infinite potentiality (that is the infinite cognition of being, or the infinite capacity to be). Schelling introduces this caesura in a manner that strikes philosophy with the creative violence of lightning flash. In that flash is disclosed, in a momentary manner, that which is concealed in the infinite potentiality of being. What is concealed is the *gigantic* beginning (Bensussan 2006: 323–42), that inexhaustible promise immemorially given, the immeasurable excess over all its consequences and results, the anarchy of an exuberance that is the origin of history, the ecstasy of eternity from which time erupts bearing the mark of death, and from which the transiency of the worldly receives its existence and meaning. This means that there must be more than one beginning, as is realised by both Schelling and Heidegger (Hühn 2014: 16–34). At its epochal closure, philosophy becomes caesural. Caesura is *de-cision* (*decidere*), a *cutting off*: it is an exit of philosophy from out of the innermost ground of philosophy.

Caesura of philosophy

In Schelling's works such a caesura manifests itself in all its creative violence. This alone makes his thought of singularising actuality closer to his friend Hölderlin's 'caesura of the speculative' (Lacoue-Labarthe 1989: 208–35) rather than to the Hegelian speculative-dialectical logic of subsumption. In this sense, a thoughtful consideration of the Schellingian deconstruction of the metaphysics of presence is still due. It is not necessary to suppose that Schelling – the individual philosopher bearing the proper name 'Schelling' – deliberately brought this violence upon himself and calculated in advance all the consequences, effects and results that would be unleashed from it. *Decision* (*Ent-Scheidung*) – and we will discuss shortly what this means in Schellingian thought – cannot be thought merely as a choice to be exercised by the will of an individual thinker, however great may he be, and as such it exposes us to the limit of the thinkable. Decision, far from being the essential attribute of the subject, is rather that event which exposes us to the extremity exceeding the measure of knowledge.

The place of *de-cision* (*decidere* in the sense of cision, caesura or cutting off) is tied up, in its innermost mode, with Schelling's painful and yet liberating awareness that Occidental metaphysics has come to its epochal closure, which means that not only a certain epoch (the epoch that grounds itself on the metaphysical principle of the Subject) but the entire metaphysical history of the concept of being has come to its closure. De-cision, since it is an event, no longer allows itself to be thought on the metaphysical basis of the will or the Subject; de-cision can no longer be thought on the metaphysical basis of potentiality. The intensification of this *difference* would be an essential gesture or style of our reading of Schelling's singular deconstruction of the metaphysics of presence, a difference that he intensifies between 'the maximising thrust' of potentiality (the universalising trait of being) and the singularising breakthrough of actuality where there is no potentiality. As in Hölderlin's 'caesura of the speculative', this caesura (between 'negative' and 'positive' philosophy) has to make itself manifest like a lightning flash in all its creative violence. This is why Schellingian thought, enigmatic as it is, still appears to us difficult to bear, for its 'operative gesture' consists of seizing truth which appears, in its suddenness, at the instance of its arrest which is also its very acceleration. It is, thus, not for nothing that Schelling could say that 'system' means none other than stagnation: far from seizing truth at the instance of its advent, system petrifies truth in the law of the concept. The verbality of truth, its eventive arrival, is then transformed into a cognitive category: the operation of the concept, then, works just like the nomothetic operation of what Schürmann calls the 'hegemonic fantasm': it produces chimeras of 'actuality' or 'reality', demanding from us a normative obligation to conform to this actuality, while it is nothing other than a fantasm, of what Nietzsche would call 'the last wisps of smoke from the evaporating end of reality' (Nietzsche 2005: 168). The law of the concept is the chimera that hegemonies need so as to elicit from us 'normative obligations'.

At the epochal closure of metaphysics (where Schelling sees himself), the task would then be to think the question of truth without the law of the concept, truth unimpaired by the violence that the concept inflicts on phenomena, truth un-enclosed in the economy of worldly values which the hegemonic fantasm imposes upon us. But such a task implies a decision, in the sense outlined above, that does not restitute in turn the sovereignty of the Subject. Truth, like the event of decision, does not endure; its duration is the duration of the lightning flash, momentary and incalculable, always on the verge of disappearance like the comet in the night sky. Therefore it can't be 'endured'; it does not have 'the suffering and patience of the concept' (Hegel 1998: 10) to linger on in each stage of the great march of world-historical becoming, slowly enriching itself by subsuming what is particular, preserving only the essential in it – namely, the universal immanent in it – while discarding its sensuous garb till the moment arrives when it becomes pure thought (thinking that thinks nothing other than thinking itself, as though there is a law of thinking, proper to itself, that *necessarily* has to attain the concept, that ineluctably has to pass over into the concept). Against this, we must evoke, like Schelling, the impatience of language-thinking that does not have to convert itself into concept. This explains the oft-accused protean nature of Schellingian thinking. In encountering the *un-pre-thinkable* event, that immeasurable *actuality without potentiality*, the cognitive apparatus of categories and predications lose their potentiality. This instance of the absolute transcendence *breaking into* the immanent movement of the categorical is like the lightning flash, suddenly appearing against the dark sky of identity: this instance of caesura breaking-in, interrupting the immanence of self-presence in its most intense gathering, releases in its blazing light the irreducible *differend* and welcomes the singularising event of actuality. The *differend*, always shifting its terrain, is never adequate to the concept; it is either too much of an excess or it is impoverished, below the concept and, as such, never its contemporary; it is absolutely heterogeneous in respect to worldly values, which are those of the law at the service of world-historical hegemonic regimes.

In Schellingian thinking, such a *differend* breaks into the discourse of philosophy with the creative violence of a lightning flash at the instance when the caesura between positive and negative appears like an irreducible wound, *separating* and *setting apart* (positive) philosophy from (negative) philosophy. The whole complex of gestures, through the incalculable shifting and re-shifting of terrains that Schelling performs in his long philosophical career, consists of opening up philosophy, in so many different ways, to its possible exit, even though that may not always be his conscious intention. It is rather that the *act*, or better, the *actuality* of freedom itself, working and unworking through the inner movement of his thinking, like an invisible life of thought or like a secret energy, continuously engages in a Jacob-like struggle with the *un-pre-thinkable* event beyond being (*Überseyn*). In this failure of thinking to express the absolute, that is, its inability to attain a systematic completion, the caesura (between negative and positive philosophy) opens up an irreparable wound, a fissure or a fracture at the heart of metaphysics, disrupting the univocity of philosophy's immanence. What Schelling touches in this ceaseless struggle with the *un-pre-thinkable* is the *heart* of metaphysics itself, and he discovers that this *heart* of metaphysics is an irreducible caesura, a fragile *topos*, an inflicted wound or an injury for which there is no longer any metaphysical surgeon. At the instance of epochal closure, Schelling, already *stepping beyond* and yet *still* speaking the language of metaphysics, touches the heart of metaphysics in all its fragility and finitude. The metaphysical investment in being with powers (it's capacity to be), with its *arché* and *telos*, suddenly appears precarious, incapable of securing a good return or profit, a useless expenditure, an extravagance. When being thus disinvests or divests itself of its potentiality, this metaphysical economy loses the force of its gaze and the power of its legitimation; the exigency then reveals itself in the utter urgency that we leave philosophy (metaphysics) to itself without return.

Such an exigency animates the philosophy of Schelling. As far as I know, he never used the term *Ausgang* (exit) to name the task of his thinking, a thinking that is at once fragile (unarmoured with the power of the concept) and rich (for being open to the infinite): there is an abundance in all abandonment that defies the metaphysical economy of worldly (world-hegemonic) values. If we follow Gérard Bensussan (2007) here, it is perhaps Karl Marx who first made this term crucial to his own thinking. Yet it is already an essential component of Schellingian thought, which comports itself, in an essential manner, toward a possible *Ausgang*. This is what needs to be shown, and is what constitutes the task of the following pages. Marx's thought takes place in the space opened up in this *Ausgang*, in this *exit* (of philosophy) from philosophy which is already revealed in Schelling's works, most decisively in his Berlin lectures on mythology and revelation. In the Schellingian caesura of philosophy between negative and positive, the *Ausgang* of philosophy from philosophy takes place indiscernibly, because of the peculiar mode of its manifestation – like a lightning flash, suddenly appearing only to disappear at once, an event of encounter and not a static state. But this sudden apparition of the inapparent does not take place only once.

In the exigency of abandoning philosophy to itself from itself, while still speaking the language of philosophy, lies the ambiguity of the whole Schellingian undertaking. But this ambiguity is such that, far from inhibiting thought and constricting its exuberance, it rather opens thinking to truth without the law of the concept. Heidegger, as the first to call us to attend to it, shows more clearly than anyone this ambiguity in its fecundity as much as in its essential failure (Heidegger 1985). Although it receives decisive expression in Schelling's later thought, when he introduces the eschatological caesura between negative and positive philosophy, the ambiguity is already there in his early works, glowing like an invisible glow 'within the coarse and ponderable':

> Whoever has to some extent exercised their eye for the spiritual contemplation of natural things knows that a spiritual image, whose mere vessel is the coarse and ponderable, is actually what is living within the coarse and the ponderable. The purer that this image is, the healthier the whole is. The incomprehensible but not imperceptible being, always ready to overflow and yet always held again and which alone grants to all things the full charm, gleam and glint of life, is that which is at the same time most manifest and most concealed. (Schelling 2000: 61)

What is this gleam latent in all that exists which is 'at the same time most manifest and most concealed' if not that immeasurable generosity of *actuality* beyond all potentialities? This *generosity* of actuality, this giving by withdrawing from all appropriation, could not but be ambiguous for the mortals: there is a paradoxical generosity that consists in making oneself weak and fragile. Schelling knows that an unmediated access to this generosity is destructive for man. We must, then, participate in the generosity of divine excess only by abandonment (*Gelassenheit*), by abandoning all potentialities of the world, by mortification of all egotism and all worldly triumph. It is the profundity of Schelling's tragic knowledge that abandonment is a pathway of indirection that alone enables us to participate in it by separating from being (for all participation is at the same time separation). Participation *separates*; in being partitioned, we participate in the generosity of the divine excess, the un-pre-thinkable event to come. In the following sections of this introduction I present a sketch of Schellingian political theology in bold strokes, which will be substantiated and elaborated upon in the following chapters.

Destitution of sovereignty

There is hardly anyone in the history of philosophy who, with all the profundity and originality of his thought, is read so little and understood even less. This enigmatic thinking has failed to be contemporaneous with the settled mode of an epochal condition – but it is this essential failure (Heidegger 1985: 7) that is for us more interesting and more fascinating today than the success or victory of a completed philosophical system. Schelling failed remarkably: his attempts to arrive at a definitive system could only give rise to a plethora of attempts to produce one, each of them destined to fail, as though by an ineluctable necessity that is singular to his thought. It is as if there is a 'worklessness' or 'unworking', to use a phrase from Maurice Blanchot, that is at 'work' each time his thought attempts to institute itself as *work*. To come to terms with this *worklessness*, with this vertigo of thought, is something of a task today, and it is from Heidegger, more than anyone else, that we know that this failure has something essential to do with confronting mortality *as* mortality, death *as* death; that is, with encountering the event that *singularises* each one of us in turn and each one singularly. The question of mortality that is the vertigo of thought, the event that fractures the regime of 'constituted phenomenality', that absolute singularity that remains in *differend* with regard to 'the maximising thrust' of hegemonic fantasm – so fraught with pain – is fundamental to Schellingian thinking as well; and we will soon see that this question of pain, tied up with the tragic 'experience' of the singular event *as* singular, is an inevitable element of the Schellingian phenomenology of nature as much as of spirit. We have learnt from Heidegger and, very recently from Reiner Schürmann, that essential thinking is *singularised* by mortality; or, to put it another way, singularity is marked by mortality in such a manner that thinking is singular to the measure by which it is measured by mortality. One can say that what interests us today, more than ever before perhaps, is this experience of a finite thinking that is fragile, bereft of sovereignty; a thinking marked by destitution and by the nakedness of a confrontation with what exceeds all measure: the immeasurable that is always incommensurable with the accustomed mode of our being in the world. Schelling has a name for this, a strange name, and all the more so because of its provisional character, and because it names in a manner which, at once, leaves the unsaid to its provenance. It is a name that is less a (certain) theological pretension to name the name, than a bearing witness, in finitude, to that which must be left to its excess. Schelling calls this *Überseyn*, above or beyond being. The event of encountering the glory of that which is even *beyond being* – the immeasurable par excellence – is also violence, but it is a violence that redeems and expiates; it is not the violence of the 'maximising thrust' of Reason which transforms phenomena into a hegemonic fantasm. The task here will be to show how in Schelling's works there is a singularising intensity at work that undoes at the same time the instituting impulse in his thought.

We are thus already introduced to what fundamentally concerns that discourse which we name here as 'religion', wherein the question is not so much that of being, but of what exceeds being – any being, whatsoever, even the being of God. If 'being' is, in a pre-eminent sense, a hegemonic fantasm (Nietzsche is not far away here) of Occidental metaphysics, then this 'God without being' indicates *the singularising event* that would release us from the hegemonic impulse of 'constituted phenomenality'. This gesture, which comes to Schelling from Meister Eckhart (Cattin 2012), consists of intensifying a distinction between God as the principle or *arché* of beings (God as *hegemonikon*: the sovereign principle, or the principle of sovereignty that founds the order of creation) and, on the other hand, the idea of a Godhead without sovereignty (because it is without principle, without *arché*: *an-arché* of Godhead). We must learn to exist without principle and without *arché*: so Eckhart says, so says Schelling too: an enigmatic saying, for it implies that what we call 'religiosity' demands that we learn to abandon, not only any being whatsoever and the whole domain that we call 'worldly', but even God. One must abandon even God: a strange idea of *religiosity* (Schelling 1992), as though religiosity must abandon even religion, abandon it to the extent that it is ruled by *arché* or principle: the glory of the lord is *kenosis*. In such a case, where religion is ruled by an *arché* called 'God', it would not be qualitatively different from the hegemonic powers of the world. The crucial idea here is 'abandonment' (*Gelassenheit*), the Eckhartian word that will eventually be crucial for Heidegger himself in his later period. Schelling combines here the Greek philosopher and the Christian speculative mystic, in order to open up the strange idea of 'religiosity': *religiosity is Gelassenheit*, abandonment of all that is *arché* or principle, all that serves as the *hegemonikon* of earthly powers. Religiosity would then amount to none other than a gesture of impoverishing or destituting 'the sovereign referents' of the world (Schürmann 2003).

This is the fundamental 'thesis' that Schelling attempts at various periods of his philosophical career: to think religiosity or *religion without sovereignty*. I thus argue in this work that this is the very precise point of his contention with Hegel (with the discourse called 'German Idealism'), and that it was this scandal of religion that led him eventually to break with German Idealism, inaugurating a new thinking beyond metaphysics, while passing through this passage of the deconstruction or destitution of metaphysics. 'The sovereign referents' here enter into destitution. Religion would now come to mean something like the passage through which the worldly hegemonies enter their destitution. Schelling has a word for it, very close to Eckhart's *Gelassenheit* and Schürmann's 'destitution': 'mortification', which implies that the hegemonic referents confront their utter insufficiency and utter non-sovereignty. The late Schellingian idea, the idea of *actuality without potentiality* – taken up from Aristotle and yet reading him against the grain – has immense political-theological consequences for us (Schelling 1990: 55–67). In this Schellingian reading, the actuality of the divine is seen as irreducible to any potencies or powers of the world; the divine, being actuality, is a non-power. In confronting the *actuality without potentiality*, the worldly powers enter into destitution. The Pauline messianic idea of *kenosis* resonates here: actuality without potentiality means the *emptying out* of the predicates, potencies or attributes of the world.³ The idea of *divine mourning*, which is to be found in Schelling as much as in Hölderlin, opens up the event of the apparition of the divine (which Hölderlin calls 'the holy') which is without sovereignty and which, as such, interrupts the 'constituted phenomenality' of worldly hegemonies (Schürmann 2003: 4). It is not an apparition that constitutes regimes of worldly truth; rather, the divine appears without appearing, appears as disappearing and is thus an inapparent apparition, irreducible to worldly cognition. It is Hölderlin who poeticises the condition of modernity wherein the divine is in constant flight from the world, abandoning the whole of nature and history to its profound lament. Very close to his poet friend, Schelling too conceives of the divine as in mourning (albeit remaining only a possibility in him and never actualised); likewise the fundamental attunement (*Grundstimmung*) of the mortal is this indestructible veil of profound melancholy that affects the whole contiguity of beings (since the mortal is the link between the divine and nature). Such a mournful, absconding divine cannot itself serve as the sovereign foundation for earthly powers in the worldly order. Between the divine and the worldly, between the religion of *religiosity* and the profane, political order of the world, lies an abyss of *separation* or an irreducible distance: the world is *separated* from its foundation with the advent of the *eschaton*; or, in the breaking-in of the *eschaton*, the foundation is unavailable to the world.

The scandal of eschatology

Let me now, in a very schematic form, articulate the main points I hope to elaborate in the following pages:

1. What Schelling conceived as 'philosophical religion', of which we find only a very schematic outline in his later works, was posed against both the Kantian idea of 'rational religion' and the Hegelian speculative dialectical idea of a theodicy of history. Here one can see Schelling fighting on many fronts:

i) Against the Kantian or Enlightenment subjugation of religion to the normative-regulative principle of reason, Schelling evokes the ecstatic or exuberant *existential* opening to the positivity of the *that* which is singular, irreducible and historical. Schelling thus undertakes a genealogy of the philosophical discourses of modernity in order to make manifest what is forgotten or repressed in that history, where self-consciousness rules as the sovereign referent of the epochal condition of modernity. He thereby destitutes (in a way similar to Johann George Hamann and Friedrich Heinrich Jacobi) the epochal condition of modernity in the name of the revelation (*Offenbarung*) of religion. The event of revelation, which cannot be thought by the pure rational religion of reason, is the event of the *historical*. As the word *Offenbarung* implies, what revelation *opens up* is not anything occurring *in* history, nor anything like the universal truth of pure Reason, but the *historical* itself in a fundamental sense. Between revelation, which is a historical category, and the mythic, there lies a radical discontinuity of origin. The ahistorical, a-linguistic and universal pretension of reason's claim of sovereignty here undergoes destitution or deconstruction. The whole Enlightenment pretension to being the de-mystifying and de-mythologising work of pure reason is here un-masked. Far from reason being de-mythologising, there is indeed something like a myth of reason. Religion, receiving its essential sense from revelation (*Offenbarung*), is, then, fundamentally incommensurable to the mythic constitution of the worldly order. Schelling, from very early on, categorically insists on this distinction between religion and myth, a distinction that remains fundamental even to the later work. In the later Schellingian thought of positive philosophy as distinguished from negative philosophy, this distinction is intensified to the point of a tragic *differend*. Religion, in a fundamental sense, is historical in contrast to mythology, not because it happens *in* history, but rather because *the historical* is for the first time opened up, disclosed, manifested as this absolutely singular event of revelation.[4]

ii) Against Jacobi's insistence on the irreducible ineffability of the heart wherein the divine manifests itself as a profound feeling, Schelling envisages a 'metaphysical empiricism' which keeps the Kantian critical thinking alive in spirit, while at the same time ceaselessly interrogating the closure of its a-historical and purely rational pretension. This is a difficult gesture on Schelling's part: a deconstruction of rational religion doesn't imply that one has to endorse an irrational religion of inscrutable feeling governed by a blind faith in an indemonstrable and ineffable being beyond all reason.

iii) As if that is not enough, Schelling also fights on a third front, this time against perhaps his strongest adversary. The Hegelian speculative dialectic claims to have brought to a synthesis the opposition between reason and revelation. Kant (the advocate of reason) is now made to enter into reconciliation with Jacobi (the advocate of revelation) in the name of Reason in an expansive sense, where it is necessarily *historical* and processual and not a static, fixed, petrified Reason in the Kantian sense. We know that later, following Schelling, Kierkegaard will turn violently against the Hegelian abuse of this idea of *mediation*, and for the same reason as Schelling: what triumphs once again in Hegel (despite his own fight against Kant), so Kierkegaard will argue, is 'the maximising thrust' of Reason, the hegemonic fantasm of the law (which is the Hegelian normative order of empty universality: the ethical stage), at the cost of the life of the singular relation which absolutely exceeds the *nomos* of the worldly (the religious stage). Thus absolute knowledge is a fantasm: *nomos* in itself is empty, void of the passion and intensity with which alone the opening of the depth of the world to the Other is possible. The key term here, crucial for both Schelling and Kierkegaard, is *Wirklichkeit* (Kierkegaard 1957: 9–21): *actuality* or *reality* is not an affair of Reason; it refuses the bourgeois solution of finding everywhere mediation and only mediation, the easy solution for all those philosophers who work like 'the civil servants of humanity' (Schürmann 2003: 8); it does not comfortably get inside the nomothetic operation of Reason without being violated. Against the Hegelian false synthesis in which the sovereignty of the epochal principle of modernity (that is, the principle of the Subject) is not radically deconstructed, Schelling conceives a philosophical religion that opens up the idea of a post-secular thinking of the secularising project of modernity.

2. From this, one thing becomes clear, at least provisionally: what Schelling calls 'philosophical religion' is neither Kantian rational religion, nor Jacobi's wild, almost fanatical, religion of the heart, nor the Hegelian theodicy of history; it is rather an *eschatology*, where eschatology would signify an infinite task of deconstruction of whatever assumes the name of sovereignty and *hegemonikon* in the worldly order. If, in the Kantian subsumption of the event of the historical and revelation to the empty, formal law of morality, the epochal principle of modernity – that is, self-consciousness – does not yet sufficiently enter destitution, this is because in the Kantian idea the divine is reduced to a mere guarantor of the world-order, a harmless cohesive principle of the moral law, the legitimising principle of Reason (Schelling 1980: 156–218). In Kantian discourse, the existence of the divine is deduced from the necessity of the moral law, while it ought to have been thought in entirely the opposite manner: the exuberance of the divine existence must make the moral law a necessity so that the world remains open to its outside, beyond the rule of necessity. Only then may the divine justice, eschatologically thought, be a task of world politics. We must imagine an eschatological, incalculable arrival that is free even not to be free; such an eschatological arrival is a *justice* that suspends the *nomos* of the world-historical hegemonies. Far from being a guarantor of the cosmic world-order, or a functionary of the moral laws governed by the unifying, necessary ideals of Reason, the divine is rather to be thought as an interruption, or de-legitimisation, of the *nomos* of the world-order. We must, so Schelling would say, go beyond the epochal principle, the *arché* of the Subject that legitimises the hegemony called 'modernity'. God is no Subject; the divine is, to use a phrase from Schürmann, *anarchic* in excess of the world-order, a surplus

to the normative ideals of Reason. *Deus absconditus* is not a nomothetic principle of the world; he is not the truth of the world: the divine truth, thus, a folly, the folly of Christ on the cross, is an unbearable expression of the suffering and evil of the world. On the other hand, and at the same time, religion must also be distinguished from the mystical foundation of political authorities. That the political authority of a hegemonic worldly order may ground itself on a mystical foundation – this is the danger of *Schwärmerei* that Schelling sees in the mysticisms of Friedrich Jacobi and Baruch Spinoza. In one of his most well-known works from his younger days, the *Philosophical Letters on Dogmatism and Criticism*, Schelling names such a mystic foundation of authority as 'dogmatism'. Freedom, now uncoupled from necessity, turns demonic and arbitrary, knowing no severity of justice. The complicated gesture that Schelling undertakes here is remarkable. Against the Kantian *nomothetic* order of Reason he deploys Spinozistic realism, only in order to surpass the mystical foundation of political authority implied in the Spinozistic *Schwärmerei*. The result is the double strategy of deconstruction, implied in his idea of a tragic double bind wherein dogmatism and criticism, each in turn, are torn open to the third, the tragic thought understood as the *belonging*-together of singularity and universality in their *differend* without dialectical mediation.

Dialectic is the third enemy of tragic thought. One can see already in these youthful writings, even before Hegel came to write his great works of speculative philosophy, that a deconstruction of dialectics under way. In the Hegelian theodicy of history, the divine is conceived as embodied in the immanent order of world-historical politics; as such, the modern state of Prussia can become, for Hegel, the figural expression of the Absolute. Against such pantheism, which the Hegelian 'cunning of reason' realises by means of its dialectical manoeuvring, Schelling conceives of philosophical religion as eschatological. This eschatology, based upon the idea of *difference without dialectical mediation*, de-legitimises all worldly power based on a divine foundation. Hence, unlike in Hegel's theodicy, the state can never be the figure of the Absolute; the state as much as the visible Church is merely a state of apostasy (*Abfall*), an order of transiency or passing away. The state, and so also the Church (in so far as it comes to ally itself with the state for world domination), are thus deprived of their sovereign claims on us; they cannot claim to elicit from us normative obligations and bindings. As merely part of the order of passing away, the visible Church is only an indirect way to open up the restitution of the messianic Kingdom which is always *to come*. In this sense eschatology is the future of religion as much as the religion of the future: this *eschaton* can never be enclosed with the dialectical time of self-presence, within the historical time of any earthly (Hegelian) theodicy of history. Redemption is the surprise coming from an extremity of the future; it's *Noch Nicht* (as Bloch says, taking inspiration from Schelling) is forever incommensurable and non-contemporaneous with any (worldly) historical *hic et nunc*. Here Schellingian eschatology turns into a critique of historical Reason. The modern Prussian state of the nineteenth century is not even a poor embodiment of this coming redemption. Anticipating Marx's eschatological atheistic denunciation of the Hegelian apology for the given world-order, as well as Kierkegaard's eschatological Christian deconstruction of eighteen hundred years of Church history, Schelling cautions his contemporaries not to misjudge their time. Thus the prophetic intimation that Schelling refers to in the first pages of his *Die Weltalter* is only the intimation of a surprise, in excess of historical Reason, of what is always *to come*, in relation to which the world as it exists loses its ultimate sovereignty and legitimacy. This moment marks, more explicitly than ever before, the dissolution of German Idealism. What remains a 'scandal' to German Idealism, and what brought about its dissolution, is nothing other than this scandal of religion, or more properly, this 'eschatology'.

This is important: Schelling, considered to be the initiator of German Idealism along with Fichte, even before Hegel came on the scene, is also the thinker of destitution and dissolution – it is in his thought that two thousand years of Occidental metaphysics becomes *epochal*. In this strict sense, Schelling was never a German Idealist pure and simple. Even in his early thinking (which is supposed to be more 'Idealist' than his later works), the scandal is *always already* made manifest as something that cannot be thought and that must remain something like an 'irreducible remainder' of all thought. This unthought, for Schelling, remains essentially tied to the question of religion. At stake in the later Schellingian introduction of the caesura between 'positive philosophy' and 'negative philosophy' is none other than the immense question of the exit from philosophy itself (Bensussan 2007). It is Schelling who, while belonging to German Idealism and to Occidental metaphysics, always already somehow escapes it and has already somehow exceeded it. This occurred not so unequivocally and not in such certain terms, but precisely by and through an instituting of the movement that we call 'speculative metaphysics', which is supposed to be the highest standpoint of an Occidental metaphysics more than two thousand years old. And yet, by instituting this speculative metaphysics called 'German Idealism', Schelling has, at the same time, unleashed the forces of dissolution or destitution in such uncertain terms, by constantly changing terrains, by incessantly *unworking* that which has just come to be instituted. The result is, to use Schürmann's tragic term, a 'broken hegemony', a fundamental failure, a ruin whose ravages or breakages are more important for us now than the grand Hegelian success of the system. At the instance of the highest fulfilment of metaphysics, the demand now arises to think what could not be thought within its two-thousand-year history: namely, this most difficult thought, so fraught with pain, made fragile by the singularising trait of mortality – *actuality without potentiality*. If one wants to read Marx today, and to read Kierkegaard and Nietzsche seriously, then this scandal of thought, this unthinkable within metaphysics, must be decisively taken into consideration.

Political eschatology

I will now try to present, in the quickest possible way, an outline of Schellingian eschatology. Schelling discusses the question of religion in detail for the first time in his 1804 essay *Philosophy and Religion*. Therefore this essay is of decisive interest for us. It seeks to find a solution to the problem that lies at the heart of his Identity philosophy, a solution that would, so I will argue, break from the traditional metaphysical principle of identity. The question here is: how to explain the eternal birth of all things and their relationship to God? Schelling's discussion takes up, one by one, the previous solutions to this question, of which the most important, influential and profound is the idea of emanation that found such moving expression in the Neo-Platonist Plotinus. What is the fundamental principle of emanation if not continuity? The idea here is that the phenomenal world emanates from the absolute in an ever diminishing order. However, Schelling argues that neither the possibility of radical evil, nor the very birth of the phenomenal order, can be explained on the basis of the idea of continuity, for,

> In the absolute world there are no confines anywhere, and just as God can only bring forth the real-per-se and absolute, so any ensuing effulgence is again absolute and can itself only bring forth something akin to it. There can be no continuous passage into the exact opposite, the absolute privation of all reality, nor can the finite arise from the infinite by decrements. (Schelling 2010: 24)

As such, the birth of the phenomenal order can only be understood by way of the idea of an event of radical disjunction, a fundamental fall, a discontinuity marking an indelible caesura between the divine and the world. The birth of the phenomenal order involves, then, a *remove*, an irreducible *distance*, an event of *discontinuity* from its ground. The idea of a *remove* or *falling away*, taken up from the German mystic Jacob Böhme, is the fundamental eschatological idea that will remain decisively important for Schelling even during his later period. An abyss of *distance*, a *setting apart* of the world from its foundation, alone explains the existence of the world. Schelling here, in Gnostic-Kabbalistic mode and so very influenced by Böhme, turns the creation theology upside down: there is as if an abyss or non-being within God himself, an idea that Schelling will expound more fully in his 1809 essay on freedom and in his incomplete magnum opus *The Ages of the World*. The ground, the foundation of the phenomenal world, can't now be traced back to the absolute directly but only to the abyss of a freedom that is the counter-image of the absolute. 'No finite thing', writes Schelling, 'can directly originate from the Absolute or be traced back to it whereby the cause of the finite world is expressed as an absolute breaking away from the infinite world' (2010: 29). Like Meister Eckhart's *Godhead beyond even God*, the Schellingian absolute too cannot even be called a principle, an *arché*, as sovereign cause or as the original foundation of the phenomenal order. This absolute is not even potentiality but *actuality without potentiality*, a *non-arché*, a non-sovereign Good before the distinction between good and evil; the later distinction comes to be only with the fall of man. This Platonic thinking (the thinking of Good beyond being), which is also taken up by Emmanuel Lévinas, is the Schellingian ethical task par excellence: the task is precisely to think the ethical beyond essence or beyond ontology. Here is the instance which releases the trait of singularity from the onto-theological constitution of metaphysics: the divine cannot be thought as 'Being' at all; he is not the Being which is the ground of beings, but what infinitely exceeds being as such. As such, the question of the divine is not an ontological problem. Schelling here uncouples God from the question of being: God is not the *arché* of beings, and thus cannot be the legitimising principle of any hegemonic order.

The idea of the soul that Schelling adopts here is the Gnostic-Kabbalistic principle of *Pneuma* that he combines with the Platonic 'Good beyond being'. It is the remainder of that divine spark that is left over in the fallen world, the remnant of a light that is now imprisoned in the cages of the law. It is the acosmic, spectral Gnostic principle, now eschatologically conceived by Schelling, which must be released from the cages of the world-historical order of earthly sovereignty. The soul is the other principle, otherwise than a 'principle': worldless, independent of time, a dim reflection of the absolute. Rather than bearing the positive knowledge of the phenomenal order, it rather bears witness to the non-being of all that is earthly (the transiency of even the most powerful regimes of world-historical politics). This eschatological *Pneuma*, by virtue of its discontinuous relation to the *nomos* of the world, does not have its equivalent in the external, conditioned relationships of worldly existence. The absolute *breaking away* from the Absolute undoes all attempts to embody the divine on the immanent plane of world-historical politics on the basis of analogy. The *antinomic* insistence of Schelling's eschatology is unmistakable here, and one sees it rising in sharp contrast to the Hegelian theodicy of history which for Schelling, as later for Marx and Kierkegaard, turns out to be a mere apologetic for the given, epochal world-order, a theodicy which is at worst a mere bourgeois conformism bent on glorifying what exists in the world-historical order, the modern state of Prussia.

Some six years later in 1810, in a series of private lectures at Stuttgart, Schelling further intensifies and brings to concretion this antinomic idea of *distance* or *remove* by elaborating on an eschatological conception of history. The emergence of the world is thought again, in contrast to all principles of homogeneous continuity, as a divine *de-cision*: a fundamental *cision* or *separation* by which alone the world can come into being must, then, have its source in the Godhead itself. This event is an event of *setting apart*, an *event* – in a decisive sense of the term – that *sets apart* being (*das Seyende*) from Being (*Seyn*). The coming of the world *separates* itself from its foundation.⁵ In contrast to Hegel's *Logic* (which does not distinguish non-being from nothingness), Schelling here distinguishes this principle of non-being (which Being –*Seyn* – is) from nothingness: this non-being can't be included in the logical system of Hegelian dialectics; it is extra-logical, extra conceptual and not a category among categories in a philosophical system. This is the point that Schelling will raise against Hegel from 1830 onwards.

God *contracts, withdraws, restricts* so that the world may come into being. In an important article, Gershom Scholem traces this Schellingian conception to the Lurianic form of Kabbalah (Scholem 1995: 412). This irreducible *separation* of the world from its foundation, so central to Schelling's eschatology of being, makes their *difference* irreducible to dialectical mediation. Gilles Deleuze's reading of Schelling here touches the heart of the Schellingian task: to think difference *as* difference without representation of difference.⁶ Life is to be found, and this includes even divine life, only in this *separation* of ground and existence, a *separation* full of strife because it arises out of an un-thinkable abyss of freedom. Hence this nexus of beings – divine, mortal and nature – which is opened up in the groundless ground of freedom, can also be broken, for this freedom is such that it is free even to be un-free. Schelling now incorporates the idea of *remove, distance* or *falling away* into this eschatological schema of *separation*: the Fall marks the event of a breakage of the nexus of beings. The jointure of beings is disjoined. That the jointure is now out of joint marks the birth of history. Thus the realm of history is an *apostasy* (*Abfall*), and as such, it is a predicate of freedom, and not the other way round, that is, freedom being predicated upon history. The actuality of radical evil presupposes this fundamental discontinuity at the heart of the jointure of beings.

Schelling's deduction of the state and the Church is to be understood from this absolutely singular event of the Fall that affects the entire jointure of beings. The profound melancholy of nature, which Schelling finds in the elemental rustling of leaves as in the bellowing waves of the ocean, echoes man's profound melancholy that mourns the lost unity. The state is the impoverished creation of man who can't restitute the lost unity by his own power, as though what has happened out of his freedom now escapes his own capacity like a tragic fate. As the poor, mortal supplement of an absolute impoverishment, the state is merely an order of 'passing away'. Far from seeing the state as a figure of the spirit as Hegel did, Schelling offers here an eschatological deconstruction of the world-historical politics embodied in the state. The state is thought as precarious and mortal, fragile and transient, not as the site where the cunning of Reason realises itself via its opposite. In these lectures of 1810, the irrationality of the state is seen to be not just an attenuated variation of a triumphant Reason, but fundamental to the very constitution of the state, in so far as it continuously demands legitimisation and normative obligations from us. In these demands lies the violence of state power.

It is in this sense that even the Church, when it forgets its promise and its origin and allies itself with the world-historical powers, functions exactly like the state. Thus the eschatological deconstruction of religion must accompany the critique of the state. This may be accomplished in the Marxist style, or in Kierkegaardian mode: both Marx and Kierkegaard adopted the Schellingian critique in two entirely different ways. The Schellingian gesture, perhaps closer to Kierkegaard, consists of releasing that element which he calls 'religiosity' from its enclosure either in the secularisation of the theological project of modernity on the one hand, or, on the other hand, from the enclosure of religion that assumes the form of law. This shows that religion is incommensurable with the worldly; far from founding worldly politics on a secure ground, religion rather exposes the world to the imminent but incalculable explosions that continue to disrupt the mythic foundation of the worldly *nomos*. Ernst Bloch, the 'Marxist Schelling' (Habermas 1985: 61–78), accomplishes something like this, albeit in a less Kierkegaardian than Marxist manner, by finding atheism at the very heart of Christianity – a paradoxical move, but a fascinating one.

This brings us to the point I am trying to articulate here: that there is in Schellingian eschatology something akin to what we call today, following Jacob Taubes and Walter Benjamin, a 'negative political theology' (Taubes 2003, 2009), which consists of thinking *the relation of the political and the theological as one of separation*, but not separation in the way that neoliberal secularism speaks of today. It rather consists of *weakening sovereignty in any worldly order*. Both the state and the Church, in as much as the later allies itself with the former, belong to this worldly truth; religion, on the other hand, is not the truth of the world. This demands a re-thinking of religion today: a re-thinking of *religion without sovereignty*, without legitimation and without normative obligation. It was Schelling, even before Marx and Nietzsche, Kierkegaard and Heidegger, who attempted to re-think religion in this new sense: religion as *abandonment* or *releasement*. As mentioned earlier, the latter is Meister Eckhart's word, later taken up by Heidegger in his own deconstruction of Occidental metaphysics. One must abandon everything that claims sovereignty in the worldly order, for this order itself, by definition, is only that which must pass away and therefore lacks ultimate sovereignty.

Reception of Schelling

Contemporary scholarship credits Martin Heidegger's 1936 lectures on Schelling's *Freedom* essay as the beginning of the Schelling renaissance in our time. Though placing Schellingian thinking within the history of nihilism – as he will also place Nietzsche's thought – Heidegger discovers in Schelling 'a new, essential impulse [that] enters philosophy's fundamental question of Being' (1985: 98), thus seeing him in close proximity to Hölderlin's caesura of metaphysics and anticipating Nietzsche's attempt at overcoming metaphysics through its reversal. The raging discordance seething within Schelling's work between two incommensurable claims – the irresistible claim of freedom in its utter groundlessness on the one hand, and the unavoidable allegiance to system on the other – is painful for thought, a pain that constitutes the very fecundity of thinking, (un)working from within that which it helps found. Such an essential failure – rather than the success of being able to create a grand system *à la* Hegel – allows philosophy to enter into its most fundamental question, and precisely thereby prepares philosophy for its *Ausgang* (exit). Such a (Heideggerian) reading indeed opens up Schelling's work for the future of thinking beyond the closure of metaphysics. More than anyone, it is Heidegger who discovers for us the pain of thinking that makes Schelling a truly tragic thinker: thinking, refusing the dialectical subsumption with its logic of *Aufhebung*, is exposed to the non-dialectical *agon* between two incommensurable demands. It is, on the one hand, the claim of the immeasurable excess, the claim from the abyss of freedom even *beyond being* (*Überseynde*), the claim from the *an-arché* that is its singular trait;

while, on the other had, there is the unavoidable claim of the universal, the claim of expression that we name as 'system' wherein the totality of relations can be expressed. This tragic agony makes Schelling a truly unique thinker of the West. The tragic discordance between incommensurable traits, already piercing through at the very instituting moment of metaphysics, manifests in his thought like a lightning flash: an event or an encounter with that exuberance which is always unbearable to the discourse of metaphysics, namely, the exuberance of actuality as pure generosity, the wound of the gift before being. Still speaking the language of metaphysics, Schelling is already intimated by the irresistible claim of the unconditional that would not simply belong to the metaphysics of presence. The result, argues Heidegger, is a Schelling who belongs to metaphysics and yet who also announces, before Nietzsche, a new beginning *outside* of metaphysics, in a language of trembling and stuttering that is uniquely his, shattering the language of metaphysics in order to say the unthought of metaphysics.

Recent Schelling scholars consider Schellingian deconstruction closer to the Heideggerian deconstruction of metaphysics than Heidegger allowed himself to admit in 1936 (Hühn 2014; Bensussan 2006; Courtine 1974: 147–70). If one looks beyond what Heidegger himself said in 1936 (which was limited to a discussion of Schelling's essay of 1809 called *The Essence of Human Freedom*, and does not at all engage with Schelling's works from his middle and later periods), and sees the internal problematic of Heidegger's own thinking as a whole that opens to itself at the epochal closure of metaphysics, then the inner proximity of these two thinkers discloses itself in a surprisingly revealing light. One then can see that the Heideggerian notion of *Ereignis* out of the groundlessness (*Abgrund*) is already opened in the space cleared by the Schellingian *Abgrund*: hence the profound importance of the question of beginning for both thinkers, a question that allows itself to be thought only at the epochal closure of metaphysics; and hence also the exigency of a deconstruction of the metaphysics of the Will, and their respective attempts to think decision (*Entscheidung*) outside of that metaphysics. It then becomes difficult to place Schelling unequivocally within the metaphysics of the Subject, especially if one takes into account the later Schellingian thought of *actuality without potentiality*. Heidegger takes into account neither the middle nor the later thought of Schelling, even though there is something decisive that happens there, in more than one place and in more than one manner: the dialectical-immanent movement of categories that grasp the potentialities of being through its logic of subsumption (*Aufhebung*) is replaced with a narrative temporality that is ecstatic (in *The Ages of the World*), opened up to an immemorial beginning before beginning and to an eschatological exposure to that which is without being the last. Here the univocity of being as potentiality in all its categories, grasped by one principle (*arché*) of process, gives way to the decisive caesura between positive and negative philosophies, where for the first time the thought of *actuality* announces itself as that which can no longer be grasped, categorically, on the metaphysical basis of being as potentiality. At this instance, wherein metaphysics touches its epochal closure, an exit of philosophy could not have been missed or avoided, but this necessity is also its highest freedom: this is the unique gift of thought from Schelling to us. This gift of thought demands the abandonment (*Gelassenheit*) of metaphysics: such an idea of the gift, unthought in metaphysics, passes from Eckhart to Heidegger through Schelling. With this, a turn (*Kehre*) becomes a task and an exigency for thought which, now freed from the demand of thinking on the basis of *arché* – that is, being as potentiality – is free to think of *actuality without potentiality*. As such, the instance of Schelling marks a *Kairos*, an instance of metaphysics *turning* to its outside. When such a *turn* occurs, the idea of potentiality itself receives a new sense: no longer enclosed in the vicious circle of its eternal return, it is almost violently exposed, in a lightning flash of interruption, to that *actuality without potentiality*. That lightning flash of interruption, escaping presence-absence, is an event of temporality that disjoins and brings together existence with what is beyond being. In that sense, Schelling is the first post-Hegelian thinker: the question here, when metaphysics has received its fulfilment (*Vollendung*), is no longer that of subsuming singulars under the maximising law of the universal, but rather of *singularising* the phenomenon by *temporalising* it (that is, thinking the phenomenon as event, which Schelling calls 'actuality', 'reality' or 'existence'). With Schelling, existence ('actuality' or 'reality') can no longer be thought as a constituent element of constituted phenomenality: existence is an event, singular each time, which cannot be grasped by the maximising violence of Reason, and which has to be excluded from the universalising violence of the law. What exceeds the economy of the law is the gift; the 'logic' of the gift, immeasurable in any economy, is always incommensurable with the logic of the law.

The immeasurable generosity of what arrives to us as a gift, as that excess in which we participate only in abandonment ('Only he has come to the ground of himself and has known the whole depth of life who has once abandoned everything and has himself been abandoned by everything' [Heidegger 1985: 6–7]), frees us from the vicious circle of the law of being as potentiality, from the potentiality of being as law. What arrives outside the circular return of the law, outside the logic of fate and the iron cages of necessity, is named by Hölderlin and Schelling alike, although in different ways, as *the holy* or the divine. What Schelling calls 'actuality without potentiality' has no other meaning than this eschatological sense of the divine, the divine as holy – without law, without fate, and without power. It does not need potentiality to exist. Actuality is outside potentiality: *ex-sistence* is the 'outside', a radical exteriority without being.

Already, before Heidegger, Franz Rosenzweig in his great work *The Star of Redemption* takes inspiration from the Schellingian eschatological exit of philosophy for his messianic deconstruction of 'the whole venerable brotherhood of philosophers from Ionia to Jena' (Rosenzweig 2004: 12). Rosenzweig's existential-messianic exit of philosophy – clearly taking its point of departure from the caesura that Schelling introduces at the heart of philosophy's fundamental question – puts into question the Hegelian theodicy of history grounded on the metaphysical determination of being as potentiality. The opening to the messianic arrival, outside the historical Reason, demands *Ausgang* from the fundamental task that philosophy gives to itself, that is, grasping the world on the metaphysical basis of potentiality. Thus there is something like a 'violence of the concept', a violence that subsumes singularities into the fold of the maximising thrust of the universal. While Schelling eschatologically names this *singularity of existence* as the *that*, Rosenzweig names it as *the singular* that refuses to be subsumed under the fold of the universal *logos*. The singularity of the *that* is the unthought of metaphysics; it is that which is repressed in the whole 'brotherhood from Ionia to Jena'. Only when the fantasm of the *hegemonikon* of metaphysics, grounded upon the *arché* of subsumption, is disclosed to its outside, and the outside is manifested *as* outside, does the repressed singularity receive its *releasement* from the 'violence of the concept'.

What makes Schelling's eschatology important for Kierkegaard's own eschatological-Christian deconstruction of Christendom as much as Rosenzweig's messianic withdrawal from the triumphal march of world-historical politics is that for both of them Schelling revealed the *outside* of philosophy by almost violently introducing an irreducible caesura at the heart of philosophy. The lightning flash of the instance (*Augenblick*) that Kierkegaard and Rosenzweig understand eschatologically-messianically, rising against 'the homogeneous empty time' (Benjamin 1985: 261) of historical Reason, takes inspiration from Schelling's ecstatic vision of temporality as he elaborates it in his *Die Weltalter*, wherein the instance (*Augenblick*) is thought qualitatively, irreducible to the quantitative succession of moments that define the dialectical logic of historical time. The eschatological opening of the world to the radically new by disjoining itself from the universal march of historical Reason requires an understanding of temporality as event, which is otherwise than the historical time of universal history. Temporality must be thought as the event of bursting open, from the heart of presence, to the immemoriality of beginning and to that which is without *telos*, wherein time is not understood spatially as extension but as intensification, eternity intensified in the instance *hic et nunc*. Schelling's eschatological vision of history evokes such an intensification of time, which enables him to formulate a critique of history and of politics. In their different ways, Kierkegaard (eschatological Christianity) and Rosenzweig (existential messianism) formulate critiques of history and politics that are profoundly inspired by Schellingian political eschatology. In still another way, his eschatological deconstruction of modernity found a way into Paul Tillich's systematic theology (Tillich 1975a, 1975b).

While Rosenzweig takes up Schelling in his liturgical-existential deconstruction of Occidental philosophy, Ernst Bloch combines his messianism with the atheistic-Marxist disruption of history. The importance of Schelling for Marxist thought is well documented (Habermas 2004: 43–89; Habermas 1954; Frank 1975). Bloch transforms Schellingian eschatological deconstruction into his own unique atheistic deconstruction of historical Reason (Bloch 2009), thereby discovering at the heart of Marxist thought a utopian-messianic principle of hope (Bloch 2000). Bloch's crucial eschatological idea of 'the ontology of the not yet' (*Noch Nicht*), now atheistically thought, re-interprets in new terms not only the middle and later Schellingian idea of the 'ecstasy of reason' but also Schelling's earlier eschatological phenomenology of nature. From here comes Bloch's 'dream of a matter': 'that dream of a matter in nature and history which the matter has of itself and which belongs both to its tendency and to the settlement of its *totum* and *essence*' (Bloch 1995: 95). The Schellingian Christian eschatological insistence on the irreducible transcendence of actuality in respect to all the potencies of the world is here atheistically-eschatologically understood as *deus absconditus*. The home is not yet to be found in the conditioned politics of world-historical negotiations: such is the unconditional claim of redemption that lies as a latent potency that continuously and restlessly moves the realm of history to the *Not Yet*. This *Noch Nicht* of *topos*, which is the meaning Bloch gives to *utopia*, our non-coincidence with ourselves, is the very invisible *dunamis* of history that does not rest content in going along with the world-historical march of politics 'through homogeneous empty time', but with messianic energy radically disrupts, and keeps on disrupting, the closures of the world. The traditional eschatological idea of exodus, so important for Schelling, becomes for Bloch a Gnostic-atheistic interruption of the *nomos* of the world: this messianism, unique to Bloch, takes seriously the Schellingian notion of nature as *Phusis*, restlessly surging forth into the unknown, yearning and groaning and dreaming of redemption to come out of an eschatological future. With this, Bloch goes on to deconstruct, like Schelling, the cold technological domination wherein matter is seen as an inert, malleable, calculable entity. There is, thus, in Bloch a deconstruction of the metaphysics of the Subject that can think of *Phusis* only objectively, depriving it of its exuberance and movement, and reducing nature to something that is formed through the violent exercise of instrumental Reason.

At the epochal closure of metaphysics, Schelling's thought thus opens up to these two very different linguistic registers of thought. One may note further the profound importance of his notion of unconsciousness for both Freud (McGrath 2012) and Nietzsche. This alone is sufficient to explain the fecundity of Schellingian thought. His early phenomenology of *Phusis* allows us to think nature anew in an age when technological domination – whose essence lies in the metaphysical determination of the Subject as potentiality – renders nature as mere material at the disposal of our sovereign mastery. The middle Schelling's thinking opens up a non-dialectical thinking of time as ecstasy, eschatologically opening to what is *to come*. While in the later Schelling's introduction of a caesura between positive and negative philosophy, and in his thinking of *actuality without potentiality*, a decisive rupture with metaphysics opens thought to a new inauguration of historical thinking outside of metaphysics.

Formulation of a question

It is the aim of this study to make manifest this 'eschatological' or 'messianic' spirit in Schelling's work that insists on the 'structural opening' of the world to a radical exteriority, to the excess un-enclosed in the immanent rational foundation of the world. This 'outside' of the world – not another world as opposed to this world but an outside of the world as such, keeps the world open to the event of pure futurity: *eschaton* means for Schelling nothing but this idea of exception that explodes the continuum of the world-history to its outside. The historical Reason of the world is torn open from its foundation to the eschatological event of redemption to come. This makes impossible not only the representation of this eschatological event in any earthly sovereign figure, but also our attempts to translate such an event into the rational-secular structure of metaphysical propositions.

If the *eschaton* is the idea of exception par excellence, then it must be other than the sovereign exception. The sovereign exception suspends the normative-general order of legality by an act of de-cision only in order to make possible and legitimise a new order of *nomos*. Such a notion of sovereign exception functions like the legitimising principle (*arché*) of a given political situation in the world. In the 'concrete' context of politics, it serves as the *raison d'état*. In contrast to this legitimising principle of exception, I attempt to think a de-legitimising exception which can only be *an-arché*, an exception without 'principle', without potentiality, that is, without power. From Reiner Schürmann we know that the very idea of principle (*arché*) is inseparable from its function of legitimation. As such, this study must pass through a deconstruction of the works of the famous German Jurist Carl Schmitt, who conceived of a political theology of exception constituting sovereignty in respect of the normative order of general validity. The task of conceiving of an exception without sovereignty should, then, be able to formulate a critique of the legitimacy of all sovereign claims made by worldly regimes in the profane order. I propose to show here that this is the fundamental concern of Schellingian thought. Schelling not only deconstructs any possible political theology constructed around the figure of sovereignty, he also radically puts into question the liberal-humanist pathos of modernity that grounds itself on the immanent metaphysics of the Subject. It is in the name of eschatology, in the unique sense that Schelling gives to it, that his deconstruction of the metaphysics of the Subject turns to think an *exception without sovereignty*. He thereby turns the hinge of philosophy, at the epochal instance of the closure, towards a possible exit from philosophy, since the exception cannot be thought within the immanent task of philosophy itself. The exit of philosophy toward its outside has an immense ethico-political importance for us: his eschatological deconstruction of any political theology of sovereignty is, thus, profoundly connected with the question concerning the epochal closure of metaphysics itself.

Schelling is a thinker of transcendence, but not a transcendental thinker like Kant. Transcendence *breaking into* the world makes the world ecstatic, not figural. The 'ecstasy of reason' does not figure itself into the figure of the one who decides on the state of exception. Schelling thereby avoids the epochal task that modernity gives itself, a task that has been associated with the destinal task of Hegelian thinking: to think the universal world-history on the immanent-rational foundation provided by the absolute concept, which Hegel calls by the name *Geist*. In Hegel's thought, this name or term *Geist* is the secularised translation of the apocalyptic-eschatological concept of the *Pneuma*. The philosopher Hegel, the epochal thinker of modernity, translates the eschatological-apocalyptic notion of *Pneuma* – a radical transcendence that puts any legitimising worldly institution in question – into the immanent-rational-metaphysical notion of *Geist*. With its self-consciousness, then, *Geist* becomes the legitimising *arché* of the epochal condition of modernity. The triumphant march of the world-historical becoming, grounded on this metaphysical principle of *Geist*, can therefore be said to be a *theodicy*. Here the notion of *Geist* is *theologoumenon* par excellence, but bereft of its original eschatological sting. Schelling's attempt to think the exception (transcendence without the transcendent) thus has to *turn* the hinge that disjoins philosophy from its immanent self-foundation. By disclosing the disjointure that (de)constitutes the legitimising principle, Schelling opens us beyond the epochal condition of modernity, anticipating what Kierkegaard and Marx, Bloch and Rosenzweig were to formulate their respective critiques of the world.

By taking away the eschatological sting of *Pneuma* that makes the world disjoined and inconsistent with itself, Hegel's grand metaphysics of immanence makes the world a harmonious structure, the world closed upon itself in the circular return to the same, a world joined into a coherent totality. When such a world is governed by the supreme principle of Reason, Reason turns into the legitimising principle of the world as it exists. Reason, then, becomes the instrumental principle of constituted phenomenality: with its 'maximising thrust', it subsumes particulars under a hegemonic regime that pretends to universal validity and normative truth. In contrast, Schelling shows the irreducible ecstasy of a Reason whose ground is not the rational-logical order of necessity but that of the highest, inscrutable freedom. He makes such freedom into the alpha and omega of his thinking. Freedom is the apocalyptic event par excellence; it frees us for the 'singularisation to come' (Schürmann 2003); it introduces the element of highest contingency into the immanence of world-history and thereby destitutes world-historical hegemonies. In so far as the subject of history is freedom, and history is the predicate of freedom, the domain of history bears that which frees itself from the iron cages of its law. The worldly sovereignties thereby lose their autonomy and necessity. At the epochal closure of metaphysics, Schelling conceives an eschatological principle of freedom that never ceases to put into question any attempt to legitimise a political situation on a theological foundation. Freedom *sets* the world *apart* from its very foundation, and thereby keeps the world open to the arrival of *the holy*.

Theory of reading

The protean character of Schellingian thinking has not gone unnoticed in the history of the reception of his works. However, the eschatological energy of his thinking manifests itself best precisely in/as these *turns*. His unique task throughout his long philosophical career passes through all these shifting explosive terrains, through all these incalculable *turns* and unforeseeable inversions, through discontinuities and interruptions, without ever congealing into a systematic expression. The result is, as

Heidegger (1985) acutely diagnoses, a 'failure' of philosophy – an essential and ineluctable failure, for it is moved by an excess which is a creative non-Reason, moved by the *pneumatic* energy of freedom. The conventional reception of Schellingian thought does not see in these turnings of the hinge, where philosophy is disjoined from itself, opportunities for new inaugurations of future thoughts, but understands them as the idiosyncratic utterances of a failed thinker who, unable to fulfill the radical promise of his earlier thinking, falls into wild theosophical speculations. It is in the space left open by Heidegger's reading that the question of Schelling's failure – which is also the failure of philosophy as such – is to receive a new understanding. It is as if the essential task of Schellingian philosophy could not be incorporated, without an 'irreducible remainder', into the epochal destiny of metaphysics. As such, his thinking itself could not have been merely epochal, that is, 'regional, dated, finite and "finished" in both senses of the word: complete as well as terminated' (Schürmann 1986: 5). The excess here allows itself to be thought as 'failure'; or, rather, the 'failure' here has no other sense than the excess of a sense, of an experience of thinking that could not have been metaphysical in the sense that Heidegger gives to us: a metaphysics that is onto-theologically constituted (Heidegger 2002).

Now it is important to understand that the energy of Schellingian thought does not so much follow a determinate movement of maturation, as in Hegel, but is moved by a fecundity whose *dunamis* is an anarchic freedom, whose fullness is at once a *kenosis*. A thinking that is moved by the anarchy of freedom, whose eschatological sense we must not miss, cannot be *destinal*. Unlike the Hegelian dialectical movement of world-historical triumph, Schellingian thought no longer seeks to grasp the event of the *eschaton* as the *telos* of an immanent, homogeneous, auto-engendering march of the universal world-historical process; rather, the *eschaton* is understood as the event that frees us from destiny because it is moved by the anarchy of freedom. Not being identifiable with the *telos* of the triumphal world-historical movement, and remaining incommensurate to all world-historical politics, eschatology gives voices to those who are oppressed by the universal world-history. Eschatology, as such, is a hope for the unhoped-for, a hope for the arrival of that which is without destiny and without fate. It is the singular contribution of Schellingian thinking to have kept alive this sting of the *eschaton* in an age whose metaphysical image is that of a grand world-historical becoming, triumphantly surging ahead to a destiny that is teleologically defined. The violence and injustice of history appears, in such an image, as a mere aberration, an inevitable and necessary suffering which will be automatically and mechanically rectified at the end of history.

When Schelling came to Berlin to give his lectures on revelation and mythology, the world stage was already determined by the metaphysical image Hegel had given to it. To pose the question of revelation (*Offenbarung*) at a time when the principle of Reason was identified as the metaphysical *arché* of modernity could only have been an anathema to his contemporaries. That is why philosophers and historians tend to appreciate his earlier rather than his later works. The image of Schelling then comes to be that of a harmless *passé* figure, transitory at best, already finished off in 1807 (by Hegel, in just once sentence), while the later Schelling is passed off as a 'failure', an obscurantist at the service of conservative political interests, or, at best, a speculative theosophical mystic. After 1807, the world of philosophy, even the world-historical stage, has changed definitively (marked by two events: the publication of Hegel's *Phenomenology of Spirit*, and the ascendency of Napoleon). The dominant history of philosophy thus marks a radical disjunction between the early and the later Schelling. The former is recognised as a transitional figure between Kant and Fichte on the one hand, and, on the other, the absolute Idealism of Hegel, who gave the most consummate expression to the secularisation process of modernity. The later Schelling, even the Schelling of 1809 is, however, an *anathema* or an eccentricity at best. The later Schelling is understood as an archaic and arcane philosopher of mythology, a theological-conservative figure of decision (the notion of decision is already a fundamental idea in 1809), a political theologian who justifies the world-historical situation as it is and who – by 1841, in a world already given over to the secular emancipatory politics of world-revolution – will come to defend archaic authority on religious grounds.

It is necessary then, now more than ever, to read Schelling anew. Taking up the question of the Schellingian notion of de-cision (*Ent-Scheidung*), this work attempts to show, contra the dominant historical understanding, that Schelling indeed radically questions every mythic foundation of the political, that his radical notion of de-cision interrupts any immanence of self-presence and opens up the sense of religion as a radical transcendence that is disjoined from both myth and politics. Such a sense of religion cannot serve as a mythical foundation for any political hegemony. Far from participating in the glories of the world, in the triumphal march of world-historical hegemonies and the ideology of progress, religion opens up the world to its radical exteriority from the depth of its foundation. Schelling envisions such a *taking place* of the radical event of exteriority eschatologically. On its own account, the stage of history (so Schelling argues) cannot reach this eschatological event; the immanence of the world's self-presence has to be *broken* through; an abyss of *distance* has to *set* the world *apart* from its foundation. The political hegemonies of the world can't thus have an auto-engendering, mythic foundation. To open the world to the outside, the secularised metaphysics of immanence needs to be left behind. The late Schellingian caesura between positive and negative philosophy is this eschatological deconstruction of metaphysics. It is clear from the above that Schelling's deconstruction arises in confrontation with the Hegelian theodicy of history, which finds its 'objective' expression in his dialectical account of the modern state: here he sees, in a pantheistic-immanent manner, the embodiment of the *eschaton* in the immanent plane of a world-history that progressively fulfils itself and expresses itself objectively in the figure of the Prussian state of the nineteenth century. An examination of Schellingian political theology must, then, take up his critique of the nineteenth-century philosophy of history based on this fundamental idea of progress.

Such an examination will need to foreground his idea of the *(de)cision* which is an instance of exception, an event of exception without sovereignty. I try to show this by taking into account the place of religion in Schellingian thought and relating his conception of religion with Meister Eckhart's notion of *Gelassenheit*. Uncoupled from its function as a foundation for political sovereignties in the profane order, religion is understood here as the opening of the finite world to what is absolutely in excess, an opening that consists of the emptying out (*kenosis*) of all worldly attributes and predicates. This work argues that such a *kenosis* lies the heart of Schellingian eschatology and has no analogy with worldly sovereignties in the profane order: it empties out rather than legitimates the given order of the political. Far from glorifying the political ontology of the world (metaphysically grounded on the notion of the Subject as potentiality), religion exposes the world to the desert of the non-descript which is *actuality without potentiality*. Only on the basis of such *kenosis* can the world welcome what is outside all totality, that which is without the law and without essence. It is an exception without sovereignty.

The reading of Schelling will take a regressive path, that is, we will take the later philosophical works as our point of departure and then read him backward. Reiner Schürmann (1986) likewise adopts such a strategy in his reading of Heidegger, but with a purpose and for a reason different from that of my reading of Schelling. The dominant style of reading Schelling progressively is often undertaken in order to show that while the early Schelling is wholly an Idealist, from his 1809 *Freedom* essay onwards his works increasingly took the eccentric path of theosophical speculation under the inspiration of Jacob Böhme. In this reading, the interest of the early works is overshadowed by the immense light emanating from Hegel's consummate accomplishment, and Schelling's later works are deemed negligible as the wild speculations of a frustrated, conformist old man. This standard reading assumes the achievement of a systematic metaphysics to be the criterion of judgement. But when we read Schelling regressively, that is, starting from his decisive break with metaphysics in 1842–45, and then re-read the earlier work in light of that break, the glow concealed in the early works is suddenly manifest. Here the early Schelling surprises us by revealing himself anew. In this new light, it will now be possible to see that, rigorously speaking, Schelling never belonged to the movement called 'German Idealism' in any simple sense at all. It is rather that, in his own manner, he has *always already* broken away from the fundamental presuppositions of metaphysics at the very instance of its institution, that is, in his own works. The raging discord between 'system' and 'freedom', between the double traits of being (between the 'maximising thrust' of the universal and the withdrawing-retreating destitution in the name of the 'singularisation to come', between the economy of nomothetic Reason and the infinite transcendence of actuality as pure generosity), already pierces through Schelling's attempt at a systematic metaphysics that must equally be a metaphysics of freedom: a tragic dissonance that will ultimately break philosophy itself in two, unleashing an irreparable dissolution to Occidental metaphysics. This tragic thought is closer to that of his other friend, the poet-philosopher Hölderlin, than to the Hegel of the system. Reading Schelling backwards makes visible this break with metaphysics *already* at work in his early thinking, only waiting to receive its decisive form.

This is not to say that there is a homogeneity to Schelling's philosophical career. It is rather to show that the difficulty of thinking exception without sovereignty led him into discontinuous attempts to break with metaphysics, and that reading him regressively rather than progressively better reveals these discontinuous attempts to think the same (*belonging-*together) and not the identical (belonging-*together*) through the idea of a non-sovereign exception. Thus the later caesura of philosophy between negative and positive philosophy was already latent – even if it not visible as such – in his early career. Only retrospectively, when it has made a decisive appearance in the caesura, does the crack that hollows out the depth of immanence become thinkable at all. But this shows that the crack has *always already* been unworking metaphysics, even in Schelling's early attempts at a systematic expression, in ways that are truly unforeseeable and incalculable. Because a philosophy of freedom must also be *existentially* free, the pathways of such a thinking remained for Schelling himself incalculable and ineluctable. This is the highest necessity of freedom. The apocalyptic notion of freedom, anarchic in the sense that it is without *arché*, is necessity at its highest instance. To think together the irreducible *differend* of freedom and necessity, without reducing this *differend* to the immanent-rational principle of identity, is the highest task of thinking today. Schelling more than any one of his era – later followed by Kierkegaard in his own way – is the thinker of this *belonging*-together of the disparate, of this tragic *differend* in the sense that Schürmann gives to it. If I retain the old name of *eschaton*, it is in this sense of a *belonging*-together at whose core is an abyss of difference or caesura. This caesura that *cuts through* this today that 'we' call 'today' is the caesura that Schelling introduced at the epochal closure of modernity.

In this sense, Schelling, in his own untimely manner, is our true contemporary: not in the sense that we share the same historical presuppositions out of the depth of a world-historical immanence, but in the sense that the *eschaton* is contemporaneous to each historical epoch, since it cannot be thought as the *telos* of a quantitative movement of a long, very long, world-historical politics. The idea of contemporaneity is the idea of excess par excellence; it is also a *kenosis*: such is the paradox of 'contemporaneity'. It is the unsaturated phenomenon, unsaturated in a world filled with endless predicates, with infinite attenuations of self-presence and its countless attributes. In the world of actuality that we grasp with the rational-logical principle of necessity, the *eschaton* is the eternal but imminent potentiality of a transcendental *breaking-in*. In the world of mere potentialities – for the conceptual ordering of essences is only a potentiality – the unsaturated excess is *actuality without potentiality*: this is, in sum, the essence of Schelling's paradoxical thinking. To think the *disparate* in their *belonging*-together is to think the abyss of their caesura. To put it simply, the task of this work is to think, with the help of Schelling, the event of the exceptionality of *de-cision* which is not a prerogative of an earthly sovereign figure in the immanent plane of world-historical politics. Schelling helps us think the divine *de-cision* that *sets us apart* from the foundation of the world so that we mortals can remain open to the enclosed event of redemption. Our fragility and destitution, on account of our mortality, is the very condition of our opening to the excess. Such an excess gives us, on the basis of our poverty, the gift of existence. Our attempts to enclose this gift within the cages of law and fate, within the mythic immanence of self-presence, unleash that unspeakable destruction and unimaginable historical violence that the world bears witness to today more than ever before. Schelling helps us to think this exception without totality and without sovereignty, a thought that it remains for us to think in this era when metaphysics is abandoned to itself without restitution.

The work opens with a sketch or an overview of Schelling's political eschatology. I here pose those questions, without discussing them in detail, that will be elaborated in the coming chapters. The first chapter offers a reading of some of Schelling's last works, including the first few lectures on positive philosophy and on revelation that he delivered at the University of Berlin in 1841–42. I take up the intricate and delicate question of *actuality without potentiality* to show that Schelling here attempts to think of an exception without sovereignty that does not allow itself to be thought on the basis of worldly power. Thus there can be no analogy between the divine monarchy and earthly sovereignty: between them there lies an irreducible caesura where the divine decision happens, and the world opens to us out of this divine decision. I will show how Schelling's exit of/from philosophy is tied up with this task of thinking the radical transcendence of actuality outside worldly potentialities.

In the next chapter I go on to read the posthumously published fragment *Die Weltalter* to show that the deconstruction of sovereignty demands a re-thinking of the question of history. Confronting Hegel's pantheistic-immanent philosophy of history, I attempt to reveal an eschatological vision of history at work in Schelling's *The Ages of the World* which radically puts into question the secularising theodicy formulated by Hegel in his lectures on the philosophy of history. He thereby opens up the possibility, later elaborated by Søren Kierkegaard, Franz Rosenzweig and Walter Benjamin, of a messianic-eschatological critique of historical Reason. I here argue that such an eschatological-messianic conception of history, by withdrawing from the triumphal march of universal world-historical politics, gives voice to those who are oppressed by the irresistible demand of progress.

In the next chapter I read the much-neglected novella *Clara*. In my exposition of this beautiful work, I present Schelling as offering an imaginative-creative expression of what may be called the 'beatific life', a life that is moved not by the power of the law but is released from the cages of the law. Beatitude, then, is the fundamental attunement that, by releasing life from the foundation of the worldly *nomos*, attunes it to the eschatological *advent* of *the holy*: the result is a political theology that destitutes sovereignties in the worldly order. Our exposure to the gift of our very existence, the gift that wounds us in the outpouring of an unconditional beatitude, is not mere life at the disposal of the law but the being which exists just 'like a rose, without a why'.

I then go on to read Schelling's magnum opus, the *Essay on the Essence of Human Freedom*, of 1809, in order to elaborate on the concept of a finite politics. Taking up the question of freedom anew, and posing it in the context of contemporary thought, I renew the Schellingian thought of an 'irreducible remainder' that does not allow itself to be enclosed in the cages of the world. The 'irreducible remainder' of the world keeps the world open, immemorially, to the incalculable arrival of the new and of the absolutely heterogeneous. In 'The Non-Sovereign Exception' I read the Stuttgart lectures of 1810 to show how Schelling is again concerned with elaborating an eschatological conception of being. Irreducible to any and all possible enclosures in the immanence of self-presence, religion is thought here in a new sense: as unenclosed opening to *the unconditional*, a sense and a passion that it shares with philosophy. Existing in neighborhood to each other, philosophy and religion – each in its own manner – infinitely open us to the generosity of *the unconditional* which can neither be demonstrated in the predicative structure of the speculative proposition nor understood on the basis of the tasks of world-historical politics. Religion and philosophy, in their different ways, open us thereby to an *unsaturated excess* outside the *nomos* of the worldly powers in the profane order and outside the predicative structure of the dominant Occidental metaphysics. In the 1810 private lectures in Stuttgart we find Schelling understanding eschatology in terms of infinite disclosures of the divine that constantly open us to a future *to come* that refuses to embody itself in the immanence of the world-historical potencies. These world-historical powers thereby lose their autochthony and autarchy, their legitimacy and sovereignty, their power to elicit from us absolute obligation. They can at best be understood as belonging to the order of 'passing away', as the impoverished attempts of mankind to supplement the Fall (*Abfall*). Such a Fall, with which the history of mankind itself is inaugurated, will henceforth mark the world-historical powers with an indelible caesura that can never be redeemed by these powers themselves. This caesura will forever haunt any attempt to construct a strict analogy between the political and theological, the divine and the profane. For Schelling, religion is nothing other than this constant exposure to the abyss, without which neither promise nor hope can ever exist for us. He thereby prepares for us a *political theology without sovereignty*, where religion in its spirit and promise – uncoupled from the world-historical foundation – keeps us alive to an absolute beatitude *to come*, an unconditional beatitude which alone redeems mankind from the violence of history.

Finally, in the chapter titled 'The Tragic Dissonance', I take up the justly famous early essay *Philosophical Letters on Dogmatism and Criticism* to show that Schelling here attempts to think the tragic as the *belonging-together* of freedom and necessity in a manner that already exceeds speculative-dialectical Idealism at the very moment of its institution. Bringing Schelling's tragic thought closer to Hölderlin's tragic 'caesura of the speculative', I hope to show that what is at stake in his thought is the sense of a tragic *differend* that cannot be thought within the onto-theological constitution of metaphysics.

Intervening in contemporary debates on 'post-secularism' and the 'return to religion', this work is an attempt to construct the elements of a negative political theology of messianism or eschatology by thinking through the notion of an exception without sovereignty. I try to show that Schelling's work correctly traces the epochal closure of the philosophical discourse of modernity, thereby putting into question not only the liberal-humanist pathos of modernity that grounds itself on a pantheistic immanent metaphysics of the Subject but also any political theology that would seek to legitimise the sovereign power of the state by an appeal to a 'divine' or 'theological' foundation. I thereby argue, with the help of Schelling, that thinking such an exception without sovereignty is the very task of our destitute time.

Notes

1. In his little essay 'The Principle of Identity', Heidegger juxtaposes the understanding the principle of identity as belonging-*together* with the principle of identity as *belonging*-together. While Occidental metaphysics understands the principle of identity in the former sense, it is now the task of thinking – at the epochal closure of metaphysics – to think the *belonging*-together, wherein difference *as* difference is not subsumed under 'the unifying center of an authoritative synthesis'. Heidegger writes: 'If we think of belonging *together* in the customary way, the meaning of belonging is determined by the word together, that is, by its unity. In that case, "to belong" means as much as: to be assigned and placed into the order of a "together", established in the unity of a manifold, combined into the unity of a system, mediated by the unifying center of an authoritative synthesis. Philosophy represents this belonging together as *nexus* and *connexio*, the necessary connection of the one with the other. However, belonging together can also be thought of as *belonging* together. This means: the 'together' is now determined by the belonging . . . this reference makes us note the possibility of no longer representing belonging in terms of the unity of the together, but rather of experiencing this together in terms of belonging' (Heidegger 2002: 29).
2. 'First of all, the holy is separation (*Aussonderung*) and setting apart (*Absonderung*); being holy means being apart. The holy is the terror that shakes the foundations of the world. The shock caused by the holy bursts asunder the foundations of the world for salvation [das *Heil*]. It is the holy that passes judgment in the court of history. History exists only when truth is separated from error, when truth is illuminated from mystery. History is elucidated from the mystery of error to the revelation of truth' (Taubes 2009: 194).
3. Schelling writes in his 1804 *Philosophy and Religion*: 'This view which is as evident as it is noble, also represents the true Platonic doctrine put forward in the aforementioned writings and carries most purely and distinctively the imprint of its founder's spirit. According to Plato, the soul can descend from its original state of beatitude and be borne into the temporal universe and thereby torn away from the truth only by means of a falling away from the originary image. This was the tenet of the Greek mystery cult's secret teachings, to which Plato alluded quite explicitly: that the origin of the phenomenal world should not be imagined, as popular religion does, as *creation*, as positive emersion from the Absolute but as a falling away from it. Hereupon was founded its practical doctrine that the soul, the fallen divine essence in man, must be withdrawn from and purified of its relation and association with the flesh as much as possible so that by mortifying the sensate life the soul can regain absoluteness and again partake of the intuition of the originary image' (Schelling 2010: 27).
4. The political-theological implication of this Schellingian caesura or separation between

mythological and revelation is unmistakable here. In this work I am attempting to show that this *separation* or disjunction of the mythological and religion, the latter understood on the basis of revelation, is fundamental to Schellingian eschatology. This idea, which found such decisive expression in Schelling's Berlin lectures on mythology and revelation, had already been announced as early as 1802–3. Thus in his lectures on *The Philosophy of Art*, Schelling says that Religion 'necessarily assumes the character of a revealed religion and is for that reason historical at its very foundation. Greek religion, as a poetic religion living through the collectively itself, had no need of a historical foundation, as little as does nature, which is always open. The manifestations and figures of the gods here were eternal. In Christianity, on the other hand, the divine was only a fleeting appearance and had to be held fast in this appearance' (Schelling 1989: 69).

5. Of this primordial separation, Schelling writes: 'Hence, once God has separated Himself internally, He has separated Himself *qua* being from his Being . . . whoever does not separate himself from his Being considers this *Being* essential rather than his inner superior, and more truthful essence. Likewise, if God were to remain as immersed in his Being, there would be no life, now growth. Hence, He separates Himself from his being precisely because it is merely a tool for Him' (Schelling 1994a: 208–9).

6. In Deleuze's remarkable words: 'The most important aspect of Schelling's philosophy is his consideration of powers. How unjust, in this respect, is Hegel's critical remark about the black cows! Of these two philosophers, it is Schelling who brings difference out of the night of the Identical, and with finer, more varied and more terrifying flashes of lightning than those of contradiction: with *progressivity*. Anger and love are powers of the Idea which develop on the basis of a *më on* – in other words, not from a negative or a non-being [*ouk on*] but from a problematic being or non-existent, a being implicit in those existences beyond the ground. The God of love and the God of anger are required in order to have an idea. A, A^2, A^3 form the play of pure depotentialisation and potentiality, testifying to the presence in Schelling's philosophy of a differential calculus adequate to the dialectic' (Deleuze 1994: 190–1).

Chapter 1

Actuality Without Potentiality

> Potency is the Latin *potentia* – power – and is opposed to the *actus*. (Schelling 2007a: 132)

> Whence its 'existence', i.e. its being outside itself, being outside the one place where it ought really to be, namely, outside the inside? (Schelling 1994b: 176)

On the exit from (of) philosophy

The famous lectures of 1841–54 that Schelling delivers at the University of Berlin, on what he comes to call 'positive philosophy' in distinction from 'negative philosophy', have as their premise the following: if one undertakes a history of the concept of being from the inception of metaphysics till its fulfilment in Hegel, then one can see from the instance of its epochal closure what that history represses, namely, the unthought of that history. The task of thinking the unthought of metaphysics presents itself as an exigency only at the instance when the history of metaphysics has reached its epochal closure. The unthought of the history of the concept of being, by not belonging to that history, marks a fissure or an excess of that history. Now visible more than ever before, the manifestation of this excess destitutes that fundamental principle on which the immense edifice of the given metaphysics has built itself. The edifice of that history, looking more fragile than ever and in such undeniable visibility for the first time, must now open itself to a new inauguration of thinking. In the later period of Schelling's philosophical career such a new inauguration would be thought in terms of an opening to a new philosophical investigation that he comes to call 'positive philosophy'. If the historical juncture can be said to be predicated upon freedom, then this juncture is also the instance of the fundamental disjointure or discordance out of which the event of history itself erupts.

All throughout his long career, Schelling tirelessly insists on the indemonstrable actuality of freedom. This indemonstrability of freedom is the subject of history that introduces into the realm of history the possibility of *the otherwise* of what it has been. Because the realm of the *historical* itself is opened by the abyss of freedom, the historical juncture may also be disjoined. At its highest instance, freedom manifests itself – without manifesting as 'this' or 'that' phenomenon (because freedom is indemonstrable and inscrutable) – as the highest necessity. But this necessity does not strike us as fate or the law: higher than the necessity of fate, the necessity of freedom exists fatelessly, without destiny and without the law. At the epochal closure of metaphysics, Schelling conceives the task as that of thinking this *belonging*-together of freedom and necessity outside the law and outside the logic of sovereignty. It is now a question of this (dis)jointure being made manifest as historical necessity, out of the (un)ground of freedom, a necessity that goes beyond the intentionality or decision of a particular thinker. It is this *belonging*-together of freedom and necessity (of what Hölderlin calls 'monstrous copulation'), this tragic *holding* together of incommensurable traits (mortality and natality, singularity and university, revelation and Reason), which has remained unthought in the history of metaphysics: such becomes a task only outside the history of metaphysics (which thinks the tragic as belonging-*together*). With the destitution and exhaustion of the history of metaphysics, this unthought manifests itself as task (*Aufgabe*) for the first time, the task of releasing the *singularisation of existence* (its 'actuality' or 'reality') from the hegemonic fantasm of Reason. Schelling understands the task on the basis of an *eschatology of being*; positive philosophy is interested in constructing or grounding such an eschatology.

In the first few lectures, where he attempts to ground positive philosophy and its historical necessity, Schelling discusses how a thinker's thinking arrives as a call from philosophy's innermost necessity itself. In that sense, an *exit* from philosophy (understood as metaphysical system) is a simultaneous *opening* to the futurity of philosophy (as *philo-sophia*, philosophy without system). That there is a futurity of philosophy or that philosophy has a future (*philo-sophia* is, as the very term indicates, essentially futural): this unconditional claim of the futurity of philosophy demands an exit *from* philosophy itself, from a *certain* philosophy that has come to its epochal closure. Futurity is here to be understood, not as the futurity that comes to pass away (as attenuated variation of presence), but eschatologically, as that which is always *to come* (and never presently present, a given present). This difficult gesture of thinking, enigmatic and ambiguous for us now, makes Schelling's thought at once fascinating and yet not immediately accessible. If one takes only the lecture on 'The History of Negative and Positive Philosophy' (Schelling 2007a: 155–70), one can glimpse the Jacob-like struggle with which Schelling attempts to name that which could not have been allowed to be thought within the given history of the concept of being. In just fifteen pages of the published lecture, Schelling sketches in bold strokes that which haunts like a spectre in the history of the concept of being from Socrates to Hegel via Aristotle: the eschatology of an advent that does not belong to the truth of the world (and more specifically to 'our' world of secular-liberal democracy). Since the spectral makes itself manifest (manifesting without manifesting, without any 'this' or 'that' manifestation: such is the spectral manifestation), by calling us to an undeniable responsibility, to an unavoidable demand or task (*Aufgabe*), the history of the concept of being calls us to think that which is unthinkable within that history, namely, the *that* that is without concept at all. It thereby opens up a new philosophical discourse, hitherto unrealised, now called 'positive philosophy'. As if (a certain) philosophy must *leave* itself, abandon itself; or, even better, must preserve itself while abandoning its fundamental *arché* in the name of a philosophy still *coming*, which is 'philosophy' nevertheless (in the absence of any other name), even philosophy for the first time – philosophy without system, without closure, without totality. Perhaps we may call it 'non-philosophy', philosophy opening to non-philosophy, philosophy infinitely opening to the *that*, that event of eruption which he names, in the still trembling language of metaphysics, as 'existence' ('actuality', 'reality').

While still speaking the language of metaphysics, Schelling makes that fantasmatic language of the concept tremble by introducing an irremissible resonance of *verbality* into the name of existence: existence is not opposed to essence, is not a mere inversion of essence; it is rather *ex-sistence*, the radical outside or radical *exteriority*, the absolute transcendence without the 'transcendent' (the latter having been demolished by Kant's refutation of metaphysics). Hence it cannot be 'philosophical', if philosophy is to bear the meaning of 'system', and if the concept of 'system' has to bear no other signification than 'the maximising thrust of the universal' at the cost of the singular phenomenon: 'for ancient physicians, system meant stagnation'. And yet, what name is there other than this strange name 'philosophy' to think that infinite opening of the future out of the very heart of finitude? 'A future opens up for positive philosophy which will not be anything else than a progressive demonstration. While negative philosophy is a closed system, the positive is no system in this system' (Schelling, from an unpublished translation by Vater). Only as non-system is an infinite opening to the outside possible:

> There emerges at this point yet another difference between the negative and positive philosophy. The former is an entirely self-enclosed science that has arrived at an unchanging conclusion, and is, thus, in *this* sense a *system*; in contrast, the positive philosophy cannot in the same sense be called a system precisely because it is never absolutely closed.

And yet,

> If, on the other hand, one understands by 'system' a philosophy that determines and distinguishes itself through positive assertions – in this second sense, under which one understands a totality of knowledge that serves as the basis for a magnificent declaration, in this sense the negative philosophy is not a system. Positive philosophy, in contrast, as pre-eminently affirming is, in this sense, in an eminent way, a *system*. (Schelling 2007a: 182–3)

Compare these words, written in 1841–42 with the following, written as early as 1795:

> The genuine philosopher has never felt himself to be greater than when he has beheld an infinity of knowledge. The whole sublimity of his science has consisted in just this, that it would never be complete. He would become unbearable to himself the moment he came to believe that he has completed his system. That very moment he would cease to be creator and would be degraded to an instrument of his own creature. How much more unbearable he would find the thought if somebody else should want to force such fetters on him! (Schelling 1980: 172)

The conventional reading of Schelling according to which his early philosophy belongs to the movement of speculative Idealism now appears to require a radical revision. Already in 1795, that is, at the instituting instance of dialectical-speculative thought, Schelling opens up a split, a *setting apart* and a *separation* between the unconditional demand (the demand for the unconditional) and a never to be accomplished totality of conditional predicates. He thereby exposes a wound or a caesura that is never to be repaired but only to be intensified in the wake of Friedrich Jacobi's deconstruction of philosophy. Gestures toward the exit *of* philosophy *from* philosophy are already manifest in the early Schellingian thought; the injuries of destitution would already have marked the instance of institution; the exit of philosophy is already the unconditional demand at this very instituting instance of 'speculative Idealism'. Like an event of the future anterior, the demand of the unconditional arrives *proleptically* as though from elsewhere, from a utopian origin (from 'no-place'), but announcing itself *here and now*, in each *hic et nunc*, disjoining each *hic et nunc* from any mythic immanence of self-presence. Each instance, swelling and surging ahead with the power of *institution*, is simultaneously an opening toward its *destitution*. Absolute freedom is simultaneously necessity at the highest instance: the highest coincidence of opposites that would forever open us, by exposing us to the singularising trait of mortality, to the immeasurable infinitude of knowledge ungraspable in the concept and unbound by the grasp of the law. It is as though the immeasurable itself must *always already* measure all worldly predicates, all our assertions and negations, all our attributes and qualifications. The caesura between positive and negative philosophy interrupts the mythic closure of the system and its claim to univocity. In Schellingian thought, the metaphysics of presence withers away. After Schelling, the question for philosophy can no longer be: how to ground the self-presence of the world in the labour of the concept? It would rather be: with the withering away of the metaphysics of presence, how to think the event of the unconditional free from the cages of the law, from the mythic foundation of fate?

Already at the turn of the century, in his philosophy of nature (which the later Schelling would call 'negative philosophy'), the Pauline eschatological resonance is irremissible.[1] The protean nature of *Phusis*, groaning and yet opening to the outside like a wound, bearing that excess which would burst it out from all immanence of self-presence, is understood more radically and in a more originary manner than the Idealist metaphysics of the time was able to think. Despite the protean nature of his own thought – or rather because of it, since it nourishes itself on this tragic agonal strife that rages within – the abyss of this interruption haunts Schelling throughout his long philosophical career, bringing the whole of modernity to its epochal closure so that the unthought, *the actuality without potentiality*, may make itself the task of a new thinking. The thought of immanence, which was the epochal task of the history of being, is not thereby suspended but preserved, not in the same mode of its being (that is, as potentiality) but as transformed. A new thought of immanence must be conceived in such a way that immanence is exposed to the surprise of the eschatological event. This event erupts as the absolute transcendence of *actuality without any potentiality*. Along with the thought of actuality, that is absolute transcendence breaking through like a cut or cision, the thought of immanence is not abandoned but made necessary for the first time. A new immanence is now to be thought, a thought of *exposed immanence* (immanence torn from all autochthony and all autarchy), opened to the surprise of the event out of its essential groundlessness, an immanence that Schelling has been attempting to think, from very early on, with his conception of 'potency'. The event is a surprise: it surprises us for the laws of thought valid for the general order are no longer applicable to it. All that matters here is singularity, an absolute transcendence in respect to worldly hegemonies.

Thus positive philosophy and negative philosophy *belong*-together: a new philosophy of immanence in which Schelling puts into effect his doctrine of potencies, and a new philosophy of transcendence in which *actuality without potentiality* is thought as *the event*, untouched by potencies, for it does not need potentiality to exist. Hence *the event is not even being*, but beyond or above being (*das Überseynde*). The event is thereby released from its subjugation to the ontological (or onto-theological) ground of metaphysics. Later, Heidegger will renew such a thinking of the event in the name of *Ereignis* with its double bind, without having to subjugate it to the self-presence of being. With this, the unthought of actuality is loosened and freed from the onto-theological determination of being *as* power. The event *as* event lets itself be the task of thinking when it is no longer a question of grasping being on the principle of power, but rather as that of non-power, as that which *ex-sists* infinitely as an immeasurable and un-pre-thinkable *actuality without potentialities*. It thereby infinitely puts into question every *arché* on the basis of which worldly hegemonic regimes exist. The event is *eschaton*. At the epochal closure of metaphysics, Schelling eschatologically opens up thinking to its non-power, to the non-power of being, not as non-being but as transcendence of all beings and of being as such. The power of being has its source in its infinite capacity to be (*Seinkönnen*), which, as such, is non-being, namely, potency itself; while actuality is without capacity, without power, without the possibility to be: it does not need potentiality to exist. Such actuality is not that which is powerless as opposed to the powerful; it is not incapacity as opposed to capacity, or impossibility as opposed to possibility, but the outside of this opposition, on *this* side of their tragic *differend*. Therefore, *the actuality without potentiality* eludes the grasp of the dialectical razor. Dialectics, Schelling would say, is the enemy of the thought of the event. If philosophy at the moment of epochal closure assumes the dialectical as its achievement, then the abyss of this caesura (that opens up here) escapes, like a lightning flash, this destinal closure: the event is the lightning flash, the momentary apparition without destiny. Arriving without destiny, the event is fateless. That which escapes the potentiality of being, the un-pre-thinkable event out of *Abgrund*, cannot be understood on the basis of the law. This is the point the later Heidegger himself takes up from Schelling, without naming him or explicitly acknowledging the debt. The *that* that arrives *fatelessly* is named by Schelling as *beatitude*. It is that which *beatifies* the very being of being, and takes up all beings into itself in their redeemed condition. It is an old theological name wherein Schelling attempts to hear the enigma of the fateless, out of the mortality of existence, and on the ground of a freedom that is groundless. It is this paradox that does not begin with the thinkable, for the simple reason that it is the very beginning of thinking. The event, in that sense, is also the event of thought. And yet, just for that reason, it does not begin with the thinkable. This is the essential insight of Schelling's later thought which he comes to call 'positive philosophy' in distinction from 'negative philosophy'.

History of negative and positive philosophy

The sixth lecture of Schelling's *Philosophie der Offenbarung* concerns 'the history of negative and positive philosophy'. The title, supplied by the editor, is misleading. Schelling speaks here not so much about two already realised philosophies existing side by side in a two-thousand-year history (from the Ionic physicists to Hegel), but rather of how *actuality without potentiality* has remained unthought and unthinkable within the history of the concept of being. It is the unthought of that history, which nevertheless presents itself as 'anticipation' or as an object of love (*philo-sophia*) at certain exceptional instances of that history, that interests Schelling. As such, there has never been a fully present 'positive' philosophy existing side by side with another already fully present 'negative' philosophy; rather, positive philosophy – a philosophy without system (closure) and in that sense already a non-philosophy – could not have presented itself because negative philosophy itself had not yet come, properly speaking, into its own. Schelling appears to make an exception here for Aristotle, who grasps the determination of being as potentiality in a far more profound manner than Hegel. This decisive exclusion of actuality from 'the fires of the purest analysis' is a profound renunciation: 'to remain with God as *terminus* and not to want him again as a generative cause' (Schelling 2007a: 164). For Schelling, Aristotle remains, in decisive contrast to Hegel, the purest thinker of immanence. Hegel claims to be able to think the absolute transcendence of actuality on the basis of cognitive categories that can only grasp in the concept what is a *presently given* entity. The question here is not merely that of thinking of the absolute transcendence of *actuality without potentiality*, but also that of the necessity of thinking immanence in an originary manner. This means that the positive philosophical thinking of transcendence does not nullify or displace the negative philosophical thinking of immanence, but rather truly welcomes it for the first time, in a manner that is appropriate, that is, in the manner of immanence *belonging*-together with transcendence where their difference *as* difference is underlined. When *difference as difference* becomes a task of thinking, the epochal closure of metaphysics becomes more clearly visible.

Schelling's deconstruction of the categorical foundation of Occidental ontology here anticipates the early Heideggerian deconstruction of ontology: categories grasp (*Begriff* means 'grasping') only the entities

Vorhandenheit and *Zuhandenheit* and not existence as *ex-sistence* (which is *event*). Hence the necessity for Heidegger to undertake an existential analytic of *Dasein* who (*Dasein* is *who* and not a *what*) is neither *Vorhandenheit* nor *Zuhandenheit* but is *existence*, opened by mortality, out of its groundlessness. Such is the Heideggerian *Destruktion der Ontologie* as set out in *Being and Time*: the de-sedimentation of the presuppositions that underlie the categorical de-phenomenalisation of Being. To *phenomenalise* Being is to *temporalise* the being that is ontico-ontologically privileged, that is, the *Dasein* each one of us is, the *Dasein* who is singular (who is thus an existence and not an entity *Vorhandenheit* or *Zuhandenheit*), singularised by an irreducible event of mortality which is, each time, always *futural*. Temporality, in an originary sense (as distinguished from the vulgar concept of time), *singularises Dasein* and thus exposes *each one* of us to that event which is repressed in the context of 'constituted phenomenality' (which Heidegger names as 'metaphysics'). While for Heidegger *Dasein* is a *who*, for Schelling it is *that* without *what*. In this positive philosophy, as much as in the Heideggerian existential analytic of *Dasein*, it is always a matter of thinking *the event of existence* non-categorically, out of its *Abgrund*, putting into question the exclusive determination of being in metaphysics as 'what', as potentiality, on the ground of reason: each time it is the question of releasing the *singularity* of existence from 'the maximising' grasp of the categorical fantasm. The cision or caesura between negative and positive philosophy, now becoming the task of thinking, shows that in the history of the concept of being this *difference* itself remains unthinkable, for that history could not think existence otherwise than on the basis of ground, on the basis of the grounding *arché* of Reason. This is in so far as it is the essence of Reason (or, reason of essence, Reason as essence, Reason as essential determination, Reason that determines entities in terms of their essence, Reason that determines being in its potentiality, that is, its mere infinite capacity to be) to ground, to give ground, to act as *arché* or principle, to supply the 'why' of entities. Being determined as potentiality is the *self-giving as ground*. Being here, being as such, is either thought ontologically or theologically, as permanent ground or universal ground. Both thinkers, each in his own way, understand this logic of being as constitutive of metaphysics. At the epochal closure of this metaphysics, *the event of being* arrives to us out of *Abgrund*: if Schelling here speaks of God, and Heidegger of *the holy* (Heidegger 1982: 159–98) (das *Heilige*, which means *setting apart* and *separation*), this God is not the God which serves as onto-theological ground, as *arché* or principle of the *hegemonikon* called 'metaphysics'. It is rather the *eschaton*, the other is the *coming* God that *sets itself apart* or that *separates* itself from worldly potentialities, the divine without a 'why', the 'singularisation to come' (Schürmann 2003).

It is this idea of the divine without a 'why', the anarchic God, that each of them thinks along with Meister Eckhart: to live like a rose, without *arché* and without a 'why', that is, without any hegemonic fantasm.

Thus the *actuality without potentiality*, actuality that *ex-sists* without a 'why', could not have been thought on the onto-theological determination of being as potentiality, for the advent of this actuality marks *kenosis*, the emptying out of worldly potentialities. A true immanent-negative philosophy is that which progressively leads the movement of potencies, through 'the fire of purest analysis', to the point of their *kenosis*. Like Heraclitus, Schelling is the thinker of fire par excellence. Here the fire of analysis is the fire that empties out attributes, qualities, predicates so that the whole immanent movement, at the instance of its closure, comes to a standstill in confronting *that* which, in an *a priori* manner, *always already* excludes itself from this movement of potentialities, namely, the un-pre-thinkable event or the exuberance of being. The *telos* of the immanent movement of thought that determines being as potentiality is the arrest of that movement itself, opening to the exuberance of the event in *astonishment* or *wonder*.

Looking back at 'the history of philosophy', not to reify that history but rather to open the Book of history once again to its outside, to open fissures that have already marked that history at the instance of its very inception (in Socrates, in Plato): such is the deconstructive strategy that Schelling performs here. In that history, Socratic ignorance, which is also a profound knowledge,[2] and Platonic (Socratic) astonishment in encountering 'the Good beyond being', occupy places of decisive importance. If one undertakes a study of the importance of Platonism for Schelling, the early Schellingian philosophy in particular would appear to be a Platonism par excellence, the negative philosophy at its best. Such (true) immanence is not the immanence that ever achieves closure by its own means. Socrates' profound ignorance, which is also a profound knowledge, constantly opens to an outside or to an excess which is of an exuberant nature (*Überschwenglichkeit*). The instance of arrest of the whole dialectical movement at its fulfilment is also an opening to the *Überschwenglichkeit* in utter astonishment or wonder. The infinitude of the potentiality of being is still *finite* when it *prophetically* encounters the other, the otherwise than being, the 'Good beyond being'; it is the infinitude of true knowledge that Socrates disavows and is in love with (*philo-sophia*, love of wisdom). That is why for Socrates astonishment or wonder is *the fundamental attunement* (*Grundstimmung*) of philosophy. The Socratic negative-destructive deployment of 'bombast and pomposity as a type of smoke to be blown in the face of his opponents' (Schelling 2007a: 157) is still negative, immanence opening to the infinitude of the unthinkable. Herein lies the paradox of the Socratic dialogue. Socratic *dia-logue* is a conversation in the mode of an infinite 'dia', which means *setting apart* and *separation*, as opposed to 'sync' which means contemporaneity or 'on the same plane'. The Good *separates* itself from being; or, the Good is *distance* in regard to being (therefore the Good is not merely an attribute or a quality of God). Being is *separated* from itself by the Good. The Good thereby infinitely exceeds being and is otherwise than being. The beyond being (*Überseynde*) of the Good, at the instance of the standstill of the dialectical questioning-answering, arrives as from the future. Therefore 'Socrates and Plato both relate to this positive as something of the future: they relate to it prophetically' (Schelling 2007a: 159). In encountering the immeasurable Good, dialectics comes to a standstill. This is true even when, 'in the *Timaeus*, Plato becomes historical and breaks through, albeit violently, into the positive, with the result that the trace of a scientific transition is barely or hardly to be detected since it is more a cessation of what has preceded (namely of the dialectic) than a transition to the positive' (Schelling 2007a: 159). In one of his last lectures in Berlin, Schelling could thus say, so approvingly, of this Platonic 'Good beyond being':

> If we were capable of being surprised by anything at all today, it would have to be at hearing even Plato or Aristotle ranged on the side of those who put thought above being. Plato? – well, now, perhaps if one overlooks that one passage in the sixth book of the *Republic*, where he says of the *agathon* (the Good), i.e., of the highest in his thought: that the highest is no longer *Ousia*, essence (*Wesen*) or Whatness (*Was*), but is even beyond essence, preceding it in worth or power. Even the word *presbeía*, which in the primary meaning signifies age and only in a secondary sense signifies superiority, worth, was not chosen for nothing, but rather itself expresses the priority to the essence. If we overlook this passage, then it might appear as if Plato gave thought precedence over being. (Schelling 1990: 66)

This is an important passage. True immanent philosophy does not give precedence to the potentiality of being but to the absolute transcendence of actuality in respect of any potentiality, even though and precisely because such true immanent philosophy cannot be concerned with the exuberant event of the beyond-being. This is why Aristotle's philosophy of immanence is a truly immanent philosophy, a true negative philosophy:

> But Aristotle? Aristotle, to whom more than anyone the world owes the insight that only the individual exists, that the universal, the [*determinate*] being is only an attribute (*kategóremamónon*), not a self-being, as that which alone is *prótos* (first), has the foremost claim to be designated – Aristotle, whose expression 'whose substance is actuality' alone would demolish all doubt. For here Aristotle characterizes *Ousia* (substance) in the way he normally does the *tí estin*, the essence, the *Was* [i.e., as *enérgeia*]: and the meaning is that in God no *Was*, no essence precedes, but that in the place of the

essence the *Actus* steps, the actuality precedes the concept, the thought. (Schelling 1990: 66)

Here it appears as if the positive philosophy almost arrives in the Aristotelian *actus*. This *actus* is always in excess of *ousia*. The fundamental metaphysical presupposition of Greek (Occidental) thought – its *ousiology* – here undergoes destitution. It is *actus* and not *ousia* that is the object of Platonic prophetic love and of Aristotelian immanent thinking. *Actus* is inaccessible to potentiality: it is an exception that *ex-sists* without power, without *potentia*, and without sovereignty. This is even more the case when Aristotle, in his passion to exclude anything mythical or prophetic, distinguishes his thinking from logical philosophy, even from that of the Platonic doctrine of the 'participation of things in the ideas'. Being is indeed thought here, but as potency 'leaping toward being':

> The truly logical, the logical in real thought, has in itself a necessary relationship to being: it becomes the content of being and necessarily passes over into the empirical. The negative philosophy as an *a priori* philosophy is therefore not in this a merely logical philosophy that would exclude being. Being is indeed the content of pure thought, but only as potency. But what potency is, according to its nature, is, so to speak, a leaping toward being. (Schelling 2007a: 160)

The Aristotelian movement of thought, then, begins with a potency that leaps *toward being* and not with actuality. *Actus*, which Aristotle understands as *pure entelechy*, is merely the *telos* of the movement of potentiality; it is *that* to which all potentiality is *attracted* (*Angezogen*) and for the sake of which potentialities enter into the continual fire of purification until the pure *actus* is approached when being comes to 'rule over non-being, the *actus* over the potency. 'The final telos is, thus, no longer potency, but is rather the potency fixed entirely as *actus*. This final *telos* itself does not again become a member of the series like everything else, but is rather that being which exists in its own right above and independent of the entire series' (Schelling 2007a: 162). Aristotle indeed understands this *actus* which is the *telos* of this path of *a potentia ad actum* as that which actually exists (*das Wirklich Existirende*), for the whole movement begins with a presupposed being, with experience in its givenness. In that sense, it is indeed empiricism. However, the entirety of the Aristotelian movement of potencies, although it begins with the presupposed being (this being for it is just this, a *presupposition* and only a point of departure), is none other than negative philosophy itself. Aristotle does think of *das Wirklich Existirende*, but only as the *telos*, as a result of the immanent movement of potentialities. As such it is *actus* but only the *actus* that negative philosophy, at its best, can attain:

[Aristotle] employs that which actually exists as the final telos only because it grounds his entire science in experience. He thereby incorporates this entire world, which the rational philosophy has in thought, as the existing world. Nonetheless, it is not a question of existence, for existence is, as it were, the contingent element in all this, and has worth for him only as far as it is that from which he can extract the whatness of things. His real goal is the essence, the whatness of things, and so, for him, the final telos – which is the same as that which actually exists according to its *nature* – is pure *actus*, and precisely this being, which according to its nature is *actus*, is the final telos of rational or negative philosophy. (Schelling 2007a: 162)

Thus, *actuality without potentiality* has remained unthought in the Occidental history of the concept of being. In the Aristotelian *actus*, there is *still* potentiality, in so far as this *actus* is only a *telos* that *attracts* and thereby *grounds* the entire science of potentiality. In this ground of *actus* (*actus* serving as ground), potentiality triumphs once more. *Actus* is still the *arché*, the ultimate principle par excellence in which one hears the *nomothetic* and *monothetic* operation of powers. It is the highest instance that a truly immanent philosophy can attain and yet, precisely at this instance, immanence is also opened to *that* which exceeds its power and its infinite capacity to be. At this instance of its highest fulfilment and of its highest power, immanence loses its autarchy and autochthony; it renounces the sovereignty of its *nomos* and gives way to that which exists without *nomos* and without categorical fantasm, namely, *actuality without potentiality*. For Schelling, Aristotle is the profoundest thinker of renunciation, precisely because he alone was able to think, in the history of the concept of being, immanence *as* immanence.

For Schelling, Aristotelian negative philosophy remains a paradigmatic example of immanent thinking, in relation to which the Hegelian philosophy looks like a mere caricature. While Aristotle never makes use of this final *telos* (namely, God), and renounces thinking this *telos* as 'efficacious beginning as well' (he therefore remains the thinker of the *end* rather than the *beginning*), Hegel wants to makes use of God, which he reaches only at the end of the movement of potentialities, as 'efficacious beginning as well' (Schelling 2007a: 162). Hegel thereby closes up *that* which can only be prophetically announced in that philosophy, *that* infinite opening of futurity and *that* infinite futurity of opening, beyond the self-enclosure of potentialities that constantly returns into the same as in a vicious circle. Schelling here takes up the Aristotelian distinction of the *prótos ón* from the *hepoménos ón*, the latter understood as 'that being which is posited merely as the consequence and supplement of another; just as he distinguishes the *energéia ón* from the merely *hylikôs ón*, and makes the latter equivalent to the *dynámei ón* or the *mè ón* (carefully to be distinguished from the *oúk ón*, which is the absolute non-being, or nothing at all)'.

> Thus, regarding the material nature of this co-posited being there surely was no doubt. What was unresolved, and remained resolved even unto our own time, consisted not in its constitution, but rather in the fact that this secondary being, though in its own nature merely an ability to be (*Seinkönnendes*), yet had to have some sort of relationship to God. (Schelling 1990: 58–9)

Schelling's critique of Hegel is based upon this distinction, drawn from Aristotle, between the *prótos ón* and the *hepoménos ón*, the latter further carefully distinguished from the *oúk ón*. From this irreducible caesura – via his deconstruction of Hegelian onto-theology – Schelling deduces the following:

> That which comprehends all possibility, as itself merely possible, will be incapable of *self-being* and only be able to be in the mode of relating itself as mere material to another [pure actuality], which is its being and over against which it [the pure potentiality] appears as that which is not through itself. I offer these characterizations without further ado, because they are all based on well-known Aristotelian propositions. 'The hyletic, which is only capable of a material being cannot be said of itself, it can only be said of another', to which other it therefore belongs. For if I *say* (predicate) B of A, then I am saying that A *is* B. That other, however, which is this (the [potentiality] incapable of self-being), that would have to be the self-being, and indeed in the highest sense *the Self-Being* – God. The real relationship, then, would be that God is that being which is not for itself and which now, insofar as it is – *Is*, namely, in the only way it can be – will appear as the *ens universale*, as the essence in which all essences, i.e., all possibilities, are. (Schelling 1990: 63–4)

One must not miss the Schellingian (and Aristotelian) distinction made here between 'is' and 'Is'. It is not that potentialities (the infinite capacity to be) have no relationship to being or God at all. It is rather that its 'is' relates itself to 'Is' as non-being, in the way that *hepoménos ón* relates itself to *prótos ón*. The latter is not predicative being at all; it is not a capacity for signification and predication. Therefore it *Is, actuality without potentiality*, or the *un-pre-thinkable* event, the pre-predicative or the non-predicative in the eminent sense.

> Thus the relationship is not indeed determined in such a way that God is the universal essence; but God *is* not as it *is*, nor *is* God it in consequence of the necessity in it. With respect to the '*as*', it is understood even without reference to the foregoing that God is the totality of possibilities in an eternal manner, hence prior to every act and thus also prior to every volition. And yet *he himself* is not this totality. In *himself* there is no 'whatness', he is the pure 'thatness' – *actus purus*. (Schelling 1990: 64)

This God outside totality and outside closure, *God without being*, exceeding ground and grounding, is not the onto-theological God. He does not act as the *nomothetic arché* of worldly potentialities; he is not the mythic origin toward which the *nomos* of the worldly can be traced back apophantically.

Schelling makes this distinction in the manner of Meister Eckhart: between the Godhead and God, between the God of *actuality without potentiality* and the God of pure potentiality. The fire of the *pure that* (*das reine Daß*) dissolves the potentialities of the world. It is Origen's eschatological *Apokatastasis*, the fire that dissolves the *nomos* of the worldly hegemonies. The *pure that* does not embody or incarnate itself in any worldly figure; nor does it *figure* as a worldly institution. As absolute transcendence, it deprives the worldly potentialities of their claim to sovereignty. What alone rules is that which is without power and without potentialities. If one says, in still another way, that the one who rules is he who possesses power, then the following citation from Aristotle (who further cites from Homer), of which Schelling approves, would mean that the pure *Daß* does not rule at all. It is without sovereignty: *heîs koíranos ésto* ('let one be the ruler').

With this, the link between ruling and power is dissolved. Schelling's tireless critique of all political theology based upon the theological principle of emanation is well-known (see Schelling 2010, 1992). Following Aristotle (and Homer), Schelling advocates monarchy, but it is divine monarchy that is at stake here, a monarchy that has no analogy with any earthly sovereignty at all. The divine singularity that infinitely exceeds all closures and totality (in that sense the divine is the true *life* rather than system) suspends and delegitimises the ultimate *arché* of earthly hegemonies. The earthly sovereignties rule by the violence of power, and hence in them an analogy links power and ruling. On the other hand, the divine monarchy does not rule by power, and in that sense it rules without ruling; it is violence without violence, monarchy without sovereignty. Like Walter Benjamin's conception of 'divine violence', it is the violence of the *pure that*, 'without spilling blood', in contrast to the 'mythic violence' that is 'bloody power over mere life for its own sake' (Benjamin 1986: 297).

Schelling carefully distinguishes the divine monarchy from earthly sovereignties, the one from the multiple, the absolutely individual that rules without power (and therefore does not rule) from the multiplicity of powers: *heîs koíranos ésto*. The absolutely individual is not dialectically opposed to the multiple so as to be subsumed under a speculative totality; nor does it transit into the multiple, as in the Neo-Platonic model of emanation, in an ever decreasing manner. Were the latter the case, the divine would then serve as the originating *arché* of worldly powers. Schelling's Gnosticism, coming to him via Jacob Böhme's Kabbalah, decisively puts into question the political implications of the theology of emanation from which the legitimation of earthly sovereignties is drawn. It is rather that the absolutely individual, in an absolutely incommensurable manner, takes exception from the powers of the worldly, not so as to ground/institute/found them, but in order to make them fragile, to destitute or *unground* them. It is the Origen-inspired eschatological conflagration (*Apokatastasis*), the fire that overwhelms the order of the profane and redeems it in violence 'without spilling blood'. Hence the anarchy of love that precedes the nomothetic violence of potentialities: love interrupts the law of the eternal return of the same. Therefore the absolutely individual – which is not a particular as opposed to the universal – is not part of the series or chain of potencies once more; as singularity, it is always incommensurable to any 'hegemonic fantasm'. Love is outside totality: by interrupting the vicious chain of conditions and disrupting the mythic violence of eternal return, it opens the depth of being to the infinitude which is no mere modification of the law. Hence love does not know judgement, for in every judgement the law institutes itself with renewed force. The infinite divine excess of love is excessive, not on account of the power of its individuality, but rather out of its utter non-potentiality. Hence the worldly potentialities may participate in the divine excess only by following the infinite task of mortification, that is, by letting themselves be *impotential*. The divine exception without sovereignty is at once the *im-potentia* specific to the divine.

The citation from Aristotle (*heîs koíranos ésto*) is preceded by a discussion on the question of the absolutely individual and multiplicity. Multiplicity is not traced back to the absolutely individual as to an origin or a foundation. Between them there is a *hiatus*, an interruption and a diversion that remains like an irreducible remnant, *setting apart* and *separating* the un-pre-thinkable from the circle of potentialities. Going with and against Leibniz at the same time, Schelling thinks of this *cision* within God himself. The actuality of existence cannot be grounded on the nature of God, while the potentialities are ungrounded in the divine will. Thus one cannot make use of the divine will as an explanatory and originary principle of potentialities. The divine will can't be thought as the legitimising *arché* of potentialities: 'as the most singular (*tòmálista choristón*), i.e. as the most individual, is rather that from which nothing universal follows' (Schelling 1990: 65). Here singularity is not reduced to the particular so as to be subsumed under the universal. Rather, singularity (*Absonderlichste*) is that *Absonderung*, that which *sets apart* and *separates* and hence is *that* which is unsubsumable within totality; it is *that* which *always already* sets itself *apart* and *departs* from 'the maximising thrust' of empty universality. Singularity *absolves* itself from totality. Here the unity of thought and being is not abandoned (which is also the Hegelian task), but they are understood as *belonging*-together, that is, outside the onto-theological constitution of metaphysics. Nowhere but here does Schelling so forcefully exhibit the limit of metaphysics, while speaking the very language of metaphysics itself: 'In this unity, however, the priority does not lie on the side of thought; being (*das Sein*) is the first, thinking only the second or following. This opposition is likewise that of the universal and the absolutely singular' (Schelling 1990: 65). 'The opposition' of this 'unity', opposition from the heart of unity: such is the thought of the *belonging*-together of the trait of singularity and the trait of universality wherein their *difference as difference* is emphasised; it is the tragic *differend* of the traits of mortality and the trait of natality, wherein the emphasis is put on the trait of mortality (that we understand as *belonging*-together), seeing the 'unity' *from* the side of being, from mortality, from singularity as such. Like Kierkegaard and Heidegger, Schelling is the thinker of mortality that singularises the phenomenon, existence, being: singularity destitutes the 'maximising thrust' of universality and disjoins itself from the totalising *arché* of the *common* (*Koinon*). When one emphasises the trait of natality, 'the maximising thrust of the universal' (the potentiality of being or the de-phenomenalisation of being through the determination of it *as* essence), then there occurs the onto-theological grounding of worldly hegemonies. According to Schelling, this is what happens in Hegelian hypostatisation. In Hegel's metaphysics, the realm of apostasy (*Abfall*) and transiency (the worldly realm of history where earthly sovereignties rule) is divinised. This, as we have seen, is Hegel's theodicy of history, whose fundamental principle of movement is grounded in the Hegelian logic of the *Logic* itself, and which ends up discovering the objective expression of the absolute in the nineteenth-century Prussian state. This is how metaphysics and politics are conjoined in Hegelian logic. The result is an apology for the world.

Schelling, on the other hand, is the thinker of destitution and mortality, the tragic thinker of the *belonging*-together of singularity and university, of *that* (*Daß*) and *what* (*Was*), of actuality and potentiality in their *differend*. In this non-contemporaneity and incommensurability, an essential freedom is eschatologically emphasised. On account of the abyss of his freedom, God is essentially *free* in respect to the world, and in respect to his own nature.[3] He can thereby bring the entire world-order of *nomos* to an epochal closure and initiate an entirely new state of *just* existence. Thus the God in his Godhead is to be distinguished from the God bearing the mythic principle of *nomos*. Schelling discovers this thought of incommensuration and non-contemporaneity in Aristotle's idea of *symbebekós*: all religious ideas are ideas of incommensuration and distance. The absolute singularity opens up a generosity because it is *free* in relation to all potentialities, a generosity whose measure is not that of powers or potentialities, but that of justice. It is as though the immeasurable must, in any event, measure the measures of the world, and precisely thereby de-measure all wordly measures (*Apokatastasis*). The fire of *Apokatastasis* which found such decisive expression in early Christianity is understood here as a *de-measuring* of the worldly. Intensifying this distinction between *Daß* and *Was*, Schelling goes on to say:

> The way in which both are connected to each other requires a more precise expression. God is the universal essence, the Indifference of all possibilities. He is this not in a contingent, but in a necessary and eternal manner; he has it *in him* to be this Indifference: 'in him' in the sense that one might say of a human being that he has something 'in him', in order to express that he did not 'want' it, indeed sometimes even that he did not know about it. But precisely because God is that other without any additional action on his part, not in a wilful manner, hence *with respect to himself in a contingent manner*, it is to him a supervenient complement, a *symbebekós* in the Aristotelian sense, indeed a necessary complement, an autô kath' hautòn hypárchon, but still [something] that is not in his essence (mè en tê Ousía on). Hence [the supervenient universal is something] over against which the essence remains free. (Schelling 1990: 66)

The immeasurable singularity of the *Daß* in which there is no potentiality, and which precedes the concept, is thought here otherwise than as particularity. Singularity is not a particular illustration of the universal nor is it deducible, *axiomatically*, from the universal. The absolutely singular absolves itself from the universal, not as result or consequence of a given totality, but in an *a priori manner* that opens to the infinitude of the always un-enclosed futurity of manifestation. The negative philosophy *de-phenomenalises* the event by enclosing it in the necessary movement of potentialities (where the hegemonic fantasm triumphs); the positive philosophy, in contrast, opens us to the *phenomenality* and *re-phenomenality* of the event, out of the abyss of mortification (that is, by subtracting its worldly attributes and predicates, by *kenosis*), where, for the first time, we encounter the nakedness of the immeasurable being that *ex-sists* without predicates and attributes. Here the potentiality of the phenomenon is not denied, but is now understood in its 'proper' light, that is, out of the gift of mortality, out of the generosity of singularity, as the *donation* of freedom out of its groundlessness. The 'lordship' over potentiality is not here that of the power of sovereignty, but rather that of an immeasurable generosity which is, at once, the non-power. Such sovereign non-power is the holy; it is the holiness of Love without judgement, without the law. It is this exception that Schelling attempts to think with Aristotle: *heîs koíranos ésto*. With this notion of exception, the divine lordship (*herrshaft*) is uncoupled from sovereignty. As early as 1809, Schelling writes in his *Freedom* essay that Love precedes the distinction between good and evil; in other words, the language of Love precedes the language of judgement. As pre-judgement, Love is without fate, for there can be fate only on account of judgement: judgement strikes us as the fateful power. Therefore Love does not have to end with fate; or, fate is not the end of Love, for the beginning-less beginning of Love is a beginning before the beginning of judgement.[4]

It is the task of truly immanent thinking, according to Schelling, to keep itself open at the limit of possibilities to the generosity of this immeasurable gift, and to receive this gift out of abandonment and mortification (*Gelassenheit*). In the history of the concept of being, the gift of the immeasurable remained un-thinkable; this history did not understand the *that* as the *that* (*Daß*). In Plato, it is still thought prophetically as that which is *to come* out of the future. In Aristotle's renunciation, it is freed from his immanent thinking as *that* which is un-enclosed and irreducible. Hence Aristotle kept on multiplying distinctions so as not to enclose it within the immanence of potentialities. In these two different ways, immanent thinking arrives. This possibility is foreclosed when Hegel onto-theologically grounds singularity on the immanence of the absolute concept thereby reducing it to a mere particular instantiation of the universal: the tragic *differend* is denied by the 'hegemonic fantasm' of the dialectical cunning of Reason. Reason totalises; love singularises. The result is an immanent thinking, despite Hegel's claim to include actuality in the categorical movement of concepts. However unlike the Platonic prophetic immanence and Aristotle's immanence of renunciation, the Hegelian dialectical immanence not true immanence. Therefore, at the epochal closure of metaphysics, it is necessary to think not only a philosophy of transcendence (which is already non-philosophy in a certain manner), wherein *the actuality without potentiality* is the task of thinking, but also a true immanent philosophy that is concerned with true potentiality, exposed to the pure exteriority of the *that* which *ex-sists* without potentiality.

In that sense, in the history of the concept of being, *actuality without potentiality* has remained unthought and unthinkable. Only when the continuum of that history is torn open by a creative violence, and its movement brought to a standstill, does a new inauguration become thinkable. The major contribution of Hegel lies here – and this is not denied by Schelling – in that the immense movement of the history of philosophy is brought to a *respite* by him bringing it to its fulfilment. Because Hegel alone could think the closure of the history of philosophy by *gathering* that history into its innermost unity on the basis of the principle of a dialectical *continuum*, a radical discontinuity may now, even if momentarily, take its breath. Schelling is the lightning flash that makes visible, momentarily, the eschatological image of the event standing still in the burning landscape of redemption. This standing still of the image of redemption is also, because it is a lightning flash, an utmost intensification of time. In *The Ages of the World* Schelling opens up the possibility of thinking the eschatological event of temporality that bursts open the dialectical continuum of historical time. This intensification of time, the time of Schelling, in its utter transiency, bears another logic of endurance than that of the speculative-dialectical petrification of time and event. To come closer to Heidegger, it is a question of 'perdurance' (*Austrag*), which is not a lengthening of qualitatively indifferent time,[5] but a matter of *epochal breaks* without precedence. An ecstasy of interruption, this event of time is pregnant with eternity at each instance of its apparition, for it arises out of the gift of eternity itself. Schelling thought this exuberance eschatologically: the *eschaton* as *difference* that *separates* and *sets itself apart* from the *Koinon* (from the world-historical movement of quantitative, homogeneous and empty time). With this, Schelling's thought expresses its eschatological reserve toward any absolutisation of that which is only passing away: the divine event of redemption thus does not have, strictly speaking, a 'political meaning' (in the way that the state or the visible Church has). The unconditional event of *coming* does not coincide with any given historical presence; it bears neither any empirical historical 'date' nor any meaning as fate or destiny. The empirical-historical categories cannot congeal the originary event of decision. In that sense, the event of the *eschaton* is beyond history. In his Berlin lectures on mythology, Schelling elaborates on this idea of the excessive event of *de-cision* (*Ent-Scheidung*) which, as though in an *a priori* manner ('always already'), makes the *historical* possible for the first time, and which, *as such*, cannot be grasped in the categorical codification of the concept. Being not a 'presently given entity', it eludes the law of the concept. It does not become reconciled in speculative-dialectical mediation with the worldly regimes of the earthly order; rather, it radically puts into question the law of the worldly and opens up the futurity of the event from the heart of the finite world, that is, from the heart of the transient realm of history.

The actuality without potentiality is the other trait that withdraws from investment in an eschatological meaning in the worldly realm of potentiality. The positive philosophy insists on the *non-economy* of actuality. The logic of being, categorically grasped as potentiality, is always the logic of economy. In Hegelian universal history, the transition from one world-historical epoch to another is only a quantitative interruption which maintains, through the discontinuity, its fundamental continuum. Each circle of potency opens up to the other in an immanent manner, transitively, on a linear-progressive scale. Therefore, Hegel does not need to introduce radical breaks into his conception of universal world-history. In contrast, the advent of *actuality without potentiality* brings radical discontinuity into the vicious circle of the potencies. For Schelling, therefore, the *eschaton* is not a transition but an epochal interruption. He calls this messianic logic of non-economy the 'positive', the absolute transcendence that is not dependent on potency for its existence. It *ex-sists* without any capacity to be, and hence is the highest freedom from the mythic law of the eternal return. In the Schellingian eschatological schema, the return of the divine does not bring the identical but something absolutely new, by interrupting the mythic continuum of the world. *The divine is an interruption of the mythic immanence.* It is the holy that *holds apart* eternity from the foundation of the world. It thereby keeps the world open to receiving that which is beyond the law, outside fate, above the guilt. What is beyond fate is none other than blessedness or *beatitude*, the highest Good of mortal existence. This idea of beatitude, which has such a profound relation with the task of mortification of the worldly *nomos*, is already a decisive question for Schelling during his Platonic period, and it runs through his entire philosophical oeuvre. Throughout his career, Schelling never thought of beatitude as the *telos* of the triumphal march of world-historical Reason. For him, it is only by *abandoning* the logic of triumphalism and the work of law that one can open oneself to *beatitude*. As Paul Tillich informs us, it is Christ himself in his divine folly who works toward this abandonment of the law: 'But the Gospel is the perfect law of freedom whereby the external law, the external necessity that underlay all consciousness, is annulled. In Christ the whole cosmic religion died.'[6] The glory of the lord dying on the cross is *kenosis*: glory is *kenosis*; it is utter foolishness and not the truth of the world.

The acosmism of Schellingian thought is of Gnostic origin. Unlike Hegel's immanent pantheistic metaphysics, Schelling's thought does not make Christ into the prince of the world. In his idea of an acosmic God, a soft resonance of the old Gnostic notion of the *deus absconditus* can still be heard. *Freedom is the possibility of being free from potencies*: potentiality therefore has only a transitive meaning; in itself, potentiality does not have an ontological ground. Man is *spirit* on account of his freedom (not on account of his nature), which he never exhaustively actualises. Being essentially spirit, he receives the gift of freedom by which he remains free with respect to the *logos* of the worldly. 'As long as man chooses to be the universal essence, he remains in the center and is the lord of the potencies' (Tillich 1975a: 74). The task of his existence lies in releasing this spirit from the cages of the law through the infinite work of the mortification of self. From this Schellingian-Gnostic idea of the *deus absconditus* the Marxist Schelling Ernst Bloch develops the revolutionary-utopian possibilities of radical transformation. He thereby comes to think history itself as consisting of incalculable messianic disruptions that never allow the world to be totalised once and for all. For Bloch, hope is this eschatological principle of *difference* which he discovers at the very heart of the religion of exodus. Taking his inspiration from the Pauline messianic patience of the cross and from Marcion's Gnostic doctrine of the 'alien God', Bloch develops the idea of exodus as an atheistic-eschatological interruption of the mythic (Bloch 2009, 2000). The paradoxical Pauline messianic logic and Marcion's Gnostic doctrine of *Pneuma* are also of decisive importance for Jacob Taubes' political theology (Taubes 2010: 137–46). In Paul's messianic suspension of the law and his opening of a new covenant (*Verbund*) free from ethnic ties as much as from the *nomos* of the Roman Empire, Taubes discovers a radical political theology of exception without sovereignty. Already in his *Occidental Eschatology*, Taubes shows that the holy (*das Heilige*) means *separation* (*Aussonderung*) and *setting apart* (*Absonderung*), the holy that *sets the world apart* from its foundation. This being set apart lies at the heart of Occidental eschatology. The holy interrupts the mythic foundation of the *cosmos* (Taubes 2009: 194). The world is thus delivered from the law of the eternal return of the same into a radical transformation in which the voices of the oppressed can be heard. Taubes sees in Gnosticism such an apocalyptic flight from the iron cages of the law, a flight that still resonates in Schelling's philosophy of nature as much as in Surrealism (Taubes 2010: 98–123).

Deconstructing potentiality

By insisting on the provisionality of all worldly potentialities, the theodicy of historical Reason is eschatologically deconstructed. Here religion is understood eschatologically and not mythically: *religion as interruption of mythic foundation*. *The holy* is that which *sets apart* the world from its foundation. By interrupting the mythic immanence of the worldly, the eschatological event of revelation opens up the historical decision of existence to its new inauguration. As early as 1804 in his famous lectures on the Philosophy of Art, Schelling shows this disjunction *historically*. The circle of potencies that follows the law of the eternal return to the same is mythically founded. The horror and violence of this law, always returning to the same, is 'mythic violence'. Actuality introduces a *cision* into the vicious circle of the eternal return of potencies, and by virtue of its freedom suspends the law of return and opens the potentialities to the non-potential, to the un-pre-thinkable event of futurity that does not, in turn, belong to the totality of potencies. In such an eschatological provisionality, freedom introduces contingency and transiency into the domain of profane history.

The unconditional thus cannot 'express' itself objectively in the figure of any worldly hegemony without reserve.

Schelling arrives at this thought of *eschatological provisionality* by way of the famous 'pantheism controversy' that was raging at the beginning of nineteenth century. The profound importance of Friedrich Jacobi for Schelling's own thinking is often dismissed by Schelling scholars. They make Jacobi out to be a vicious figure, incapable of original thought and only good at inventing lies and creating controversies. However, in Jacobi's critique of philosophy as such (Spinoza is his paradigmatic example), thinking in nineteenth-century Germany took a decisive turn. Here is Jacobi's argument: If philosophy's self-given task, according to its own claim, is none other than Reason's determination of being as such, then philosophy can only end up in fatalism and nihilism. This is because the purely rational categories bear no intrinsic, unconditional being at all, and therefore can only begin and end with the conditioned. Since no conditioned being is 'being' in a proper sense, philosophy in a fundamental way can begin only with non-being. Beginning with non-being, Reason cannot help but open itself to still further non-being, and an endless progression from non-being to non-being is thereby released. Thus philosophy never arrives at the unconditioned, for the unconditioned cannot be said to be the result of an infinite chain of conditionals. Jacobi is horrified by the law of the eternal return of the same non-being, as if this nihilism is the necessary fate of philosophy. According to him, even Spinoza's pantheism (which treats God as immanent in the world) exemplifies the fatalism or nihilism with which all philosophical investigation must inevitably end up. In that sense philosophy is essentially atheistic; it can't be concerned with religion's insistence on the absolute irreducibility of the divine in respect to the world.

The theologico-political consequences of such an argument are undeniable. Jacobi decisively puts into question the purely immanent task of philosophical thinking that has become the epochal task of 'modernity'. He thereby warns of the immense theologico-political consequences that arise from such fatalism. The divine that is seen as embodied in the profane figures of worldly hegemonies is not truly divine. It is merely an idea of Reason that grasps the world in its iron necessity. This idea of Reason is a mere principle of the coherence of the world; it can be made to serve as the theological foundation of world-historical regimes. The pantheistic God is the pure potential being. He is, thus, the mythic God; he is the mythic power that bestows legitimacy on worldly powers in the profane order of eternal conditionality.

Schelling's early works grapple with this critique of the secularising project of modernity. This alone shows the decisive importance of Jacobi for Schelling's own deconstruction of historical Reason. The pantheistic immanent metaphysics of history that arises in nineteenth-century Europe with the secularisation of the theological is interrogated intensively by Schelling via Jacobi. Even though he refuses to accept the early Jacobi's solution to this nihilism, Schelling carefully attends to his critique. What he calls 'metaphysical empiricism' in his lectures on positive philosophy is a decisive and singular attempt at a way out of the alternative posed by Jacobi: neither the pure immanent determination of being as potentiality alone (the Spinozistic-Hegelian Path), nor mysticism's claim to attain the actuality of the divine in the ecstasy of interior feeling (Jacobi's path); to participate neither in the secularising project of modernity (Hegel's project), nor in the obscurantist mystical project of spirituality (Jacobi's project); neither to seek the unconditional in the infinite chain of 'not-not' (as in Hegel), nor to found the actuality on the basis of the 'mystical foundation of authority' (Derrida 2002: 228–98). Schelling's deconstruction here passes through a double reading: on the one hand, he puts into question the self-proclaimed authority of Reason that would arrive at the unconditioned by its own means, Reason that turns into the mythic foundation of worldly powers (Hegel is the target here); on the other hand, he recognises a terrible authority that founds itself on a mystical foundation, on the fantasm of the heart, in the name of the ineffability of God. In both these ways the divine is transformed into the theological-mystical foundation of worldly powers. In both, the divine is understood as the power of being, as the being that empowers, that is the source of power, as the *nomothetic* and *monothetic* principle of worldly hegemonies in the profane order. Therefore his metaphysical empiricism must radicalise immanence as much as transcendence, potentiality as much as actuality. A radicalised thinking of potentiality must pass through the deconstruction of potentiality itself; in the same way, a radicalised thinking of actuality, too, must pass through a deconstruction of actuality as it is known in the history of the concept of being. Both in his Munich lectures of 1833–34 and later in his Berlin lectures on positive philosophy, this deconstruction is carried out in such a way that the unthought event of *actuality without potentiality* is made apparent as the task of thinking. Such a deconstruction is *historical*, in two different and inseparable senses of the term: 1) it not only has to encounter the history of the concept of being in order to make manifest the logic of that history; 2) it also thereby has to raise, for the first time, the question of the *historical* itself, in a way that could not be thought in the concepts of being that determined the destinal passage of Occidental metaphysics. This *historical* deconstruction (which is also a deconstruction of 'history' [of historicism]) is different from the Hegelian project of a philosophy of history. In distinction from

Hegel's philosophical logic of history or historical logic of philosophy, Schelling's historical thinking does not ground itself on the speculative-dialectical logic of *Aufhebung*; he doesn't aim to reach the closure of metaphysics by taking up, one after another, the previous epochal stages through the very act of their negation. The task here is not to remember or re-trace the historical continuum of the world-historical movement from the 'dusk of history' back to its origin; it is rather to trace the fissures of the given history of the concept of being to disclose *that* which does not have to terminate in the epochal *telos* called 'modernity'. It is with this in-de-terminability, and with the in-de-terminable, that the question of the *historical* must again be posed, this time without the accompanying auto-engendering dialectical movement of *Aufhebung*.[7] The ecstasy of historical time, whose eschatological *energeia* is an inscrutable freedom, opens up the world to an arrival from the future that must not be teleologically determinable; it must be an un-pre-thinkable event of arrival, incalculable and yet imminent.

In his Munich lectures of 1833–34 on the history of modern philosophy, Schelling demonstrates how the event of existence, an *ex-sistence* that *spaces* being and thought (for *ex-sistence* is this *spacing*), could not have been thought in the philosophical discourses of modernity. This metaphysics of the epoch of modernity, from Descartes to Hegel, constitutes itself as a metaphysics of the Subject. The Subject is the ultimate *arché* of the modern *hegemonikon*. As *suppositum* of existence (this, so Schelling reminds us, is the meaning of the Subject), which exists *necessarily*, the Subject is the legitimising onto-theological ground or the nomothetic principle of the modern *hegemonikon*. Schelling thus underlines the decisive importance of Descartes and Hegel, the former representing the instituting moment of the epochal condition of modernity, while with the latter this epoch reaches its fulfilment and closure. At this instance, the question that presents itself to us is no longer: how to continue further with the fundamental onto-theological project of the modern *hegemonikon*? The question is rather: how to bring about a decisive rupture with the logic of the Subject by introducing an irreducible *spacing* within philosophy itself? The *disparate* of the 'positive' and the 'negative' is not a return to Kant, 'but a going beyond Hegel'. 'With this last event in the history of classic German philosophy begins the "philosophy of existence" which Marx and Kierkegaard developed in opposition to Hegel, the one externally, the other internally' (Löwith 1991: 115). The Schellingian caesura between negative and positive philosophy opens the history of metaphysics to its outside, to the eschatology of the historical materialism of Marx on the one hand (passing through Feuerbach, Ruge and Bakunin), and, on the other hand, to the Kierkegaardian eschatological-Christian deconstruction of Christendom.[8] With Schelling, followed by Marx and Kierkegaard, the principle of the Subject withers away.

Descartes institutes the *hegemonikon* of modernity by grounding it on the onto-theological *suppositum* of being, i.e., the Subject that *necessarily* exists. The famous Cartesian first principle, *Cogito ergo Sum* (the indubitable principle he arrives at), must be thought by Descartes in such a way that thought and being are considered to be immediately identical. This means nothing other than that the *Sum* is already 'enclosed in the Cogito': 'the opinion of Descartes is then that the *Sum* [I am] is enclosed in the *Cogito* [I think], already comprised in it, and given without any further mediation. From this it follows, then, that the *Cogito* really means the same as *Cogitans sum* [I am thinking].' But since '*Sum Cogitans* cannot mean that it is as though I were nothing but thinking ... thinking is, therefore, only a determination or a way of being' (Schelling 1994b: 46). From this Schelling concludes:

> The *Sum* which is contained in the *Cogito* does not, then, have the significance of an absolute I am, but only the significance of an 'I am *in one way or another*', namely as just thinking, in that way of being which one calls thinking. Hence even in *Ergo Sum*, 'I am absolutely' cannot be contained, only: 'I am in one way or another' ... it is just as right to infer: I doubt the reality of things, therefore they are, or at least: therefore they *are not not at all*. For if something is not at all in any way, I also cannot doubt it. Therefore, from my doubt itself about the reality of things, it does not follow that they indubitably and absolutely are, but it does follow that they are in one way or another; but, as was shown, no more follows from the I think than that I am in one way or another. (Schelling 1994b: 47)

The principle of the Subject that legitimates the modern *hegemonikon* determines being as 'not not'. It is this 'not not', which is *necessarily* an infinite capacity of being (and therefore is not itself an *existence*), that Schelling calls 'potentiality'. From this potentiality it does not follow that being *exists* necessarily: the singularity of existence, for existence is always irreducibly singular, cannot be deduced from the concept of being. The ontological foundation of the modern *hegemonikon* – which Descartes provides here – is the determination of being as potentiality and necessity, an instituting that Hegel perfects by giving it expression in an absolute system: at the heart of the modern hegemony lies a categorical fantasm, a fantasm of category. The law of being, the concept, is emptied of all singularity. A split, a caesura, a cleft already opens up at this very instituting instance of the modern *hegemonikon*: the rift between the 'what' of being in its mere capacity to be (the universalising thrust of Reason) and the 'that' of being as really and freely existing (the singularising trait of existence) – as if such *arché* violence must *always already* mark any instituting moment so that any such moment can only be a dehiscent, exposed, wounded opening. Because the act of institution can legitimise itself only by *representing* to itself its own act, and by *reflecting* upon this act, an ineluctable movement of *doubling* unconsciously opens up at the instance of institution. This shows that each event of institution is at once a doubling, exposed to the other trait of being that refuses to be enclosed in the nomothetic operation of Reason. It is this fate of reflection (*re-flection*) that haunts the epochal condition from Descartes to Hegel: the reflection never reflects without distortion or inversion; it never returns to the identical. Schelling reveals such an abyss already opening up at the instituting movement of the modern *hegemonikon* – that is, in Descartes – thereby disrupting the onto-theological constitution of modern metaphysics at the decisive instance of its fulfilment. To arrive at the certainty of *Sum Cogitans*, Descartes must open the movement of thinking to its *iterability*, to the logic of *differance*: on the one hand, thinking must go on in me, irrespective of whether I am aware of it or not and independent of my thinking of this thinking; on the other hand, there is the thinking of this thinking, that is otherwise than this thinking. If 'I am' to be absolutely certain of my existence, then I will have to arrive at the instance when the spectre of *differance* is definitively and decisively surmounted and negated (*Aufheben*). Contrary to Descartes' manifest desire, the *differantial* structure of all representation and reflection will have made any reflective positing of self-presence (in the form of 'I am') non-unitary. Since such reflection in an *a priori manner* proceeds from 'non-not' by positing only the entity which *necessarily* exists, it thus already excludes *that* which *exists* at all, for that which *exists* is not the 'not not at all'. Schelling shows this spectre of *differance* unworking the speculative logic of the Hegelian concept at the instance when the absolute spirit is supposed to have arrived to itself in absolute knowledge. This Hegelian absolute concept is not any 'this' or 'that' concept but the concept of the concept as such. The power of the concept, its metaphysical violence, lies in its thetic positing and grasping (for *Begriff* – coming from *Greifen* – means to seize, to grasp, to grab, to take hold of and to possess) of the entitative mode of being in a way that being is fundamentally determined as potentiality (it's *one way or the other*, its 'not not' character). In that sense Hegel's achievement is just to have brought to its consummate expression the metaphysical violence that already emanates from Descartes' instituting moment of the modern *hegemonikon*: that is, the violence emanating from the 'maximising thrust' of the concept. Since this whole movement of thought has to begin with the 'not not', with the *necessary* existence of God, and proceeds through reflection, it is still enclosed – even at its *telos* – within the infinite chain of conditionals, within the vicious circle of the eternal return of the same, within the mythic context of fate and the law. It appears as though reflection does not have the necessary resources to break with the original mythic context of the law in order to open itself to the historical existence. The *historical* cannot begin with what exists *necessarily*. What exists *necessarily* is not the actuality with which alone the realm of the historical can begin. From the infinite potentiality of being, 'it does not follow *that* He exists' (Schelling 1994b: 50).

Descartes attempts to bridge the gaping abyss (the famous Cartesian dualism) that opens up at this instituting moment of modernity by invoking a *deus ex machina*, the God who must exist *necessarily*. The God demanded by Descartes, the one who must exist necessarily, cannot not be, for it is impossible for such God not to be. 'But that for which it is *impossible* not to be cannot ever *possibly* be – for that possibility of being also includes the possibility of not being in itself – therefore that for which it is impossible *not* to be is never in the possibility of being.' In its impossibility not to be, God is the blind being 'which could never *not*-be and thus also could never really *be*' (Schelling 1994b: 53). What this God is – for it is none other than *what* is – is none other than the absolute concept of reason, the concept that reason supplies us with, the God who 'exists necessarily and blindly'. The hegemonic fantasm of the concept produces only the blind being: 'But if He is that which exists blindly, then he is for just this reason not God' (55), not the God that is *life*, for

> Life (*Lebendigkeit*) consists precisely in the freedom to negate its own being as immediate, posited independently of itself, and to be able to transform it into a being posited by itself . . . in the concept of God it must be thought that He is free in relation to His existence, not bound to it, that He can make it itself into a *means*, can negate existence in its absoluteness. Even if those who pronounce and assert God's freedom are not accustomed to proclaim it in this way – to think of it as freedom of God in relation to His existence, as a freedom to negate this existence as absolutely posited, it is still *in general* the case that in the concept of God absolute freedom of activity is thought. (Schelling 1994b: 55–6)

The God that Descartes invokes is the 'philosophical' God, where 'philosophy' is already determined as the metaphysics of the Subject. The God who is invoked here is the onto-theological Subject. He is *What Is*, the *suppositum*, the *arché* or the ground of beings, but not *that it is*, namely, *life* or *existence* that is moved by the exuberant energy of freedom. As concept of Reason, God is the ultimate principle (*arché*) of the world, the principle that guarantees the coherence and unity of the world as it exists, the rational principle that explains how God himself steps in to 'produce the corresponding movement in the body' when 'a desire or a wish arises in the mind, which the body should carry out' (Schelling 1994b: 59). It is the fate of this 'philosophical' concept of God – the God who exists in a *necessary* manner – to always have to supply and to legitimise the *nomos* of the world. The ultimate *arché* of God functions here as the *nomothetic* principle of the worldly: the laws of the world draw their justification and apology from this principle of ground. As such, it is the God of the myth on whose foundation the *hegemonikon* of modernity, from Descartes to Hegel, is founded. Schelling distinguishes this mythical foundation of authority from the God of religion whose existence is moved by a freedom that is groundless, who groundlessly opens the new world of history. The absolute singularity of God, his infinite transcendence with regard to worldly potentiality, makes him the *wholly other* of all hegemonic fantasms of the law. With the affirmation of the highest contingency within God himself – affirmed out of groundless freedom – the mythic continuum of *nomos* is eschatologically blasted open. The irreducible event of revelation is this blasting open of the mythic continuum, and in this sense it is the historical event par excellence. In his Berlin lectures on revelation, Schelling elaborates such an eschatological deconstruction of secularised modernity. If the Hegelian project is to consummate this neutralisation of the eschatological sting of religion, which is already begun with Descartes, then there can be no surprise of the future in the Hegelian pantheistic-immanent metaphysics of history. This is because Hegel has retained from Descartes only the concept of God as mere potentiality. According to the demand of the system, it cannot be open to the wholly other God, the other objectionable God who is not merely 'not not', who can't be included with a system of immanent categories. This 'wholly other' God is not the nomothetic principle of the world-order but *life* or *existence* itself.

In Hegel's renewal of the ontological proof of God in the wake of the Kantian critique, the Cartesian metaphysics of the Subject is given a decisive and consummate foundation. Schelling shows how such an onto-theological constitution of metaphysics has to determine God to be mere the result or *telos* of a rational movement that is *necessarily* progressive. The system demands that nothing is presupposed. Therefore Hegel has to begin with the pure subject-less (or purely objective) beginning: *being in general*.

> But that supposed necessity, of thinking *being in general* and thinking *all being in being* – this necessity is itself merely pretence, since it is an impossibility to think *being in general*, because there is no *being in general*, there is no being without a subject, being is rather necessarily and at all times something determinate, *either* essential being, which returns to the essence and is identical with it, or objective being – a distinction which Hegel completely ignores. (Schelling 1994b: 139)

To this subject-less pure being or *being in general* where nothing is presupposed – and in that sense pure being is really equal to nothing – to this barren, utterly empty being a movement, a transition, an inner restlessness is attributed:

> For the fact that he does, by the way, attribute a movement, a transition into another concept to this pure being, indeed attributes to it an inner restlessness which drives it on to further determinations, does not prove that he nevertheless thinks a subject in pure being, it only proves something or other of which it can only be said that is not *not*, or is not nothing at all, but in no way proves that it already is something – if this were his thought, the *progression* would have to be completely different. The fact that he nevertheless attributes an immanent movement to pure being means no more, then, than that the *thought* which begins with pure being feels it is impossible for it to stop at this most abstract and most empty thing of all, which Hegel himself declares is pure being. (Schelling 1994b: 138)

The result is a false claim on Hegel's part: a purely immanent movement of *not not*-movement that begins with *not not*, and can arrive only at the *not not* on the basis of the self-cancellation of the negative: this merely conceptual process is supposed to be the real movement of God's becoming of himself. Hegel substitutes the singularity of existence for a conceptual fantasm, arrived at purely through a conceptual process of subsumption: 'Becoming is supposed to follow' (Schelling 1994b: 140) from this pure, empty being which is equal to nothing. Here Schelling uses the famous Aristotelian distinction between 'the nothing' which is true potentiality and 'nothing at all'. In an immanent fashion, Aristotle opens up a true immanent thinking of potentialities, pushing it to the *telos* where the entire movement comes to a halt in encountering the exuberant being. Aristotle does not attribute actuality to this purely immanent movement. On the other hand, Hegel attributes actuality to the purely immanent movement of categories, beginning with an empty, barren *being in general*. But 'becoming cannot be there before something becomes, existence not before something exists' (Schelling 1994b: 145). Everything happens in this immanent movement of categories 'quite peacefully – there is no opposition between being and nothing, they do not do anything to each other. The translation of the concept of *process* onto the dialectical movement, where no struggle is possible, but only a monotonous, almost soporific progression, therefore belongs to that misuse of words which in Hegel is really a very great means of hiding the lack of true *life*' (143). Hegel's beginning that supposedly begins without any presupposition already opens this empty being to becoming and then goes on to unleash, in purely automatic fashion, the entire movement of dialectics:

> The Hegelian concept is the Indian God Vishnu in his third incarnation, who opposes himself to Mahabala, the giant prince of darkness who has gained supreme power in all three worlds. He first appears to Mahabala in

the form of a small, dwarflike Brahmin and asks him for only three feet of land (the three concepts of 'being', 'nothing', 'becoming'); hardly has the giant granted them than the dwarf swells up into a massive form, seizes the earth with one step, the sky with the other, and is just in the course of encompassing hell as well with the third, when the giant throws himself at his feet and humbly recognizes the power of the highest God, who for his part generously leaves to him the power in the realm of darkness. (Schelling 1994b: 148)

This immense logical movement of the concept at its conclusion is supposed to begin again in the realm of nature by virtue of 'the agony of the concept' (153), and is supposed to reach its *telos* with God the absolute spirit. In this entire movement, Hegel 'puts the fact that in the Last everything goes as into its ground; one ought rather to say: everything preceding grounded itself by the fact that it lowers itself to being the ground of what follows, i.e., to that which is no longer itself being but is itself ground of being for an other; it grounds itself by its going to ground (*Zu-Grunde-Gehen*), it itself is ground thereby, not what follows' (158). The distinction here is crucial. When God is seen as the Last into which everything goes 'as into its ground', we have the onto-theological constitution of metaphysics; but when God is thought otherwise than the ground of beings, then this God is not thought metaphysically as the ground of worldly potentialities: he is free in respect to all potentiality, and therefore is transcendent in relation to the world. Such freedom alone groundlessly opens up a new world, and it alone can be the true principle of beginning. What Hegel could not think, because he thinks God metaphysically as ground, is the event of arrival or the beginning of something – that is, the *historical* itself. The surprise of the event, groundlessly opening something out of the extremity of future, remains unthought and un-thinkable within the onto-theological constitution of metaphysics. As Schelling writes:

> For the God in so far as He is only the *end*, as He can only be in the purely rational philosophy, the God who has no future, who cannot initiate anything, who can only be as final cause, and in no way a principle, an initiating, productive cause, such a God is only spirit according to *nature* and essence, thus in fact only substantial spirit ... but just according to its essence, for how should *real* spirit be that which cannot move away from the end where it is posited, be that which only has the function of taking up all the preceding moments into itself as that which brings *everything* to an end, but not itself be the beginning and principle of something? (Schelling 1994b: 156)

As the principle of ground of the world, God is the *nomothetic* principle of the world's coherence: 'in the Last everything goes as into its *ground*'. But since this God is the absolute spirit only according to its *nature*, he 'is not free of the world, but burdened with it instead':

> As such, therefore, this doctrine is Pantheism, but not the pure, quiet Pantheism of Spinoza, in which the things are pure, logical emanations of the divine nature; this is given up, in order to introduce a system of divine activity and effect, in which divine freedom is all the more ignominiously lost because one had given oneself the appearance of wanting to save it and sustain it. The region of the purely rational science is left, for every externalization is an act which is freely decided and which absolutely interrupts the merely logical succession; and yet this freedom as well appears as illusory, because at the end one nevertheless sees oneself unavoidably pushed towards the thought which negates all having-happened, everything historical, because one, on reflection, must return again after all into the purely rational. (Schelling 1994b: 159)

This God is the mythic God; the ground of the world. As such, it is the pure potential God, the God of potentiality, God according to nature, and not the God that opens the world by absolutely disrupting the mythic circle of eternal return. The pantheistic God of immanence *necessarily* exists; it is impossible for him not to exist. As such he exists as fate or the law. But the divine actuality, in whom there is no potentiality, is the eschatological-messianic suspension of potentiality. Because he is free of the world as the groundless event, the worldly potentialities cannot draw legitimacy and justification from the divine actuality. As the groundless event, God decides, that is, *separates* himself from any claim of sovereignties (*decidere* meaning separation or cision). *Actuality without potentiality ex-sists*, that is, remains outside as *non-potestas*, as the *non-power*. It is the event of *cutting* (*decidere*), the un-pre-thinkable (*Unvordenkliche*) interruption of the mythic circle of the law and the opening of the realm of nature to the surprise of the future. What Schelling wants is not God as the mere rational principle of the worldly, the principle of harmony of the *cosmos*, but the God who, by the free act of revelation, initiates a new relationship, a new messianic covenant with man.

> In Schelling's concept of revelation, the rationalistic antithesis of revelation and redemption is overcome. By his personal act, God has revealed himself as personal. By the act of redemption, that is, the self-sacrifice of his natural sovereignty, he has redeemed mankind from the unfree, natural and servile relationship to him and has become truly personal toward mankind. God has entered into a new relationship with man, one that is personal instead of natural, evangelical instead of legalistic, spiritual instead of unfree. (Tillich 1975a: 139)

The divinity of this God is not an attribute or predicate which Reason supplies; his divinity lies in his incalculable *coming*: he is the *coming* God, the God of the future, 'the principle of hope', who initiates a new order of existence by suspending the coercive order of worldly hegemonies.

If the epochal principle of modernity, the principle of Reason or ground, totalises, then the other trait of mortality ungrounds out of the abyss of freedom. Schelling attempts to think the two traits in their *belonging-together* out of their difference *as* difference by introducing a polarity within God himself. The worldly potentialities cannot be traced back to the exuberant being of actuality; they lose their legitimacy and sovereignty in encountering the exuberance of being. They bow down as grounds – as non-being – to that which follows.

> Knowledge assures itself of exuberant being by its self-destruction; but it does not see exuberant being as long as there is still a residue of objectivity in itself, as long as it has not destroyed itself; it therefore only destroys itself in the *belief* that it will reach what is exuberant *by* this self-destruction – so to speak, as the price of its surrendered selfhood. Nonetheless, since it destroys itself only in its objectivity, but not in its subjectivity as well, and since it is rather only completed *knowledge* in subjectivity, then it would stand still *as* knowledge, and the last and simultaneous result would be – knowledge which was completed and which destroys itself in belief, but precisely thereby posits what is truly positive and divine. (Schelling 1994b: 176)

Therefore the totalising principle of Reason cannot really be total. There always remains the eternal remnant outside, a radical exteriority of the world, an unsaturated over or beyond being. It is the messianic remnant that holds the possibility a new inauguration of a just existence. It is the unsaturated excess without being. In confronting this *un-suture*, dialectics comes to a standstill at the very moment of its *telos*. Therefore the principle of Reason cannot claim itself to be the ultimate *arché* that elicits from us 'normative obligations' (Schürmann 2003). In confronting the anarchy of the divine without sovereignty, Reason retreats into the mere principle of ground. The epochal principle of modernity that determines being *as* potentiality is thereby destituted in this attempt to think the event out of the *Abgrund* of freedom.

In his 1809 essay on human freedom and in his 1810 private lectures at Stuttgart, Schelling shows that it is the devouring malice and the insatiable hunger of the non-being for being that is the source of radical evil. What evil is in the realm of history, disease is in the realm of nature: it is the insatiable desire of the non-being to actualise its inexhaustible potentialities that unleashes the demonic on the stage of history. When the non-being claims being for itself (while constantly falling short of being), it determines the whole of beings in totality as potentiality, as the infinite power-to-be. Radical evil erupts not from the power of being but from the infinite power-to-be. The more the non-being falls short of being, the more terrible becomes its hunger for being. If the principle of Reason determines beings only in their potentiality, this principle is always in danger of degenerating into demonic totalisation, for it recognises none other than its infinite power-to-be. This infinite power is not just *this* or *that* power, but power as such and at all; it is this infinite power-to-be that fascinates us, blinds us, provokes us to do evil. In making beings blind, they become blind being, which is being according to *nature* or *essence*. The world of the blind being is the mythic world of the eternal circular return of powers. But there is also the divine being, who is indeed outside being, who *is* not according to nature and essence but is Love; it is he who alone inaugurates the *historical* by interrupting the mythic circle of law. Therefore the immemorial Love precedes the lawful or lawless world of judgement, and thereby also follows it, like an eternal remnant, promising redemption in the new world. Love then cannot be thought on the basis of the law. It is neither lawless nor lawful, neither law-positing nor law-preserving, but that which precedes the language of judgement per se. If it bears power at all, the essence of this power would be *im-potentia*, that is, pure actuality in which nothing potential remains. *The divine actuality is therefore the non-sovereign exception*: it *ex-cepts* itself, puts itself *outside* of the potencies or powers-to-be, *separates* itself or *sets itself apart* from the mythic ground of the law. It therefore does not need a ground to *ex-sist*: it is pure anarchy of freedom, without legitimacy or legality, and yet in accordance with the highest necessity. Such necessity is not the necessity of the mythic law but the necessity at one with the highest freedom. Schelling's philosophy considers this highest necessity which is also the highest freedom to be the fundamental task of thinking at the epochal closure of modernity. Such a task is only thinkable when we put into question the secularising project of the modern epoch.

Metaphysical empiricism

The philosophical discourse of modernity reaches its epochal closure with Hegel's claim to have sublated dialectically the opposition between *quid sit* (what a being is) and *quod sit* (that it is). However, this sublation (*Aufhebung*) is only a conceptual sublation, a sublation only within the concept. For Schelling, such a dialectical opposition still belongs to the epochal condition of metaphysics, albeit bringing that metaphysics to its decisive closure. The true relation between *quid sit* and *quod sit* is to be understood in a manner that demands a step outside metaphysics. 'The former – the answer to the question *what* it is – accords me into the *essence* of the thing, or it provides that I understand the thing, that I have an understanding or a concept of it, or have it *itself* within the concept. The other insight however, *that* it is, does not accord me just the concept, but rather something that goes beyond just the concept, which is existence' (Schelling 2007a: 129). The result of Hegel's self-proclaimed 'reconciliation' of this difference within the concept is a pantheistic-immanent metaphysics of history. Hegel ends up divinising the profane world-order which anyway must pass away. Against this secularisation of theology, Schelling insists on an eschatological intensification of difference between the profane order of transiency, the realm of 'not not' which is destined to pass away, and the arrival of the absolutely singular event of actuality that is always *to come*. The dialectical reconciliation and its speculative totality laboriously achieved by Hegel's patient work of the concept are torn asunder once again. A qualitative *differentiation* bursts forth between the *real* (*Wirkliche*) that becomes within the mobile nature of the concept and the *reality* (*Wirklichkeit*) that is the event: the former attracts us with the gaze of power while the latter singularises us in an undeniable withdrawal. The logical nature of what is in *real* space (order, symmetry and definition) does not coincide with the indivisibility of space that is *reality*. The invisibility is *really* the life of the event. It is therefore is not the real (*Wirkliche*). In the same way that the indivisible event of *spacing* is not reducible to the logical categories of *space* (order, symmetry, definition), the event of phenomenality is not exhausted in the constituted order of signification.[9] With this *spacing* which is not space, the constituted order of the phenomenon (which Reason accomplishes through its nomothetic operation) is broken: it is this breaking of metaphysics, which Schelling introduces by interrupting the metaphysics of immanence, that anticipates both Marx's atheistic eschatological deconstruction of bourgeois society and Kierkegaard's qualitative distinction between eternity and time in the name of a Christian eschatological deconstruction. Marx and Kierkegaard, in opposite ways, quarrel with Hegel precisely on the question of 'reality', the former in an atheistic eschatological manner in the name of the messianic communist society, the latter from the Christian eschatological insistence on a qualitative distinction between the absolute claim of religion and man's pursuit of happiness in the order of profane history.

This *sundering* already manifests itself in the qualitative distinction Schelling sets out here between the *real* that is the immanent content of the concept *passing over* into being and that which does not exist in order to pass over into being (and therefore is not potentiality but pure *ipseity*). Schelling does not contest that there is a process or movement involved in Hegelian logic in which dialectical oppositions may pass over into each other and sublate themselves. He only contests that this movement of passing over – 'mediation' is the Hegelian keyword here – is other than a mere movement of potencies, and that it involves 'reality' itself. The conceptual movement of Hegelian phenomenology cannot *phenomenalise* existence, which is each time singular and irreducible, singular on account of its mortality. The inner restlessness of the concept lies in this potentiality, for there is indeed a restlessness of *quid sit*, which is to be distinguished from the aleatory manner in which *quod sit* erupts groundlessly. True, there is *necessarily* a restlessness in the concept itself (Hegel's claim is indeed true if he means no more than just this, but he claims much more), but it is a *necessary* restlessness of *quid sit* because reason has the compulsion 'to go forth into all being' and because only '*all* of being' (Schelling 2007a: 132) corresponds to its *infinite* potentiality. It thus 'immediately discovers therein its own thoroughly mobile nature and, with this, a principle of movement is provided':

> But the infinite *potency* of being – or that immediate content of reason that has the *infinite capacity to be* is not just the ability to exist, it is also the immediate *prius*, the immediate *concept* of being itself. In this way it subsists in accordance with its nature – hence always – and in an eternal manner. It must, as soon as it is thought in the concept, pass over into being, since it is nothing other than the concept of being. It is, therefore, that which is not be held back from being, and therefore, that which immediately *passes over* from thinking into being. Because of this necessary transition, thinking cannot remain as that which has the capacity to be. (Schelling 2007a: 133)

However, in this *necessary* movement *a potentia ad actum*, in this *essential* movement of pure potency *passing over* into being, it is the *quidditative* being involved and not the *quodditative*. In so far as a being (*ein seyendes*) which is concept – and thus is a potency – *passes over* into being, it shows itself to be 'not that which *Is*' in a movement which has to be *essential* and *necessary*. Thus in this movement one can only have the negative concept of being, the not not of being: 'it has no concept for the being that is other than that of what is not non-being, of that which does not pass over into otherness, that is, a negative concept' (Schelling 2007a: 137). The successive elimination of *potentia*, this infinite self-cancellation of the negative, never attains the exuberant actuality of being. The actuality of being can only appear at the end (*telos*) of this immanent movement of successive elimination as that which is exuberant (result of a process, a consequence), and precisely thereby it cannot be said to have already been included in the immanent movement *a potentia ad actum*. What alone is attained in this immanent-successive movement of self-cancellation of the negative is rather the 'intensification of the concept which in its highest potency remained just a concept, without there ever being provided a transition to *real* being, to existence' (139). Since such necessary-immanent-successive movement cannot but think something otherwise than *transitively* – as relative non-being *passing over* into being – it cannot but determine, by the logic of the ineluctable (namely, the speculative dialectical logic), *all* beings in its *all-ness*, in its totality or in its intensification of the universal trait of being. The hegemonic fantasm of totality, its 'maximising thrust', triumphs only at the cost of the other trait, i.e., singularity. Hegel's dialectical phenomenology does not remain faithful to the event of phenomenality itself; it does not attend to the double traits of being in their tragic *differend* (*quid sit* and *quod sit*). In the ever-expanding movement of totalisation, the intensification of the concept (and its subsumption of singularity under universality) is justified in the name of its *telos*, which is absolute spirit or absolute knowledge. At the level of world-historical politics, such a theodicy justifies the violence and suffering of the past, for it judges an event as meaningful only on the basis of its consequence, of its possible success in the visible light of the world-historical day. It constitutes itself as universal history wherein singularity is subsumed in the name of a future *telos* which is determined beforehand, a *telos* toward which the movement of history is irresistibly moved by the energy of the concept.

Against this triumphal march of the world-historical movement *a potentia ad actum*, Schelling discovers an eschatological *that*, a *that* which is never 'a transitive capacity to be', which 'does not pass over into being' (Schelling 2007a: 138), and which is not 'drawn into the process' of 'intensification of the concept' by passing through dialectical becoming. It is *that* which is neither the God of the ultimate *arché* nor the foundational principle (the onto-theological ground) of this immanent movement. The latter, being the *arché* of the infinite movement of the return of potencies, serves as the nomothetic foundation of the world-historical hegemonies. Against such a God who is the 'necessary idea of reason', who is the 'necessary consequence' (138) of the immanent movement of transitive potencies, and therefore which is still a concept even at the instance of its utmost intensification, Schelling must think the event of the *un-pre-thinkable actuality* in a *non-transitive* manner. He must think of an *eschaton* that does not pass over into being; an arrival that does not come to pass away; a transcendence that is not drawn into the immanent process of potencies again; a future that never becomes a *passed* past; a God who does not serve as the theological-nomothetic foundation of worldly potencies; an infinite singularity that does not get subsumed into the 'maximising thrust of the universal'; an absolutely individual that does never knows the logic of subsumption which the concept again and again thrusts into the world; an anarchy without any calculable, conditioned, practical negotiation with the pre-determined *telos* of the dialectical *Aufhebung*. If the fundamental *ethos* of the epochal condition of modernity is now visible more than ever, if 'it was from beginning to end an immanent philosophy' (138), then the task now is to think *difference as difference*, the difference, hitherto unthinkable, between negative and positive philosophy, which is *difference* outside of metaphysics.

From very early on Schelling attempts to think the event in a *non-transitive* manner. It is possible to show how the Heideggerian *Ereignis* – the event outside of metaphysics – is profoundly intimated by the Schellingian event of *non-transition*, if one takes into account the profound importance of the question of freedom for both thinkers. For both Schelling and Heidegger, as also for Kierkegaard, the event is not a transition but a *leap*, which Heidegger thinks in his own enigmatic way as *origin* (*Ursprung*), the *primordial leap* of *Ereignis* (Heidegger 2001: 75). Thus Schelling's 1804 essay *Philosophie und Religion* endeavours to deconstruct the Neo-Platonic metaphysical discourse of emanation that explains the phenomenon of the world from its source transitively and incrementally. Grasped retrospectively, the divine is seen in this process as the end result of a necessary-immanent movement of potencies, as the origin and legitimising ground or principle (*arché*) of potentialities. The worldly legitimising powers then can be traced back to God as foundation. Schelling understands the various discourses of the epochal condition of modernity – the Cartesian *deus ex machina* that is needed to explain the connection between two substances; the Spinozistic Substance-God that eternally exists *ad-geometrico* and which does not need to become; the Kantian regulative demand of God as necessary Ideal of Reason; the Hegelian God of theodicy as the *arché* of the profane world-historical order of potentiality, etc. – as so many attenuated variations of the determination of the divine as immanence. On the other hand, positive philosophy invokes the exuberance of the beyond being (*über dem Seyn*). 'Positive philosophy begins with [this] *completely transcendent being* and it can no longer be just a relative prius like the potency that serves as the basis of science . . . it must be the absolute *prius*, which has no necessity to move itself into being' (Schelling 2007a: 179). Profoundly important here is the question of freedom, which Schelling grasps eschatologically. The positive philosophy that Schelling names as 'metaphysical empiricism' is concerned with the free act with which the whole historical realm is inaugurated by bursting open the immanence of the mythic continuum: 'if it passes over into being', Schelling continues, 'then this can only be consequence of a free act, an act that can only be something purely empirical, that can be fully apprehended only a posteriori, just as every act is incapable of being comprehended a priori and is only capable of being a posteriori' (179).

When the epochal closure of metaphysics is in sight and the epochal principle of Reason withers away, the question of *the event* presents itself as the task of thinking anew the *historical beginning* out of the unground (*Abgrund*) of freedom. This free beginning, lacking an *arché* or ground in any necessity, cannot be grasped *a priori*; 'it is only capable of being a posteriori'. 'It freely determines its object'; it receives the demand of beginning 'solely from itself' and, 'likewise, it can provide itself with its own actual beginning. For this beginning is of the type that requires no foundation: it is that which through itself is the certain and absolute beginning' (Schelling 2007a: 154). At the closure of the onto-theological constitution of metaphysics, the question can no longer be that of instituting another order of hegemony by grounding it on the principle of necessity, but is rather that of opening a new *historical beginning without foundation*. Still speaking the language of metaphysics ('the certain and absolute beginning'), still naming this event of thought metaphysically ('metaphysical empiricism'), and yet thinking already outside, Schelling brings into play all those 'names', 'terms', 'symbols', 'emblems', 'hints' that will take on a decisive importance for post-metaphysical thinking after Hegel: the question of *event* and *decision*, of *existence* and *freedom*, of the *unground* and the *historical*, of *difference* and *finitude*, etc. In each of these names, the event of temporality — out of the disjointure marked by freedom — opens to the outside as that which is the ungroundable 'pre-supposition', the immemorial presupposition before of system (before *suppositum*, before the subject), the absolutely other of all self-presence, which, as such, can only come to us (it is the future anterior of the event) from the extremity of the future as posterior without finality: 'it is only capable of being a posteriori' (179).

Schellingian metaphysical empiricism is an empiricism that knows *a posteriori* what *always already* exists and knows this immemorial actuality without finality. This is indeed a paradoxical empiricism, for it is never the empiricism of what exists as present-at-hand or of what gives itself as an immediate and 'empirical' fact or datum of 'experience' to be finally subsumed under the general, universal law of cognitive categories. In this sense, metaphysical empiricism is neither empiricism nor rationalism in their already well-known senses as epistemological positions. The event exceeds destiny or fate; it rather concerns us with the task (*Aufgabe*) of *philo-sophia* – thinking that is 'always advancing' and thus always 'opens onto a future' (Schelling 2007a: 182) – that cannot be called 'system' 'precisely because it is never absolutely closed' (183) and is 'independent of all authority' (185). If the *hegemonikon* of modernity is instituted with the Cartesian *arché* of the Subject ('Cogito ergo Sum') as the legitimising authority of all that exists, the impoverishment of this principle opens up the futurity of thinking outside the authority of the Subject. In metaphysical empiricism, the Subject undergoes *kenosis*.

Thus it is no longer a question of substituting the epochal principle of modernity, namely the principle of Reason, with another principle of revelation. Metaphysical empiricism is not an empiricism of *presently given entities* that replaces the rationalism of the infinite potentiality of being.

Being neither mere rational cognition of the potency of being nor an empirical cognition of *presently given entities*, metaphysical empiricism is 'a new creation', 'a new phenomenon' (Schelling 2007a: 174) of opening to *the event of the world*. If the event of the world has some essential relation with the event of revelation, Schelling does not see in this event an *arché* or principle of the world. Revelation is not another principle displacing the sovereignty of Reason. Revelation is, therefore, not a source of authority. Metaphysical empiricism cannot be said to be *revealed philosophy*, as though philosophy, as such, could exist only on the basis of revelation. On the other hand, Schelling permits himself to speak of a 'philosophy of revelation' 'in exactly the same sense as in similar constructions – philosophy of nature, philosophy of history, philosophy of art and so on – that is, that in this construction, revelation is proposed as an object and not as a source or authority' (187). This is because he does not want to think of another hegemony (a Christian theological hegemony founded upon a principle of revelation) by displacing the given secularising *hegemonikon* of modernity (grounded upon the principle of Reason). That is why it is necessary for philosophy itself to 'advance beyond the merely logical systems', 'a necessity that lies in philosophy itself' (186) for 'an expansion of philosophy beyond its current limits' (190), beyond the universalising fantasm of Reason as much as the fantasm of mystical authority.

As true empiricism, the metaphysical empiricism of event must not be content with substituting one legitimising authority for another. While mere negative philosophy grounds itself on the legitimising authority of Reason, various other empiricisms ground themselves on the legitimising authority of mysticism. In two opposing ways, both negative philosophy and theosophy are unable to understand the *event as event*: they are 'familiar only with pure essential relations. Everything merely follows from it [from its *arché*] *modo aeterno*, eternally, which means in a merely logical manner, through immanent movement' (Schelling 2007a: 177). Such immanent thinking is essentially unhistorical. The source of its authority comes from the vitality that emanates, if it can be called a 'process' at all, in that it is *necessarily* engaged in a mythic process of becoming:

> In its essence, theosophy is no less unhistorical than rationalism. The God of a truly historical and positive philosophy however does not *move*, but *acts*. The substantial movement in which rationalism is confused starts out from a negative *prius*, for example, starts out from something nonexistent that must first move itself into being; but the historical philosophy starts out from something positive, that is, from an existing *prius* that does not first have to move itself into being. This *prius* thus posits only with complete freedom without being somehow required by its nature to posit a being. (Schelling 2007a: 177)

The divine, being the absolutely transcendent and absolutely irreducible *prius* of all thought, is not drawn into the mythical movement. As absolutely outside of all mythic foundation, the divine opens up a messianic futurity outside myth. Both the negative determination of being as mere potentiality that passes over into being (the Hegelian speculative theology of history), and the theosophical intuition of the birth of God and of the world (Jacob Böhme's 'wheel of nature') are enclosed in mythic eternity. Despite Hegel's claim to be able to really introduce history into being itself, thereby making Reason itself processual, Hegel's God remains, just like Böhme's 'wheel of nature', 'still enclosed in his eternity' (Schelling 2007a: 175). Therefore Schelling must put into question, in the same instance, both rationalism and theosophical empiricism. The rotatory movement of Hegel's absolute Spirit in returning to itself and the rotatory movement of Böhme's birth of God are both equally incapable of initiating a real event out of the *Abgrund* of freedom. Their God 'is incapable of ever changing over into real motion, instead of circulating around the very same point' (177). The result is the system of fate that encloses even the divine being in the law of the eternal return of the same.

Against the nihilism of Hegel's speculative theology of history that encloses even the divine being in the mythic law of necessity, Schelling thinks the event of revelation as the true event of the world. Such an event does not begin as potency passing over being into a conceptual and cognitive 'actuality' (as in Hegelian logic), but with the absolute *prius* of actuality. The world, beginning thus, does not have to end with a God at the *terminus* of the immanent movement as its unavoidable necessary result. As infinite *a posterius*, a continuously advancing demonstration of *that* which is absolutely *prius*, the world 'still opens onto a future'; it is always 'still incomplete', always already a limitless exposure to the outside (namely, the *dis-enclosed event*). Revelation, understood in this manner, is not one event among others. Independent of any authority, revelation is the state of existence of the world opening to infinitude, an 'ecstasy of reason': 'it contains something that exceeds reason, something that is more than what reason contains' (Schelling 2007a: 189). This excess or outside of the world, irreducible to the economy of the law, is precisely what makes the world incommensurable with itself. This 'beyond of the world', opening 'before the foundation of the world', is not *in* the world. It is not enclosed in the law of 'worldly' becoming. Yet being 'beyond' of this world, it precisely thereby opens up the world for the first time and thus cannot be grasped in the logical-immanent categories of worldly cognition.

> The content of revelation is first of all a historical content, but not in the vulgar or temporal sense. It is a content that indeed is *revealed* at a deter-

minate time, that is, intervenes in worldly phenomena. Yet according to its subject matter it is nonetheless veiled and hidden, as it was present and prepared 'before laying the foundation of the world', before the foundation of the world has been laid, whose origin and proper understanding thereof leads back to that which is beyond this world. It is this type of content that should become the content of philosophy within the philosophy of revelation. (Schelling 2007a: 188–9)

Here is Schelling's decisive response to the secularising project of the epoch of modernity. Against such a secularising historical Reason, Schelling does not posit the revealed philosophy of Christianity. The event of revelation is not thought *Christianly* in the name of revealed philosophy, for it is not a particular divine act that interests him, but 'what is *general* in revelation' (Schelling 2007a: 188). Without excluding this great historical phenomenon of Christianity and yet without positing itself as Christian philosophy, metaphysical empiricism is concerned with *that* event that opens up the realm of history, and which, precisely because of that, cannot be grasped through empirical historical categories (see Tillich 1975a: 117–58).

At stake here is the question of philosophy itself. Schelling calls metaphysical empiricism *philo-sophia*. It is not philosophy, if philosophy has no meaning other than 'system' and if system means absolute closure. Yet it is *philo-sophia* itself in the true sense of the term, if *philo-sophia* were to open up to an infinite affirmation without closure and without finality. In that sense the event of revelation opens up non-system in philosophy, as though the sense of *philo-sophia* is not exhausted in the finality that the system imposes upon itself. If, on the other hand, the meaning of system affirms the immeasurable outside, the unsaturated phenomenon of the un-pre-thinkable, then the Hegelian speculative system of dialectics cannot rightly be called a 'system'. If metaphysical empiricism is still 'empiricism', it is in the most unorthodox sense of the term. Such empiricism is *philo-sophia*, an infinite affirmation of the future and the outside without closure and without finality. It is *philo-sophia* 'beyond its current limit' (Schelling 2007a: 190). This may mean that the history of philosophy of the last two thousand years and more has now exhausted its possibility; it is finished, terminated, fulfilled, closed. Philosophy has become 'epochal'. But it also hints at the futurity of philosophy in entirely new sense of the term, at a philosophy that is still *to come*, that is *spaced open* by the hyphen: *philo-sophia*, the name of a thinking-opening to the infinitude of an affirmation of being that is 'above being'. If the epoch of modernity, out of its fundamental ground, determines being as potentiality, then it can be said that Schelling prophetically proclaims the end of that epoch. With this proclamation or declaration, the exhaustion of the discourse called 'philosophy', but also its possible renewal, announces itself in Schelling's attempt to think at the epochal closure of modernity.

Sublime event of history

Schelling conceives 'philosophical religion' as a religion of the future that is always open-ended; eschatology is the essence of this religion. Philosophical religion is not the particular truth of a *religious philosophy*. In that sense, metaphysical empiricism 'will nonetheless refuse to call itself, or allow itself to be called, a *religious* philosophy' (Schelling 2007a: 183); it does not ground itself on the theological dogma of a specific religious system to counteract the secularising project of modernity. In a certain sense, it is correct to call philosophical religion 'post-Christian' (Tillich 1975a: 149), and yet it does not participate in the secularising project of modernity derived from the Enlightenment's neutralisation of the eschatological sting. Since the metaphysical discourse of modernity itself is founded upon a certain theological principle that in turn neutralises the eschatological sting, positing a *religious* philosophy or even a mystical religion opposed to the former would be nothing more than its mere inversion. Therefore, metaphysical empiricism, of which the philosophy of revelation is an important constituent part, should not simply be understood as a 'return to religion' or 'return of religion', in the simple sense of returning to the pre-modern mythic idea of the aboriginal. It is not *religion* in the sense of *re-legio*, if that means binding us back to an aboriginal nature; with the event of revelation there occurs a decisive break with the mythological. If we follow Schelling here in spirit and not just in letter, philosophical religion ought rather to be thought in terms of the *eschatological suspension of the mythic foundation of the law of origin*. From this eschatological perspective, the political state appears to be an external form of the law as much as rational religion appears to ground the principle of the law onto-theologically. 'The oppressive power of the state and the public religion that is bound inseparably to it keep religion in original paganism within the boundaries of the nation and do not allow freedom to arise there' (Tillich 1975a: 99).

Freedom from the cages of the law means freedom *from* the worldprocess itself, *from* the rational law of morality as much as *from* the mythic law of nature. Schelling thinks this freedom by introducing a distinction in God himself. 'Just as it is necessary to distinguish in the concept of God between nature in God and the divine Self, so it is also necessary to distinguish between logos as cosmic potency and logos as personality within God' (Schelling 2007a: 102). This is because the self 'desires a God "who is outside of and above reason, to whom is possible what is impossible to reason, who is equal to the law, that is, a God who can set one free from the law". The ego finds its salvation only when it possesses God in actuality, and when it is united to him, that is, when it is united to him by means of religion, that is, by means of a voluntary, spiritual, personal religion that brings the old world in its entirety to its end' (102).

The divine is the *spirit*; as divine, he is free from worldly *nomos*. This divine is not a mythic principle burdened with the weight of the world-process. Schelling uses the term 'revelation' 'for the action of God as personality, or since it is the logos who acts, it is the term for the action of the logos as personality within God' (Schelling 2007a: 103). The spirit of God or God as spirit is freedom from the world, from worldly potencies, from the mythic law of nature. While the Hegelian secularised-rational version of the eschatology of spirit (*Geist*) divinises the earthly law of world-historical politics by introducing the dialectical principle of 'mediation' or 'reconciliation', Schelling's eschatology of spirit renders the mythic realm of potentiality transient and non-autarchic. The world is burst open to the miracle of revelation with which history begins groundlessly. Revelation is the event of the new and the incalculable outside the law. 'High above it as spirit is above nature': this spirit could not be anticipated in the Hegelian onto-theological metaphysics.

> In mythical forms God was perceived as nature, for man was related only to the cosmic potencies. In Christ the divine self is revealed as a spiritual personality who acts historically and who breaks through all the limitations of nature. This, then, is the content of all of history: the works of Christ, namely, to sacrifice his natural being in order to find himself again in spirit and in truth; this is the content of history because it is the essence of spirit. (Schelling 2007a: 111)

Thus, according to Schelling, Hegel's use of 'spirit' to refer to God is misleading. The process by which Hegel's God *releases* (*Entlassen* – an expression that Hegel borrows from Jacob Böhme) himself from himself and returns to himself does not break away from the mythic circle of presence (175). In the Hegelian term 'spirit', it is the mythic God that operates as the nomothetic *arché* of the worldly hegemonies. This process inevitably has to constitute itself as a pantheistic philosophy of history, going from one stage to the other in necessary movement of the concept, in which the apocalyptic sting of the new event *breaking through* is neutralised and removed.

Against this immanent pantheistic philosophy of world-history, where the world necessarily and in a determinable manner moves toward its *telos*, Schelling offers a catastrophic or apocalyptic vision of history that draws an entire world to its eschatological consummation and brings an entirely new world into being. The eschatological event of consummation can't be thought on the basis of the immanent plane of secular world-history. If Hegel speculatively grasped the world-historical movement on the basis of a dialectical logic immanent in the world process itself, it was only by deploying the principle of Reason. However, the principle of Reason, 'in which everything develops of necessity, knows nothing of a decision, of an act or even of a deed' (Schelling 2007a: 211). For the event of history to really be opened up, we must begin with a beginning that groundlessly opens up the world out of an unthinkable abyss of freedom, that is, we must begin with an immemorial beginning, with a beginning before any speculative memory, before any grounding process of the concept.

In history of the concept of being, the ontological proof of God provides the principle that guarantees the necessity and unity of the world. In his Munich lectures and later in his Berlin lectures of 1941–42 Schelling shows how, from Anselm to Hegel, passing through Descartes and Leibniz, the ontological proof really supplies the onto-theological foundation of the world. In the ontological proof, existence is the 'consequence of the concept or of the essence' (Schelling 2007a: 207). This is what is really at stake in Anselm's proof as much as in Leibniz's idea of God as *Deus et Ens, ex cujus essentia sequitur existentia*: 'But in eternity', Schelling objects to Leibniz, 'there follows from the essence, from the nature, from the concept of *God*, nothing more than this: that God, *if* he exists, must be that which a priori, in no other way can he exist, but *that* he exists does not follow from this concept' (199). With this *intensification of difference between the nature or essence of God*, God as potentiality and the existence of God, the world is eschatologically dis-enclosed from the cages of the law. For God himself is not merely the law, whether he is seen as the moral law or as the law of the world, 'for then it would not be that which necessarily and thus groundlessly exists'. This is because 'that which necessarily exists is precisely that which exists not in consequence of an antecedent concept, but rather exists *of itself* – as one used to express it, *a se*, that is, *sponte, ultra*, and which exists without an antecedent ground' (207). In Hegel's renewal of the ontological proof, this *nomothetic* principle of God is substantiated once more and this time as the very constitutive principle of a theodicy of history. The event of existence that exposes us to 'the abyss of reason', to the sublime decision of history – because it is so absolutely singular – is once again brought back to the universality of the concept instead of letting the law of the concept go.

In contrast to the Hegelian grounding of the worldly *nomos* on the theological principle of God, Schelling sees in the Kantian antinomy a *Wink* or a *hint* to the abyss of Reason 'in which no thought can discover a ground or beginning' (205). This hint to the absolutely transcendent and groundless being (*ein grundlos seyendes*), in confronting which Reason 'becomes motionless, paralyzed, *quasi attonita*' (206), occurs in the following passage:

> Even the idea of eternity, terrible and sublime as it is, as depicted by Haller, does not produce upon the mind such a feeling of giddiness; for although it only *measures* the duration of things, it does not *support* them. We cannot bear nor can we rid ourselves of the thought, that a being, which we regard as the greatest of all possible existences, should say to himself: I am from eternity to eternity; beside me there is nothing, except that which exists by my will; but *whence then am I?* All sinks away from under us; and the greatest, as the smallest perfection, hovers without stay or footing in the presence of the speculative reason, which finds it as easy to part with the one as with the other.

These lines, quoted by Schelling from the *Critique of Pure Reason* (Kant 1993: 418; A613/B641), 'express Kant's profound feeling for the sublime nature of the being that precedes all thought' (Schelling 2007a: 204). What Kant's antinomy exhibits, then, is not only that the principle of Reason cannot, on the basis of its categories, attain the unconditional, but also that such absolute transcendence can't be thought in terms of the relative transcendence of the old metaphysics. Kant's refutation of the ontological proof, then, was really only meant to show that *the sublime event of being* does not allow itself to be thought as the onto-theological 'support' or 'ground' of the world. Kant, however, does not really open himself to a new 'science' of the positive. With the notion of religion as non-potency, Schelling decisively surpasses Kant's idea of rational religion.

At the epochal closure of metaphysics, Schelling's positive philosophy shows the withering away or *kenosis* of the law of Reason, for Reason itself 'possesses nothing *on its own account*, it only watches as its content *dissipates*' (Schelling 2007a: 197). Therefore, the negative philosophy has as its content, 'properly speaking, only the constant *overthrow* of reason' (196). The exuberance of being, that which is *beyond being* or outside the potentiality of being, 'crushes everything that may derive from thought, before which thought becomes silent and before which reason itself bows down' (202). The *eschaton* is the divine anarchy that *groundlessly* opens history for the first time. Schelling thus argues for the abandonment of the principle of the ground. We must impoverish the *nomos* of the worldly and expose ourselves thereby to that which initiates without the law, the sublime event of history:

> For either the concept must come first and being must be the result of the concept, so that it would no longer be the unconditional being, or the concept is the result of being and we must then start from being, devoid of the concept, which is precisely what we want to do in the positive

philosophy. But in God it is precisely *that* by virtue of which he is what groundlessly exists, which Kant calls the abyss of human reason, and what is this other than that before which reason stands motionless, by which reason is devoured in the face of which it is momentarily nothing and capable of nothing? (Schelling 2007a: 205)

Such being is not the onto-theological God: 'Of this being Hegelian philosophy knows nothing – it has no place for this concept' (204). To open ourselves to the messianic event of history, even God (as *arché*, as ground, as *nomothetic* operation) needs to be abandoned. We are not opened to the groundless opening of the world starting with the law of the concept or with the consequence of an essence given to us beforehand. Just as Heidegger, in *Being and Time*, will later think the ecstatic *phenomenalisation* of existence (which is not just an inversion or consequence of essence), where Being is to be understood as 'to-be' – that is, in the infinitude of its verbal resonance – Schelling, too, here thinks existence not as a 'consequence of the concept or of the essence, but, rather, that which exists is here itself the concept and itself the essence' (207). Thus the saying 'existence precedes essence' or 'being precedes the concept' – which looks like a mere inversion of the metaphysical distinction between essence and existence – does not really keep the metaphysical opposition intact. Though Schelling himself sometimes describes it as an 'inverted capacity to be', in so far as the exuberant *actuality without potentiality* 'does not exist via transition *a potentia ad actum*' (199), he has already radically destabilised the metaphysical opposition between the two and thereby disrupted the unitary movement of Reason. Between God as the *nomothetic* operation and the divine being that groundlessly opens up the world beyond the law, there is no transition *a potentia ad actum* but an irreducible interruption, an unthinkable caesura, an abyss without reason, the event without foundation. Therefore negative philosophy does not *automatically* pass over into positive philosophy: 'Positive philosophy could begin of its own accord since it starts out from the absolute *prius*' (197). At the closure of negative philosophy, positive philosophy has to begin again – without foundation and groundlessly. Between them, as it were, there is inscribed a halt, a bringing to a standstill of Reason, a momentary paralysis of the law. The entire movement of the worldly *nomos* is, as it were, brought to a momentary nothing. The *Augenblick*, this absolute eschatological moment, actualises the passing away of *nomos* and inaugurates a new world. The momentary nothing is the sublime instance of history. There is therefore more than one beginning in Schellingian philosophy. The second beginning is not merely an indifferent and quantitative repetition of the first, but is a *differential* repetition, a bringing forth of *difference as difference* 'out of the night of the Identical' (Deleuze 1994: 190–1). Schelling shows how Hegel's speculative use of the incarnation of God reduces *difference as difference* to a difference that is a mere attenuated variation of identity. In that sense, Hegel did not remain faithful to the spirit of dialectics: that the event is always more than unitary; that being bears two traits that are always incommensurable, that cannot be subsumed under an overarching unifying principle. In Hegel's speculative idea of God becoming man and man becoming God, which he conceives dialectically, the absolute transcendence of the groundless opening is domesticated, neutralised, subsumed under the power of the concept. Difference becomes a dialectical energy that propels the triumphant march of world-historical politics. The result is a justification of the world as it exists.

The eschatological *Augenblick* can also be understood as an instance of revolution within history, when the time of the clock stops and the calendar time may begin. Ernst Bloch develops this Schellingian messianic, apocalyptic idea by combining it with the historical materialism of Marx. Kierkegaard, however, develops the Schellingian idea of *Augenblick* by thinking an *impossible* (outside potentiality, outside the concept) Christian interruption outside 'Christendom'. Rosenzweig in his turn develops the Schellingian eschatological idea of existence by elaborating an existential messianism outside the totalising grand narrative of Hegelian world-history. In all these philosophies, it is always a question of thinking, *outside* the epochal closure of metaphysics, *that event* which does not just issue from the power of being, which does not have to emanate *necessarily* from the 'violence of the concept'. The divine violence that crushes the power of being is violence in the sense that it suspends the law of the concept. In that precise sense, it is also without violence. Schelling is one of the few nineteenth-century thinkers who attempted to think the event of history in the name of a new *philosophical religion* without foundation. He thereby opens up the abyss of Reason, which Kant alone in his half-hearted and timid way hinted at, without decisively releasing it from the demands of the system. Only when the claim of the non-system becomes an unavoidable demand, bringing metaphysics to its closure, does the foundation-less event of history become the task of thinking. It thereby comes to disrupt the mythic foundation of the worldly constitution by introducing an eternal remnant of the pure future that will not come to pass away. Such a sublime event of history will no longer allow itself to be included within the predicative structure of a speculative history. In the post-Schellingian era, philosophy will have to begin with the un-pre-thinkable event which, as groundless *prius*, opens up a limitless and infinite thinking without closure.

Notes

1. Stanislas Breton in his work on St Paul underlines the proximity of the Pauline eschatological vision of nature to the Schellingian phenomenology of *Phusis*: 'Schelling . . . attempts "a derivation, on the grounds of principles, of a determinate system of our knowledge, that is to say the system of total experience". In both Schelling and in Pauline theology, the fundamental thought that emerges is of a "decline and slavery of a nature" waiting for its liberation. The speculations on the "world soul", on the *nisus formativus*, and on the "potencies" at work in the great organism show that the "mechanism" is at once a kind of waste or cadaver of extinguished life and a permanent yearning to surmount it. "Full of soul" and of a trembling sensitivity, *phusis* suffers the pains of childbirth that it might attain the spontaneity of which it is the obscure or unconscious reminiscence. The categories of immanent finality, the vision of a finality without an end, borrowed from *The Critique of the Power of Judgment*, but without the Kantian corrective of their critical usage, authorise a "hermeneutics of nature"' (Breton 2011: 124).
2. Schelling writes: 'The Socratic ignorance must be preceded by a profound and even exceptional knowledge: a knowledge of which it is worth the trouble of saying that it is not knowledge, or that nothing is known with it. Ignorance must be a *docta ignorantie*, an *ignorance savante*, as Pascal has expressed it. Without a profound knowledge that precedes it, the pronouncement that one knows nothing is merely ridiculous; for if one who is actually ignorant asserts that he knows nothing, then what is so strange about that? . . . Socrates presupposes a knowledge in this explanation of ignorance' (2007a: 158). The Socratic bombast and pomposity is thus a knowing ignorance, in contradiction to the bombast and pomposity of the sophists whose is an unknowing ignorance: 'for the one is unknowing or ignorant due to a lack of science, whereas the other is an ignorance caused by the exuberant nature (*Überschwenglichkeit*) of what is to be known' (159).
3. In his first monograph on Schelling, Paul Tillich dwells on how Schelling's attempt to think God free from the world-process comes out of a necessity to think 'a principle of difference [that] exists in indifference, a principle of self-defection, an irrational principle' (1975a: 48). Schelling thinks this principle of difference by developing a qualitative notion of time. 'It is possible to think', Tillich quotes Schelling, 'that the unconscious and the conscious were included in God in the same indivisible act of becoming conscious, the conscious as the eternal present, but the unconscious as the determination of the eternal past.' Tillich then comments on these lines: 'The qualitative notion of time that emerges in the concept of "eternal becoming" is a foundation stone of Schelling's system, especially of his philosophy of history. It will be examined more closely in that connection. In any case, at this point it frees the concept of God from a way of thinking that joins it indissolubly to the world process' (58).
4. The holiness of love overcomes the radical evil *groundlessly*: 'Therefore, as duality comes to be in the groundless, there also comes to be love, which combines the existent with the basis of existence' (Schelling 1992: 89).
5. Heidegger thinks of *perdurance* as the abyss of difference between overwhelming and arrival: 'The perdurance of that which grounds and that which is grounded, as such, not only holds the two apart, it holds them facing each other. What is held apart is held in the tension of perdurance in such a way that not only does Being ground beings as their ground, but beings in their turn ground, cause Being in their way. Beings can do so only in so far as they "are" the fullness of Being: they are what is most of all' (Heidegger 2002: 68–9). And again: 'The onto-theological constitution of metaphysics stems from the prevalence of that difference which keeps Being as the ground, and beings as what is grounded and what gives account, apart from and related to each other; and by this keeping, perdurance is achieved . . . this origin of the difference can no longer be thought within the scope of metaphysics' (71).

6. Tillich 1975a: 112. Tillich quotes from Schelling, *Sämtliche Werke*, ed. K. F. A Schelling (1856–61, 14: 239).
7. In a similar manner Kierkegaard offers an eschatological critique of historical Reason: 'the essence of passion is that, in contrast to the conclusive "termination" of Hegel's system, it compels a de-termination which decides "either" one way "or" another. A decision par excellence is the *leap*, this "decisive protest against the inverse, methodological process", namely, dialectical reflection. The determined passion of a decision ready for this leap determines an immediate beginning, while the beginning of Hegelian logic truly starts not with the "immediate" but with the product of an extreme reflection: pure being in general, abstracted from all real existence' (Löwith 1991: 150).
8. Löwith writes: 'To the bankruptcy of this "world grown old", Marx opposed the proletariat; Kierkegaard the solitary existence before God   reduction of human existence to the elementary questions, to the bare question of existence as such; this was for Kierkegaard the other side of what Marx called the "secular question as to the value of life". Thus both criticisms are based on the same hostility toward the existing order: to Marx's secular criticism of the bourgeois-capitalist world there corresponds Kierkegaard's equally radical criticism of the bourgeois-Christian world, which is as far removed from primitive Christianity as the bourgeois state is from the *Polis*. Marx confronts the external, existential situation of the masses with a decision, and Kierkegaard the internal, existential relationship of the individual to himself; Marx philosophised without God and Kierkegaard before God' (1991: 160–1).
9. 'Thus, for example, the indivisibility of space is not a matter of real space, and what is in real space – order, symmetry and definition – is all of a logical origin. In this way one may comprehend the importance of that distinction. Reason provides the content for everything that occurs in experience; it comprehends what is *real* (*Wirkliche*), but not, therefore, *reality* (*Wirklichkeit*). This is an important distinction' (Schelling 2007a: 131).

Chapter 2

The Rhythm of History

Political theology and the philosophy of history

It has been suggested by some of the most important scholars and philosophers of our time (Löwith 1991, 1957; Taubes 2009; Schmitt 2005) that the philosophical discourse of modernity is theological in its origin and that the epochal project of modernity can be understood as the secularisation of the theological notion of history.[1] This secularising project of modernity, best expressed as what we come to call 'philosophy of history', 'begins only in modern times' (Löwith 1957: 2), and is unique to the philosophical discourse of modernity. From Karl Löwith we know that the term 'philosophy of history' was first used by Voltaire. 'This philosophy of history', writes Löwith, 'originates with the Hebrew and Christian faith in a fulfilment and . . . ends with the secularization of its eschatological pattern' (2). In contrast to the Greek conception of history, whose fundamental principle is 'verification of prognostications concerning historiconatural events' (9), the philosophy of history opens up 'the temporal horizon for a final goal', 'an eschatological future' which 'exists for us only by expectation and hope' (6).[2]

However, the secularising project of modernity has not left its eschatological origin intact. On one hand, the philosophical discourse of modernity legitimises its condition by an appeal to the eschatological opening up of the future as the pre-eminent temporal horizon out of which our historical condition, at any instance, is to derive its meaning; on the other hand, the historical Reason of modernity, by relegating the *eschaton* to an indefinite goal, takes away the eschatological sting of the Judeo-Christian thought. The result is an immanent-pantheistic metaphysics in the form of a philosophy of history which maintains the insistence on futurity while at the same time liquidating its urgency and imminence. Hegel's speculative-dialectical philosophy of history, with its immanent movement presupposing no transcendental foundation, is the utmost realisation of the secularising project of modernity. According to Carl Schmitt, it is in Hegel's organic theory of the state that such a pantheistic-immanent metaphysics finds its utmost systematic expression. With the withering away of transcendence in today's world, the state now can no longer appeal to any transcendental (or 'theological') foundation for the legitimacy of its existence. With Hegel's dialectical 'reconciliation' and 'mediation' of the divine and the worldly, such a transcendental foundation 'has lost all validity'. This, however, does not mean that after Hegel the question of the legitimacy of the state itself has lost all validity. It is rather that a new form of legitimacy has come into being, no longer on the basis of the transcendence of the sovereign figure with respect to the legal order, but on the basis of a dialectical 'mediation' that is effected, in an auto-engendering manner, in the very immanent-processual order of universal world-history.

This process of secularisation can take place only by removing the apocalyptic throne of transcendence. For a political theologian like Schmitt, the result is disastrous: with the liquidation and neutralisation of sovereignty – and, along with it, the loss of authority and apocalyptic possibility in the political order – there occurs a neutralisation of the very possibility of *the political* itself. Schmitt's political theology laments this loss of sovereignty, this loss of exception in regard to the legal order, and the loss of decision that alone keeps alive the apocalyptic passion of the sovereign figure who, being the exception, knows no dialectical 'mediation' or 'synthesis'. It is this unmediated character of decision that Schmitt finds expressed in the theological passion of Kierkegaard, whose negative dialectic resolutely refuses any dialectical 'mediation', 'reconciliation' or 'synthesis' (Kierkegaard 1957: 9–21) between the radical stage of the religious existence and the immanent order of normative generality. The yawning abyss that Kierkegaard finds in his own existence is the very condition of possibility for decision, the decision that must be taken at the limit of all situations and 'outside' the general order of validity and normativity. No doubt it is Kierkegaard who, more than any other nineteenth-century thinker, understood the apocalyptic sense of *decision*, where the event of *de-cision* is affirmed in all its exceptionality (in the sense of *decidere*, that is, of *setting apart* or *cutting off*). Schmitt discovers in Kierkegaard's eschatological deconstruction of the immanent-pantheistic metaphysics elements of a political theology that maintains the loneliness and the sovereignty of the authorial figure. To Schmitt, Kierkegaard appears to maintain an exception in respect to every positive-general order of equality and legal rights, an exception that is the privilege of the sovereign power alone.

Schmitt's political theology, centred on the concept of sovereignty, arose as a critique of the secularising project of modernity. Against the pantheistic-immanent metaphysics of history which grounds the Hegelian dialectical conception of a world-historical movement, Schmitt erects a counter-revolutionary apocalyptic political theology, drawing on counter-revolutionary political thinkers such as de Maistre, de Bonald and Donoso Cortés. Exception, argues Schmitt, cannot be thought on the basis of the pantheistic-immanent conception of history, for the question of legitimacy does not allow itself to be included in the immanence of the positive-legal order. In this post-secular turn, the Schmittean conception of *exception* interrupts the mythic immanence of the Hegelian theodicy by showing that the fundamental political concept of modernity (the concept of 'progress') has its origin in theological discourses, and thus cannot be explained without evoking the theological in turn.

While participating in this 'post-secular turn', and going along with the Schmittean deconstruction of the Hegelian theodicy of history (and thus of the pantheistic-immanent metaphysical discourse of modernity), I attempt to construct here the elements of a political theology that puts into question the logic of sovereignty itself. This double reading or double deconstruction puts into effect *a non-sovereign political theology* in the name of a messianism or *eschatology without sovereignty* – if such a political theology allows itself to be conceived at all. Naming such a messianism or eschatology, destitute of sovereignty, as a 'political theology' is a gesture I borrow from the works of Jacob Taubes (2013, 2010, 2009, 2003), in which he conceives of a 'negative political theology' from below rather than (like Schmitt) from above. The hypothesis I propose here is the following: in Schelling's deconstruction of Hegel's pantheistic-immanent metaphysics there can be found the elements of a political eschatology (or a political theology) that puts into question the secularising project of modernity without having to invoke the figure of the sovereign (the one who decides on the state of exception). This is because Schelling was able to think, at the closure of the epochal condition of modernity, *an exception that does not in turn become a rule*. Such an exception does not serve as the legitimising principle of sovereignty; it is without *arché*, incapable of founding any worldly hegemony in turn. We find in Schelling's *Hegel-Kritik* just such a *radical political theology of exception* that constantly interrogates, through an *eschatological intensification of the difference* between the profane order of the political and the theological, any attempt to legitimise worldly sovereignty. Schelling attempts to think such exception not onto-theologically but as *outside being* altogether: as the *un-pre-thinkable* (*Unvordenkliche*) *event* that does not exhaust itself in any immanence; as the transcendence of the *beyond-being* (*das Überseynde*) that does not have to pass over into potentiality. Such a political theology, unlike Schmitt's, does not recognise the political to be total. Against the Schmittean totalisation of the political (which is a political theology of sovereign exception), Schelling's radical political theology thinks an exception and a decision that has only 'religious' meaning.[3] In the unique sense that Schelling lends to *religiosity*, the political encounters here what it cannot include, what is prior to political Reason, what exceeds the logic of the law. This insistence of the surplus exposes the domain of the political to the wound of an eschatological justice that keeps the possibility of the future alive. The future is, then, thought to be the unsaturated event that makes Reason ecstatic (outside of itself), un-enclosed in the cages of the law. Such an eschatological future does not allow itself be grasped as 'progress' in the realm of universal world-historical politics: the *eschaton* is the *surprise of the future* that may suddenly and incalculably erupt in the very midst of history. Anticipating the *politics of world-nihilism* of Benjamin and the messianic disruption of Bloch, Schelling — from very early on — conceives the worldly domain of phenomena eschatologically as the order of mere passing away, and thereby insists on a *dis-investment* from the world as it exists.

This disinvestment from the worldly order of transiency enables Schelling to construct an eschatologically conceived philosophy of history that he decisively distinguished from the Hegelian immanent-pantheistic metaphysics of history. Closer to the Benjaminian *politics of pure means* and the negative political theology of Taubes (and thus to the Pauline paradoxical messianic logic)[4] than to the political theology of Schmitt, the Schellingian eschatology of history renders all worldly attributes empty, in the sense that St Paul gives to *kenosis*. This paradoxical logic of the *kenotic* eschatology does not think the domain of the world-historical as theodicy: *kenosis*, being surprise, cannot be envisaged as a goal to be pursued in the plane of world-historical politics. *Kenotic* eschatology puts into question the ideology of progress that constitutes the fundamental metaphysical presupposition of modernity. We know from Benjamin that such an ideology serves the interests of the victorious and the dominant. In the name of the future good that is placed at an infinite distance (in Kant, as we know, it is a mere regulative principle: an infinite idea or task), the ideology of progress justifies the past sufferings of mankind. Against the Hegelian dialectical vision of the universal world-historical movement, Schelling envisions *epochal breaks* that do not have to be the mere attenuated variations of a fundamental, underlying continuum that Hegel calls 'Subject'. Only such a vision of history, consisting of so many messianic instances of disruption, can give voice to the muffled cries of those who are oppressed by the triumphal march of world-historical politics. It is in such an *antinomianism* — this eschatological interruption of the mythic continuum of history – that Benjamin too, following Schelling (without, perhaps, reading him), sees the possibility of expressing the irremissible past suffering of the oppressed and the downtrodden and thereby redeeming them from the violence of history. For Schelling, as for Rosenzweig and Benjamin, the unconditional claim of redemption is tied up with the immense question of the past that does not have to become *passé*. Conceived thus, the past *remains* the past of presence without being *passé*; in waiting for redemption it thereby elicits from us the messianic obligation not to invest wholeheartedly in the profane order of world-historical politics. Schelling names this *surplus* over the political 'religiosity', while Rosenzweig and Benjamin name this religion in excess over the political 'messianism'. At stake here is the task of thinking the unconditional that is always *in excess* of the conditioned realm of world-historical politics, whether we name this excess 'religiosity' in the manner of Schelling, 'Christianity' (without 'Christendom') in the manner of Kierkegaard, or 'messianism' in the manner of Rosenzweig and Benjamin.

In his magnum opus *The Ages of the World* we find Schelling attempting to formulate such an eschatological vision of history. As such, incomplete though it is, this work occupies an important place in the Schellingian oeuvre. In this fascinating document we see Schelling posing some of the decisive questions that will occupy him for the rest of his life. *The Ages of the World* appears to be the threshold that opens the negative philosophy to the positive philosophy, the doctrine of potencies to the actuality of the un-pre-thinkable event of freedom. This threshold is conceived not as an immanent transition of the potencies into the actuality of freedom but as a caesura that lends this fascinating text its enigmatic beauty and inexhaustible profundity. Schelling's political theology is born out of this eschatological vision of history whose fundamental principle is not the idea of progress, as in Hegel, but that of epochal breaks exposing the world to the eruption of the incalculable and the unthinkable. This incalculable *eschaton* – incalculable because its principle is not necessity but the abyss of freedom – tears open the mythic continuum of (Hegelian) historical Reason to the explosion of catastrophes.

In *The Ages of the World* Schelling discovers as the ground of history not the metaphysical principle (*arché*) of the Subject but the groundlessness of freedom. History is the predicate of freedom. This idea – that history is the predicate of freedom and not vice versa – makes history eschatological, that is, exposed to the absolutely new, to the unanticipated, uncalculated event of the absolutely heterogeneous and dissymmetrical in respect to the worldly. What arrives out of the abyss of freedom is the un-programmable *event*. It is the *differance* in the heart of the same that opens up the realm of the historical in the first place: *differance* is the structural condition of the birth of history.[5] In this eschatological vision, history appears to be nothing other than the order of apostasy (*Abfall*), transient in its inner rhythm, exposed to the wound of eternity that breaks it open, and that keeps breaking open any attempts at the closure of history. It is this possibility of *the arrival* that frees us from the law of necessity and opens the worldly to that which is neither lawful nor lawless but of the redemptive order of justice. Freedom frees us from the law of necessity into the Open of history by putting into question any justification of past suffering in the name of a never-to-be attained future *telos*. The *dunamis* of such an eschatology, whose intensity is given by its infinite interruption of any mythic continuum, is that of *rhythm*. Schelling's eschatology expresses itself as *the rhythm of history*.

Theodicy of history

It is no accident that the birth of historical Reason in modern times is tied up with the liquidation of the eschatological sting. The Kingdom of God is to be established *hic et nunc* in the worldly realms of the profane order. The *coming* of the Kingdom of God which (by virtue of its absolute heterogeneity in respect to any legitimising earthly *hegemonikon*) puts into question any worldly sovereignty, is now domesticated, reformulated as the *telos* of *saeculum*. 'Thus for Hegel', writes Karl Löwith, 'the so-called secularization of original Christianity – its spirit and its freedom – by no means signifies a reprehensible apostasy from its original meaning' (1991: 35).[6] The result is a theodicy,[7] 'the justification of God in history' (Löwith 1957: 57; 1991: 216). Hegel grasps this theodicy of history speculatively and dialectically, tacitly presupposing a certain Christian theological doctrine of creation. It conceives the order of creation as immanent, wholly coincident with itself – as the metaphor of the circle implies – knowing nothing outside of the world: the Kingdom of God is to be established *hic et nunc* in the worldly realms of the profane order. It grasps the *becoming* of the world or the world *coming* to itself by the principle that is this *becoming* itself, presupposing nothing outside, nothing of the futurity *to come*. While everything that has come to pass away *in* the world can be questioned, there remains nothing exterior to question *the worldly* itself. Like Mozart's joyous celebration of the created order for being so beautiful and so consummate in its completion and harmony, Hegel's theodicy of history celebrates the *pleroma* of the worldly; it feasts and nourishes itself on the fecundity of this *pleroma* which presupposes nothing transcendent. As we have seen, such a celebration of what exists can turn out to be an apology for the world as it is, and a justification for the irremissible suffering of the oppressed – it accepts as a necessary and unavoidable evil the muffled cries of those who are trampled by the triumphant march of universal world-historical politics. It is against just such a theodicy of history that Nietzsche writes his 'untimely meditation' called *On the Uses and Disadvantages of History for Life*.[8] Hegel evokes the Christian idea of God's 'sojourn on earth' in order to legitimise the universal world-historical triumph in the profane order. His speculative theology thus understands the order of creation as inherently good: the world-order is inevitably, necessarily and irresistibly progressing toward the *pleroma* that is the *telos* of history, which can be none other than the Good itself. In throwing God into the world, neutralising his transcendence (where transcendence implies divine freedom in respect of the created world-order), Hegel's speculative theology deprives us of the standpoint from which the injustice of the world can be judged and opened to eschatological justice. Since the world is thought to be necessarily harmonious in spite of the inevitable conflicts of world history, Hegel cannot address the question of radical evil in its radicality and immediacy. This is because the Hegelian 'cunning of reason', by the power of conversion, recognises evil to be merely the privation of the good. Hegel understood evil to be a necessary and justified aberration, a fecund necessity which gives the world-historical movement its energy, its agony and ultimately its atonement.

Hegel's theodicy of history, despite its dialectical-agonal structure, does not recognise radical evil: the question of evil and suffering is not its fundamental problem.[9] At stake in this pantheistic-immanent metaphysics is a political theology of sovereignty: a worldly figure is elevated into an embodiment of absolute Spirit, a result that does not conform to the Christian conception of 'divine foolishness', of Christ dying on the cross, with its appeal to abandon worldly privileges for the sake of redemption from sin.[10] Secular historical Reason, founded upon the political-theological principle of sovereignty, here turns out to be an 'apologist of the factual' (Nietzsche 1997: 106), of the world-historical situation as it exists. But this celebration of the 'power in history' that constantly evokes the Christian theological conception of creation is, in fact, a distortion of the true Christian eschatological impulse. Here the outstanding element is not the celebration of the consummate beauty of creation, but the profound experience of evil and suffering (Löwith 1957: 3). It is Hegel's faith in the world-historical march of universal history that neutralises the true eschatological intensity and ignores the impatience of the unconditional demand for redemption in its urgency and imminence. The indeterminate and indeterminable eschatological eruption in the immanent plane of history, outside of all calculation and programme, is transformed into a 'goal' or 'aim' at the end of the triumphant world-historical movement of progress. The true eschatological interpretation of history, however, is not one of triumph or success but one of 'boundless suffering'; it demands an eschatological history that is qualitative not quantitative, consisting of so many instances of messianic intensity.

Eschatology and history

Birth of non-dialectical thought

Schelling's departure from speculative Idealism, already markedly visible in the 1809 Freedom essay, appears even more decisively in *The Ages of the World*. In his *Phenomenology of Spirit* of 1807 Hegel achieves the most consummate expression of speculative Idealism: here dialectics is no longer a mere method but the very *dunamis* of being that *phenomenalises* itself as processual and historical. In his later works (for example in his lectures on philosophy of history), Hegel does little more than put to work this speculative-dialectical ontology, performed, of course, 'in a grand style and with rich certainty' (Heidegger 1985: 6). Because for Hegel the question of freedom was never the singular question it was for Schelling, the decisive *polemos* between freedom and system — which leads Schelling to depart from speculative Idealism — never appears in Hegelian thought in all its worklessness. Hence for Hegel, at least according to his intension, philosophy can have no meaning other than that of 'system'. Accepting the consequences that follow from this self-understanding of philosophy, Hegel places his own philosophical system of absolute Idealism at the end of metaphysics, that is, at its epochal fulfilment, thereby unintentionally opening up the imperative or task, later taken up by the young Left Hegelians, of thinking without 'system', that is, without dialectics in its speculative investment. Schelling thus remains for us, even now, the enigmatic figure who appears at this incalculable *juncture* where thinking must *disjoin* itself from the claim of the 'system', and in that sense he can justly be called the first post-Hegelian thinker. The question of freedom, now freed from 'system', has retained — thanks to Schelling — its irreducible singularity and its sublime inscrutability. The question of history is now allowed to manifest itself as something heterogeneous, dissymmetrical and inaccessible to the dialectical method, for freedom (which is the subject of history) shows itself to be incommensurable with 'system' each time it is evoked. Now the question of history, as the predicate of freedom and not vice versa, is approached from an eschatological standpoint, and no longer only dialectically. Freedom is the eschatological principle that moves history toward an *eschaton* which is not a 'goal' (*telos*) attained by a necessary and immanent movement of Reason but an *end* which is at once incalculable and imminent. This distinction (between 'goal' and 'end') has for us a profound theologico-political significance.

This is why Schelling could say in his Berlin lectures on positive philosophy that only positive philosophy (whose subjects are *actuality* and *freedom, existence* and *event*) is *historical*, while negative philosophy (by which he means the pure rational and immanent philosophies of Kant and Hegel) is a-historical. Here the meaning of history is understood eschatologically: *eschaton* understood as *an event of transcendence* (which is actuality) *breaking through* the world, tearing open the fabric of the world to the *outside*, not to another world but the *outside* of the world *as such*. This event of *eschaton*, because it is the work of freedom and transcendent to history, cannot be set as a goal to be progressively realised in the immanent-movement of secular history; therefore, the event of the *coming of God* does not manifest itself as a 'worldly' reality. With this, Schelling puts an end to the theodicy of history, displacing it with an eschatological vision that insists on the radical difference between the idea of a secular-immanent progress dialectically realised in history and the messianic event of radical interruption which is not progress but an object of hope *contra* hope (hope for the unhoped for). The messianic *paradox* of this hope for the unhoped for cannot be thought dialectically; its paradox lies in its effect preceding its eruption; its affirmation precedes any dialectical act of negation. The effect of messianic disruption precedes the dialectical resolution of intra-mundane conflicts between worldly *potestas*. That is why the messianic paradox does not operate by the principle of sublation (*Aufhebung*): paradox, we learn from Kierkegaard, is not a (speculative) dialectical process, and that is why dialectic, when it is taken to be absolute without taking the question of the historical seriously, becomes only an 'empty semblance and shadow'. *The Ages of the World* begins with this deconstruction of dialectic:

> There are two beings, a questioning being and an answering being, an unknowing being that seeks knowledge and an unknowing being that does not know its knowledge. This silent dialogue, this inner art of conversation, is the authentic mystery of the philosopher. From the outside this conversation is thereby called the dialectic and the dialectic is a copy of this conversation. When the dialectic has become only form, it is this conversation's empty semblance and shadow. Therefore everything known, in accord with its nature, is narrative. (Schelling 2000: xxxvi–xxxvii)

In *The Ages of the World* Schelling replaces the 'empty semblance and shadow' of dialectic with a hermeneutic of narrative. This constitutes a significant *step back* from the dialectical method of onto-theological metaphysics. Since what is to be known is not already given and, as such, is not supposed to be lying there in its finished condition, it is 'only the striving toward *anamnesis* and hence more of a striving toward knowledge than knowledge itself'. 'For this reason . . . to regard the most consummate dialectic as knowledge itself, betrays more than a little narrowness. The very existence and necessity of the dialectic proves that it is still in no way actual knowledge' (Schelling 2000: xxxvii). Such a hermeneutic of narrative grants 'a principle outside and above the world' (xxxv). Contra the dialectical method of Idealism which must pre-suppose nothing outside the *worldly* (outside the *saeculum*), the hermeneutic of narrative opens with a presupposition of 'the supramundane principle' of *anamnesis* (xxxvi), outside the closure of the world. Because the Hegelian secular dialectic of history must not presuppose anything 'outside the world' it cannot recount its own past. The past – which must be presupposed as the abyssal ground of presence – can only be narrated, for all narrative, being recollection (*anamnesis*) of the immemorial, grants itself a 'principle outside the world' and is a *dis-enclosing* of the world from itself. On account of this *dis-enclosure*, the world or Reason becomes ecstatic. Now philosophers, like poets, are not imbecilic bureaucrats of Reason who know no ecstasy and are without 'a constant solicitation of madness',[11] who are satisfied with what *already* exists in the world as something finished and dead. Unlike these 'civil servants of humanity' dreamt of by Husserl (1954: 15), the true philosophers are those who are exposed to *the event of the world* itself and who are intimate with it. This alone explains their ecstasy (being outside of oneself, enamoured, transported): 'Not only poets, but also philosophers, have their ecstasies. They need this in order to be safe, through the feeling of the indescribable reality of that higher representation, against the coerced concepts of an empty dialectic that lacks enthusiasm' (Schelling 2000: xxxvii). Here is a critique of the metaphysical 'violence of the concept'. Because the labour of the concept (*Begriff* – Schelling has Hegel in mind throughout) is essentially the dialectical operation of positing, grounding or founding, the concept is essentially coercive. The metaphysical 'violence of the concept' is same violence that emanates from the law, which is a thetic operation of founding out of nothing. Such an operation does not have to presuppose anything apart from this very act of founding itself (Benjamin 1986: 277–300; Derrida 2002: 228–98). The metaphysical 'violence of the concept' (Derrida 1980: 97–192), which is the violence of metaphysics, is none other than this law positing violence of founding, grounding or instituting out of nothing.

What Schelling asks us to attend to, though it is not clearly brought out here, is political authority based on a theological foundation in the absence of any given foundation: such a founding without given foundation is the source of the law and of its violence. According to Schelling, the dialectic does not radically put into question the coercive law of the concept; instead, presupposing nothing that is given, it radicalises the possibility of founding in an immanent fashion. The metaphysical violence of the concept lies in this very mythic *auto-poesis*; the violence of the concept is mythic violence. The politico-theological legitimisation of authority may conceive the divine figure as immanent in the secular world, on the stage of world-historical politics, and objectively embodied in the state. Thus Schelling's deconstruction of the pure rational religion – wherein God is either subjected to ethical necessity (as in Kant) or embodied in the figure of the state on the stage of world-historical politics (as in Hegel) – is essentially a politico-theological critique. The later Schellingian thought of a 'philosophical religion' cannot, then, be understood mythically or mythologically; rather, as the *religion to come*, it interrupts the mythic foundation of the law. The religion of the future is truly 'religion' – so Schelling would say – for it preserves the transcendence of God without subjecting him to the law of (ethical or juridico-political) necessity and at the same time without subjecting him to the lawlessness of fanatical mysticism (as in Jacobi). The challenge and task for Schellingian political theology is to think this eschatological suspension of the law and necessity without giving way to the mysticism of lawlessness. If Reason is the *arché* of the hegemony of modernity, the deconstruction of modernity demands a re-thinking of religion as an 'ecstasy of reason' which Reason itself cannot grasp, for it is not mere unreason dialectically opposed to Reason.

The coercive law of the dialectic lies in its repression of that tragic *differend* which does not automatically sublate itself into a dialectical opposition: the *differend* desists the law of the concept and stands outside thought as 'something impregnable so that the philosophy that would explain everything found nothing more difficult than to provide an explanation for precisely this Being. They had to explain the incomprehensibility, this active counter-striving against all thinking, this active darkness, this positive inclination toward darkness' (Schelling 2000: 7). This demands thinking contradiction that is without *Aufhebung* as its operating principle, contradiction that does not have to sublimate itself into the 'maximising thrust' of the universal that constitutes the hegemonic fantasm of modernity. Understood in this sense, the dialectic with its operating principle of *Aufhebung* is the enemy of that 'philosophy' that attempts to think *actuality without potentiality*. This *actuality without potentiality* is the 'singularity to come' without hegemonies. Following the tragic-Gnostic thinking of Jacob Böhme and Franz Baader, Schelling conceives (as already prefigured in his *Freedom* essay) *existence* itself, whether divine or human, as the agonal site of contradiction without *Aufhebung*. This tragic contradiction without *Aufhebung* does not allow itself to be thought under the jurisdiction of Reason, for it is not contradiction that is immanent in Reason: it is not Reason's own *othering* of itself, and hence is not lifted up into the fold of Reason, for Reason in its demand for totality cannot account for the very event of its *coming* to itself. The contradiction that dialectical Reason, with *Aufhebung* as it operating principle, can think is only the contradiction that must be immanent to it (this is the coercive law of the concept) and it must repress that which is counter-striving against thought, that which is 'prior' to Reason:

> Idealism, which really consists in the denial and nonacknowledgement of that negating primordial force, is the universal system of our times. Without this force, God is that empty infinite that modern philosophy has put in its stead. Modern philosophy names God the most unlimited being without thinking that the impossibility of any limit outside of God cannot sublimate that there may be something in God through which God cuts itself off from itself, in a way making itself finite for itself. Being infinite is for itself not a perfection. It is rather the marker of that which is imperfect. (Schelling 2000: 7)

Idealism's denial of 'that negating primordial force' is the *tragic denial* of the disparate; it is the tragic denial of the incommensurable traits of being: what Schelling discovers here (closer to Hölderlin's 'caesura of the speculative' than to the Hegelian negativity of the concept) is the tragic difference at the heart of identity, 'a doubling that already lies at the bottom of the simple concept' (Schelling 2000: 7), and the event of decision, that is, the *de-cision* (*decidere*) that does not sublimate itself into identity. It is this contradiction as *differend* – without necessarily passing over into identity – that gives vitality to God's as much as to the mortal's life: 'therefore, without contradiction would be no movement, no life and no progress. There would only be eternal stoppage, a deathly slumber of all the forces' (12). The imbecility of dead intellectuals as much as the idiocy of the Idealist bureaucrats ('the civil servants of humanity') lies precisely in this *Hemmung*; for these civil servants who know no ecstasy, contradiction is none other than unitary contradiction. Such unitary contradiction is, in fact, only a *clotting* or *inhibition* of an *ecstatic* contradiction that is outside the law of the concept. Unitary contradiction, precisely because of its unitary character (difference grasped as an attenuation of the identical), can then be subsumed, by the violence and power of negativity (the labour of the concept lies precisely in this), under the 'maximising thrust of the universal' and be fixed under the gaze of the 'hegemonic fantasm'.

> The principle of contradiction actually only says as much as that the same *as the same* could not be something and also the opposite of that something. But the principle of contradiction does not disallow that the same, which is A, can be an other that is not A . . . expressed in other words, this would

mean: of two things exactly opposed that stated of one and the same thing, according to the law of contradiction, if one is in force as the active and as that which has being, then the other must become that which is respectively not acting Being. (Schelling 2000: 8–9)

From this ecstatic contradiction, life – divine or mortal – nourishes itself. Here life is an event, unfinished and unenclosed, not a coagulated product of inhibition that dead intellectuals grasp and subsume under a conceptual category. In this ecstatic contradiction, Schelling finds an ecstasy of contradiction in God himself:

> It does not follow that in God one force is active and the other is inactive, but rather God itself is of two different kinds; first the negating force (B) that represses the affirmative being (A), positing it as the inwardly passive or as what is hidden; second, the outstretching, self-communicating being that in clear contrast holds down the negating power in itself and does not let it come outwardly into effect. (Schelling 2000: 9)

This ecstatic contradiction – the ecstatic polarity in God himself – cannot be subsumed, by the force of the concept, under a unitary principle. There is, thus, always more than one affirmation and one negation, more than one being and more than one non-being. Invoking the names of Plutarch and Aristotle, Schelling invites us to think this ecstasy of contradiction that is without the logic of subsumption, an ecstasy where non-Being (*nicht Seyn*) is non-identical to not-having-being (*nicht seyend Seyn*):

> this distinction, entirely easy to learn and which can be found, if nowhere else, certainly in Plutarch, between non-Being (*nicht Seyn*) (μή εἶναι) and Being which has no being (*nicht seyend Seyn*) (μή Ὄν εἶναι). This lets one also defend the expression 'privation' with which Aristotle indicated the other, the opposed τοὐναντίον, namely, insofar as the negating force, which contracts the being, does not posit that it is-not, but rather that it is not that which has being. (Schelling 2000: 14)

The fundamental argument Schelling puts forward here hinges upon this ecstatic *intensification* of *difference* that can't be subsumed under the 'maximising thrust' of a unitary principle (*arché*) called reason or ground: the non-identity of non-Being and not-having-being does not admit of dialectical resolution. Schelling's Gnosticism of is nowhere more apparent than here: God is not just nature but also freedom (this is the polarity in God). The event of decision, erupting out of the abyss of freedom, cannot be grasped on the basis of the principle (*arché*), the principle of the 'why' (reason or ground). Therefore this contradiction or difference is not a speculative-dialectical (Hegelian) contradiction of Reason; rather, it is this contradiction that makes Reason *ecstatic*, that is, a contradiction not immanent in Reason itself. Only a non-dialectical hermeneutic of narrative, opening to that which is outside the 'web' of Reason, can narrate the primordial past of the world, a past which is not an attenuated variation of presence (once present) but an immemorial past that is always past. This immemorial past – this always *outside* the world – cannot be understood on the metaphysical (onto-theological) ground of being as presence; it is thereby not merely empty nothing – despite what the Hegelian speculative dialectic thinks – but 'the primordial force', something 'impregnable', a counter-striving; it is an active nothing that must nevertheless be constantly overcome; a madness without which the law of Reason becomes coercive and violent, and which must nevertheless always be regulated; an unconscious past without which consciousness cannot account for its own condition of eruption, and which nevertheless consciousness can never completely sublate into the light of intelligibility. It is this 'irreducible remainder', this radical *outside* without ground, this immemorial past of all that exists, that can never be dialectically sublated into the light of Reason:

> There is no dawning of consciousness (and precisely for this reason no consciousness) without positing something past. There is no consciousness without something that is at the same time excluded and contracted. That which is conscious excluded that of which it is conscious as not itself. Yet it must again attract it precisely as that of which it conscious as itself, only in a different form. That which in consciousness is simultaneously the excluded and the attracted can only be the unconscious. Hence all consciousness is grounded on the unconscious and precisely in the dawning of consciousness the unconscious is posited as the past of consciousness. Now it is certainly not thinkable that God was unconscious for a while and then became conscious. But it is certainly thinkable that in the same inseparable act of the dawning of consciousness the unconscious and the conscious of God were grasped at the same time. The conscious was grasped as the eternally present but the unconscious was grasped with ascertainment of what is eternally past. (Schelling 2000: 44)

This ground or the past of Reason – that is, the madness without which there are only dead intellectuals – is not sublated into Reason without an 'irreducible remainder'; it is the 'principle', in a manner of speaking, outside Reason in the sense that it is never exhausted in the light of Reason. This *outside* is not the dialectical other of contradiction but is the other of ecstatic contradiction which, when regulated, gives life its beauty and grace, gleam and glint,[12] redeeming it from 'the violence of the concept'. What Hölderlin calls 'happiness' (life redeemed from fate), Schelling would call 'beatitude': the paradisiacal blissfulness redeemed from 'the force of law' and from the power of the concept; an ecstasy nourished by a contradiction that (Hegel's) Idealism cannot imagine. The coercive concept of the Hegelian dialectic does not know this *other* contradiction or difference that is ecstatic and redeeming and a 'path to glory'.[13] Schelling sees such an ecstatic contradiction at work in the divine life as much as in mortal life:

> Pain is something universal and necessary in all life, the unavoidable transition point to freedom. We remember growing pains in the physical as well as the moral sense. We will not shun presenting even that primordial being (the first possibility of God externally manifesting) in the state of suffering that comes from growth. Suffering is universal, not only with respect to humanity, but also with respect to the creator. It is the path to glory. God leads human nature down no other path than that down which God himself must pass. Participating in everything blind, dark and suffering of God's nature is necessary in order to elevate God to the highest consciousness. Every single being must get to know their own depths and this is impossible without suffering. All pain comes only from Being. Because all living things must first involve themselves in Being and break out of the darkness to transfiguration, so, too, in its revelation, the divine being must first assume nature and, as such, suffer it, before it can celebrate the triumph of its liberation. (Schelling 2000: 101)

There must be contradiction such that it is an unavoidable 'path to glory', a path to redemption from the violence of nature; there must not be dialectical contradiction that coerces us by the force of its law, that *inhibits* the flow of life by erecting dams along the way. A 'critique of violence' in a Schellingian spirit must, then, affirm a redemptive contradiction in distinction from the coercive contradiction of the concept. Since God is life, and therefore must pass through Being (and is therefore 'beyond being'), his suffering is a pathway to redemption from the violence of nature and from the coercive subjection of divine life into ethical or politico-legal necessity. Schelling here attacks the metaphysical violence of the law of Reason that dialectically subsumes difference or contradiction into the unitary, indivisible figure. Where the logic of sovereignty constitutes itself as unitary and indivisible, the ecstatic contradiction of the divine life escapes the ban of sovereignty: it is *life* and as such it is freed from the ban of the law. This is because for Schelling the law of nature or of Being (from which violence is inescapable) is not the Godhead, truly speaking. Outside the nature of God – that means, outside God himself – there *ex-sists* the Godhead *as actuality without potentiality*, as an exception without sovereignty. Such is God's freedom in respect of his own nature: he suspends the law of nature and transfigures it into glory. It is this contradiction, this irreducible *distance* between God and his nature, this contradiction as the pathway to redemption, that the empty dialectic of Hegel cannot imagine. Therefore, despite the Hegelian insistence on the agonal structure of dialectic, there is always the danger of a conflation of the world and God which results in a pantheistic metaphysics of history, a theodicy that glorifies the profane history of the secular world as expressive of the absolute. Such a metaphysics, as Nietzsche rightly points out, is an apology for the world, for the successes and triumphs of the dominant. Against the Hegelian dialectical subsumption of contradiction under a unitary principle, it is necessary to invoke an ecstatic contradiction that is mindful of the irreducible *distance* between God and the world and between ground and existence. Religion, in this sense, is the *spacing* of God and the world, an immeasurable distance that incessantly measures the worldly order of transiency. The world thus loses autochthony and autarchy. The history of the profane order is the order of passing away, and not worth much of our wholehearted investment: this is the essence of Schelling's political theology.

Spectres of pantheism

The famous 'pantheism controversy' that F. H. Jacobi unleashed against Moses Mendelssohn and others has profound politico-theological consequences for us. Jacobi's argument can be succinctly summed up thus: the philosophical discourse of immanence (a discourse that presupposes nothing of transcendence, because it does not begin with anything determinate) inevitably ends up in a pantheistic metaphysics which hurls God down to earth, turning him into the worldly figure of a finite knowledge which philosophy deifies into absolute knowledge, a result that Jacobi terms 'nihilism'. At stake in this nihilism is the inability of philosophical thinking to think the irreducible difference between God and human Reason (or the human world). In response to this argument, Schelling comes to conceive of an ecstatic contradiction that moves life in ways that makes Reason itself ecstatic, a contradiction opened up by 'an irreducible remainder' that *ex-sists* (remains outside) without ground, by that which is not immanent in Reason itself.

Schelling's response starts with his critique or deconstruction of the theory of emanation, which is already visible in his 1804 essay *Philosophy and Religion*. Contrasting his own Platonism with that of the Neo-Platonic thinkers, Schelling argues that a philosophical system (like that of the Neo-Platonists) that explains the origin of things in a descending manner by positing the One or Reason or the Absolute as the originary *arché* inevitably ends up in pantheism, because such a thinking cannot conceive radical, qualitative breaks between the originary *arché* and the (non)being at the lower extreme, which is for it nothing but 'a shadow of the being', 'a minimum reality'. In such a philosophical system there is no 'active negation', no radical 'counter-striving against thought': everything flows immanently and 'harmlessly' by the logic of necessity, from more to less in an attenuated diminution. Here nothing actually happens, for the idea of the event demands an *ontological voiding*, an incalculable interruption in the continuum of being, an un-anticipatable eruption of the absolutely heterogeneous, an explosion of eternity in the very midst of time. Such an event of dissymmetry cannot be a mere attenuated diminution of the One. For an event to open itself for us, the link between beings (or between being and non-being) must be disjoinable, momentarily and suddenly, like a lightning flash. Only an exuberant freedom, a sublime freedom that makes beings ecstatic, may interrupt the mythic auto-poesis of Reason and produce the event as *de-cision*. The event is thus an un-pre-thinkable (*Unvordenkliche*) decision that introduces a qualitative *disjunction* between what is before and what is after, which Schelling names *Abfall* (Fall). Contra the logic of immanent movement as thought by the philosophical system of emanation, the principle of 'active negation' is not a mere attenuated diminution of the originary *arché* but a challenge, a counter-striving, an 'impregnable' contradiction:

> The systems that want to explain the origin of things as descending from above almost necessarily come to the thought that the emanations of the highest primordial force sometime or other reach their extremity below which there is nothing. This extremity can itself be called only a shadow of the being, a minimum of reality, only to some extent still having being, but not really. This is the meaning of non-being according to the neo-Platonists, who no longer understood Plato's real meaning of it. We, following the opposite direction, also recognize an extremity, below which there is nothing, but it is for us not something ultimate, but something primary, out of which all things begin, an eternal beginning, not a mere feebleness or lack in the being, but active negation. (Schelling 2000: 31–2)

Where there is no such 'active negation', there is no ecstatic contradiction, and where there is no such ecstatic contradiction, everything is made immanent to the One. In such a system it is possible to trace, in a movement of return, the extreme below to the One as its originary *arché*: the One becomes the legitimising principle. This has immense politico-theological consequences: the One here, as the originary *arché* of existent power of being, can be evoked as legitimising principle of worldly powers. Against such system of explanation, Schelling therefore conceives of an ecstatic contradiction wherein eternity 'always remains free with respect to Being':

> God, in accordance with his highest self, is not manifest. God manifests Himself. He is not actual. He becomes actual. It is precisely by this that God may appear as the most supremely free being. Hence something else emerges between free eternity and the deed, something that has a root that is independent from eternity and which is something commencing, albeit

eternally so. Thereby, there may eternally be something through which God could draw nigh to creatures and communicates himself to them. Thereby, pure eternity may always remain free with respect to Being. And Being may never appear as emanation from the eternal capacity to be and hence, there may be a distinction between God and his Being. (Schelling 2000: 80–1)

Note Schelling's insistence on the verbality here: God is not manifest but *becomes* manifest; God is not actual but *becomes* actual: manifestation and actuality are not mere attributes of God; God is not an entity that has such and such properties, attributes and predicates. With this distinction between God and his Being – a distinction that is erased in the theory of emanation – Schelling decisively confronts Jacobi's allegation of pantheism. Far from fusing God and the world, he insists on this *radical disjunction*, not only between God and the world but also between *the Godhead in so far as he actually is* and *God as nature*. It is as though God himself must resist and regulate the 'inner self-laceration of nature', 'that inner madness' (Schelling 2000: 103), the unconscious and blind force that counter-strives: 'Panthers or tigers do not pull the carriage of Dionysus in vain' (102–3). This contradiction and the existence of a 'principle' that 'resists revelation' – unlike the conceptual contradiction of Idealism – explains the very vitality of God:

> Without this principle which resists thinking, the world would actually already be dissolved into nothing . . . this principle is the eternal force of God. In the first existence, there must be a principle that resists revelation, for only such a principle can become the ground of revelation . . . an irrational principle is at work in the first existence which resists confrontation and which is hence, contrary to the creature. This principle is the real might in God, just as in the supreme gravity of tragedy it is Might and Violence, servants of Zeus, that chain the philanthropic Prometheus to the crag around the roaring sea . . . it is necessary to acknowledge this as the personality of God, as the Being in itself and for itself of God . . . this is the principle that, instead of confusing God with the creature, as was believed, eternally divides God from the creature. Everything can be communicated to the creature except for one thing. The creature cannot have the immortal ground of life in itself. The creature cannot be of and through itself. (Schelling 2000: 107)

Schelling's conception of God has often been criticised as anthropocentric. Such readers are advised to reread these passages from Schelling's works. It is true that Schelling conceives the passage through which God runs his course – overcoming 'the self-laceration of nature' through love, overcoming the force of gravity by the spirit of grace – as being the same as the passage run by the mortal. But he then goes on to make this qualitative distinction: while the mortal cannot have the ground of life in itself, so that the link/jointure between the principles can undergo dissolution (which results in radical evil), in God, this link is indissoluble. This explains not merely the qualitative difference between divine freedom and mortal freedom, but also the qualitative difference between the possibility and the actuality of evil. Because of this qualitative difference (not just between the God and the world, but also between God as he actually is on account of his freedom and God as nature), the finite being cannot return to an originary *arché* on the basis of his own capacity or power. The Godhead, then, cannot be understood as *arché*, as the legislative-legitimatising origin of worldly powers. Might and Violence, the servants of Zeus, bow before the gentle fire of freedom: 'the blind will cannot grasp gentle freedom. Rather, freedom is for the will an overwhelming and incomprehensible spirit and that is why the will is frightened by the appearances of spirit' (Schelling 2000: 102). Might and Violence, not just the violence and power which belong to the mortal but even that which belongs to God's own nature, must be abandoned and mortified in order to participate in this gentle flame of love. Schelling alludes to the vision of Elijah in the Old Testament:

> In the nocturnal vision where the Lord passed by the prophet, a mighty storm first came which rent the mountains and shattered the rocks. After this came an earthquake and then finally a fire. But the Lord himself was in none of these, but was rather in a soft murmur that followed. Likewise, Power, Violence and stringency must come first in the revelation of the eternal so that the eternal itself can first appear as the Eternal Itself in the soft wafting of Love. (Schelling 2000: 83)[14]

The Godhead as he actually is (God as freedom) is not the source or originary *arché* of worldly powers: between them there exists something relatively independent, a principle that actively strives against revelation, an unconsciousness, a past that never ceases to be past, that ought not to be and yet which, at the same time, cannot be annihilated, for without this 'active negation' there can be no active-creative intellect. On account of his freedom 'with respect to Being', the Godhead is not subjected to necessity and the grim fate of its law. This transcendence of God with respect to the world – a transcendence confronting which the Violence and Might of necessity must give up Being – renders all worldly powers illegitimate. Contra Jacobi's fear, Schelling neither gives up freedom to necessity nor does he end up conceiving God as the legitimising *arché* of the world; on the other hand, fearing the dangers that Jacobi's mysticism can lead to, Schelling maintains a philosophical standpoint that does not have to end up in the nihilism of the endless return of the conditional. The divine freedom is maintained without sacrificing it to the grim fate of necessity, but also – unlike the Idealist discourses of Kant, Fichte and Hegel – without repressing the ecstasy of nature that yearns for freedom and brings the *cision* to itself. Schelling thus avoids not only the mystic enthusiasm that ends up reifying the eternal law of nature but also the coercive concept of rational-ethical necessity that subjugates nature to the violence of 'the maximising thrust of the universal'. In a double reading, he conceives of nature groaning to be released from the oppressive wheel of its annular drives, and yet, at the same time, he conceives of nature as also released from the coercive law of instrumental Reason. His is a conception of freedom which is otherwise than the law of nature and above the law of Reason, a freedom without *arché* (thus *an-arché*) and without a 'why' (without ground). If all hegemony demands an ultimate legitimising principle (that is, a principle of ground) in order to claim 'normative obligations' from us, then here is a political theology without hegemony.

Freedom and necessity

Freedom is *an-arché*, the event of un-pre-thinkable decision. The philosophy of the event cannot ignore the question of freedom as *Abgrund*. The raging *polemos* between freedom and necessity recurs throughout Schelling's philosophical career, and appears already in his 1795 essay *Philosophical Letters on Dogmatism and Criticism*. There the relation of freedom and necessity, in all its discordance, is understood as a tragic paradox: freedom is affirmed by the tragic hero precisely at the instance of his downfall; at the very instance of the triumph of the objective power of necessity, there is the highest affirmation of freedom! More than a decade later, in *The Ages of the World*, Schelling comes to think of freedom as the eschatological principle that suspends, without annihilating, the horror of the law of the eternal return of the same. The primordial wheel of nature as eternal past that is always yeaning for rest is thereby released from its self-obsession and self-laceration. Therefore, the abyss of freedom cannot be understood on the basis of the law, nor can freedom be understood as mere arbitrariness or lawlessness.

This, then, is the essence of Schelling's Gnosticism: by virtue of divine freedom, which is force without force and violence without violence ('divine violence', as Benjamin calls it), not only the worldly powers (which Schelling calls 'potency') but even the law of God's divine nature is suspended, interrupted and released to the desert of non-potency. This desert with which, for Schelling, religion is concerned is the desert of the spirit: spirit is the desert where the *arché* of worldly hegemonies as much as the might of divine nature lose their potency, their force, their sovereignty. The divine freedom puts into question, not just the worldly powers in the profane order, but the law of his very divine nature. The difficult question that Schelling is grappling with here is this: how to link force to non-force, power to non-power, the law to that which *ex-sists* without the law, not in the manner of transition (as in the Neo-Platonic emanation theory of Plotinus) but in a manner that consists of the *intensification* of their difference. This political theology is a *negative political theology*: in the desert of religion all sovereignties (that exist in the name of power and force) are submerged, and our finite existence is thereby released from all 'normative obligations' to worldly potencies. Even nature yearns to be released from the oppressive wheel of potencies in which it is imprisoned, caged, bound. Religion would, then, mean nothing other than this *de-linking* and *unbinding* from the cages of the law, from the wheel of power, in order to *re-link* or *re-bind* or participate (which is the meaning of the word *Verbund*, that is, 'covenant') with that which *ex-sists* without sovereignty, without the law, as *pure actuality without potentiality*. But this *participation* with divine excess (to be distinguished from the excesses of divine nature) is also a *partition*, a *departure*, a *setting apart*, a *separation* from all egoism and masterful will; it is at once poverty, an impoverishment, a renunciation. It is as if no *participation* is possible without *departing* from all worldly privileges. Since the Godhead cannot serve as the originary principle of *potestas*, religion cannot serve as the legitimising authority of worldly hegemonies. It is rather that religion opens us to the radical outside of the world, to the desert of all deserts wherein all worldly attributes undergo *kenosis*.

Schelling thus differentiates between the Godhead of freedom in so far as he is spirit, and the God of necessity in so far as he is nature: 'there is necessity insofar as it is before freedom . . . Necessity lies at the foundation of freedom and is in God itself what is first and oldest' (Schelling 2000: 5). Necessity is the ground of freedom, but, in creation, freedom overcomes necessity and rises above it. The Godhead is *free* in respect to his nature which is his Being. With this Eckhartian distinction between the Godhead and God, Schelling releases God as he actually is (God as spirit or freedom) from the eternal law of divine necessity: God (as freedom) 'is' not; that is, the Godhead cannot be understood as Being or as having-being.[15] Thus there can be no *analogy* in any simple terms between God and Being:[16] God (in so far as he is *actuality without potentiality*), without or *above Being* (*Überseynde*), marks his exuberant freedom, transcending the law of necessity. The politico-theological consequence that arises from this distinction is this: no earthly sovereignty can have any analogical relation to the Godhead above Being and, hence, any claim of sovereignty by any world-historical figure in the name of the principle of analogy will always be unjustified and illegitimate.

Schelling here introduces his doctrine of potencies to explain that the divine nature will eternally return to the same unless, confronting the overwhelming and immeasurable divine freedom (which is above Being and thus above the wheel of potencies), the potencies bring *cision* into themselves and give up Being. The potencies have to bring this *cision* into themselves because they are driven by the excesses of an obsession which can end only in a confrontation with that which is above and outside potency, God as the pure fire of *actuality without potentiality*. It is as if there is in nature itself a *spark* (a typical Eckhartian metaphor), an animating *Pneuma* that cannot be contained within the rotary movement of potencies, and which yearns to break out of the circle of nature, out of the oppressive wheel of eternal return, by interrupting nature's form. Thus, nature itself does not remain content with the law of its form; there is in it something like a potentiality, a *not yet*, that makes it restless and ecstatic. In the divine nature itself is there a polarity between the trait of constricting-withdrawing (the negative trait = B) and the actual being of God that is expansive and infinitely giving (the affirmative trait = A). This polarity does not sublate itself within nature's immanent movement. Only by welcoming what is above nature – that is, the Spirit of God – can nature find what it seeks: its Sabbath from the horror of its eternal imprisonment in the eternal return of the law.

The vitality of nature, its animating force, lies in its Being as potency: nature has life in its very impregnable contradiction; but the exuberant freedom of God lies in its freedom with respect to the potencies, and precisely because of this, nature which resists and negates revelation is made the ground of revelation: 'precisely that which negates all revelation must be made the ground of revelation'. Hence the 'beginning is founded on that which is not': 'Since a being that has nothing outside of itself can want nothing other than simply itself, the unconditional and absolutely first beginning can lie only in self-wanting. But wanting oneself and negating oneself as having being is one and the same. Therefore the first beginning can only be in negating oneself as that which has being' (Schelling 2000: 16).

The first beginning is, then, God's self-restricting and withdrawal which has 'happened since all eternity'. Since eternal beginning is beginning and yet eternal at the same time, 'it has no beginning of its beginning . . . that is, a beginning that was, as such, from all eternity and still always is and one that never ceases to be a beginning' (Schelling 2000: 17). There is, then, in the first potency itself an originary contradiction. Schelling always emphasises this against Hegel: unlike the Hegelian dialectical contradiction, with sublimation (*Aufhebung*) as its operating principle, which begins with a beginning emptied of all determination (hence with Being which is equal to Nothing; a unitary 'nothing'), beginning here is an originary, immemorial, un-sublimated contradiction; a *gigantic* beginning that never ceases to be beginning, an immemorial that Reason at the conclusion of its process cannot uplift into its speculative memory; an immemorial that, *always already* falling outside, is always in excess and always unavailable to the grasp of historical categories and yet, precisely thereby, keeps alive a *place still available* (*Khora*) outside history (Derrida 1995: 126).

The first potency is, then, an originary contradiction (A = B) between the restricting-withdrawing principle and the outpouring-expansive principle. There is already in the first potency something that is being (A), but posited as *not-having-being*. Since both A (being) and B (non-being) cannot be posited at the same time as *having-being* (they oppose each other, so that if B is posited as *having-being*, A (being) is posited as *not-having-being*) in the first potency, B is posited as *having-being* (because the first potency must begin as originary negation [as wanting, yearning, seeking, and not the empty, banal and sterile 'Being as such' of Hegel]: in the first potency, the non-being posits itself as-*having-being*. So, in the first potency the principle of non-being (B) is posited as *having-being*, while the principle of being (A) is posited as *not-having-being*. Thus, the principle of being can be at one instance *not-having-being*, while the principle of non-being may be posited as *having-being*: it is this difference between *being* and *having-being*, or *non-being* and *not-having-being* that makes the nothing multiple (unlike the unitary Nothingness of Hegel) as much as being.[17] This idea of multiple nothings is an important element in Schelling's critique of Hegel. There is, then, an originary contradiction: being is posited as *not-having-being*. 'In accordance with the presupposition, that which is begot by it is posited as that which has being such that it has being. It can in this way be called that which has being to the second power (A^2). And from this it would be clear that if that originary No is the beginning or the first, then the being opposed to it is the second and successive being' (Schelling 2000: 18). These two potencies stand opposed to each other without being able to sublimate or sublate (*Aufheben*) their contradiction, and yet desiring the unity which is now torn apart. 'Hence facilitated by eternal necessity through the force of indissoluble life, they posit outside and above themselves a third, which is the unity. This third must in itself be outside and above all antitheses, the purest potency, indifferent to both, and the most essential':

> Yet having arrived at its peak, the movement of itself retreats back into its beginning; for each of the three has an equal right to be that which has being. The former differentiation and the subordination that followed from it is only a differentiation of the being, it is not able to sublimate the equivalence with regard to that which is as what has being. (Schelling 2000: 19)

The result is the eternal return of the same. This explains the mythic vitality as well as the abyssal horror of divine nature, its eternal commencing and re-commencing and eternal devouring of itself. The myth of the eternal return of the same explains, not the divine freedom with respect to Being, but of the abyss of the divine nature; it is the life of nature 'that eternally circulates within itself, a kind of circle because the lowest always runs into the highest, and the highest again into the lowest' (Schelling 2000: 20). Borrowing from Jacob Böhme the metaphor of the 'wheel of nature' and from Heraclitus the metaphor of a tireless fire (which is to be distinguished from the fire of divine freedom), Schelling speaks of nature's unremitting and involuntary movement as that of a systole and diastole that re-ascends (systole) and retreats (diastole). This wheel of genesis or annular drive of potencies that is 'without beginning and without end' (20) is the unconscious of God, the past posited by God himself: 'nature is the abyss of the past' (31); it is what is terrible in God, the dark principle that is the principle of potential evil; it is nature's 'insatiable obsession' (*Sucht*) with Being, an eternal 'exhaling and inhaling', a 'universal ebb and flow' (21); it is the blind force of necessity which, as such, is the mythic foundation of the law. The metaphor of the circle or the wheel is the metaphoric expression of the law. The potencies are the determinate powers of Being, and as such, the concept of potency is expressive of the metaphysical ground of the law and its violence. The law and its violence threaten to return eternally in this unremitting rotatory movement of potencies.

A life eternally enclosed in the blind necessity of nature, imprisoned in the cages of the world – such a life is not true, actual life. For true, actual life to be possible, life must be redeemed from this metaphysical violence of the law. How could life be redeemed from the metaphysical violence of the eternal return of the same if there were not a divine freedom that suspends the eternal circle of necessity, interrupts the circular return of the same, and breaks the mythic foundation of the law? Such divine freedom, then, would have to be otherwise than the power of Being and, hence, without potency. This exception of divine freedom is a non-sovereign exception: it is not the exception of potency but the exception without potency; it is the *im-potency* of the Godhead: God as he actually is, without power, not bearing the force of the law. The link of force with non-force, power with non-power, and the law with the non-law (justice or Love) – this link without a link – is possible, not on account of divine freedom forcing nature to give up its Being (for divine freedom is without force), but only on account of the potencies in so far as they '*all* communally and voluntarily sacrifice being that which has being and hence debase themselves into simple Being . . . A reciprocal inexistence is demanded because they are incompatible and when one has being, then the others must be without being. Hence this necessity can only terminate if all of the potencies have sacrificed, in the same fashion, being that which has being' (Schelling 2000: 22).

Redemption, then, lies in life released from the ban of the law. By suspending, without force, the mythic foundation of the law (which is the eternal return of the same), divine freedom *frees* life to Love or justice. As such, divine freedom is absolutely heterogeneous to the abyss of divine nature; it is 'the Other [that] cannot be posited by that eternally commencing nature in a continuous series as a potency that belongs to it. Rather it is outside and above all potency, a lack of potency in itself' (Schelling 2000: 23). Released from Being, freedom is above fate and the blind necessity that coerces us: 'There is a univocity in all of the higher and finer teaching that the highest is exclusively above all Being. The feeling is present in all of us that necessarily follows from all existence as its grim fate . . . an inner feeling tells us that the true, eternal, freedom only dwells above all' (23). This, then, is the paradox of divine freedom: its exuberance demands the impoverishment of the law, the *kenosis* of all worldly attributes. Existence cannot participate in the divine excess without sacrificing its Being. This sacrifice or mortification and the de-cision of the potencies to renounce their Being are the utmost intensification of their crisis or cision:

> Only when the relationship to the highest actually emerges into being on account of this inner beginning is the cision first confirmed; and it first becomes abiding only when eternal nature, placed into freedom by the confirmed cision itself, by virtue of an eternal wanting or decision . . . eternally and inseparably allies itself to the highest as its immediate subject and becomes its unwavering Being, its abiding substratum. (Schelling 2000: 29)

Schelling's Gnostic-inspired conception of two different kinds of God is an attempt to save the divine freedom from necessity. Love cannot be understood on the basis of the law; it infinitely exceeds the power of Being. Life, enclosed in the terrible annular drive of potencies, can never attain beatitude on the foundation of the law. Only on account of the gentle fire of freedom, the soft wafting of Love, can life be redeemed:

> If there were nothing outside that blind necessity, then life would remain in the dark, chaotic state of an eternal and hence never commencing movement, of an eternal and never ending movement. But in view of eternal freedom, the summit of nature is also elevated to freedom and with it all the other forces simultaneously come to continuance and being in that each force enters into its appropriate place. Hence, each partakes in the higher influence of which it is in foremost need, although indirectly all partake in the divine. (Schelling 2000: 37)

We must, then, give up our normative allegiance to the *nomos* of the earthly. It is not through that *nomos* that redemption is possible but through what Benjamin calls a politics of world 'nihilism' that 'strives after such passing, even for those stages of man that are nature' (Benjamin 1986: 313). Schelling would say that it is not just man but God himself who must allow the *passing* of his divine nature:

> God itself must feel the utter depths and the terrifying forces of its own Being. It is even dialectically evident that that in which the pure Godhead itself acts just as nature is equivalent to eternal nature. Hence, here is the moment where, according to Plato, God can be thought of as in a struggle with wild, unruly matter or nature. But the God for which this can be said is only the possible God, or God in so far as God is just nature and hence, not actually God. (Schelling 2000: 94)

It is as if God himself (God as nature) is eternally transient and must eternally pass away. Schelling's concept of nature, just as much as Benjamin's, is Pauline in spirit: visible nature, groaning and yearning, is an allegory of the invisible – of the *Pneuma* that is concealed in it, and thus not altogether lacking. Freedom is the *pneumatic* principle that releases what is concealed, which nature itself cannot release on the basis of its own means; freedom releases that 'gleam and glint' of spirit from the coercive law of the earthly *nomos*. Here is Schelling's evocation of St Paul:

> Hence, nature subjugated itself right at its primordial beginnings, but not by dint of its own or a natural will, but rather forced by its neediness (this is the sense of the οὐχ ἑκοῦσα, Romans 8:20), although the talk here is of a later subjugation. But this was for the sake of what subjugated nature and with the hope that nature should also thereby become free and should become elevated from the slavery (blind necessity) of that eternally transitory, self-consuming essence to an everlasting lordship. (Schelling 2000: 47)

Likewise, Benjamin refers to the eternal transiency of nature (Benjamin 1986: 312–13). This insistence on the transiency of worldly existence is the spirit in which Pauline messianism moves. Pauline messianism conceives *Pneuma* as the consummate beauty that shines through the form of matter only to shatter its coarse vessel. Schelling incorporates Pauline pneumatology into his philosophical conception of nature in its transiency: nature itself yearns toward *Pneuma*, toward that unnameable Good which attracts it by its consummate beauty, and which demands that nature bring cision to its undifferentiated state. Through cision, by an un-pre-thinkable decision, it voluntarily sacrifices its claim to Being and thus liberates the pneumatic sparkle that glistens in the darkness of matter: 'the whole life process is founded on this bipartite quality of that which we call matter and of that inner side, converted from our senses, that we intimate but do not discern. An image or inner spirit of life constantly emerges out of the corporeal and it always again becomes embodied through a reverse process' (Schelling 2000: 62).

Schelling, like St Paul, reads nature allegorically, as does Walter Benjamin. In the darkness of matter lies a spark which nature itself cannot discern; the visible reflects a consummate beauty that is the inner spirit of nature. An allegorical reading must make manifest, through the mortification of the visible and the empirical, that which is the truth, beauty or the Good. Thus purgation or mortification is essential to the allegorical reading which sees in the letter not just the letter but the spirit that 'dwells within them': 'Everything that occurs around us is, if you will, a constant alchemy. It is every inner process, when beauty, truth or the good are liberated from the attached darkness or impurity and appear in their purity' (Schelling 2000: 63). In the following lines, Schelling uses Eckhart's keyword *Gelassenheit* which, translated as 'releasement', implies freedom. But 'releasement' does not capture still something else that both Eckhart and Schelling want us to hear in this word, that is: *lassen*, to take leave, to give up, to renounce, to abandon. Taken together, *Gelassenheit*, for both Eckhart and Schelling, means freedom and abandonment together, inseparably, at the same time. Freedom demands the mortification or abandonment of that which inhibits and constricts the 'gleam and the glint' of spirit:

> What is it, by the way, about corporeality that so offends spiritual arrogance that it regards corporeality as of such humble descent? In the end, it is just corporeality's humility and external lowliness that so offends spiritual arrogance. But the lowly is precisely highly respected in the eyes of the one according to whose judgment alone the worth and worthlessness of things is determined. And perhaps precisely that releasement (*Gelassenheit*) shows that something of the qualities of the primordial stuff still dwells within them, of the stuff that is passive on the outside but on the inside is spirit and life. (Schelling 2000: 63)

Here the humility of nature is Pauline as much as it is Eckhartian. In *Gelassenheit*, what is abandoned is the worldly itself. By mortification of the worldly *nomos*, *Pneuma* is released. Such is, for Schelling, the work of the divine freedom which effects Love without force and without the law. *Nomos* is not what is ultimate for life; it is beatitude that sanctifies life and redeems it from the violence of the worldly *nomos*.

Time and eternity

Necessity is subjugated to freedom and the law is overcome in love. Overwhelmed and frightened by the appearance of freedom which arises before nature 'like lightning' (Schelling 2000: 102), the potencies are aroused and intensified to their utmost power. Here 'anxiety is the governing affect that corresponds to the conflict of directions in Being, since it does not know whether to go in or out. Meanwhile the orgasm of forces increases more and more and lets the contracting force fear utter cision and complete dissolution' (101). Confronting the gentle and pure spirit, the severity of the blind will gives up Being and 'discerns itself as already past' (101):

> God can never come to have being. God has being from eternity. But what follows from this? Nothing but that the cision likewise happened from eternity; from eternity the necessity is subject to freedom. On account of the Godhead that has being, on account of that supernatural being of freedom, the primordial state of the contradiction, that wild fire, that life of obsession and craving, is posited as the past. But, because the Godhead, having being from eternity, can never come to have being, that primordial state is posited as an eternal past, as a past that did not first become past, but which was the past from the primordial beginning and since all eternity. (Schelling 2000: 38–9)

This eternal past is past from all eternity, a past that has never come to be sublated into a present; this immemorial past of freedom is the divine nature itself in all its self-obsession and insatiable hunger for being, which, when regulated, becomes the very condition of a creative-beatific life. The positing of nature or necessity as past is the event of an un-pre-thinkable (*Unvordenkliche*) de-cision (*Ent-Scheidung*) that interrupts and ruptures the mythic law of the eternal return of the same. The wheel or the circle eternally self-seeking and eternally never-finding is here broken, giving birth to God as actuality. When the nature of God is governed by the mythic law of the eternal return of the same, there can be no actual beginning be, for

> A true beginning is one that does not always begin again but persists. A true beginning is that which is the ground of a steady progression, not of an alternating advancing and retreating movement. Likewise there is only a veritable end in which a being persists that does not need to retreat from itself back to the beginning. Hence we can also explain this first blind life as one that can find neither its beginning nor its end. In this sense we can say that it is without (veritable) beginning and without (veritable) end. (Schelling 2000: 20)

The mythic law of the eternal return – expressed geometrically as a circle – knows no time and hence is without an actual event. The true event, which is the event of time, is incommensurable with the law, for it is the product of freedom; it interrupts the mythic foundation of the law. The work of time is the worklessness of the law: temporality singularises the phenomenon and makes it non-identical to the concept. Conversely, the law can come into being only by coagulating, clotting, inhibiting (*Hemmung*) the event of time. The concept – the Hegelian concept of the concept – is this act and product of coagulation, of clotting or of inhibition. Hence, so Schelling would say, there is no temporality, no event, no actuality and thus, no life in Idealist dialectical thought. This is the critique that Kierkegaard is to renew in his own existential-Christian way. The metaphysical 'violence of the concept' is this act of coagulation. Therefore in the dialectical thinking for which the Absolute Concept is the *telos*, temporality is determined quantitatively, additively, accumulatively, wherein instances on the temporal scale are qualitatively indifferent to each other. Benjamin calls this quantitative determination of time 'homogeneous empty time', against which he evokes a catastrophic vision of an intensification of time which consists of so many messianic instances, each qualitatively different from the other and thereby opening the continuum of history to an imminent but indeterminable explosion.

A political theology without the law must, then, think the event of time qualitatively and ecstatically; it must think time as cision (*Scheidung*) and de-cision (*Ent-Scheidung*), opening to the Other that is absolutely dissymmetrical and heterogeneous to the law. That is why the divine freedom has to disrupt its own nature, not by sovereign power but by the soft wafting of Love; it interrupts the rotatory movement of necessity which is 'without (veritable) beginning and without (veritable) end' by introducing a true beginning and a true end. This veritable beginning does not have to return, once again, to the same self-laceration of nature. The divine freedom is so exuberant that it is free even not to be free, free from all being and from Being as such (above being: *Überseyn*). It is only such (divine and human) freedom that can inaugurate new life by arresting the mythic return of the law. The Godhead (who is beyond God, beyond the God of nature), by virtue of his freedom, inaugurates such a veritable beginning by making the divine nature itself, in all its self-laceration and frenzy, its past (there is no beginning without a simultaneous past). This making past of nature is the divine act of *cutting off*: the Godhead effectively cuts itself off from the divine nature by an un-pre-thinkable decision.[18]

This is crucial: an immemorial cut, a *never sublated* split, runs eternally through divinity. The divine (freedom) *cuts itself* off from itself (nature), *separates* itself from itself: this *separation* (*Absonderung*), eternally happening, is the very opening of the world. The holiness (*das Heilige*) of God (as freedom, as Godhead) is this *separation* or *setting apart* that is eternally occurring. The divine is *holy* because, by virtue of its freedom, it *separates* and *sets itself apart* from its nature. This idea of *setting apart* and *separation* – the un-pre-thinkable event of decision – distinguishes Schelling's eschatology from various theologies of emanation of which the pantheistic-immanent metaphysics of Hegel is the pre-eminent example. Where this separation is at work, the *eschaton* becomes the principle of de-legitimation. The divine, by virtue of an un-pre-thinkable freedom, sets itself *apart* from the world governed by necessity and law. Freedom renders the law of the worldly illegitimate. The *eschaton* bursts open the world from its very foundation. From this arises Schelling's idea of two beginnings. There is the beginningless beginning of nature which, as such, is not a (veritable) past; but there is another inauguration by freedom which tears open – by the divine power without power – the fabric of temporality from its imprisonment in the terrible eternal return of the same. The veritable beginning, borne out of freedom and released from the cages of necessity, is a tearing into the circle, an interruption of the rotation, a disruption into re-turn:

> There is no past without a determinate and decisive present. How many take pleasure in such a present? The person who does not overcome himself/herself has no past, or rather never comes out of the past and lives constantly in the past. It is charitable and beneficial to a person to have, as one says, gotten something over and done with, that is, to have posited it as the past. Only on account of the future is one cheerful and is it easy to get something done. Only the person who has the power to tear themselves loose from themselves is capable of creating a past for themselves. This is also the only person who enjoys a true present and who anticipates an actual future. (Schelling 2000: 42)

It is as if God himself must tear himself loose from himself: on this account the divine being is infinite *distance* (*Abstand*). But the Godhead does not thereby exclude and completely annihilate the abyss of the past of his nature ('Nature is the abyss of the past' [31]) but 'subjugates [it] within itself'. What is rendered past is kept subjugated, in the way that the good does not annihilate the evil but keeps it constantly subjugated, or in the way that a true Reason does not annihilate madness but allows it to be constantly solicited by the other, constantly regulating the irrational principle, and thereby making this other, the irrational principle, the very groundless ground of the creative-pregnant Reason (contra those 'civil servants of humanity', those 'sober spirits', those 'dead intellectuals'):

> The true eternity does not exclude all time but rather contains time subjugated within itself. Actual eternity is the overcoming of time, as the richly meaningful Hebrew language expresses 'victory' and 'eternity' with a single word (*naezach*). There is no life without simultaneous death. In the act itself by which being that which has being is posited, one of the two must die so that [the] other may live. For that which has being can, as such, only elevate itself over that which does not have being. In the moment when an organic body should come to be, matter must lose its independence and come to be mere form for its actual essence. (Schelling 2000: 43)

The true eternity is not indifferent to time but is pregnant with it. It is neither the result nor the *telos* of a quantitative movement, nor is eternity a very long time toward which we must proceed, progressively, step by step. From his Munich lectures on the history of modern philosophy onwards, Schelling always tirelessly criticises the Hegelian conception of God as the result or *telos* of a process. Such a processual understanding that introduces a *necessary* movement into the divine existence itself ends up with a conception of a God who is not freedom but an eternal necessity. Such a God is embroiled and eternally caged in the eternal self-obsession and self-laceration of its nature; it is the unredeemed God who cannot break loose from the return to necessity; it is the mythic God of the law who brings nothing actual into being, because it is forever a mere possibility and not actuality.[19] Hence the true eternity cannot be attained by going through a progressive movement (as though eternity is the goal of a temporal process waiting at the end of a line) that is empty in itself, because the instances are not qualitatively differentiated. Understood in this manner, eternity never arrives anytime, just as the self-lacerating nature – if there were no freedom – would forever seek itself and never find itself.

The true relationship of time with eternity is not mythic-auto-poetic; it cannot be understood as dialectical synthesis. The succession of potencies (A^1, A^2, A^3) is not here a temporal-historical succession, but at once simultaneity '*in* eternity itself': 'The succession in God is actual and hence not one that has happened in time. In one and the same act (in the act of the great decision), 1 becomes what has gone before 2 and 2 becomes what has gone before 3 and hence the whole (1, 2, 3) is again posited as what has gone before 4, that is, it becomes a succession *in* eternity itself, an included time. It is not an empty eternity but that which contains time subjugated within itself' (Schelling 2000: 44). This eternity is not the eternity emptied of time but an eternity, in *polemos* with time, that is a 'victory'; it is not the totality of additive, successive, indifferent moments, but *nunc stans*: an eternity pregnant with time within itself, a qualitatively different *eternity* from the *eternal* of nature. In a manner that Benjamin will follow, Schelling here displaces the secularised theological philosophy of history as progress (which is also, as Benjamin reminds us, the ideology of the dominant) with an eschatological *nunc stans* that does not happen *in* time; it does not belong to the present of any self-presence nor is it the arrest of the flow of time by the force of the law; it is rather the arrival of the Other who inaugurates a new world outside the bounds of necessity.

The *nunc stans* of the un-pre-thinkable event, borne out of divine freedom, suspends and brings to a halt, without annihilating by force, the form of eternal nature. This does not happen *in* time and *in* profane history; it does not occur on the stage of world-historical politics, precisely because it is eternity as actual and not a mere possibility. It is not the eternity of the law (eternity that is abstracted from time, eternity in the form of circle or wheel) but the eternity where freedom *is at play*, where freedom opens up the historical to the sublime event of the *eschaton*. Therefore, the true eternity is neither accessible to (profane, worldly, secular) historical categories nor is it merely emptied of historical time; it cannot be fixed as the *telos* of fate or destiny. In that sense, the event of the *eschaton* opens us to the fateless and to that which arrives without destiny. Eternity is the eschatological event that, each time, whenever it erupts incalculably (thus without *telos*), brings an entire historical order to a sudden halt. Therefore, the true eternity as *nunc stans* cannot be said to occur on the stage of the universal world-historical politics. This means that the events of revelation and redemption are not cognitive-conceptual categories but events of the eruption of eternity that tears open the fabric of time and subjugates time within itself. *Nunc stans separates* and *sets apart* history from its mythic foundation; the unconditional event takes place in an eternal Now and makes historical Reason ecstatic.

As such, eternity does not grow with time; therefore, it is always newer than the latest and always more ancient than any first. Schelling here eschatologically puts into question the fundamental metaphysical presuppositions of the Hegelian theodicy of history. By thinking eternity as *surplus* to (profane, worldly) history (it does not happen *in* time, *in* history), the realm of the *historical* as much as the realm of nature is exposed to the judgement that measures the law beforehand, and which as such, immeasurably exceeds the law. It is in this sense that freedom is above necessity: freedom makes necessity itself its own past and this event of making past, eternally happening, is itself not a necessity; it is an un-pre-thinkable decision, an exception outside the law, that eternally subjugates the law without annihilating it. The violence of divine freedom that annihilates nothing must be violence without violence; a paradoxical violence, for it arrives without fate. Therefore, necessity does not have the prerogative of judgement over freedom. The judgement on the realm of necessity, on the violence that emanates from necessity, is a free judgement, a judgement out of the immeasurable freedom that infinitely puts into question the attempt to apotheosise what happens *in* the universal world-history. Therefore it is a mistake and dangerous (Hegel is the example here) to consider an event of world-historical politics as an eschatological occurrence.

Just as eternity subjugates time without annihilating time (because it is a force without force, violence without violence), the subjugation of nature (by making it an eternal past) preserves nature's dignity as the ground of freedom and as the past of all consciousness. Therefore there is no consciousness without a simultaneous unconsciousness as its past. The dignity and nobility of nature lies, properly speaking, in its humility:

> There is no dawning of consciousness (and precisely for this reason no consciousness) without positing something past. There is no consciousness without something that is at the same time excluded and contracted. That which is conscious excludes that of which it is conscious as not itself. Yet it must again attract it precisely as that of which as it conscious as itself, only in a different form. That which in consciousness simultaneously is excluded and attracted can only be the unconscious. Hence all consciousness is grounded on the unconscious and precisely in the dawning of consciousness the unconscious is posited as the past of consciousness. (Schelling 2000: 44)

The event of revelation does not annihilate nature but, making nature its past, gives it its nobility and dignity. Thus the past is not sublated (*Aufheben*) into the presence of revelation; the past *ecstatically* remains, existing *simultaneously* with the presence of revelation and with the *coming* redemption. The past is not the dialectically annihilated once-present (therefore is not a presently given entity), and is not merely an attenuated variation of self-presence. Taking up the event of temporality as an eschatological index, Schelling here decisively puts into question the onto-theological metaphysics of presence. Neither the past (on which account the past is truly *immemorial*) nor the coming advent of the *eschaton* (on which account the future is incalculable and radically indeterminate) is a mere attenuated variation of self-presence; rather, the past is (so also the indeterminate future) the ecstatic outside, *ex-sisting* simultaneously with that which is excessive in relation to it. The divine violence of freedom does not annihilate its own nature and sublate its own past: it *lets* the past remain, as an 'irreducible remainder', as the ecstatic past of Reason or consciousness.[20] This means: Reason or consciousness is never total and is never totalisable; there always remains, simultaneously, the ground of Reason that is never annihilated, but only constantly regulated. The constantly regulated madness or the always remaining unconscious past un-totalises the metaphysical violence of Reason.

The political theological critique of violence must, therefore, be double edged: it must put into question not only the dialectical 'violence of the concept' (that seeks to annihilate its unconscious past: the discourse of speculative Idealism) but also the mystical violence of nature (when nature is abandoned to itself: the mystical violence of Jacobi[21]). What is demanded, then, is the constant reciprocal existence of incommensurable forces *at the same time*: the unity of divine freedom existing *simultaneously* with its abyssal past, without annihilating this 'irreducible remainder'. Only this vision of different *times* ex-sisting *simultaneously* articulates the link or the jointure that brings-together-while-holding-apart the eternal past, the eternal presence and the eternal future of redemption. Such a vision of different times existing at the same time cannot be imagined within speculative-dialectical thought.

In *The Ages of the World*, Schelling tries to think how 'different-times may *ex-sist* at-the-same-time'. His response leads him away from the metaphysical pre-suppositions of speculative-dialectical thought (that is, what he later names as 'negative philosophy') to the truly *historical* philosophy (what he later comes to name as 'positive philosophy'): the task here is not to account for what happens *in* history (as if history is a line, linear, irresistibly moving forward to a pre-determined *telos*) but the gigantic, sublime event of the *historical* as such that escapes necessity and welcomes, out of the *Abgrund*, that event without destiny and without the law. To think this, one must *step back* from the onto-theological metaphysics of presence and from the Idealist dialectical notion of contradiction. Here is Schelling's account of this ecstatic time as that which conceives time, each time qualitatively new, and each time 'immediately knotted to eternity':

> For different times (a concept that, like many others, has gotten lost in modern philosophy) can certainly be, as different, at the same time, nay, to speak more accurately, they are necessarily at the same time. Past time is not sublimated time. What has past certainly cannot be as something present, but it must be something at the same time with the present. What is future is certainly not something that has being now, but it is a future being at the same time with the present ... hence the contradiction only breaks with eternity when it is in its highest intensity and, instead of a single eternity, posits a succession of eternities or times. But this succession of eternities is precisely what we, by and large, call time. Hence, eternity opens up into time in this decision. (Schelling 2000: 76)

Such a vision of *different-times-at-the-same-time* can only be thought when being as well as non-being, eternity as much as time, is released from a unitary principle. Schelling's invocation of Plutarch and Aristotle is exemplary here (see above). Time is ecstatic because it is 'immediately knotted to eternity': 'for no being can begin the course of its existence without immediate divine reinforcement. Each new life commences a new time existing for it that is immediately knotted to eternity. Hence, an eternity immediately precedes each life' (Schelling 2000: 67). Thus each new time, qualitatively differentiated (and not as one instance among others belonging to a homogeneous scale), is an 'atom of eternity' (Kierkegaard 1957: 79). Time is ecstatic on account of this immediate knot with eternity, and not by virtue of belonging to a temporal scale consisting of successive, additive, accumulative instances. Each new life is new time, and therefore each new life is 'immediately knotted to eternity' (an ecstatic life and not the lifeless banality of intellectual bureaucrats), because each new time is qualitatively new. Each new life is new time because each new time is disjoined by freedom from the law. Freed from the violence of the law, life is *renewed*: such life is beatific and redemptive for being always new. In so far as life remains trapped in the grasp of the law, life is no life; life is true life only in its beatitude or redemption. Only that life is beatific which, being released from the violence of the law, does not need to annihilate the law by a dialectical opposition, for a dialectical opposition to the law is only the inverse of the law. What life needs, then, is 'being-posited-outside-of-oneself' (*das Außer-sich-Gesetz-werden*), which can also be understood as 'being-placed-outside-the law', which is: to maintain duality in unity and unity in duality without *Aufhebung*:

> 'Being posited in oneself' (*das-in-sich-Gesetz-seyn*) hinders the person. 'Being posited outside of oneself' (*das Außer-sich-Gesetz-werden*) helps one, as our language magnificently indicates. And so then we see, to stick now only with spiritual production, how the inner freedom and independence of the mental forces also conditions all spiritual creation and how all diffident people, insofar as they are as such, become ever more incompetent at spiritual production. And only one who knows how to maintain that divine duality in unity and unity in duality is blessed with that sportive desire and level-headed freedom of creation that mutually regulate and condition each other. (Schelling 2000: 71)

Such is the blessed life! It is not the sublation or annihilation of duality into unity that beatifies and sanctifies life, but the maintenance of this ecstatic duality in unity and unity in duality[22] by the soft wafting of Love, by the gentle spirit of freedom whose force is without force, whose potency is actuality without potency (hence is *im-potent* and non-sovereign). The good person is good not because he has annihilated evil – for the other principle is in itself not evil – but because he has, by the power of non-power, subjugated it within the loving unity of his freedom. There is no real good without its ground outside of it; in the same way, the reasonable person is reasonable not because he has annihilated madness, but because he has regulated this madness by the soft wafting of his spirit. There is no living Reason without a 'constant solicitation of madness' (Schelling 2000: 103). Amongst those intellectual bureaucrats for whom everything is concept and not life, there is no touch of that living madness which makes Reason ecstatic and alive. This Reason (becoming instrumental, the executive and administrative Reason of the civil servants) is coercive and destructive of life.

Schelling conceives the divine life itself passing through the terror and darkness of its own nature only in order to redeem itself from the mythic violence of the law. It thus posits its own nature outside of itself as its very ground, as its past through which it posits itself as eternal presence and eternal future. Hence there arises the succession of eternities *simultaneously*. This outside is time, from which divine freedom must free itself by a loving spirit: it is not the coercive concepts of the dialectic but Love which, without power and without the law, releases that *spark* or *Pneuma*, 'that gleam and glint', that is the animating divine nature itself. That *spark* is untouched by time (successive, linear, and additive): it is the standing still, in the midst of time, of the eternal Now, an exception without sovereignty:

> Were the Godhead eternally actual (in the adequately determined meaning of 'externally revealed'), then it would not be the power to actualise itself. But since the Godhead can only actualise itself from out of its free eternity, there must be something between free eternity and the deed of actualisation that separates the deed from eternity so that eternity remains free and inviolable. This something can only be time, but not time within eternity itself, but rather time coexisting with eternity. This time outside of eternity is that movement of eternal nature where the eternal nature, ascending from the lowest, always attains the highest, and from the highest, always retreats anew in order to ascend again. Only in this movement does eternal nature discern itself as eternity. The Godhead counts and gauges in this clockwork – not its own eternity (for this is always whole, consummate, indivisible, beyond all time and no more eternal in the succession of all times than in the moment), but rather just the moments of the constant repetition of its eternity, that is, of time itself, which, as Pindar already says, is only the simulacrum of eternity. For eternity must not be thought as those moments of time *taken together*, but rather as co-existing with each single moment so that eternity again sees only its (whole, immeasurable) self in each single one. (Schelling 2000: 79–80)

Here is a qualitative vision of time and eternity: eternity is not a totality consisting of successive moments like a circle consisting of circles within it. The true eternity is that which exists 'with each single moment' so that each single moment, immediately (without being mediated by the concept or by dialectical synthesis), knots itself with eternity. Eternity arrives not after a very long time, as though eternity were the goal of a historical process toward which the historical movement irresistibly presses. Rather, each single instance is a threshold through which the Messiah, incalculably, may arrive. Each single instance is pregnant with an eschatological-messianic possibility that may arrest, at any time, the triumphant march of the world-historical process by de-formalising the temporal scale ('the homogeneous empty time'). Each single moment is the possibility of a transcendental breakthrough that erupts out of a divine freedom which is always a 'perhaps'.[23] It is a 'perhaps' for us mortals who always measure events and things in the world by that which must already be given from an immeasurable 'principle' (without principle). But that immeasurable is *outside* the world, *outside* the totality that we call 'the world'. It precedes the world in the way that eternity precedes time. And it is always a 'perhaps' because it is such a freedom that it is free not to be free. Schelling never tires of reminding of this paradox of freedom: 'something that is free is free precisely in that it does not have to reveal itself. To reveal is to be active, just as everything that is active is a revealing. But the free must be free to remain within mere capacity or to cross over into deed. If it were to cross over necessarily, then it would not do so as what it really is, namely, as free' (Schelling 2000: 79). Freedom is the risk that God himself takes and which he affirms by that *de-cision* which is *un-pre-thinkable* (*Unvordenkliche*).

With this theory of duality in unity and unity in duality Schelling puts into question the pantheistic theodicy of the Hegelian metaphysics of history, without having to go back to the Kantian rift that leaves behind a God subjugated to ethical necessity, a God domesticated by the law of Reason (God as 'the civil servant' of the world). Schelling, then, comes to a vision of God who, by virtue of his freedom, keeps himself outside the law without having to legitimise worldly sovereignty in the profane order. Since such freedom cannot be understood by the measure of analogy, the divine *im-potentia* (that marks his freedom) remains irreducibly *distant* with regard to the worldly powers in the profane order. The secularising eschatology that to a great extent determines the dominant tendency of modernity is subjected to deconstruction in the name of a non-secular eschatology that opens up the world to its *outside*, to that which is not an onto-theological ground of beings but an *Abgrund*, the event that refuses to be embodied in the universal world-historical politics.

Notes

1. Thus Carl Schmitt writes: 'All significant concepts of the modern theory of the state are secularized theological concepts not only because of their historical development – in which they were transferred from theology to the theory of the state, whereby, for example, the omnipotent God became the omnipotent lawgiver – but also because of their systematic structure, the recognition of which is necessary for a sociological consideration of these concepts. The exception in jurisprudence is analogous to the miracle in theology. Only by being aware of this analogy can we appreciate the manner in which the philosophical ideas of the state developed in the last centuries' (Schmitt 2005: 36). However, the meaning of the term 'secularism' and the thesis that the philosophical discourse of modernity is theological in origin is criticised by Hans Blumenberg in his magnum opus *The Legitimacy of the Modern Age* (Blumenberg 1985). The debates that Blumenberg had with Löwith, with Taubes and with Schmitt cannot be discussed here. For Schmitt's response to Blumenberg, see Schmitt's *Political Theology II* (2008); for the debate between Blumenberg and Taubes, see the essay 'Notes on Surrealism' in Taubes 2010: 98–123.

2. 'The Christian and post-Christian outlook on history is futuristic, perverting the classical meaning of *historein*, which is related to present and past events. In the Greek and Roman mythologies and genealogies the past is re-presented as an everlasting foundation. In the Hebrew and Christian view of history the past is a promise to the future; consequently, the interpretation of the past becomes a prophecy in reverse, demonstrating the past as a meaningful "preparation" for the future. Greek philosophers and historians were convinced that whatever is to happen will be on the same pattern and character as past and present events; they never indulged in the prospective possibilities of the future' (1957: 6). Löwith goes on to say further: 'The Greek historians wrote pragmatic history centred around a great political event; the Church Fathers developed from Hebrew prophecy and Christian eschatology a theology of history focused on the supra-historical events of creation, incarnation, and consummation; the moderns elaborate a philosophy of history by secularizing theological principles and applying them to an ever increasing number of empirical facts. It seems as if the two great conceptions of antiquity and Christianity, cyclic motion and eschatological direction, have exhausted the basic approaches to the understanding of history' (1957: 19).
3. Such a question of the exception that has only religious meaning is the central concern of Walter Benjamin, Ernst Bloch and Jacob Taubes. In one of his early fragments, named 'Theologico-Political Fragment', Benjamin thus writes: 'Only the messiah himself consummates all history, in the sense that he alone redeems, completes, creates its relation to the Messianic. For this reason nothing historical can relate itself on its own account to anything Messianic. Therefore the Kingdom of God is not the *telos* of the historical dynamic; it cannot be set as a goal. From the standpoint of history it is not the goal but the end. Therefore the order of the profane cannot be built up on the idea of the Divine Kingdom, and therefore theocracy has no political, but only a religious meaning. To have repudiated with utmost vehemence the political significance of theocracy is the cardinal merit of Bloch's *Spirit of Utopia*' (Benjamin 1986: 312). Juxtaposing Schmitt with Benjamin, Taubes writes: 'In some respects this [comparison with Schmitt] represents Benjamin's legacy and here he sees eye to eye with Carl Schmitt: "the tradition of the oppressed teaches us that the 'state of exception' in which we live has become the rule. We have to find a concept of history corresponding to this. Then our task will come to be the creation of a real 'state of exception'; and in this our position in the struggle against fascism will improve." Schmitt's fundamental vocabulary is here introduced by Benjamin, made use of, and so transformed into its opposite. Schmitt's conception of the state of exception is dictatorial, dictated from above; in Benjamin it becomes a doctrine in the tradition of the oppressed. "Contemporaneity", a monstrous abbreviation of a messianic period, defines the experience of history on the part of both Benjamin and Schmitt; both involve a mystic conception of history whose principal teaching relates the sacred order to the profane. But the profane cannot be constructed upon the idea of God's empire. This is why theocracy did not, for Benjamin, Schmitt and Bloch, have a political meaning but solely a religious significance' (Taubes 2013: 17).
4. Nowhere is Benjamin's notion of transiency more decisively expressed than in these lines from 'Theologico-Political Fragment': 'The profane, therefore, although not itself a category of this Kingdom, is a decisive category of its quietest approach. For in happiness all that is earthly seeks its downfall, and only in good fortune is its downfall destined to find it. Whereas, admittedly, the immediate Messianic intensity of the heart, of the inner man in isolation, passes through misfortune, as suffering. To the spiritual *restitutio in integrum*, which introduces immortality, corresponds a worldly restitution that leads to the eternity of the downfall and the rhythm of this eternally transient worldly existence, transient in its totality, in its spatial but also in its temporal totality, the rhythm of Messianic nature, is happiness. For nature is Messianic by reason of its eternal and total passing away . . . To strive after such passing, even for those stages of

men, that are nature, is the task of world politics, whose method must be called nihilism' (Benjamin 1986: 313).
5. Freedom is, in this manner, the eschatological principle par excellence. 'Freedom, however, can only reveal itself in apostasy. For as long as freedom is caught up in the divine cycle of Nature, it is subject to the necessity of God and a Nature. A *non posse peccare* is no different from a compulsion to do good. Only mankind's answer to the Word of God, which is essentially a negative one, is evidence of human freedom. Therefore, the freedom of negation is the foundation of history' (Taubes 2009: 5).
6. 'The ultimate basis of Hegel's eschatological system lies in his absolute evaluation of Christianity, according to which the eschatological end and fullness of time occurred with the appearance of Christ. But because Hegel displaces the Christian expectation of the end of the world of time into the course of world process, and the absolute faith into the rational realm of history, it is only logical for him to understand the last great event in the history of the world and the spirit in the consummation of the beginning. In fact, the history of the "idea" comes to an end with Hegel; in recollection, he understands all history "up to this time and from this time" as fulfilment of all ages' (Löwith 1991: 35).
7. Hegel writes in his *Lectures on the Philosophy of History*: 'Our intellectual striving aims at realizing the conviction that what was intended by eternal wisdom is actually accomplished in the domain of existent, active Spirit, as well as in that of mere Nature. Our mode of treating the subject is, in this aspect, a theodicy, a justification of the ways of God . . . so that the ill that is found in the world may be comprehended, and the thinking Spirit reconciled with the fact of the existence of evil. Indeed, nowhere is such a harmonizing view more pressingly demanded than in Universal history' (Hegel 1900: 16).
8. Protesting against such a theodicy of history, Friedrich Nietzsche writes in *On the Uses and Disadvantages of History for Life*: 'I believe there has been no dangerous vacillation or crisis of German culture this century that has not been rendered more dangerous by the enormous and still continuing influence of this philosophy, the Hegelian. The belief that one is a latecomer of the ages is, in any case, paralysing and depressing but it must appear dreadful and devastating when such a belief one day by a bold inversion raises this latecomer to godhead as the true meaning and goal of all previous events, when his miserable condition is equated with a completion of world-history. Such a point of view has accustomed the Germans to talk of a "world-process" and to justify their own age as the necessary result of this world-process; such a point of view has set history, insofar as history is "the concept that realizes itself", "the dialectics of the spirit of the peoples", and the "world-tribunal", in place of the other spiritual powers, art and religion, as the sole sovereign power' (Nietzsche 1997: 104).
9. Karl Löwith says: 'The outstanding element, however, out of which an interpretation of history could arise at all, is the basic experience of evil and suffering, and of man's quest for happiness. The interpretation of history is, in the last analysis, an attempt to understand the meaning of history as the meaning of suffering by historical action. The Christian meaning of history, in particular, consists in the most paradoxical fact that the cross, this sign of deepest ignominy, could conquer the world of conquerors by opposing it. In our times crosses have been borne silently by millions of people, and if anything warrants the thought that the meaning of history has to be understood in a Christian sense, it is such boundless suffering. In the western world the problem of suffering has been faced in two different ways: by the myth of Prometheus and by the faith in Christ – the one a rebel, the other a servant. Neither antiquity nor Christianity indulged in the modern illusion that history can be conceived as a progressive evolution which solves the problem of evil by way of elimination' (Löwith 1957: 3).
10. Hence Hegel could find in the figure of the Prussian state of his time an objective expression of the absolute. Marx and Kierkegaard are not very far from Nietzsche's critique of Hegel: 'History understood in this Hegelian fashion has been mockingly

called God's sojourn on earth, though the god referred to has been created only by history. This god, however, became transparent and comprehensible to himself within the Hegelian craniums and has already ascended all the dialectically possible steps of his evolution up to this self-revelation: so that for Hegel the climax and terminus of the world-process coincided with his own existence in Berlin. Indeed, he ought to have said that everything that came after him was properly to be considered merely as a musical coda to the world-historical rondo or, even more properly, as superfluous. He did not say it: instead he implanted into the generation thoroughly leavened by him that admiration for the 'the power of history' which in practice transformed every moment into a naked admiration for success and leads to idolatry of the factual' (Nietzsche 1997: 104–5).

11. The violence of the administrative rationality in today's world (a rationality which is purely functional and instrumental at the service of totality) lies not so much in its mere irrationality as opposed to reason but in its lacking 'a constant solicitation of madness', in its utter imbecility and idiocy. Schelling writes: 'Since Aristotle it is even customary to say of people that nothing great can be accomplished without a touch of madness. In place of this, we would like to say: nothing great can be accomplished without a constant solicitation of madness, which should always be overcome, but should never be utterly lacking. One might do well to assess people as follows. One could say that there is a kind of person in which there is no madness whatsoever. These would be the uncreative people incapable of procreation, the ones that call themselves sober spirits. These are the so-called intellectuals whose works and deeds are nothing but cold intellectual works and intellectual deeds. Some people in philosophy have misunderstood this expression in utterly strange ways. For because they heard it of intellectuals that they are, so to speak, low and inferior, and because they themselves did not want to be like this, they good-naturedly opposed reason to intellect instead of opposing reason to madness. But where there is no madness, there is also certainly no proper, active, living intellect (and consequently there is just the dead intellect, dead intellectuals). For in what does the intellect prove itself than in coping with and governance and regulation of madness. Hence the utter lack of madness leads to another extreme, to imbecility, which is an absolute lack of all madness' (Schelling 2000: 103).

12. Schelling says: 'whoever has to some extent exercised their eye for the spiritual contemplation of natural things knows that a spiritual image, whose mere vessel (medium of appearance) is the coarse and ponderable, is actually what is living within the coarse and the ponderable. The purer that this image is, the healthier the whole is. This incomprehensible but not imperceptible being, always ready to overflow and yet always held again, and which alone grants all things the full charm, gleam and glint of life, is that which is at the same time most manifest and most concealed' (Schelling 2000: 61).

13. 'All life must pass through', Schelling says, 'the fire of contradiction. Contradiction is the power mechanism and what is innermost of life. From this it follows that, as an old book says, all deeds under the sun are full of trouble and everything languishes in toil, yet does not become tired, and all forces struggle against each other. Were there only unity and everything were in peace, then, forsooth, nothing would want to stir itself and everything would sink into listlessness. Now, however, everything ardently strives to get out of unrest and attain rest' (Schelling 2000: 90).

14. Schelling here refers to the vision of Elijah: 'For the LORD was passing by: a great and strong wind came rending mountains and shattering rocks before him, but the LORD was not in the wind; and after the wind there was an earthquake, but the LORD was not in the earthquake; and after the earthquake fire, but the LORD was not in the fire; and after the fire a low murmuring sound' (1 Kings 19:11–12). I am indebted to Jason Wirth, the translator of *The Ages of the World*, for this allusion.

15. Martin Heidegger writes of Eckhart: 'In the middle ages, *the analogia entis* – which nowadays has sunk again to the level of a catchword – played a role, not as a question

of being but as a welcomed means of formulating a religious conviction in philosophical terms. The God of Christian belief, although the creator and preserver of the world, is altogether different and separate from it; but he is being in the highest sense, the *summum ens*; creatures – infinitely different from him – are nevertheless also being *ens finitum*. How can *ens infinitum* and *ens finitum* both be named *ens*, both be thought in the same concept, "being"? Does the *ens* hold good only *aequivoce* or *univoce*, or even *analogice*? They rescued from this dilemma with the help of analogy which is not a solution but a formula. Meister Eckhart – the only one who sought a solution – says: "God 'is' not at all, because 'being' is a finite predicate and absolutely cannot be said of God." (This was admittedly only a beginning which disappeared in Eckhart's later development, although it remained alive in his thinking in another respect.) The problem of analogy has been handed down to the theology of the middle ages via Plotinus, who discussed it – already from that angle – in the sixth *Ennead* (Heidegger 1995: 38). It is possible to say that Schelling follows Meister Eckhart in this respect: at stake, as Heidegger rightly points out, is the question of analogy itself.

16. The theological-political consequences of the question of analogy are much debated today. The political theology of Carl Schmitt, which develops a notion of sovereignty out of exception, presupposes this theological concept of the analogy of being (Schmitt 2005: 36). Erik Peterson, in his famous essay *Monotheism as a Political Problem*, criticises the political exploitation of this theological concept of analogy by insisting that the divine monarchy has no analogy with earthly sovereignty, and thus, the political use of the theological concept of analogy is illegitimate (Peterson 2011: 68–105). In our time, it is Erich Przywara, the famous Catholic theologian, who seeks to renew the Catholic theological concept of *analogia entis* (Przywara 2013). Karl Barth, the Protestant theologian, criticises the doctrine of *analogia entis* as 'the invention of the Anti-Christ' (Barth 1975: xiii), and later subsumes the *analogia entis* under the question of *analogia fidei*. Hans Urs von Balthasar, in his important work on Karl Barth, seeks to bring both of these theologians into a dialogue by arguing that *analogia entis* and *analogia fidei* are not incommensurable doctrines (Balthasar 1992). Keith Johnson's book on Karl Barth presents an exhaustive discussion of this question (Johnson 2010).

17. Franz Rosenzweig makes Schelling's insistence on the multiplicity of nothing crucial to his thought. In his *The Star of Redemption*, Rosenzweig develops an account of three nothings (God, Man and the World) by using the mathematical model of differential calculus. Following Schelling, Rosenzweig here attacks the unitary principle of Hegelian nothing by opposing system with revelation.

18. Schelling says: 'only when the relationship to the highest actually emerges into being on account of this inner beginning is the cision first confirmed; and it first becomes abiding only when eternal nature, placed into freedom by the confirmed cision itself, is able to *decide*. And now, by virtue of an eternal wanting or decision, it eternally and inseparably allies itself to the highest as its immediate subject and becomes its unwavering Being, its abiding substratum' (Schelling 2000: 29).

19. In the following lines Schelling has in mind none other than Hegel: 'all attempts that want to answer that question through some kind of movement in God itself, even if it were an eternal movement, are in themselves inadmissible. For if there would be a necessary or a voluntary movement through which God merged into Being as distinct from essence, then God in the first case, would straight away in the primordial beginning not be free and not, as God is and must be, eternal freedom' (Schelling 2000: 40).

20. 'In nature', writes Schelling, 'the spirit knows itself as the one who was because it posits nature as its eternal past. Hence, the spirit knows itself as what eternally must have being since nature can be the past only in relationship to it, what has being. Thereby the spirit again gives eternity as the ground of its own eternity; or rather it gives eternity as something wholly without ground which is again based on an eternity. The spirit knows itself in nature as the one who is, as the eternally present in contrast with

something before it which is eternally past. The spirit knows itself in nature as the one who *will be* because it sees itself as eternal freedom in relationship to nature and as such sees nature as the possible project of a future conation' (Schelling 2000: 45–6).

21. Schelling says: 'The eternal nature is the same in God as what in the person is their nature, provided that if by nature one thought that which consists of body, soul and spirit. If abandoned to itself, this nature of the person, like the eternal nature, is a life of loathing anxiety, a fire that incessantly consumes and unremittingly produces itself anew' (Schelling 2000: 46). And: 'likewise in God, there would be no life and no joy of life were the now subordinated forces not in constant possibility of fanning the flames of the contradiction against unity, albeit also unremittingly calmed anew and reconciled by the feeling of the beneficial unity that holds the forces down' (47).

22. Schelling brings together oppositions that do not have to sublate themselves into an overarching unity. In this sense, again, Schelling is closer to Hölderlin's 'monstrous coupling' than to Hegel's dialectical synthesis. He illustrates this 'duality in unity' and 'unity in duality' by reading a passage from the Old Testament where God is named once as Elohim and another time as Jehovah: 'This presupposed, the doctrine of the unity of the divine essence in that duality shows itself as profoundly interwoven with what is innermost, even with the language itself, of the Old Testament. First of all, insofar as the plural of Elohim is connected to the verb in the singular, where the meaning, for example, *of bara Elohim* is "the one who created is Elohim". This is also the case with the frequent liaison of Jehovah-Elohim. The doctrine of the duality in unity is also just as clearly impressed in the language of the Old Testament. Hence, the passages where the verb in the plural is connected with Elohim (in the meaning of the unique, true God) are an indication that Elohim does not cease to be for itself because of its unity with Jehovah. Also in the passages where Jehovah swears by its soul (A3) as something that is distinct and separate from Jehovah. For incontrovertibly many things that sound too natural to more contemporary interpreters are said or narrated of Elohim, without at the same time applying to Jehovah. The most conspicuous appearance of the latter relationship is no doubt the angel of the countenance or, as it is really called, the angel of Jehovah. The angel of Jehovah, itself distinct from Jehovah, appears to Moses in the flaming bush. Yet Elohim calls to Moses from the bush (Exodus 3:2). Soon afterward the one who speaks to him is Jehovah from which it is obvious that, according to the understanding of the narrator, the angel of the countenance is also Jehovah, yet both are still distinct. The meaning of the narration is perhaps just that Moses was deemed worthy of a vision of that higher vitality, of that inner consuming yet always again reviving (and in this respect not consuming) fire that is the name of the Godhead' (Schelling 2000: 52–3).

23. Derrida analyses the logic of this 'perhaps' in an interesting way in his *Politics of Friendship* (Derrida 2006).

Chapter 3

The Beatific Life

Experience of thinking

At the end of metaphysics,[1] *being* is given over to absolute cognition. This is the 'achievement' of absolute Idealism. In the movement where being *phenomenalises* itself – the movement that we name 'dialectic' – being is given over to the absolute concept that grasps itself, seizes itself, appropriates itself absolutely. This is self-expressed in the very concept of the concept: *Begriff*, arising from the verb *greifen*, points toward this act of seizing or getting hold of or grasping: the absolute concept is the concept of the concepts that seizes, grasps and takes hold of itself absolutely. Thus this absolute cognition is not the cognition of 'this' or 'that' being but of beings in totality where this totality is understood not as an aggregation of all beings but of *being as such*: in absolute knowledge, it is *being as such* that is given over, without remainder, to the grasp of the absolute concept, as though being itself must elevate itself in a movement from which an essential act of negativity would not be separable. To lift itself up to presence, to rise to the concept (*Aufheben*), thinking must undertake the labour of negativity, that is, the *work* of seizing, grasping, taking hold of itself. At the end of metaphysics, being is absolutely *abandoned* to its grasp, to this seizure, to its be-holding of itself. At the instance of its closure, metaphysics determines thinking as this absolute act of grasping, seizing, taking possession of being as such and as such, of beings in totality. Thinking *uplifts* itself to the absolute concept by *positing* itself (grounding, founding or instituting itself, installing or placing itself) – as the verb *setzen* implies – in a manner that is self-originary, autochthonic and autarchic (*auto-arché*: self-ruling; meaning also, by the same gesture, the self that rules, the self as the *arché* or principle of beginning). From this is derived the ultimate legitimising principle (*arché*) of the modern *hegemonikon*: the notion of the Subject is understood by absolute Idealism as absolute self-grasping. As such, the Subject is the ultimate legitimising principle of the modern *hegemonikon*: it institutes itself, grounds itself, founds itself, installs itself or places itself (*setzen*) as autarchic (self-ruling), autochthonic (inhabitant in its own place) and mythic (self-saying, the auto-saying, saying that says itself, is mythic). Together, simultaneously, the auto-generative logic of the Subject (it has to be generative) constitutes itself as the sovereign exception. From the figure of the Subject a certain logic of sovereignty is inseparable: autarchy, autochthony and myth. It is not for nothing that Carl Schmitt could write: 'to great politics belongs the "arcanum"' (Schmitt 1996: 34). By virtue of its sovereignty, the Subject legitimises itself (it does not need anything outside it to legitimise it) as the very generative principle of the law (*Gesetz*), claiming from us 'normative obligations' (Schürmann 2003). In other words, the law is brought into being by an auto-generative and auto-legitimising sovereign principle in an act of placing, positing, grounding, founding and instituting. The sovereignty is the *auto-arché* that founds (grounds) the law (*Gesetz*) by an act of positing (*setzen*).

That is why Benjamin could say that violence (*Gewalt*) is inseparable from the positing act of the law (1986: 277–300). The metaphysical essence of the violence of the law lies in this positing. Myth is the original guilt-context of the law. The concept posits, out of an aboriginal and autarchic foundation (foundation without foundation; an exception), being that can be seized, grasped and taken hold of; presupposing nothing, the concept here structurally opens itself (and is opened to itself) in a founding-grounding act of law-positing; the metaphysical foundation of violence ('the foundational violence', the violence of founding or grounding) is this thetic violence that *places* (hence 'thetic') being under the gaze of the law. Only on the basis of already-being-placed and being-placed in the original mythic guilt-context can the law of the concept seize, grasp or strike being by its force. The law strikes us as a fate that, appearing unavoidable and ineluctable, *necessarily* seizes us in the gaze that fixes us, immobilises us, paralyses us. The metaphysical 'violence of the concept' lies in its power to arrest, to fix and paralyse, what wants to call itself 'life'. The law fixes life by denuding its face: life, under the gaze of the concept, is rendered naked, bare, a mere being alive. Life under the ban of the law is mere life or bare life; it is not 'true' life: true life is without fate, released from the grasp of necessity; it is the redeemed life aglow with the purest fire of redemption.

When metaphysics comes to its closure (which is, at the same time, its opening to the infinite), it is this 'true' life that comes to be the task of thinking. The *end* of such thinking ('end' and not *telos*, since in the idea of goal lurks the power of fate or the force of destiny) is redemption: life beatified, made beautiful and blessed, aflame in the purest fire of beatitude. Such a fire does not strike us with the mythic violence of the law; rather, it burns within us, without annihilating us, exposing us to that which immemorially exists without fate and without destiny. There thus exists an immemorial promise that, before the force of the law becomes operative, promises redemption. In other words, redemption is the 'state' in which the work of the law becomes inoperative, and in relation to which the force emanating from the mythic foundation of violence gives up its being. The true task of thinking, then, can no longer be measured by the measure of the concept. Thinking now, released from the metaphysical principle of ground (or the principle of reason, the principle of 'why'), must no longer orient itself to the *telos* of absolute knowledge (Heidegger 1996); it does not have to be and does not *necessarily* have to be *uplifted* or *elevated* to the absolute concept. Thinking no longer has to be subsumed to the servile function (which Nietzsche calls 'resentment', the pathos of slave morality) of being the legitimising principle (*arché*) that elicits from us 'normative obligations'; thinking does not have to supply a ground or reason ('why') for its supposedly legitimate rule at our cognitive disposal. When metaphysics comes to its closure, thinking is no longer at our cognitive disposal. It may exist without ground (*Abgrund*), without *arché*, without 'why', and the true life is that life, now beatified and redeemed, that exists without 'why'.

When metaphysics comes to its closure in modernity, absolute knowledge is no longer imposed as a demand on thinking. The seizing, grasping, positing law of the absolute concept is loosened from its mythic foundation. Redemption, which is now the task of thinking outside metaphysics, interrupts the mythic foundation of the concept. It un-fixes the gaze of the concept, de-paralyses the force of the law, releases life from the immobility which the concept effectuates with its violence. Therefore the unconditional claim of redemption cannot be effectuated or established dialectically by absolute knowledge; or, absolute knowledge cannot fulfil the unconditional demand of redemption. A thinking whose task is to contemplate the unconditional untainted by violence (the phenomenon in its redeemed 'state') no longer has to make absolute knowledge its end. This task of thinking, being no longer at our cognitive disposal, is attuned to the immemorial promise before all beginning, given to us in a beginningless beginning, as it were. Thinking must remember, in gratitude, that which is immemorial: this paradox is the heart of any essential thinking, which recognises in its finitude the exteriority that exceeds thinking in each instance; it is that which is presupposed each time we begin to think.

Here thinking is touched by a finitude or mortality which does not convert it into the concept by the power of negativity. A touch without touching 'anything' (where what is touched is not an empirical datum), a sense that is not sensible of 'anything' (subsumable under the universality of the concept), is a mortal touch, a finite sense, opening to infinitude, without touching 'anything' in us. Touch in its absolute purity is the intimation of redemption for us. Such a possibility of thinking, touched by finitude and opened to infinitude, arrives only when the metaphysical violence of conceptual thinking is impoverished, rendered fragile or weakened. But this is already, in an uncertain manner, a step beyond the onto-theological constitution of metaphysics.

When metaphysics comes to its closure and absolute knowledge, having been realised, is no longer an imposition on thinking, thinking confronts anew or perhaps for the first time the poverty of the world and the fragility of existence. This marks the beginning of a new thinking that gives itself the task of a redemption which, as we have seen, can no longer be understood on the basis of absolute knowledge. Such thinking is no longer conceptual thinking: it does not posit itself as the principle of ground, its task is no longer to seize hold of the world by the violence of the law. The true beginning of philosophy, then, begins in an *abandonment* without reserve, abandoning everything and everyone, abandoning even God: a fragile beginning, beginning in utter weakness, for it is abandoned even by God. The experience of thinking – if at all can it be called 'experience' (which in its true sense [*Er-fahrung*] opens us to the infinity of a voyage without return to the self-presence of the Subject) – is, first of all, at the instance of its inauguration (that does not institute itself by the power of thetic positing), an irreducible experience of fragility, a fragile experience. Schelling writes:

> He who wishes to place himself in the beginning of a truly free philosophy must abandon even God. Here we say: who wishes to maintain it, he will lose it; and who gives it up, he will find it. Only he has come to the ground of himself and has known the whole depth of life who has once abandoned everything and has himself been abandoned by everything. He for whom everything disappeared and who saw himself alone with the infinite: a great step which Plato compared to death. (Quoted by Heidegger 1985: 6–7)

Schelling speaks here of the fragility of metaphysics. A free philosophy – free from the legitimising principle of worldly hegemonies, the principle of 'why' – must abandon even God in so far as this (onto-theological) God operates as the principle of 'why', and in so far as such a God (understood as the principle of ground) is not the God of redemption but the God of the worldly hegemonies, the secular God that guarantees and justifies the *nomos* of the earthly. This God is the principle of sovereignty; it is the sovereign exception that legitimises the laws of the worldly existence. He is the principle (the commencing and commanding authority) who holds-*together* the worldly world (*saeculum*) in its coherence and totality, and maintains the harmony and beauty of the created order. This God wants us to accept that there is nothing radically disjoining and disrupting in the world, that, following the inviolable and necessary law of its existence, the world is closed in on all sides and is, thus, the best of all possible worlds. This God, then, is the God of theodicy. The God who is known metaphysically and who arrives at absolute knowledge dialectically by a necessary process whose law can be grasped categorically. It is only this God who can embody himself, objectively, as a worldly figure in the profane order, whether this figure is the visible Church or the modern state of Prussia.

A truly free philosophy, whose task is an unconditional redemption, demands a thinking that abandons even (this) God. It does not, then, begin with a self-positing; it begins in *abandonment*, when the *nomos* of the earth is at its weakest and most precarious, confronting the mortality that touches it, not by the power of the law but by a power whose essence is an absolute non-power. A truly philosophical thinking involves an abandonment of the law, not through a power that opposes the law but in *an exception without sovereignty*. In that sense, if we understand Schelling in this spirit, thinking is exceptional: thinking *ex-cepts* itself from the law of the world. The true free thinking is that which introduces, through abandonment of the worldly *nomos*, an ontological void; it is *kenosis*, an emptying out of the worldly attributes, an indigestible remainder, and an inhospitable question mark thrown into the world. A truly free philosophical thinking is, then, an 'experience' of exception: it does not occur *in* the time of the world; its time is not the secular time that measures, weighs, judges – based on an economy of values – the worldly values that are to be made equivalent. Rather, this thinking opens itself to an exceptional judgement on any equivalence of the values and, as such, opens us to the *outside* of the world *from within* the heart of the world. By not belonging to the economy of the world, or by abandoning it, thinking introduces that immortality or infinity for which death is a passage or a step (as Schelling, following Plato, rightly says). How can the non-economy of the world be a judgement – for there is always violence in any judgement – if it does not occur in the name of redemption?

Now this is precisely Schelling's point, visible in the instance when the closure of metaphysics becomes apparent for us. If absolute knowledge becomes the parameter/paradigm that enables an absolute judgement on the values of the world (as in metaphysics), then the world can never be redeemed from violence. Thinking, rendered completely conceptual by coercive laws, will forever carry, as in the terrible eternal return of the same, the violence that endlessly exposes the world to still further violence: in this sense, there is truly a 'violence of the concept'. Thinking that knows nothing other than the act of thetic positing will never be open to the unconditionality of redemption. For redemption to be opened up, thinking must arrest – without force – the mythic continuum of the same. What can that be if it not a judgement without judgement, judgement without means, pure judgement, if one can call it that? Unconditional redemption, then, abandons any 'means-end' relation that would determine worldly values in the economy of the profane order, for what is a value if not a 'means-end' relation that can thus be understood on the basis of the law? Thinking, opened up by an immemorial promise of the redemption that is yet *to come*, must also, then, be free from the economy of 'means-end' relations. Such, for Schelling, is a truly free thinking, free on account of its freedom from being a means to an end. It is on this account, Schelling would say, that the dialectical knowledge which puts thinking in the service of the concept is not free. It is always a means to knowledge, for it recognises nothing other than that which must pass over into the concept. For Schelling then, there is something (which is not 'anything', any 'this' or 'that') about thinking that is not at our cognitive disposal, that somehow never simply belongs to the dialectical movement of the concept, that never belongs to the absolute Subject as its property. If absolute knowledge has made the world *secular* (made the world *worldly*), completely and totally – for knowledge of the 'means-end' relation has no other aim than this – then redemption is not an event that occurs *in* the world, *in* the grand world-historical politics, *in* the profane history of the law. Therefore the messianic or the eschatological (as the arrival of redemption) cannot belong to the secular world of politics; rather, the unconditional demand of redemption abandons 'everything and everyone', that is, abandons all predicates designating the values of the worldly. Which means that no redemption is to be found in the immanent plane of the world-economy, for redemption cannot be thought as the pre-determined result of an economic process. This makes the messianic or eschatological event radically incalculable. Redemption is not the result of a programmatic solution of the world's problems, for such solutions are not equal to the unconditional demand of messianic redemption. One does not necessarily reach messianic redemption by passing through an infinite 'means-end' relation in world-history. A truly free philosophical thinking – freed by and freed for redemption – begins by abandoning this relation, by withdrawing from the intra-mundane equivalence-making of all values, for such equivalence has, for the suffering who cry out for redemption, only a formal meaning: despite every instant being filled with the worldly attributes of the law, time is still a 'homogeneous empty time' stretched to an indefinite horizon.

That is why Schelling replaces the absolute knowledge of the speculative dialectic – which marks the closure of metaphysics – with redemption as the task of a truly free philosophical thinking that begins with the utter abandonment of all worldly values. Since such redemption cannot occur in the world made secular by absolute knowledge, Schelling's atheism (atheism because it abandons even God) is profoundly religious at the same. On the other hand, one can say that Hegel's absolute knowledge, which takes up the Christian theological pattern of history in its speculative meaning, is also an atheism, but in a qualitatively different sense. Schelling abandons God in a movement of thinking that is exposed thereby to the Godhead that is not of the earthly *nomos*; Hegel's speculative cunning makes God immanent in the *nomos* of the earthly, thereby denying the messianic or eschatological suspension of the law, denying that divine arrival which *separates* the world from its foundation. For Schelling, the Godhead is *the holy* that *separates* the world from its foundation. The arrival of *the holy* does not occur as absolute knowledge dialectically realised; even at the instance when absolute knowledge occurs – if we suppose that such is possible – the world does not let itself be thought as 'finished': the world is still incomplete because of its ecstatic remainder claiming redemption; it is still and always outside the law of the concept. In that sense, the experience of thinking for Schelling – in its utter weakness and fragility, abandoned by God – is a fragile experience of the messianic or eschatological. Thinking is messianic, not because it is full with absolute knowledge, but on account of its abandonment of the *oikonomia* of worldly values. If Schelling still retains the name 'religion' or 'religious' – and he does so till the last days of his philosophical career – it is in this messianic or eschatological sense. This is the profoundest connection between philosophy and religion, and one which he sees as early as his 1804 essay *Philosophy and Religion*: philosophy too, which has to do with essential thinking, is messianic or eschatological; it too, in its own manner, partakes in the gift of divine excess in an infinite abandonment of all worldly consolations and salvations. Philosophy, too, like religion, is an opening to the desert of the Godhead: it demands the most severe and austere task of *de-linking* from all worldly powers. In this desert, all earthly glories are submerged. *Re-linking* or *re-binding* (in the sense of 'covenant') with the divine (which is the meaning of *re-legion*) must pass through a *de-linking* from all worldly glories, including God himself. Even though Schelling mentions Plato here, he follows Eckhart throughout to the bottom of the abyss. What Eckhart calls *Grund* ('Ground') is nothing other than this abyss wherein all worldly attributes enter destitution.

Though their paths are different, the task of philosophy and religion is the same, namely to share or to partake in beatitude, in the redemption that is *to arrive*. But for that we have to *depart from* and *set apart* the values of worldly glories. The path is severe, austere, bereft of earthly consolation and worldly happiness. Running counter to that worldly happiness, eschatological suffering welcomes absolute beatitude as the divine gift. Since the terrible and demonic powers of the world cannot withstand the blissful profundity of this divine gift, they must give up, abandon, and renounce their Being. By passing through the severity of abandonment, essential thinking participates in this blissful profundity of the spirit. Following Böhme and Hamann, Schelling here puts into question the secularising project of modernity. In this regard, both Kierkegaard and Rosenzweig follow Schelling. The difficult atheism of Schelling (in so far as he puts into question the God of the visible Church as much as the God of world-historical politics) is not far from Bloch's idea of a 'theology of revolution'. Revelation and redemption are not rational categories. As such, they are not worldly realities on the secular level: they don't occur on the stage of profane history. In that sense, Schelling here renews the old Pauline eschatological understanding of the Christ of the cross whose folly runs counter to the triumphant glories of world-historical expansion. The innermost concern of religion is redemption and as such it cannot be understood as an apology for established world-historical hegemonies. Religion does not follow the law of the world. Opening us to an unfathomable exteriority, religion deprives worldly attributes of their onto-theological anchor. The experience of a truly free thinking is that of unfathomable *outside* in all its enigma and profundity, in relation to which thinking gives up the attributive-predicative logic of the concept.

Promise of language

In his critique of the dialectical principle of Reason, Schelling tirelessly demonstrates how events of revelation and redemption cannot be grasped in the law of the concept. The law of the concept – the concept of the law – must be emptied of all sensuous singularities of phenomena so that it reaches its purity of self-presence; in the same way, the very concept of the law, as the pure form of self-positing, must be without language. The irreducible sensuousness of the phenomenon makes it *non-identical* and inadequate to its concept, either because this sensuousness does not rise up (*Aufheben*) to the concept without losing its *phenomenality*, or because the concept does not *suture* the exuberance of its life, as though the very event of *phenomenality*, in its way, is to remain *unsaturated*. Language that never ceases carrying an eternal remnant of materiality, can, therefore, never be exhaustively at the cognitive disposal of the absolute Subject. The law of the concept, in that sense, is without language. The pure form of the law cannot bear to be contaminated by this eternal remainder. Therefore, the concept has to eliminate, by the power of negativity, any possible remainder of the *non-identical*. Since the Idealist discourse knows no other phenomenon other than what is at its cognitive disposal, it must perpetuate an endless circulation of violent thetic-positing that always returns to the same. Idealist dialectics that sacrifices the phenomenon to the law of the concept (all hegemony is founded upon this act of de-phenomenalisation) is without language, for language, truly speaking, which carries over the non-identical as its irreducible element, always transcends the mythic context of the law. That is why the formal purity of the law emptied of the non-identical, this banal intellectual product of sober 'civil servants of humanity' (lacking the creative touch of madness), is – precisely for this reason – the most violent work of negativity. 'The violence of the concept' lies in making banality exceptional, or in allowing the exception to degenerate into banality. This is the force of the law which, metaphysically, the Idealist discourse perpetuates in its very structural condition, the operative principle of which is the master-Subject as the self-grasping intellect of cognition.

In many of his works, especially from the 1809 *Freedom* essay onwards, Schelling shows himself to be growing increasingly more critical of the Idealist dialectic. The coercive law of the concept represses what is living, active and spiritual in nature by determining the whole realm of nature in advance as a totality of inert material objects whose laws can be discovered by the mechanistic physical sciences of the nineteenth century. The figure of the nineteenth-century mechanical physicist is analogous to 'the civil servant of humanity' in the human sciences, and to the ethical, purely rational Subject in the context of nineteenth-century rational religious thought. In the last pages of *The Ages of the World* Schelling goes as far as to privilege the truly Realist philosophy over the empty dialectics of Idealist metaphysics:

> If one paid attention to its greater age, then Realism undoubtedly has the advantage over Idealism ... just as *Being* is the force and the might of the eternal itself, Realism is the force and might of every philosophical system ... Every single system acknowledges that the force of contraction is the real and actual beginning of everything. The greatest glory of development is not expected from what easily unfolds. It is expected from what has been excluded and which only decides to unfold with opposition. Yet many do not want to acknowledge that ancient and holy force of Being and they would like to banish it straightaway from the beginning, before it, overcome in itself, gives way to Love. (Schelling 2000: 107)

The result is idiocy or imbecility: the sterile intellect blindly serving the totalising system simply because its order is supposed to be 'lawful'.

The violence of the law lies precisely in this idiocy or imbecility which uncritically serves the reason of the totalising order. Therefore, neither the mechanical physics of the nineteenth century, nor the 'civil servants of humanity', nor the purely rational subject of ethics, is neutral; they all embody a value which they cannot question because the force of law has already enclosed them in its originary mythic guilt-context.[2] Against this imbecilic dialectic of the law, powerful in its sterility, Schelling revises once again the Pauline eschatological view of nature: nature groaning for redemption and surging ahead, longing for freedom from the mythic violence of eternal return, yearning to partake once again in the contiguity of beings.

This demands a re-thinking the fundamental question of language once again. Following Böhme, Hamann and Baader, Schelling constructs elements of a philosophy of language that is not at the cognitive disposal of the dialectical Subject. Rosenzweig, following Schelling here too, constructs what he calls *Sprachdenken*: *language-thinking* un-enclosed in the 'means-end' relational context of signification. This means that *the event of language* cannot be thought on the basis of the predicative logic of propositional structures. The event of language is rather to be thought in a more originary manner as a *revelation* of the link that *shows* the contiguity of beings (divine, mortal and natural): language *spaces* open a *space* where the divine, the mortal and nature encounter each other while remaining apart. Therefore the event of language is intimately tied up with events of creation, revelation and redemption:[3] each of these events is a linguistic transformation affecting the contiguity of beings in an essential manner. Hence the Idealist dialectical law of language – which is 'without language', as we have seen – must be abandoned, for language is much more than a mere 'expression' of the absolute spirit at its cognitive disposal. Otherwise than at cognitive disposal (where it is reduced to the self-giving law of Reason), language bears the immemorial and originary promise with which each time it opens itself, opening thereby the contiguity of beings to the event of revelation and to the *coming* of redemption. In that way, the *spacing* that opens the divine, the mortal and nature to each other is a linguistic opening and, as such, language is not a property of man through which he negates his nature (and external nature) and makes history the realm of his own dwelling by virtue of the power of the negative (as in Hegel). Language is rather a *revelation* of *the gift* that passes, like a password, from the divine to the mortal and to nature; it is the revelation (*Offenbarung*, which means opening) of the *covenant* between the creator and the creature which is the originary promise that opens itself to the event of the redemption of all that exists. Language is the passage of creation, revelation and redemption. In his novella *Clara* – written most likely after the

1809 *Freedom* essay and *The Ages of the World* – Schelling puts these words into the mouth of one of the characters:

> language contains a spiritual essence and a corporeal element . . . it would follow from this that in all languages, particularly in the original ones, something of the initial element's purity is still to be found. However, it must be the true common language that is spoken in the spirit world, where only the fully released and free corporeality follows us and where only those words can be heard that are one with the essentials or archetypes of things. For each thing carries within itself a living word, as a tie between vowel and consonant, that is the thing's heart and its inner being. There, however, language won't be requisite for communication as it is here, nor will it be a means of hiding rather than revealing its inner being; but, as here, there is – in a very limited way – communication without signs via an invisible, but perhaps nevertheless physical, influence. (Schelling 2002: 72–3)[4]

The proximity to Benjamin's conception of language cannot be missed: like Schelling, who recalls the original language that retains 'the initial element's purity', Benjamin understands 'the pure language' (or 'the language of truth') as a restitution of the paradisiacal language of the name. Both thinkers envision a 'messianic' idea of language whose 'end' (*eschaton* and not *telos*) is redemption for the mortal as much as for nature's unredeemed condition. Both think of the unredeemed condition of man (the result of a 'fault' – like Benjamin, Schelling names this event a 'fall': *Abfall*) in terms of being's enclosure in the 'means-end' language of signification (Benjamin calls it the 'language of judgement', the language of overnaming), which is the mythical guilt-context of the law. Both think the contiguity of beings as essentially linguistic, and thus the language of man, which is the *link* (jointure, bond) in this ontological contiguity, has to assume a profound importance for redemption. Redemption is, then, 'universal' or 'common' for the whole of mankind as well as for all creaturely existence. This commonality, however, is not the commonality (*koinon*) under the ban of the law (under the universality of the concept), but the commonality that restitutes the original paradisiacal language of promise. Hence the importance of the Platonic notion of the idea or archetype for Schelling (1989, 1984) as much as for Benjamin: both evoke the Platonic idea of a 'constellation' in order to think outside the totalising work of the concept (Benjamin 1998: 46). For both, redemption is not the work of the coercive concept at the service of cognitive disposal (Benjamin 1998: 36) but the condition in which phenomena redeem themselves in the language of truth.[5] While the work of the concept subsumes individuals under the general and, hence, is tyrannical and violent, the ideas forming a constellation are individual essentialities without subsumption, absolved from the conceptual order of anonymous universality. How, then, is a redeemed communality of individuals, revealing itself as the contiguity of beings, to be thought in a manner that does not admit of subsumption under a coercive universality? Schelling's response is not too far from Benjamin's: an originary promise is the *structural condition of opening* of any language at all and of *language as such*, whether we name it as 'messianic' or as 'eschatological'; it is the originary communality that passes through all transformations while still bearing, even after the Fall, the *potentia* of redemption.[6] For Benjamin, this 'affinity of languages' shows the very possibility of translation, whose messianic consummation is the universal redemption, the restitution of 'the original purity' of language wherein the whole of the past becomes citable. The arrival of this redeemed language of true universality occurs through a temporal-historical passage which constitutes a drama wherein not only the redemption of mankind but also that of nature is staged. This drama of redemption on the historical stage does not take place on the immanent plane of world-historical politics; it has its other or invisible side, hidden in visible history and yet without belonging to it. It is this secrecy which links the realm of nature to the spirit world. This is the subject matter of Schelling's posthumously published novella, *Clara*.

Divine mourning

The novella begins with the first narrator, a priest, passing through a town along with a doctor to pick up Clara, who has recently lost a beloved friend. It is All Soul's day: the town is illumined by the mellow autumnal sun; groups of people are gathering 'around individual graves' with autumn flowers, their silent tears 'sanctified by sweet melancholy' (Schelling 2002: 9): a perfect setting in which to contemplate death and mourning, and the relationship of nature with the spirit world. The priest and the doctor meet Clara in a Benedictine cloister situated in an idyllic spot far from the bustle of the town. They strike up a conversation, and are later joined by a clergyman. Schelling presents each character's viewpoint concerning death and the afterlife, and nature's connection with the spirit world, as an encounter with those of the others. As the narration progresses, we see how each viewpoint is supplemented and enriched by the alternatives. Speaking first, the priest narrates their meeting up in the cloister, where they find Clara looking out of the window:

> The direction of her eyes drew me toward the open window, and as she caught sight of the blue and remote hills, her eyes filled with tears and she said: Behind those hills yonder, which will become bluer and bluer and over which the sun is now about to sink, there lies buried everything I have. (Schelling 2002: 11)[7]

Commentators have convincingly shown that Schelling's 'divine mourning', which brings him so much closer to Hölderlin than to Hegel, was his constant preoccupation in the years following the death of his wife, Caroline (which also suggests that *Clara* was written after 1809 and not earlier). In a letter written a few days after Caroline's death, Schelling writes: 'I now need friends who are not strangers to the real seriousness of pain and who feel that the single right and happy state of the soul is the *divine mourning* in which all earthly pain is immersed' (Schelling 1975, italics mine). In another letter, Schelling writes to his friend Georgii:

> Even death, which may cause us to curse our dependence on nature and which fills a human soul's first impressions almost with horror against the merciless violence, and which destroys even the most beautiful and best without mercy when her laws demand it, even death, when grasped more deeply, opens up our eyes to the unity of the natural and the divine. (Quoted by Steinkamp 2002: xxx)

Already in 1809 a melancholic cadence resonates in the pages of his *Freedom* essay: not only in man and in nature but even in the divine being there resonates a profound melancholy. Melancholy or mourning is here the metaphysical *attunement* (*Stimmung*) of all beings, and hence the *fundamental attunement* (*Grundstimmung*) par excellence. As with Hölderlin's 'holy mourning', it is not a subjective experience or an ephemeral feeling, but rather involves, as Heidegger says with respect to Hölderlin, the 'transposition of the human being together with beings into attunement'.[8] A profound mourning passes through the divine to the mortal and to nature; it attunes all beings, in a fundamental manner, disclosing the contiguity of beings. The *Grundstimmung* of divine mourning is, then, the mood which affects being *as such*: beings are fundamentally open, in this mourning, to the ground of their existence. If finitude or mortality is intimately connected with this fundamental attunement of mourning, then mortality can no longer be understood as a mere accidental event of being but as a radical event, the very possibility and actuality of its being as such.

In this 1809 essay, Schelling thinks the finite being as the mortal gift: existence is 'loaned' to the human being. The human being is radically finite because his existence is 'loaned' to him. This finitude, therefore, is not an objection but the very possibility of his link or bond (or 'jointure': *Fuge*) with the divine and with nature: on account of his finitude, the human being is in *covenant* with the divine and the mortal; on account of his mortality, the human being is the copula between the divine and nature. He is the *spacing* open through which nature comes to be redeemed by partaking in the divine gift. One of the characters in *Clara* thus says:

> Shouldn't we suppose that a divine law is prescribed that nature should rise up first to man in order to find within him the point at which the two worlds [nature and spirit] are unified; that afterwards the one should immediately merge with the other through him, the growth of the eternal world continuing uninterrupted into the inner or spirit world? ... Man would have lived both a spiritual and bodily life at the same time, even here; the whole of nature would have risen to heaven or to an enduring and eternal life in and with man. God did not want a lifeless or necessary tie (between the external and inner world), but a free and living one, and man bore the word of this link in his heart and on his lips. Thus the whole of nature's elevation, too, depended on man's freedom. (Schelling 2002: 24)

If this immemorial promise (of redemption) structurally opens the human language as such, it is because this language is *always already* tied to mortality. Therefore the redemption of all created existence is essentially a linguistic event of transformation. This also means that the contiguity of beings is essentially linguistic in its nature: it is the jointure (*Fuge*) of vowel and consonant. Therefore nature comes to man to express her gratitude:

> Just think of nature's many bright and beneficent strengths. She still hasn't forgotten that through man she shall be raised up further and freed, that even now the talisman still lies within him when he scatters seeds on the earth, tills and waters the wild and arid ground, and why she rewards him with extravagant abundance. (Schelling 2002: 26)

Nature is thankful to man for his creative naming-language through which nature herself is redeemed. 'Nature is', then, 'the first or old, testament', since

> Things are still outside the center and therefore under the law. Man is the beginning of the new covenant through whom, as mediator, since he himself is connected with God, God also accepts nature and takes it to him. Man is thus the redeemer of nature towards whom all its archetypes strive. The Word which is fulfilled in man exists in nature as a dark, prophetic Word. Hence the anticipations which have no exegesis in nature itself and are only explained by man. (Schelling 1992: 92)

These words have a great affinity with what Benjamin (1986: 314–32) also says about the redemptive language of man. Nature's unredeemed condition lies in the mode of its being 'under the law'. If the language of man is redemptive for the stage of existence as nature, it is because the naming-language is primarily outside the law: in the creative *naming* word of man, existence is redeemed from the original guilt-context of the law. This original creative *naming-language of man* – which comes to him as a gift and on which account is he mortal – is intimated by the *Grundstimmung* of mourning. It is in this sense that this profound mourning is truly 'divine': it attunes us to beings, to nature as much as to the divine. But this mourning is not that overwhelming mourning that arises as a result of the mythic violence of the law. From both Schelling and Benjamin we know that there is indeed a melancholy of overnaming wherein the creative naming word withers away as a result of the Fall of man.

A fundamental melancholy, then, attunes nature and the human; or, rather, mourning is the fundamental *attunement* of nature and man. Nature is *sympathetic* to man and vice versa because of this profound mourning that is the deepest aspect of human nature as well as that of the world of nature:

> The most obscure and thus the deepest aspect of human nature is that of nostalgia [*Sehnsucht*], which is the inner gravity of the temperament, so to speak; in its most profound manifestation it appears as *melancholy* [*Schwermuth*]. It is by means of the latter that man feels a sympathetic relation to nature. What is most profound in nature is also melancholy; for it, too, mourns a lost good, and likewise such an indestructible melancholy inheres in all forms of life because all life is *founded* upon something independent from itself (whereas what is *above* it elevates while that which is *below* pulls it down). (Schelling 1994a: 230)

Melancholy is the deepest attunement of man with nature; and together, in a profound mourning, they are attuned with the divine. In *Clara*, Schelling expresses this through the doctor's words:

> Doesn't she [nature] mourn with us? We are able to complain, but she suffers in silence and can talk to us only through signs and gestures. What a quiet sorrow lies in so many flowers, the morning dew, and in the evening's fading colors. In only few of her appearances does nature emerge as terrible, and then always only temporarily. Soon everything retreats into its usual confines and in her normal life nature appears always as a subjugated strength that moves us through the beauty that it brings forth when in this condition. (Schelling 2002: 22)

The human being is touched by the divine and nature touches him in mourning. Nature mourns because her transiency does not lend itself to language, so 'she suffers in silence and can talk to us only through signs and gestures'.[9] There is, thus, a lament in 'so many flowers', in 'the morning dew', in the 'fading colors' of the setting sun: a lament that barely rises up to speech, as though nature's very quietness, her speechlessness, makes her lament. Nature yearns and 'longs to be released from transience', looking toward man who, bearing the gift of language, redeems her (Schelling 2002: 22). There is, then, the most profound connection of mourning with transiency. Both the realm of nature and the realm of history are affected by mourning, because they are to *pass away*. Redemption demands that what is to pass away ought to be passed away: this passing of what is to pass away is the internal rhythm of the transient order which Benjamin, in his own manner, calls 'messianic'.

The language of man, then, is not primarily conceptual signification at our cognitive disposal for expressing the absolute concept. 'Knowledge is possession' (Benjamin 1998: 29), but there always lies in the ground of all possession a metaphysical violence which affects not just the world-language of man but the very contiguity of beings. The task is then to renounce possession and the violence of the concept. But, as Heidegger reminds us, in all renunciation there lies a melancholy:

> For the calculative intellect, renunciation means relinquishing and a loss. True renunciation – that is, a renunciation that is sustained and brought about by a genuinely expansive fundamental attunement – is creative and productive. In releasing what was previously possessed, it receives, and not as some kind of subsequent reward; rather a mournful enduring of the necessity of renunciation and of letting go is in itself a receiving. (Heidegger 2014: 85)[10]

For Schelling, this *abgeschiedenheit* (detachment) is the fundamental task of thinking. *Abgeschiedenheit* brings distance into nearness; or rather it attunes us, in divine mourning, to what is distant and remote. In this being attuned to the distant through renunciation lies the nobility and dignity of the creative language of man. This divine mourning, wherein 'all earthly pain is immersed' (Schelling 1975), is, then, a path to glory, to the life beatified and sanctified through renunciation of what is external and accidental:

> The opposite is itself precisely what is nearest. Deserts, mountains, distant lands, and seas can separate us from a friend in this life; the distance between this life and the other is no greater than that between night and day or vice versa. A heartfelt thought, together with our complete withdrawal from anything external, transfers us into that other world, and perhaps this other world becomes all the more hidden from us, the nearer to us it is. (Schelling 2002: 13)

Beatific life

In his *Freedom* essay of 1809 Schelling shows that at the ground of human freedom lies the abyss of Love. The event of human freedom is the *un-pre-thinkable* decision of divine Love. Human freedom, originating from the divine decision, is given to the mortal so that she attains, through her very freedom, to beatitude. The mortal is thereby released from the power of necessity and from her *mere life*; on account of her freedom, she is no longer *necessarily* under the force of the law. Freedom marks the nobility and dignity of the creature: with the gift of freedom is also given the possibility of life sanctified and beatified. The mortal is ennobled by virtue of the gift of freedom (freedom *from* the nomothetic operation of the law and freedom *for* beatitude). This nobility and dignity of the mortal is inseparable from her inalienable mortality: she is what she is in all her dignity and nobility on account of freedom gifted to her from an immemorial origin. Death is, thus, not an objection to existence but is to be affirmed as the very passage through which the mortal being can participate in this original freedom. In *Clara*, the priest thus says:

> Even in this life we so easily imagine that our friends and companions through life are *ours*, when they are only God's; they are free beings, subject only to the One. We enjoy them as a gift; death reminds us of this even if nothing else does, although it would seem wise always to remember even in life that there isn't anything we can call ours in the true sense of the word … a moment nevertheless comes when the soul no longer belongs to us, but belongs once more to the whole, when it returns home into its original freedom and perhaps, in accordance with God's will, begins a new course that will never meet our own again and that serves to fulfil a quite different purpose from what it fulfilled here in working to develop our inner being and ennobling our essence. (Schelling 2002: 14)

But freedom, in the true sense of the name, is also the freedom not to be free: by virtue of the freedom gifted to the mortal, she is also given the freedom to abnegate this very freedom, thereby blocking the possibility of participating in the original freedom. The tendency of the mortal that resolutely turns away from the original freedom, because it cannot bear the experience of the centre which flashes before us like lightning, turns demonic.[11] Because of his freedom man is essentially demonic,[12] harbouring the very possibility of radical evil:

> And evil consists even now in a backward motion of human nature, which, instead of wanting to raise itself up into its true being, always clings onto and attempts to realize what should be only a condition of its activity and only a quiet, immobile basis of its life. What causes illness other than a churlishness toward development, other than the individual strength not wanting to continue with the whole, not wanting to die away with the whole, but obstinately wanting to be for itself? (Schelling 2002: 26–7)

This paradox – that freedom is not only the possibility of the gift of beatitude, but also bears, precisely thereby, the demonic nature of man – constitutes the very enigma of mortal existence. The economy of the law, with its hegemonic fantasm, restricts the unbearable paradox of this tragic existence (tragic because it is paradoxical!) and forcefully institutes regimes of 'constituted phenomenality' by effacing the enigma of mortality. Only a mortification of egoity through the *askesis* of man's will and a *kenosis* (impoverishment or emptying out) of his worldly privileges enables him once again to participate in the nobility that belongs to him as a gift. As the doctor says to Clara:

> Freedom is the true and actual appearance of spirit; that's why the appearance of freedom brings man down; the world bows to it. But so few know how to handle this delicate secret; that is why we see that those to whom the capacity falls to use this divine right become like a madman and, gripped by the madness of caprice, they try to prove freedom in actions that lack the character of internal necessity and that are thereby those that are the most accidental. Necessity is the inner being of freedom; thus no basis can be found to truly free action; freedom is as it is because it is so, it just is, it is absolutely and thereby necessarily. But freedom such as this is not of this world. Thus those who deal with the world can seldom exert such freedom, if at all. (Schelling 2002: 28)

We must, then, deprive the world of its glories and impoverish all worldly sovereignties; in other words, we must welcome mortality in the very midst of the world. We must *singularise* ourselves in our mortality, which denudes us from possessions and from the triumph of world-historical politics: 'each of us has the vague feeling', says the priest, 'that bliss lies in not possessing anything, for possessions cause worry and responsibility. And because poverty and privation are hard and painful things, monastic life has to appear as a true ideal, for there everyone lives a happy and leisurely life without possessing anything' (Schelling 2002: 16). What we call 'philosophy', so Clara responds to the priest, is nothing other than the task of abandoning every way or every 'why', a step that we call 'death': 'why else do we say that prior to death no one is blessed apart from him, we might say, who dies while living – and what else is this solemn vow of deprivation and renunciation of worldly things other than a death in the living body' (16)?

It is this 'why' which is the principle of all legitimation; it provides the worldly hegemonies with 'the maximising thrust of the universal'. The principle of Reason is, thus, the trait of natality, the instituting power of the law; mortality, on the other hand, introduces the trait of *singularity* that always remains as the undertow in all worldly hegemonies. To live without 'why', that is, to live as dispossessed, is to welcome mortality into the heart of existence in the name of the 'singularity to come' (Schürmann 2003). Schelling's thought here is remarkably close to that of Meister Eckhart and Angelus Silesius:

> The rose does have no why; it blossoms without reason,
> Forgetful of itself, oblivious to our vision
> (Angelus Silesius 1986: 54)

A life without 'why' is the true life, life un-enclosed in the cages of the law, life withdrawn from the worldly hegemonies. Such is the first step to the truly spiritual life of the philosopher: 'only he who really lives within the spirit – the true academic and artist – is truly spiritual. Merely exercising piety as a way of life, without combining it with lively and active scientific research, leads to emptiness and eventually even to that mechanicalness devoid of heart and soul that would itself have belittled monastic life even in times such as ours' (Schelling 2002: 17). The truly spiritual philosopher, then, may not hope to be a 'civil servant of humanity' at the disposal of a state-sponsored hegemonic apparatus. The truly spiritual philosopher is the one who, withdrawn from 'the maximising thrust of the universal', exists without 'why', that is, without hegemony: she is the eternal *wanderer* (in the sense that Meister Eckhart and Angelus Silesius understand it), a pilgrim on the earth, a stranger to the world, a *wonderer* who is released from the caves of darkness. The truly spiritual philosopher is she who never settles herself like an aborigine on any earthly territory: 'Freedom as such is not of this world' (Schelling 2002: 28). The one who bears this tragic knowledge must live without *means*: 'to live is death and death is also life'. A truly spiritual life, which may be either 'philosophical' or 'religious', is the life of pure means: it is (like) the rose that blossoms without 'why': beatific life, sanctified by mortality, abandoned by and abandoning all autochthony and autarchy. Here all that is profound becomes simple and this simplicity, like a pure crystal, enables the eternal rays of the sun to pass through it. But this crystalline 'spark' within the depth of our being is also the most severe desert: here the glories of the world evaporate like smoke, and yet it is precisely in this desert where everything becomes simple and naked that an opening becomes possible. The one who wants to receive this opening, then, herself has to be desert-like, simple and naked, exposed to the wound of the gift. One of the characters in *Clara* speaks thus:

> But there is one secret in particular that most people won't grasp: that those who want such a gift will never share in it, and that the first condition for it is composure and a quiet will. I've known some people who, though otherwise spiritual, never let their imagination rest by day and night, and who tried all means, as they were never blessed with that wish. Instead, it seems that throughout time immemorial those who didn't try anything like this, but who were simple and pious, were those who were deemed worthy of receiving openings from another world. (Schelling 2002: 75)

To receive that which exists without 'why', we ourselves must be desert-like, living death, for 'death is a kind of life' (Hölderlin 1966: 605). 'Like is recognised by the like': Schelling is here inspired by a Platonic-Eckhartian theory of analogy. However, it is not an analogy between two beings: to be exposed to the Nothing of the Godhead, the internal desert, the nothing (which Eckhart says, in a surprising way, is 'the Ground') of us, has to be released (*lassen*), has to *let being be*. Only then may 'a touching sympathy' or harmony occur; only then will *the like*, which may be separated by centuries or millennia in the external world, arrive to *the like* in a profound proximity. The priest says:

> For now it also seemed quite inconceivable to me how I could have doubted that *there like was associated with like* – namely, what is internally alike – or that any love that was divine and eternal here would find its loved one: not only the loved one that was known here, but also the unknown one for whom a loving soul longed, seeking in vain here the heaven corresponding to what was in their breast; for the law of the heart has no force in this completely external world. Here related souls are separated by centuries, large distances, or by the intricacies of the world. (Schelling 2002: 72; italics mine)

The imperative here, an imperative without the law, is to *let* (in the Eckhartian sense of *lassen*) 'the spark' (which is Eckhart's term) or 'the light' dawn in the night. The light dawns only in the night; or, rather, we let the light dawn in the nothing that we 'are', where the nothing of the night is transfigured into the daylike. Here, then, there occurs 'a touching symphony' between nightlike day and daylike night. This is why, so Clara says, the moonlit night is so beautiful:

> If a light were to dawn within night itself, she [Clara] continued, so that a nightlike day and a daylike night embraced us all, then all our wishes would find their final resting place. Is that why, she added, a moonlit night touches our inner being in such a wonderfully sweet way and, with its intimations of a nearby spirit life, makes a shudder run through our breast? (Schelling 2002: 47)

This, then, is the essence of what beauty is: the *symphony* between the nightlike day and daylike night, the *attuning* of the pondering vessel of the form to the animating grace that gleams out of the depth of the night. Perhaps of all nineteenth-century thinkers, Schelling is the most Eckhart-like. The moonlight is at once profound and blissful because it is at once daylike night and nightlike day: 'the true bliss can exist only in that greatest profundity of life' (Schelling 2002: 79). But for that one must abandon even God and even the mystical ecstasy that now and then elevates us: 'The soul is happy when it can have what it felt inwardly, as if by inspiration or through some divine thought, expressly worked out in the understanding, too, as if looking in a mirror. Profound souls shy away from this development, which they see as one in which they come out of themselves. They always want to go back into their own depths and to continue to enjoy the bliss of the center' (31). But this depth is also light, this centre or what Eckhart calls *Grund* (Ground) is also an abyss; in the same way as for Oedipus, who is singularised by mortality, 'life is death and death is a kind of life' (Hölderlin 1966: 605). Likewise the Godhead too, who is even beyond God, is Nothing: the spark is the crystal of the soul wherein eternity lights up. 'The deepest, I feel', says Clara, 'must also be the clearest; just as what is clearest, e.g., a crystal, by virtue of being such, does not seem to get closer to me, but instead seems to withdraw and to become more obscure, and just as I can look into a drop of water as if into an abyss. At any rate, depth must be distinguished from opacity' (Schelling 2002: 63). This simple coincidence of the opposites ('the deepest must also be the clearest'; 'life is death and death is also a kind of a life') is such a simplicity that it remains incommensurable to the thought that seeks a 'why' at every turn. The beatific life, living without 'why', is incommensurable not only with the sober, imbecile metaphysician but also with the mediocrity of banal life: both confuse depth with opacity. They can therefore never attain the simplicity and purity of the moonlit night. Just as opacity is never depth, so the ordinary life of mediocrity is never really simple. Thus the true profundity is incommensurable with the banal, administrated life of the imbecilic intellect for which thinking means thinking with reason (with 'why'). It thereby opposes reason with anything that is not thinking with reason (with 'why') and calls the latter merely 'irrational'. The bureaucrat of reason is just like the metaphysician: like the bureaucrat, the metaphysician opposes clarity with what he calls 'opacity'. Therefore, like the administered life of the banal intellect, they are caught up in this dialectical web of reason: they know no life without 'why'. Because they are not profound, they also do not know the true bliss which is not mere ecstasy but a life without 'why': 'this level of profundity isn't compatible with the limitations of our present life . . . the experience of the center, which floods us with a feeling of the greatest well-being, does not seem appropriate for the mediocrity of our present life' (32). Since the principle of Reason functions as the principle of legitimacy, the bureaucratic rationality always ends up serving the existing state of affairs. Since for such a sober intellect God can have no other mode of being than that of a mere rational ideal, an ethical necessity, or the guarantor and preserver of the lawful harmony of the world, he exists as the principle of legitimacy. The worldly sovereignties can, then, appeal to this divine foundation for the legitimacy of their political hegemonies. The abandonment of such a God thus becomes the essential task of thinking. This is why Meister Eckhart makes the fundamental distinction, crucial for Schellingian thought, between the Nothing of the Godhead and God as the legitimising principle of the world-order. He thereby solves the politico-theological question of *analogia entis* by thinking the Godhead as no-Being at all.

Following Eckhart, Schelling, too, thinks of the true God, the Godhead as such, as 'superactual, beyond that which has being [die *Überseynde*], therefore a sublimity beyond Being and Not-being' (Schelling 2000: 27). The Godhead beyond God, so to speak, is Nothing; it is not Being at all. The Godhead corresponds or is analogous to no being at all, 'since all Being goes up in it as if in flames'. No earthly creature or worldly order can on the basis of its own power go back to it as to its ground, for the Godhead is without ground and without a 'why'; it is the *Abgrund*. It is an exception, but not an exception which legitimises worldly sovereignties. In *The Ages of the World*, Schelling says:

> Hence, that which is without nature, which the eternal nature desires, is not a being and does not have being, although it is also not the opposite . . . it is nothing, just like the pure happiness that does not know itself, like the composed bliss that is entirely self-fulfilled and thinks of nothing, like the calm interiority that does not look after itself and does not become aware of its not Being. It is the highest simplicity, not so much God itself, but the Godhead, which is hence, above God, in the way that some of the ancients already spoke of a Super-Godhead [*Übergottheit*]. It is not divine nature or substance, but the devouring ferocity of purity that a person is able to approach only with an equal purity. Since all Being goes up in it as if in flames, it is necessarily unapproachable to anyone still embroiled in Being. (Schelling 2000: 25)

The highest simplicity and highest purity is without this 'why': it is not a composite of qualities or an aggregate of attributes; it is not a process lengthened to a very long time. One may approach it only by giving up Being and giving up their 'why': here an abyss opens up that shortens the distances between millenniums without, however, reducing even by a tiny fraction that irreducible *distance* between God and the Godhead. It is a simplicity that does not dissipate the enigma of mortality; it is the consummate purity that preserves the mystery of the moonlit night where unity dwells with duality and where duality is also a kind of unity. Its profound gentleness, its 'composed bliss' or deepest purity, is also the most 'devouring ferocity': the *nomos* of the earthly, the sovereign powers of worldly hegemonies, the violent blows of fate that emanate from the law – all go up 'in it as if in flames'. This is not the God of nature, who holds the coherence of the world-order in *nomos*; this Godhead is not to be found in creation, in nature, or in the immanent plane of world-historical politics. The work of the law in the earthly order is here de-legitimated; the *nomos* loses its ground and gives up its 'why'. The following passage from Reiner Schürmann writing about Meister Eckhart is equally applicable to Schelling:

> The *epekeina* – and this is in God himself – is substituted for the *chorismos*, which is the separation between creator and creature that effaces continuity.

> There, the beyond opens up the abyss between 'God', the name of names, the ontic foundation of teleology, and the 'godhead' which is without name and beyond principle. As we see, only non-attachment allows one to cross this abyss, and Eckhart does not hesitate to add: then *got entwirt*. Just as all other beings, the highest, too, makes itself indistinct as a result of the counter-strategies already encountered: operation, loan, event. For if God wants to look inside a detached soul, 'it will cost him all his names'. (Schürmann 2003: 307)

The simplicity and the purity of the redeemed state of existence, beatified and sanctified by abandonment, lies in existing namelessly. To receive the gift of being, it is imperative to *ex-sist* namelessly in the desert of languages, without any worldly or otherworldly consolations. Such simplicity attunes us in 'divine mourning' wherein 'all earthly pains are immersed'. Therefore even God mourns. To attain to the Godhead, even God must lose all his names. It is thus not enough to abandon the world; one must abandon even God, which is 'the step of death'. This also explains why there is so much suffering in nature: nature groans for redemption. It also wants to give up all the names that the human being, with its abused power of naming, uses to overname her; this nature too must pass away. There is, as it were, a *spark* locked even within the deepest womb of nature; she is pregnant with it but does not know how to give birth to the light: 'not only us', Clara says, but 'the whole of nature yearns in the God from whom she is initially taken' (Schelling 2002: 80). 'She longs to be released from transience' (22).

If metaphysics as the onto-theological discourse of Being as the ground of beings understands the grounding Being as Reason, Schelling's thinking of *Abgrund* leads to an abandonment of this metaphysics. The legitimising principle of the modern hegemony is thereby made destitute and impoverished. Any appeal to a theological foundation to legitimise any earthly sovereignty is then de-legitimated. And yet in this desert of deserts an *opening* takes place: an *opening* to the nameless abyss without 'why'. In this stripping bare of our worldly attributes and abandonment of all earthly privileges, the highest simplicity is attained in which (as Meister Eckhart says) the Godhead ceaselessly gives birth to himself in the eternal Now. This is what we call the 'beatific life', nameless and wandering, ceaselessly given birth in the eternal bliss of the Now.

Notes

1. I am using the term 'end' throughout this work in the sense(s) indicated by Heidegger and later by Derrida (who, while taking up the word from Heidegger and thus passing through him, invites us to think 'end' in still another sense, or other senses, beyond

what Heidegger meant by it). The English term 'end' does not really attend to what Heidegger wants us to hear in *Vollendung*. The French translation appears to be better: *achèvement* indicates not so much or not merely a *finishing off* but more a completion or fulfilment. The English translation of *Vollendung* as 'end' has led to a certain misreading of Heidegger in which he is taken to be saying that from now onwards (that is, after Hegel) one should not bother about philosophy at all; we must now do other – better – things, since philosophy has been finished off in a stroke by Heidegger himself. Carefully attending to the word *Vollendung*, however, should indicate that it is precisely now, when metaphysics (being understood as presence) has come to *Vollendung* (completion or fulfilment, the utmost realisation of the understanding of being as presence), that we must be concerned with the 'philosophical', wherein 'philosophical' thinking is now *released* from its subservience to the demand of the 'system'. Since 'philosophy' is determined to be metaphysics, both Heidegger and Derrida, in their different ways, hesitate to call themselves 'philosophers'. This should not be taken to mean that a rigorous thoughtful consideration of the great philosophical tradition is to be banished; it means that precisely now, when thinking is *released* from the constriction that being as presence imposes on us, is it possible to think this *releasing* itself, that is, the *abandonment* of metaphysics. In the following pages, I will explicate what significance this abandonment (*Gelassenheit*) has for Schelling, for whom – after Hegel, in a manner – the question is no longer 'being' or 'that-which-has-being' but that of *Überseyn* (beyond being). Such a thought demands that metaphysics (being as presence) be given up, or even abandoned to itself. It is in this sense that Heidegger uses the term *Gelassenheit*, borrowing from Eckhart, which means for him, as for Eckhart, not just releasement but also giving up, abandoning, detaching and thus to 'let-it-to-be' (or, 'let being be'). Heidegger then goes on to say that such an idea itself resonates in the very structural opening of any discourse as such. Since discourse is essentially linguistic – here language is no longer a mere means to an end – all discourse opens with an immemorial and originary *es gibt* (the 'there is' with which every sentence begins), which means, literally, 'it gives'. It is the gift, like a lightning flash, that opens language *as such*. When being is no longer grafted onto presence by the 'violence of the concept', a *withdrawal* (which already resonates in the word 'abandonment') from it welcomes for the first time – because it has been unthought – the gift of this unthought, the unthought of the gift. Hence, in the word *Gelassenheit* we must hear *giving* – the gift or being-given. In the English *abandonment* or French *abandonner* – if we translate *Gelassenheit* in these ways – we may still hear *doner*, which means giving or gifting. When we are released from the constriction that being as presence imposes on us, we are *given* the gift of what is, as Heidegger says beautifully, the unthought in metaphysics, that is, the event of the gift of being, or the event of being as gift, when being is no longer present or presence. For Heidegger the gift is that of *presencing*. In his later works, Schelling thinks this gift no longer as being at all but as that infinite which transcends that which has being.

2. In his 1809 *Freedom* essay Schelling describes the Idealist's violent negation of nature as 'self-emasculation' which is a 'dreary and fanatic enthusiasm'; it is the fanatic enthusiasm of those sterile intellectuals, 'the civil servants of humanity', who lack that 'vital basis' which alone endows the living intellect with holy enthusiasm, the divine madness that Plato speaks of: 'if a philosophy lacks this vital basis, usually a sign that the ideal principle was but weak from the outset, it then loses itself in those systems whose attenuated concepts of *a-se-ity*, modality, etc., stand in sharpest contrast to the vital power and fullness of reality. On the other hand, where the ideal principle really operates to a high degree but cannot discover a reconciling and mediating basis, it gives birth to a dreary and fanatic enthusiasm which breaks forth in self-mutilation or – as in the case of the priests of the Phrygian goddess – in self-emasculation, which in philosophy is accomplished by the renunciation of reason and science' (Schelling 1992: 30–1).

3. Rosenzweig, following Schelling here, develops a similar argument in his *Star of Redemption*. The correlation (taking this mathematical idea from Hermann Cohen) between the three nothings (which Rosenzweig, following Schelling again, calls 'actualities') – God, Man and the World – is not a correlation between three substantial entities but that of temporal 'closenesses and remotenesses, approaches and withdrawals' (Rosenzweig 2004: 118).
4. This idea that not only the mortal but also nature is essentially linguistic, and that the creative Word pronounced in nature and in man is the unity of vowel and consonant (revealing thereby the inner being of all existence) is already to be found in Schelling's *Freedom* essay. There he says: 'By reason of the fact that man takes his rise from the depths (that he is a creature) he contains a principle relatively independent of God. But just because this very principle is transfigured in light – without therefore ceasing to be basically dark – something higher, the *spirit*, arises in man. For the eternal spirit pronounces unity or the Word, in nature. But the (real) Word, pronounced, exists only in the unity of light and darkness (vowel and consonant). Now these principles do indeed exist in all things, but without complete consonance because of the inadequacy of that which has been raised from the depths. Only in man, then, is the Word completely articulate, which in all other creatures was held back and left unfinished. But in the articulate word the spirit reveals itself, that is God as existing, in act. Now inasmuch as the soul is the living identity of both principles, it is spirit; and spirit is in God' (Schelling 1992: 38–9).
5. Like Benjamin, Schelling too envisions a philosophy that has 'not merely general categories' (as concepts) but 'actual, determinate essentialities' (as ideas). In his lectures on mythology, Schelling writes the following, which reminds us of Benjaminian Platonic ideas: 'Philosophical concepts are not supposed to be merely general categories; they should be actual, determinate essentialities. And the more they are endowed by the philosopher with actual and individual life, then the more they appear to approach poetic figures, even if the philosopher scorns every poetic wording: here the poetic idea is included in philosophical thought and does not need to come to it from outside' (Schelling 2007b: 38).
6. In the fifth lecture on mythology, Schelling writes: 'In every language that is becoming, the original unity continues to be in force, as precisely the affinity of languages in part shows: the loss of all unity would be the loss of language itself, and with that everything human. For man is only man to the extent that he is capable of a general consciousness transcending his own singularity; language too only has meaning as something communal' (Schelling 2007b: 81).
7. This recalls the famous poem by Hölderlin, 'in lovely blueness ', which Heidegger is fond of quoting: 'In lovely blueness with its metal roof the steeple blossoms / Around it the crying of swallows hovers, most loving blueness surrounds it ' (Hölderlin 1966: 601).
8. As 'holy mourning', it is not an accidental, contingent or ephemeral subjective experience. Heidegger writes about Hölderlin: 'The fundamental attunement is a *holy mourning*. This adjective "holy" raises the attunement beyond all contingency, but also beyond all determinacy. Mourning is neither an isolated pining over some loss or other; and yet nor is it that floating, hazy and yet burdensome sadness about everything and nothing – what we call melancholy – which can in turn be shallow or profound depending on its fundamental difference in depth and extent. Yet even this character of the holy does not exhaust the essence of the fundamental attunement that prevails here . . . it is precisely that which attunes and it attunes all the more directly and steadfastly when human beings stand fundamentally open to beings within a fundamental attunement' (Heidegger 2014: 79–80).
9. Similarly Benjamin says: 'It is a metaphysical truth that all nature would begin to lament if it were endowed with language (though "to endow with language" is more than "to make able to speak"). This proposition has a double meaning. It means, first:

she would lament language itself. Speechlessness: that is the great sorrow of nature (and for the sake of her redemption the life and language of *man* – not only, as it is supposed, of the poet – are in nature). This proposition means, secondly: she would lament. Lament, however, is the most undifferentiated, impotent expression of language; it contains scarcely more than the sensuous breath; and even where there is only a rustling of plants, in it there is always a lament. Because she is mute nature mourns. Yet the inversion of this proposition leads even further into the essence of nature: the sadness of nature makes her mute. In all mourning there is the deepest inclination to speechlessness, which is infinitely more than the inability or disinclination to communicate' (Benjamin 1986: 329–30).

10. In another place Heidegger writes: 'But the more joyful the joy, the more pure the sadness slumbering within it. The deeper the sadness, the more slumbering the joy resting within it. Sadness and joy play into each other. The play itself which attunes the two by letting the remote be near and near be remote is pain. This is why both, highest joy and deepest sadness, are painful each in its way. But pain so touches the spirit of mortals that the spirit receives its gravity from pain. That gravity keeps mortals with all their wavering at rest in their being. The spirit which answers to pain, the spirit attuned by pain and to pain, is melancholy' (Heidegger 1982: 153).

11. In one of his earliest essays called 'Treatise Explicatory of the Idealism in the Science of Knowledge', Schelling speaks of the danger of freedom thus: 'Everything about man has the character of freedom. Fundamentally, man is a being that inanimate nature has released from its guardianship and thereby entrusted to the fortunes of his own (internally conflicting) forces. His fundamental continuity is one of a *danger* (*Gefahr*), forever recurring and forever to be mastered anew, a danger that man seeks by his own impulse and from which he saves himself anew' (Schelling 1994a: 94).

12. In the 'Stuttgart Seminars' Schelling writes of this demonic essence of human being: 'Consequently, death marks not an absolute separation of the spirit from the body but only a separation from that corporeal element which inherently contradicts the spirit, that is, a separation of good from evil and vice versa (for which reason our remains are not called a body any longer but a *corpse*). In short, it is not merely a part of man that is immortal but all of man according to his being [*Esse*], and death is a reduction *ad esssentiam*. That essence which does not remain behind – for that which does remain behind is the *caput mortuum* – but which is formed and which is neither merely corporeal nor merely spiritual, but the corporeal aspect of the spirit and the spiritual aspect of the body, we shall refer to as *demonic*. Hence that which is immortal in man is the demonic, [which is] not a negation of materiality but rather an essentiated [*essentificirte*] materiality. This demonic aspect thus constitutes a most actual essence, indeed it is far more actual than man in this life; it is what in the language of the common man (and here we may legitimately say *vox populi vox Dei*) is called – not *spirit* – but *a spirit*; such that when it is claimed that a spirit has appeared to someone we must understand such a spirit to be precisely this most authentic, essentiated being' (Schelling 1994a: 237–8).

Chapter 4

The Irreducible Remainder

Abyss of freedom

Schelling's *Philosophical Inquiries into the Nature of Human Freedom* (1809) takes up the great philosophical problematic of freedom, a problematic that is rarely mentioned in contemporary philosophical discourse, as if the question of freedom is now *passé*, or already exhausted by the determinations that have been applied to it. In other words, as Adorno (1987: 214–15) puts it, freedom appears to have now become 'obsolete' or aged. Yet freedom is precisely that which no predicates can ever exhaust and no determinations saturate. If the question of freedom no longer appears to us as compelling, this shows us only that, now more than ever before, the ecstasy or excess of freedom consists in its releasing itself, while summoning up predicates and determinations, from these very determinations and predicates. Likewise, if the question of freedom no longer appears to us as a prominent question in our contemporary critical discourses, this only shows us that those discourses – being no longer able to release the unconditioned in us – are languishing in that self-satisfaction which consists in being enclosed in the immanence of self-presence, or in various closures of totalisation, which is then predicated and determined on the basis of *presently given entities*. To most of us, then, it appears that the thought of freedom is no longer a requirement for our 'post-metaphysical' discourses; and yet at the same time, whenever we invoke an idea of 'right' or of 'justice' in our practical political debates, we presuppose the possibility of freedom; in other words, these ideas are grounded on the very possibility of freedom *as such*, whether explicitly or tacitly. In such debates we no longer feel it is a requirement to ask: But whence is this freedom?

While on the one hand, freedom is the 'catchword' or 'password' in various debates, most often determined by the mass media, in which issues like 'rights', 'law' and 'justice' are evoked, its absence in our contemporary critical-philosophical discourses is more decidedly marked. There the question of freedom is regarded as an obsolete metaphysical problem. It is extremely difficult, if not impossible, to release the idea of freedom from its various metaphysical overdeterminations – not to mention those various practical determinations that presuppose the dominant metaphysical thought of freedom – for it demands a radical deconstruction not merely of what we generally mean by 'politics' or 'ethics', but of the very ground of the *political* as such, i.e. its metaphysical foundation.

What deconstruction is concerned with, then, is to release the very presupposition of the political ontology of the world: the 'facticity' or 'actuality' of freedom that is always already presupposed in those predicates of the political that already exist, and whose validity has acquired the solidity of unquestionable self-evidence and a 'naturalised' foundation. Thus the task here is not merely laborious but also disturbing, since the problematic of freedom not only touches the extreme limit of the dominant metaphysical foundation of the political, but also radically undermines the ground of what we mean by 'politics'. This politics is supposed to involve an exercise of 'free will' as the 'property' of 'the human' who is 'the political animal' – whose animality (or better, *anima*), whose *life*, is not merely *Zoë* but that of *Bio*. We know that this distinction was made by Aristotle, with whom a moment is reached that has essentially – i.e. metaphysically – determined what has subsequently come to be thought as 'the political': a certain metaphysical determination of 'the human' as *life* and a certain determination of life as *political*.

Here, a certain determination of 'politics' is already founded upon (supposed) predicates of 'freedom' and 'the human' – and, of course, 'life' – which are *already* thoroughly metaphysical: freedom as 'the property' of the being *human*, which as 'property' is the power of appropriation or the appropriation of power. Politics *supposedly* begins here, according to this determination, at that moment when the human – already always in its very essence the proprietor of 'free will' – opens to the force of law, exposes himself to the gaze of others who are equally proprietors of 'free will' and thus of freedom. Recognising this – and granting this metaphysical determination of the human as 'the political animal' who has such a 'free will', who is thus *naturalised* and *essentialised* – the very task of the political is understood as the immanent one, the conditional one: that of negotiating, of equalising forces and gazes, economising heights and abysses, which by their own definitions refuse equality or equivalences, negotiations and economy. It is the task, itself thought to be political, of contesting power in the name of power, force in the name of force, height in the name of height, rather than the task of thinking the unconditioned that frees us to transcend these overdeterminations. The unconditioned task is that of thinking freedom outside property and the appropriation of the human, of inventing the political that would name, in its very un-nameability, the *spacing* of *the Open* for the arrival of the other and the outside, the outside of power and force, of gaze and conditioned 'rights'.

In a manner that prefigures Heidegger's (2002) later reading of Parmenides, Schelling's *Freedom* essay begins with a radical deconstruction of the metaphysical principle of identity. If the dominant notions of our juridico-political liberties and rights tacitly presuppose or have their ground in the metaphysical principle of identity – national, racial, communitarian, etc., which are naturalised and essentialised – then it would be necessary to rethink the principle of identity outside of its 'metaphysics of presence', outside the speculative principle of the unity of judgement. This also means, simultaneously, releasing it to freedom, to the *ex-sistence* of freedom, to its unconditional affirmation of the outside. Before Schelling's *Freedom* essay was published, Hölderlin, in his 'Judgment and Being' (1988a), had already broken away from speculative Idealism, while Hegel was in the process of constituting an Idealism based on the principle of identity of the Subject. What Hölderlin problematised in this short essay became something decisive, not only for Schelling but for the future of speculative Idealism, namely, that the ground of the grounded cannot itself be thought on the basis of the grounded, but remains irreducibly outside all ground, outside all appropriation and mastery. This ground does not allow itself to be thought within any circle of predicates of consciousness, because as their basis it precedes them and cannot itself be grounded on the basis of them. The ground is that non-conscious which escapes the circle of self-consciousness, not as a result of the circle, but as a moment of the origin of self-consciousness itself, or as an immemorial origin of the speculative as such. *The ground exceeds what is grounded*: this *ecstasy* or *excess* of the (non-)ground, this transcendence which can never again be grounded, this 'irreducible remainder' of the abyss in all that exists, this remnant of the non-ground, never allows identity to be the unity of I = I. It never allows the speculative unity to emerge without caesura, for it must *always already* be marked, wounded, opened by that caesura in its very origin. Therefore the principle of identity does not allow itself to be thought on the basis of the speculative unity of self-consciousness, but only as what Heidegger (2002) calls *belonging*-together – but not belonging-*together* – belonging-together as *jointure, constellation* or *configuration* which, in so far as it does not belong to the immanent form of necessity but has its ground in freedom, is *free* to be *disjoined, dis-*

installed or *disfigured*. Out of this abyss of freedom arises the possibility of a radical evil.

What this shows, then, is that our dominant juridico-political concepts – our national, racial, communitarian, etc., concepts – are based on what Jean-Luc Nancy (1991) calls 'the mythic foundation' of identity, a form of an immanence of self-presence. But more originally understood – as it is by both Schelling and Heidegger in their singular ideas of repetition – the principle of identity is the abyssal thought of an irreducible *hiatus* or caesura, of an irreducible *difference* or chasm that *spaces* open on the ground of an unground, on the unground of a jointure that is free to be disjoined. Thus, in his seminar in *Le Thor*, Heidegger (2003b), recalling his thoughts from *Being and Time* (1962), attempts to think the question of Being no longer on the basis of identity as belonging-*together* but in terms of an irreducible *ontological difference*. This means that the latter inaugurates the wholly otherwise of history no longer on the basis of an ontological ground, but as a *spacing open* in the *hiatus* between the ground of something that exists *and* that existence itself. In the following discussion I shall take up this distinction between Being in so far as it is the ground of existence *and* that existence itself. This 'irreducible remainder' that excludes itself in order to summon to itself what *belongs* together, this inscrutable ground, this undecidable of the abyss of freedom, this unthinkable abyss, summons incessantly and interminably (precisely because it is undecidable) the whole 'decision of existence' which is not 'this' or 'that' existential decision but the *decision of existence itself as such*. The 'decision of existence' is played out in this open space, in this irreducible hiatus or caesura that never allows the ground to be completely grounded, that keeps open the yawning gap or abyss between ground *and* existence, thereby making possible the eruption of something – namely, that which is *historical* as such, which is *event* as such. The thought of the event thus belongs to the open chasm of freedom where the decision of existence is played out. This decision – wherein the entirety of existence itself is played out; wherein existence in its entirety is 'thrown', as Heidegger says; wherein existence itself is decided; wherein existence *as such, essentially and in its innermost manner*, is waged and is risked *each time* – this *free* decision, this unconditional decision in pure ecstasy, is the decision for and between good and evil. It thus arises out of that freedom which releases the unconditional in us, and thereby opens us radically to the wholly otherwise arrival, to the wholly otherwise futurity free from all immanent self-enclosure. Such is the unconditional transcendence in freedom, since its ground is an inscrutable abyss: freedom is free to be free and not to be free. In that sense, the exuberant actuality of freedom is also pure potentiality: it is free to realise itself and not to realise itself; it is free to self-abnegate its own very possibility. As such, the thought of freedom is the thought of pure possibility or pure potentiality: it is the pure possibility of freedom to self-abnegate its own possibility and, in so far as freedom is this pure possibility itself, therein also lies the possibility of radical evil – that is, the possibility of its impossibility which is its most radical possibility. The political, more essentially thought – i.e. outside its merely economic-juridical delimitation – manifests itself in the open space of this pure possibility or pure potentiality of freedom. Only *the-there* where freedom opens the space of pure possibility may manifest something like what we call *the political*. It is on the basis of this spacing open in decision – of existence – that there may be revealed something like *the political*, that is, out of the unconditioned in freedom.

The political is therefore to be originarily understood no longer on the basis of the self-consuming immanence of the ground and predicates, no longer on the basis of the 'mythic foundation' of self-presence (national, racial, communitarian or linguistic), or on the basis of the metaphysics of the Subject, but rather as a *spacing* open, on the basis of an originary non-ground and non-appropriation, to the 'decision of existence' as such between good and a radical evil. If something like power, force and law in the realm that we tend to call 'political' manifests itself here, they themselves are not originary. They always already belong to a more originary, therefore immemorial, 'partitioning of forces' that throws existence into its decision, arising out of a groundless freedom that cannot be resolved in thoughts or concepts. Life is *political* not in the sense that *Zoë* is inserted into *Bio*, which already somehow presupposes a 'naturalised' existence already given. What we are attempting to understand here – and thereby attempting to think the very notion of the political anew – is that the ground of the political precedes the distinction between *Zoë* and *Bio*: that ground is the ground of freedom which 'throws' existence into the Open – to put it in Heideggerian terms – throws it open to the 'decision of existence' itself as such. Since this decision, arising out of freedom, is a decision between good and evil, and not the mere mastery of the intelligible over the sensible, it is on the basis of this decision, on the basis of a more originary distribution of forces, that there can be something like 'rights', 'power', etc.

That there should be something like the 'rights' of the 'human' against various manifestations of injustice and evil presupposes that this 'human' is the pure possibility of evil and good, and that, more essentially understood, the very 'humanity' of the human must be this possibility of radical evil itself. Thus, the notion of the *political* arising in the *spacing* of the pure possibility needs to be traced back to the more essential notion of *existence* as such, which in its *exstasis* can be understood (in so far as *ex-sistence* itself is the location of pure possibility, where this very location is to be understood in its *event-character*, in the infinitude of its verbal resonance, in the sense of a *placing* of place and not as 'this' or 'that' given place) as *placing* as such, as *taking place* as such, as *arriving* as such. Where does this pure possibility arise, which in its radical possibility is this impossibility, that is, the possibility of radical evil? Which is also to ask: Where does the very humanity of the 'human' arise, the human who is this very possibility of radical evil? The answer is: from nowhere, from nothingness. It is this nothingness or nowhere which is itself this *spacing* of pure possibility, which is the *locus* of the political or historical; it is the *topos* of the political which is not a topological or ontological site but the *taking place* of site *as such, the open space where something happens, erupts, arises*. The 'human', this 'political animal', is not merely the subject of rights – who, being the 'Subject' ('political' or 'ethical'), is the proprietor of 'free will' – nor is he merely the power or force of the negative which on the basis of its tremendous energy of converting nothing into being founds 'community', 'history', 'nation', etc. He is rather the *(a)topos* of pure possibility, the *spacing* of freedom even before he is *this* 'subject' of 'rights' and proprietor of 'free will'. As such, he is the *existence* whose essence is that of *ex-sisting* from any immanence of self-presence. In the various discourses of the 'rights' of the 'human', not only are 'rights' thought to be naturally given, but the very idea of the 'human' is presupposed as a naturalised, essentialised entity, as the bearer of those rights.

Hence, the metaphysical determination of the political is played out in the zone of distinction or indistinction between *Zoë* and *Bio*, between the animal that screams and the animal that founds community by speaking, between the natural animal and the political animal, where nature keeps on entering while being excluded, destabilising and yet founding what appears as 'history' and 'politics'. But with this overdetermination of the political – which is also the question of the 'human' and 'life' – the question of the pure possibility of this humanity itself, i.e. the question of the pure possibility of radical evil itself, remains foreclosed, although it is on the basis of freedom alone that the question of the human as bearer and *subject* of rights and the claims of justice can be asked. Now, if this pure possibility of radical evil belongs to the 'decision of existence' arising out of the abyss of freedom, then these discourses of the rights of the human subject, who is 'human' to the extent that he is 'subject', belong to the question of the essence of freedom. There then belongs to man a far more fundamental possibility than the possibility of being the subject of rights – of juridical rights, political rights, ethical rights, etc. This more fundamental possibility is that of the radical evil which belongs to the essence of freedom, freedom which in a sense is granted to man as a *gift*, forever non-appropriable, prior to man as a subject of rights, not so much because man may be evil, but because, on the basis of his disappropriation and of his mortality, he may be the very promise of an unconditional redemption. Evil is there so that there can be paradisiacal love, that promise of a redemptive, messianic fulfilment.

To release this unconditional possibility of a messianic, redemptive fulfilment is the task of thinking today. But this demands that thinking rescue this pure possibility by wrestling with the conditioned task of politics, by delivering the politics of the immanence of self-presence to unconditioned freedom, to the pure possibility of redemptive fulfilment. This in turn demands that the 'facticity' of existence itself be thought anew in its essential finitude and mortality, in its character as *ex-sistence*. In other words, it demands from us that we think *ex-sistence* as the *(a)topos* or *locus* of the open, as the site of the pure possibility of freedom, or the freedom of this pure possibility that opens up time beyond any self-presence to the incalculable arrival of the wholly otherwise. The question then arises as to why this essentially finite, mortal being is given the possibility of radical evil and, at the same time, the redemptive possibility of a messianic justice before law. Does this possibility of radical evil not undermine the very essence of freedom itself, and not merely that, but the very 'humanity' of the human, and thereby the very *sense* of the political as such? If the possibility of the messianic promise of a redemptive justice demands, paradoxically or aporetically, that one remains open, at the same time, to the 'irreducible remainder' of the possibility of radical evil, does this not undermine the very possibility of that messianic justice itself, and the possibility of that paradisiacal, redemptive love? In other words: If freedom is the open site of pure possibility, does this not imply the possibility of a radical evil which undermines the very ground of the political as such? If so, would the task not then be precisely to destroy any possibility of evil, and most desirably that radical evil, so that through this power of destruction man may finally be delivered over to that pure justice which, as such, is the *only* justice without remainder? But then, if man is an inextricably mortal and finite being (the being who, on account of his mortality, cannot completely appropriate the ground of his existence), can he on that event be the author of this justice without remainder? It is as if there adheres in the very finitude and mortality of man – i.e. *in the very essence of existence* – this pure possibility, not as the author of this possibility as a capacity, but as a *grant*, as a 'loan' or debt, or as a gift; there remains, on account of this inextricable finitude, an 'irreducible remainder', an irreducible possibility – *which as such is only a possibility and not an actuality* – of that, *in so far as this is a possibility*, which is not only the possibility of radical evil but also the possibility of a messianic, redemptive fulfilment.

It is this aporia that lies in the very 'decision of existence' as such, which makes freedom truly the limit question that renders thought groundless, reaching thereby the limit of sense. The sense of the political we are working towards is thus not the sense of a self-presence or self-foundation, but is rather the question of this limit of sense, which is the sense of freedom. Freedom is this limit of sense – which presents us with an aporia of freedom – from where the very sense of the political is derived. *How can we make sense of the possibility of radical evil and, at the same time, also demand the redemptive possibility of a messianic justice?* This aporia of freedom, taking thought to the limit of the thinkable, demands precisely at the same time that freedom be thought more than ever before, and not merely that the possibility of radical evil be explained, but also that we are opened up to the redemptive possibility of a messianic justice in the possibility of a pure future and the unconditional arrival of the wholly other.

We are now at the very heart of Schelling's thought. This irreducible aporia of freedom not only constantly pushes Schelling's thought to the limit of his demand that there be a system of freedom, but also thereby constantly summons his thinking to make sense of the possibility of radical evil, and to think at the limit of the thinkable this aporia of freedom itself. The task is *not* that of explaining away the possibility of radical evil, of minimising and reducing its terrible malice to a mere privation or a less perfect emanation of being, and thereby saving the foundational task of a system of freedom. The task is rather to render the wound of the system of freedom open to the abyss of evil, to allow it to feel in every vein 'the poisonous sting' (Rosenzweig 2004: 9) of evil, and *yet* to envision that redemptive possibility of the arrival of the event of a pure, incalculable, unprogrammatic futurity and its messianic, paradisiacal love. It is this task of undoing or unworking the possibility of system as such that Schelling's philosophical works point us toward. But that is a bigger question. Here we shall concentrate on the question asked in Schelling's *Freedom* essay. Following this introductory discussion, we can now venture to read the essay itself, not in a linear manner but in a gesture of repetitively seizing the same thought over and over again, for the reading that concerns us here is not an accumulative gathering of successive moments that arrives at a final truth, but a question of each time – which means over and over again – seizing a truth which momentarily presents itself. As such, the repetitions are different and multiple each time, in a *differentiating repetition* that attempts to 'wrest' that momentary apparition when truth itself is made known in philosophical contemplation. At stake is an attempt to think the question of freedom itself as *difference*, which demands a repetition of the dominant question of metaphysics: the principle of identity. Which is how Schelling's *Freedom* essay itself begins.

Existence and the ground(less)

In that essay, Schelling introduces a distinction 'between Being insofar as it exists and Being insofar as it is the mere basis of existence' (Schelling 1992: 31). All that exists has thus a condition or ground without which there cannot be 'this' or 'that' *thing*, and which, in precisely being a condition or ground, cannot be thought on the basis of what is conditioned or grounded. It is what remains as what Schelling calls 'the irreducible remainder', an excluded ground or basis as the very condition of possibility for some thing according to its genesis. Each thing or existent, in order to *come to itself*, presupposes as its condition of possibility this basis or ground, which cannot be resolved in it but remains independent, free and is in itself a *non-thing* (*unbedingt*),[1] not purely and simply a nothingness, but in respect to that thing that comes into existence as 'this' or 'that'. This *non-thing* of the 'irreducible remainder', this indigestible remnant of the abyss which cannot be resolved in any thing, being or existence in a form or a concept of reason, is precisely the ground of reason, being and existence, and therefore is not itself reason, neither in itself being nor existence, but is an abyss of reason or an ecstasy of being. Schelling says:

> Following the eternal act of self-revelation, the world as we now behold it, is all rule, order and form; but the unruly lies ever in the depths as though it might again break through and order and form nowhere appear to have been original, but it seems as though what had initially been unruly had been brought to order. This is the incomprehensible basis of all reality in things, the irreducible remainder which cannot be resolved into reason by the greatest exertion, but always remains in the depths. Out of this which is unreasonable, reason in the true sense is born. (Schelling 1992: 34)

Therefore no being, existence or created thing in itself is merely *this* thing, *this* being or *this* existence, self-present and self-sufficient, saturated and enclosed in its mythic, autochthonous foundation or ground; no being, existence or created thing in itself on the basis of itself attains its own ground, its own being or its self-presence and its self-foundation. There remains as the irreducible ground of all that exists *that* which has never been present, but is always already a loss – in respect of 'this' existence or 'that' existence – an *immemorial* forgetting, an irreducibly indigestible origin that no memory can ever retrieve, yet which is always *there*, as *the-there*, or what Heidegger speaks of as the *let-there*, which is not-yet-being and not-yet-existence. With this, the innermost metaphysical foundation of speculative Idealism (which is the utmost realisation of metaphysics: being grasped as potentiality) is broken and shattered. The *coming into presence* of the existent is the *diversion* – what Schelling (2010) calls *Abfall* – from its own condition or ground, whereby this condition has *always already* receded into an immemorial and irretrievable past such that it does not allow itself to be thought within the unity or identity of a ground. As a result, each created existence, being or thing – in so far as it comes into existence at all – carries this originary caesura, split, diversion or discordance between the ground of its existence and itself as *this* being or existence, a discordance or caesura that can no longer be thought as belonging-*together*, but only as a *belonging*-together: a *holding* together of irreducibly *differentiating* forces that are free from each other, that are separated from each other and, while being separated, call each to the other, summon each other, thus forming this jointure, this *Zusammenhang* (Schelling 2000) or nexus between 'Being insofar as it exists and Being insofar as it is the mere basis of existence' (Schelling 1992: 31) and *this* existence itself. Since it is free and not of necessity, this jointure, constellation or configuration (*Zusammenhang*) of that which exists *and* that which is the ground of existence allows that which exists to operate freely and independently, since what is thus being determined as this created, finite existent is not what it is in itself but that which arises out of a ground that is outside of itself. As Schelling explicates:

> But dependence does not exclude autonomy or even freedom. Dependence does not determine the nature of the dependent, but merely declares that the dependent entity, whatever else that may be, can only be as a consequent of that upon which it is dependent; it does not declare what this dependent is or not. Every organic individual, insofar as it has come into being, is dependent upon another organism with respect to its genesis but not at all with regard to its essential being. (Schelling 1992: 18)

In all existents – in so far as they exist at all – there operates this free *Zusammenhang*, this free jointure, this free *belonging*-together, this free 'partitioning of forces' (Schelling 1992: 57), or rather *assemblage* of forces. Unlike the speculative unity – unity thought as *Hypokeimenon*, as *Subjectum*, where identity is grasped as belonging-*together*, where the *Subjectum* gathers into its self-presence the disparate and the epochal discontinuities, reducing them only to the attenuated variations of the same *Subjectum* – the *belonging*-together here of *Zusammenhang*, in so far as it belongs to freedom, cannot be grasped on the basis of unity as ground or on the basis of the logical principle of identity as the underlying *Subjectum* or *Hypokeimenon*, but only as that which precedes all predicative forms of judgement, or ground or identity, as that which no ground can ground and to which no predicates apply. It is that which, preceding all ground and existence, preceding all difference and identity, all predicates and time, is the originary *unground* (*Abgrund*) or abyss, the originary time before time

– what Schelling (2000) calls the 'eternal past' – the excluded, ungrounded or 'un-pre-thinkable' (*Unvordenkliche*), where what *belongs* together cannot be thought in speculative terms – i.e. as an antithesis of concepts leading to a synthetic unity of judgement – but only as a *belonging*-together in an originary disjunction of forces, more originary than the antithetic logic of the speculative dialectic. Thus, the epochal breaks, radical discontinuities, and the originary disjunction of forces or principles – the principle of the ground and the principle of existence – cannot be thought in speculative terms: i.e. they cannot be thought to belong to the metaphysical *Subjectum* or underlying *Hypokeimenon* as an underlying identity (Heidegger 2003a). What Schelling is attempting to think here, in the manner that Hölderlin had already attempted before him, is the epochal discontinuities that define that *historicity* of history itself, the principle of *belonging*-together as the principle that inaugurates the very *event of history* itself. This principle belongs to the 'un-pre-thinkable' abyss of freedom, to that abyss to which 'no predicates except lack of predicates' applies (Schelling 1992: 87). It is the *unbedingt* – the *non-thing* of freedom – which is precisely the *absolute* of freedom: the pure actuality of freedom which is, at the same time, pure potentiality, the pure freedom which is also the highest necessity. It is the originary dispropriation, being unground or *Abgrund*, 'the originary forgetting' – to recall the words of Jean-Louis Chrétien (2002) – the 'immemorial' loss, which Schelling calls 'eternal past' or the 'dark ground':

> There must be a being *before* all basis and before all existence, that is, before any duality at all; how can we designate it except as 'primal ground', or, rather, as the 'groundless'? As it precedes all antitheses these cannot be distinguishable in it or be present in any way at all. It cannot then be called the identity of both, but only the absolute indifference as to both . . . indifference is not a product of antitheses nor are they implicitly contained in it, but it is a unique being, apart from all antitheses, in which all distinctions break up. It is naught else than just their non-being and therefore has no predicates except lack of predicates, without its being naught or a nonentity. Thus they must . . . really posit indifference in the 'groundless' which precedes all basis. (Schelling 1992: 87)

Freedom is this originary event of history, which is the event of history's inauguration. Since freedom is the decision between good and evil, this good and evil belongs to the realm of history. Only there where history arises and only there where the political arises (for the political arises as historical and, only in so far as the realm of the historico-political belongs to the abyss of freedom, arises out of freedom) does the possibility of radical evil manifest itself. The question of the possibility of radical evil is inscribed essentially and not accidentally in the very possibility of the manifestation or inauguration, in the very possibility of the revelation of the historical and the political, in so far as the historico-political belongs to the groundlessness of freedom, i.e. to the decision between good and evil. Therefore, quoting Franz Baader, Schelling speaks of the possibility of the radical evil that belongs to man alone, for man alone is that central being who is capable of something which does not belong merely to the bestiality that manifests itself in the realm of nature. For evil is the highest manifestation of spirit itself. There is granted to this central being that power of the second beginning, that other inauguration – and this is the essence of human freedom – which is to inaugurate the realm of history where the spirit reveals itself. As such, as the beginner of the 'second creation' (Schelling 1992: 58), man is not only the only creature capable of evil, but, precisely because of this capacity, in him there lies the redemptive possibility wherein the whole of nature redeems itself. 'Where danger threatens, that which saves from it also grows' (Hölderlin 1998: 231). This 'saving power', this pure possibility of redemption, is nothing other than the language itself that man utters, where mute nature finds its own redemption in the pure naming language of man. Here is what Schelling says:

> Only man is in God, and through this very being-in-God is capable of freedom. He alone is a central being and therefore should also remain in the center. In him all things are created, just as it is also only through man that God accepts nature and ties it to him. Nature is the first, or, old testament, since all things are all outside the center and therefore under the law. Man is the beginning of the new covenant through wisdom, as mediator, since he himself is connected with God, God (the last division being attained) also accepts nature and takes it to *him*. Man is thus the redeemer of nature towards whom all its archetypes strive. The Word which is fulfilled in man exists in nature as a dark, prophetic (still incompletely spoken) Word. Hence the anticipations which have no exegesis in nature itself and are only explained by man. (Schelling 1992: 92)

We are reminded of Benjamin's (1986: 314–32) notion of the pure language of naming that is redemptive, where mute nature finds its fulfilment in the mournfulness of a paradisiacal bliss. It is the Adamic language of pure naming. Man, in being capable of freedom (which does not mean that he is capable of making freedom his property but rather that he is granted the gift of freedom so that out of it, out of his being 'thrown' by freedom into the 'decision of existence', he may freely inaugurate this 'new covenant'), is thereby the one who alone inaugurates the spiritual realm of the historical – i.e. the realm of the spirit wherein the possibility of radical evil and, at the same time, of the redemptive fulfilment through him are equally primordially given.

Now, to come back to Schelling, this freedom is granted to man – i.e.

this principle of inauguration through which he can inaugurate this 'new covenant' – so that therein the entirety of created existence may find redemptive fulfilment in the paradisiacal language that man speaks. Since this redemptive possibility is granted to man on the basis of his intrinsic, inextricable finitude – on the ground of an unground, on the basis of a non-basis, an immemorial and originary forgetting, an originary dispropriation and irremediable loss – this very finitude also summons up, in the very necessity of the 'decision of existence', that possibility of radical evil, not for itself, but so that there may be redemptive fulfilment.

Exuberant life

As an unconditional principle, freedom is the transcendence of *ex-sistence*. Life is that movement that *ex-sists* any in-sistence in immanence; life is *always already* the becoming in freedom: *in so far as life is free, life becomes.* The excess of life lies in this ecstatic character: life is essentially ecstatic, i.e. it transcends any insistence in necessity and frees itself to freedom.

Thus, for Schelling, freedom as life, rather than a system of the categories of pure reason, is movement, becoming and event. Life is *free* arising. Life is this longing, desiring and willing that constantly pushes itself to its own limit, constantly touches its own limit, undermines its own foundation and summons an ever new foundation, an ever new basis for itself. Life on that account never reaches totality or unity since it is forever transcending itself, and thus life is movement, becoming and event. As life and not a mere mechanical production, freedom manifests itself as an essential strife of forces, as a 'partitioning of forces' and as a division of principles. *Life is agon* in the sense that Heraclitus speaks of strife: the bursting forth of oppositional forces out of an essential concealing which cannot be further grounded.

Thus arising unconditionally – i.e. freely – life reveals itself as a free nexus or jointure of forces, which we understand (after Heidegger) as *belonging*-together, as a 'band' or *Zusammenhang* of forces that, being free, are free to disjoin themselves from any given jointure, that themselves strive against each other. If the essence of the historical and the political is derived from the essence of this freedom, then the essence of the historico-political cannot be derived from the self-grounding principle of *Hypokeimenon*, as *Subjectum*, as the logical principle of identity underlying, as a belonging-*together* that gathers the strife and partitioning of forces and the epochal breaks into the unity of a ground. Rather, as *life*, the strife of forces, their partitioning and the epochal breaks would be traced to the more originary unground of freedom, to the unconditioned principle of inauguration that appears as movement, becoming and event. This is what Schelling (2000) calls 'un-pre-thinkable': what lies beyond the thinkable and beyond predicates, beyond being and nothing, from where the *agon* of forces immediately bursts forth, opening up in this revelation the realm of spirit – of history and the political.

The question here is not, therefore, how life is inserted into the 'political' and thus becomes 'the political life', but rather how to conceive the political in a more originary manner as always already political and historical, and which, as such, as life, precedes the famous Aristotelian distinction between *Zoë* and *Bio*. This would be Schelling's notion of life as pure transcendence, where the pure potentiality of freedom manifests itself as pure actuality. This is the reason why Schelling, setting himself against any conception of immanence and emanation, against various overdeterminations – whether mechanistic reductive or systematic logico-grammatical – over and over again conceives life as becoming, movement and event. Even God, because he is not merely a 'moral world order', or merely the regulative, necessary hypothesis of an end, but is an actual God, an actualising God and not mere potentiality, is himself a principle of beginning, and therefore is *life*. 'God is a life', says Schelling, and 'not a mere being', 'for being is only aware of itself in becoming'. What is life, then? It is that which, being finite, arises out of a ground, condition or basis, but which ecstatically *ex-sists* any ground in so far as the ground determines only its genesis but not its essence. I quote these lines again:

> But dependence does not exclude autonomy or even freedom. Dependence does not determine the nature of the dependent, but merely declares that the dependent entity, whatever else that may be, can only be as a consequent of that upon which it is dependent; it does not declare what this dependent is or not. Every organic individual, insofar as it has come into being, is dependent upon another organism with respect to its genesis but not at all with regard to its essential being. (Schelling 1992: 18)

There cannot be a system of life, though there can be a system of an understanding of life, and even though life is conditioned according to its genesis, it is unconditioned according to what it is in itself, and therefore is *free*. Here we have arrived again at the point where we began, namely, with life as a nexus, jointure or assemblage of forces or a strife of principles between the ground, the basis or the condition of existence *and* this existence itself, between the pure potentiality to exist and the actuality of something that exists. *Life constantly presents itself as a strife of forces between this irreducible basis and that which exists.* This irreducible basis is the irreducible remainder of the things that exists, the basis of all reality and all existence. Schelling speaks of this 'irreducible remainder' in the following way:

> Following the eternal act of self-revelation, the world as we now behold it, is all rule, order and form; but the unruly lies ever in the depths as though it might again break through and order and form nowhere appear to have been original, but it seems as though what had initially been unruly had been brought to order. This is the incomprehensible basis of all reality in things, the irreducible remainder which cannot be resolved into reason by the greatest exertion, but always remains in the depths. Out of this which is unreasonable, reason in the true sense is born. (Schelling 1992: 34)

Thus, even God – in so far as he is life, in so far as he is this *coming into presence* to himself – has a relation to a basis of his existence, that is, simply because it is the basis, is outside of himself, an abyss as the very condition of his existence, *except* that the relation to this basis is indissoluble in God, while this *Zusammenhang* is dissoluble in mortals. As *life*, God himself is finite in so far as the life of God has a basis independent of God himself, who is not thereby the actual God or the actualised God, yet this finitude is such only to the extent that God can take it up into himself as a moment of his realisation, an immanent finitude. Thus, there is a source of the abyss even in God, but as mere potentiality which is always subordinated to the higher principle of actuality. *Therefore God is the only being in which pure potentiality and pure actuality come to coincide*. In man, however, this strife of forces, because of the dissoluble character of the nexus or jointure, can never be resolved once and for all: there remains that 'irreducible remainder' that can never be completely resolved in reason, that can never be completely actualised; there remains the potentiality that can never be completely actualised in reason, a non-being (which is not mere nothing) that can never be completely converted into being by the energy and power of the concept. Here, Schelling's 1809 essay, coming barely two years after Hegel's *Phenomenology of Spirit*, has broken apart the very metaphysical foundation of the Hegelian speculative determination of history. For Hegel's metaphysical foundation of speculative history and the political, as readers of *The Phenomenology of Spirit* know, is based upon the energy and the 'power of the negative' that converts even the nothing into being, and thereby makes history and the political itself possible.

What Schelling, in contrast, attempts to think here is not the non-being that will be converted into being by the energy of the negative; nor does he, contra Hegel, attempt to think the possibility of universal history and the political as grounded upon the *Hypokeimenon*, upon the *Subjectum* as the self-presence of the Same that gathers the relative discontinuities and breaks of history into the principle of identity. What Schelling attempts to think is rather the indigestible remainder of non-being that can never be converted into being, that expelled ground of history that is always the irreducible remnant, the irreducible outside of universal history and of the political based on the *Subjectum*. This is the eternal remainder of non-being in being, of potentiality in actuality, the remnant of the not yet that lies unconditionally at the basis of all that exists.

What Schelling attempts to think then is the event of the outside, the remnant of history – not because it is the end, but because it is the promise of history itself. Above all, it is the thought of a finite history and a finite politics of a finite creature that initiates or inaugurates on the basis of a power which is only *granted* to him beforehand, a power that man can never appropriate but only receive as a *gift*. This 'irreducible remainder' that makes our history and our politics finite alone explains the actual strife and partitioning of forces, the actual disjunctions and the epochal breaks, as the very condition of the inauguration of history and the political, and that thereby explains the radical evil that manifests itself in the realm of history and politics. Hegel's metaphysical determination of history, therefore, cannot explain the possibility of radical evil, and therefore also cannot explain the redemptive thought of a futurity, for the Hegelian account of history explains away radical evil only as a moment within universal history, as a necessary moment of negativity that has not yet been actualised into being and which, for that matter, is not radical. For evil is radical to the extent that its possibility lies at the very basis of the manifestation of the realm of history and the political, at the very moment of history's inauguration – a possibility that remains always a possibility – and thereby keeps history and the political open to the arrival of the wholly otherwise, un-predicable, incalculable and undecidable, not merely to the possibility of radical evil, but precisely to the possibility of redemptive fulfilment. In this sense, Schelling can be called a messianic thinker, a thinker of radical futurity, of a pure futurity that is always *to come* and that will not come to pass away.

Finite politics

What is thus at stake is the very question of finitude. A finite being, unlike the divine being, is that being in whom the nexus, jointure or constellation (*Zusammenhang*) of forces is dissoluble, for 'here alone light and darkness, or the two principles, can be united in a way capable of division' (Schelling 1992: 51). While the divine being can grasp the whole of his becoming – past, present and future – simultaneously in an indissociable *Zusammenhang*, for mortals this nexus of temporality is dissociable or disjoinable. In this sense, there is radical futurity only for mortals, a futurity that is incalculable, unprogrammable and undecidable *par excellence*, which is not a futurity that will come to pass but an eternal promise of redemption that cannot be reduced to any earthly sovereignty. This radical futurity, this pure possibility that is free, is radical to the extent that at the same moment it summons, in its possibility, not only the possibility of danger but also that of an eternal promise that arrives to mortals only as beatitude. The mortal is that undecidable line that is 'thrown' into this (dis)jointure of time; he is that point of the abyss, like the ungrounded copula of a monstrous judgement that opens, at the same moment, to both sides in an equiprimordial manner: to danger and promise, to evil and good in an equal measure. Thrown into this in-*de-cision*, into this *cision*, separation or division that joins both danger and promise to evil and good, man is predisposed to both, oscillating in indecision between good and evil, for he combines in him the possibility of both in the nexus of forces:

> Man has been placed at that summit where he contains within him the source of self-impulsion towards good and evil in equal measure; the nexus of the principles within him is not a bond of necessity but of freedom. He stands at the dividing line; whatever he chooses will be his act, but he cannot remain in indecision because God must necessarily reveal himself and because nothing at all in creation can remain ambiguous. Nonetheless it seems as though he could not escape his indecision, just because it is indecision. There must therefore be a general cause of temptation, a solicitation to evil, even if it were only to bring the principles within him to life, that is, to make him conscious of them. (Schelling 1992: 50)

What is the consequence of this finitude, of this oscillation born out of the undecidable, of this not being able to appropriate once and for all the principle of the basis or ground (since there is indecision and the undecidable only to the extent that the principle of the ground remains ungrounded and unappropriated, that it remains not only unresolved into reason, but an 'irreducible remainder', a forever indigestible remnant)? The consequence of this finitude is the summoning of decision, not *that* or *this* decision, but the *'decision of existence' itself as such*, which is played out in this abyssal zone of indecision. Into this zone of indecision, the whole of existence is thrown. Since the existent cannot remain in this indecision, out of the necessity of decision there arises a constant solicitation, a predisposition to evil. Like Kant, Schelling, too, locates here the source of the radical evil in man's predisposition to evil: 'in this it is supported by man's own evil inclinations, for his eye, which is incapable of looking constantly at the glamour of divinity and truth, always gazes at non-being' (Schelling 1992: 69). It is here that the possibility of a reversal of the nexus of forces emerges (since this nexus is dissoluble): what must remain in the centre as a mere ground of existence now may attempt to come to the periphery and claim to be the All, the Universal, the totality, while it is only a particular and ought to remain only this much – a mere particular will, a mere basis of existence, a mere potentiality and not yet actuality, an always *not yet*, a remainder, so that this very remnant, this very 'irreducible remainder', can serve as a condition of possibility for the eruption of redemptive fulfilment so that there may arise *the pure paradisiacal gift of love*. Therefore, in itself, this principle of basis or this 'irreducible remainder' is not evil – simply because, as a principle of the basis, it is also the basis of love – but precisely because of this it ought to remain a mere basis, always remaining a potentiality, a mere condition. As a mere basis, it is the principle of the mere *possibility* of evil, but it becomes *actual* when, as a result of the reversal of principles and of forces (or the dissolution of forces), there occurs the reaction of the principle of basis. Evil is not a mere discord of forces but forms a false unity or false nexus of forces that has a mere simulacrum of being; in other words, the constellation of *belonging*-together becomes now one of belonging-*together*. Man in his evil forgets the originary promise of redemption given on the basis of an originary dispropriation as a *gift* and now seeks to appropriate this very gift, this originary finitude, this originary dispropriation, in the name of a self-presence of being. What is then sought to be totalised in the appropriation of the unity of ground is that which ought to remain forever outside ground – that spacing chasm – on the basis of which alone there can remain for a mortal his futurity, his radical openness to the other. In evil, the finite will – which, being particular, is always finite and never absolute – ferociously hungers for the attainment of being, for the complete actualisation of itself only because it is only the non-being, or not-yet-being, a potentiality that never attains to complete actuality. Evil lies precisely in this: in this totalising malice of the non-being, or the all-devouring lust of potentiality to attain complete actuality in this self-negating movement of finitude. In itself, however, this finitude is not evil. Schelling is explicit here: 'evil is not derived from finitude in itself'. It is, however, derived 'from finitude which has been exalted to independent being' (Schelling 1992: 46). As mere potentiality, the principle of the basis, this 'irreducible remainder' is the principle of evil, and yet, as the principle of potentiality, it is the very unconditioned principle of the basis for the future. That there is futurity for the mortal is only on account of the fact that potentiality lies at the basis, as condition; there is *not yet* so that being may *come to presence*, so that there may be *presencing* itself. This principle of evil becomes actuality only when, out of the self-affirmation that necessarily lies in this principle, it reacts against itself – i.e. against its 'not-yet' character, against its own finitude – and attempts to totalise itself into the self-presencing ground of the whole of being or existence.

Here we arrive, with the help of Schelling, at the fundamental aporia of freedom, from which we can derive the very aporia of the political. Redemptive fulfilment, which is the very thought of promise, requires that there may remain open for us the possibility of a radical futurity, for in this futurity alone lies the happiness of mortals. However, this radical openness for futurity lies in the principle of potentiality – that there ought to remain for us a basis, a condition, a ground – which is forever inappropriable, which must *always already* dispropriate us in a time before us, in an immemorial past; the principle of potentiality which is the very principle of the possibility of evil. To remain open to the radical possibility of the pure *coming* at once summons the very *possibility* of evil; but to negate this possibility of evil on that account would result in the self-abnegation of our very finitude, which is nothing but evil itself, but in its *actuality*. It is as if evil is inescapable here, the evil that ineluctably lies in our very finitude and whose terrible abyss may make itself manifest at any time in our midst, threatening our very existence with destruction and annihilation, as that against which the whole of existence itself is played out, waged and risked. It is this possibility of evil which is not the mere privation of being or a gradual emanation from perfect being (for then it would not be 'radical'), but is the decision of a particular will that in its non-being attempts to actualise itself into complete actuality of being; 'it is the hunger of selfishness which, in the measure that it deserts totality and unity becomes even needier and poorer, but just on that account more ravenous, hungrier, more poisonous' (Schelling 1992: 69). What we learn from Schelling here, and the truth of which is apparent in the most terrible manifestations of evil in our empirical history, is that evil is the particular will's attempt at a false universality, precisely where it ought to remain a mere particular will, as a mere condition of the opening up of history and of the realm of the political to the advent of the messiah. It is this aporia that Schelling articulates and which renders the highest task of the political essentially *finite*: on the condition that the mortal can never appropriate his own ground, even the highest task of mortals is unable to attain complete actuality. It is this fate of never being able to actualise ourselves completely that spreads such an 'indestructible melancholy' in our lives:

> In God, too, there would be a depth of darkness if he did not make the condition his own and unite it to him as one and as absolute personality. Man never gains control over the condition even though in evil he strives to do so; it is only *loaned* to him independent of him; hence his personality and selfhood can never be raised to complete actuality. This is the sadness which adheres to all finite life, and inasmuch as there is even in God himself a condition at least relatively independent, there is in him, too, a source of sadness which, however, never attains actuality but rather serves for the eternal joy of triumph. Thence the veil of sadness, which is spread over all nature, the deep unappeasable melancholy of all life. (Schelling 1992: 79)

While this inextricable finitude renders our historico-political destiny essentially melancholic, in that what can have the sense of the political or the historical for us can only bear a finite sense, in this abyss of melancholy there can be hope and joy in the arrival of beatitude from a source or origin that never allows itself to be reduced to the immanence of the human. It is important to recognise there is a politics and an ethics for us, that there is a history for mortals, only in this sense of finitude. There is a finite politics, not in the sense that there are other politics besides finite politics, that the latter is one amongst others, but in a more essential sense: that politics as such, not 'this' or 'that' politics, is essentially finite and incomplete, that it never attains complete actuality and complete being. There remains that 'irreducible remainder' of potentiality, that irreducible 'not yet', that infinite future, that time always to come. It is finite to the extent that, precisely on account of this finitude, it is radically open to the infinitude of *coming*. In other words, only on the basis of finitude is there a remainder of time to come, is there a messianic remnant of the future. While the inalienable finitude of our condition renders any sense of our historico-political task melancholic, it is also the very condition of our openness to radical futurity. On account of our finitude we are opened to a messianic, redemptive fulfilment. Thus, Schelling could write: 'Evil is that contradiction which devours and always negates itself, which just while striving to become creature destroys the nexus of creation and, in its ambition to be everything, falls into non-being' (Schelling 1992: 69).

A finite politics is thus in an essential sense a politics that *arises* out of finitude, in the verbal sense of its event-ness and in the sense of the *arising* of the world or the *worlding* of the world, which is a 'world' in the sense that it is the *spacing open* where being opens itself towards others out of an essential mortality. But the fact that this world *arises* – and to the extent that it *arises* it can only be finite – is what brings on that 'unappeasable melancholy'. It is out of this originary melancholy that a finite politics derives its attunement, its 'fundamental mood', as Heidegger (1980b) puts it. In his *Introduction to Metaphysics*, Heidegger says of the *polis*:

> The *polis* is the historical place, the there *in* which, *out* of which, and *for* which history happens. To this place and scene of history belong the gods, the temples, the priests, the festivals, the games, the poets, the thinkers, the ruler, the council of elders, the assembly of people, the army and the fleet. All this does not first belong to the *polis*, does not become political by entering into relation with a statesman and a general and the business of the state. No, it is political, i.e. at the site of history, provided there be (for example) poets *alone*, but then really poets, priests *alone*, but then really priests, rulers *alone*, but then really rulers. *Be*, but this means: as violent men to use power, to become pre-eminent in historical being as creators, as men of action. Pre-eminent in the historical place, they become at the same time *apolis*, without city and place, lonely, strange, alien and uncanny, without issue amid the beings as a whole, without stature and limit, without structure and order,

because they themselves as creators must first create all this. (Heidegger 1999: 152)

Why are the poets and philosophers melancholic, with that melancholy which is merely possible in God, but which in mortals attains to actuality? Because the poets and philosophers are those who first open the world by articulating this openness of the *polis*, or rather by articulating the *world-ing* of the world, and precisely on that account they become world-less, exiled and homeless. This dense paragraph from Heidegger problematises the complex relationship between the *poesis* of the opening, the originary promise that opens the *polis*, and the political ontology of the world, the political being of the *polis*, which must already have been opened by the opening falling outside the *polis*. This opening of the *polis*, which cannot be posited in the immanence of its self-presence because it must already be there for there even to be positing, is the originary promise of redemption which language offers, and which the poets and creative thinkers, through renunciation of mastery and all appropriation, keep open so that there remains the possibility of a coming redemption above and beyond the given, beyond violence and beyond the law. With the poets and creative thinkers, language, instead of being a mere means at their cognitive disposal or being a mere language of judgement that overnames, is the remembrance of the originary Adamic naming that is given to man as a gift, that naming wherein the whole of mute nature redeems itself. It is that gift which is given as a promise to mortals when mortals, on the basis of that gift, inaugurate that 'new covenant' which is the realm of history and politics. Therefore, the promise given to mortals is that of redemption, and not of evil: redemption is the secret password of history and politics that invisibly operates in the world. This naming is redemptive because it renders the offering of language as an enduring presence for us, the gift of being present to us, and opens us to the eternity of the gift. The possibility of this redemptive gift given in language is the endowment of eternity. But man, being the will of self-affirmation, seeks to enclose within the immanence of a self-consuming totality what ought always to remain outside all totality and all predicates, outside all negations and independent of time: that is, the gift of the eternity given in the naming, that promise of redemption that is 'loaned' to man when he is given the possibility of inaugurating the realm of history and politics. And this is 'radical evil', arising out of man's decision. The originary melancholy of which Schelling speaks thus lies in the very opening of existence, and in this very sense, existence is essentially *ex-static*: i.e. it remains open, on account of its finitude, to the redemptive gift of a time *to come*. As in Heidegger and Benjamin, in Schelling, too, it is language alone that carries the messianic promise of redemption.

Thus, the 'irreducible remainder' that renders the mortal essentially finite is the very condition of joyousness and beatitude for him. For the mortal it is only on the condition of non-condition that there can be the promise of happiness and redemption. Hence, 'joy must have sorrow, sorrow must be transfigured in joy' (Schelling 1992: 79). There is joy because, on account of this inappropriable finitude alone, there is for mortals futurity, that time which remains to come, out of which there arises the infinite creative task of freedom: to infinitely transfigure melancholy into joy through creative acts of freedom.

Radical evil

What, then, has remained of radical evil? In its most extreme possibility, evil *remains* in so far as there remains for mortals the eternal remnant of potentiality, that 'irreducible remainder', as long as mortals are *free* – in the sense that mortals are *granted* freedom, gifted freedom, 'loaned' freedom – on the basis of their dispropriation and finitude. Evil remains a radical possibility as long as mortals remain mortals, and therefore other than beasts and the divine; as long as man is the spacing open in the abyss where 'the new covenant' never ceases to inaugurate, in the realm of history and politics where spirit as spirit reveals itself. On this account, all politics is finite, a finitude open to the infinitude of the future where the spirit of potentiality will never cease to reveal itself, and on this event, evil remains as a most radical possibility for mortals. There is a source of melancholy even in God and there is a melancholy even in nature, not merely in the mortal's existence, in so far as, like mortals, not only nature but even God, too, is an *existence*; i.e. even God has a basis independent of his actualised existence. But the melancholy of mortals is of an entirely different nature: it arises in the opening of the realm of spirit which neither God nor nature but man alone inaugurates out of his freedom. This realm is political. In this sense, man is essentially political, not in the sense that he is the bearer of 'human rights' and rights of other sorts, nor because he is that 'power of the negative' that Hegel speaks of. Man is political because he is essentially finite.

If, for such a finite being, evil remains the most extreme possibility, then evil is the most inescapable possibility for a finite politics. Radical evil is the abyss of politics, only because politics arises out of an ungroundable, inscrutable freedom that fills mortals with what Kant calls *Achtung* ('respect', 'awe') in the face of that which is truly sublime, the immeasurable *par excellence*, in relation to which all measure fails and from which all measure is derived, which cannot be represented in our concepts or language but which, as pure ecstasy, is pure 'presentation' (*Darstellung*). This is what Schelling calls the 'exuberance of Being' or the 'un-pre-thinkable'. It is from this 'un-pre-thinkable' exuberance that a finite politics derives its sense and essence.

Evil thus remains, but only as a *possibility*. Here, Schelling makes a crucial distinction between *possibility* and *actuality*. As a mere possibility, the principle of basis is not in itself evil, but the very source of life and of the creative affirmation of selfhood, and thus of what is absolutely necessary for life: it is originary fire that gives warmth and light, and animates the spirit. In itself, the principle of basis is the very condition of man being godlike: the creator of the 'new covenant' where God reveals himself anew; it is there as a principle of contrast against which the principle of love strives and thrives. Here, then, is the saving grace: this very finitude which, when it is raised to the power of its own negation, becomes evil – this very finitude that never actualises itself without remainder, becomes the condition of our radical openness to the wholly otherwise of an ever new 'covenant'. The task of the realm of the spirit – that is, of our history and politics – is thus *not* to seek to appropriate the irreducible finitude, that 'irreducible remainder' of potentiality, for that – lacking the basis of life and spirit – would result in the most terrible evil and the most destructive forms of totalitarianism.

The task of our politics and history is thus to keep this task itself essentially finite, as that which can never be totalised, so that there may remain, on account of this finitude, a radical opening to a wholly otherwise inauguration and a wholly otherwise future; in other words, never seeking to appropriate and master this pure potentiality of freedom. If evil has manifested itself in history in its most terrible and totalising manner, it lies precisely in the absolutising and totalising decision that attempts to enclose the heterogeneity, the undecidable, unpredictable openness, of futurity in the decisionist immanence of self-presence. This is not to say that there ought not to be decisions, that one should remain forever in that zone of indecision which is obviously not only impossible but also undesirable; it is rather that one must not exhaust the radical futurity of the undecidable in an absolutising and totalising decision, so that the principle of potentiality can interminably, incessantly inaugurate an ever new 'covenant' that transcends, unconditionally, any *in-sistence* in self-consuming immanence.

What we have learned from Schelling is that there is no politics without the radical possibility of evil. In this sense, politics is essentially finite. The task of the spirit – of history and politics – is to maintain this possibility only as forever a *mere* possibility. It is this risk, this danger, that a finite politics must confront without shying away and, at the same time, make it the very conditioning principle for an ever new 'covenant' through creative acts of freedom. If, on the other hand, politics wants to appropriate or conquer its very finitude, then the most terrible evil attains *actuality*, and there results unthinkable forms of destructive totalitarianism in which politics negates the very possibility of its sense or meaning. That there is un-reason is the undeniable possibility of reasonable mortals, and this possibility, in itself, when regulated, is the very ecstatic source of divinity and freedom, of our creative acts and our joyous, ecstatic reason. In that sense, our reason is essentially finite. It is what Heraclitus invokes with the elemental name 'fire'. But when one of the principles attempts to conquer this finitude, all hell breaks loose and a terrible unruliness spreads over all of existence: then the fire no longer remains a source of warmth and light but a destructive one that, in its self-devouring hunger, attempts to destroy every bit of its own creation. In all his works, Schelling wrestles with this truth, which is not the harmless, petrified truth of propositions and logical judgements, but the truth wherein the whole of existence puts itself at stake, each time anew, from its innermost ground. Likewise, there is a melancholy that arises out of our intrinsic finitude, in that we can never appropriate the ground of our own existence, but this non-mastery and dispropriation alone gives us that 'irreducible remainder' of pure futurity on account of which alone there is happiness, even though finite, as well as paradisiacal, blissful, divine joy. Yet when this very finitude attempts to master and conquer itself and negates its own finite character, there arises the other melancholy which is truly the terrible melancholy of evil. Then it twists, with cunning power, the very promise of our history and politics into violence and the terror of totalitarianism.

In the face of this possibility of radical evil, the task of politics is an endless, interminable one: that of infinitely releasing the unconditioned element in politics from the immanence of this self-consuming hunger for the complete attainment of being. Only in this manner will mortals keep the realm of history and politics open to the 'irreducible remainder' of a *time to come*, not 'this' or 'that' time coming, but the always *to come*. If there is any sense of freedom today it is only here: in that freedom of sense, which is the sense 'to come'. Freedom is this verbal infinity 'to' – *a finite infinity* – and in that sense, an open infinity, always transcending any self-consuming immanence, in its ecstatic inauguration of ever new 'covenants'. This is what we have learned from Schelling's essay on freedom.

Note

1. The German word *unbedingt*, which is often translated as 'absolute', literally means 'non-thing' or 'no-condition'.

Chapter 5

The Non-Sovereign Exception

Gift of beatitude

Schelling's 1802–3 lectures on *The Philosophy of Art* begin with a formulation of the task of such a philosophy: to *present* the laws of art's phenomenal apparitions as ideas. It attempts a *presentation (Darstellung)* of *ideas* to *disclose* the truth of works of art rather than a representation of aesthetic objects in concepts for our cognitive possession. This task of the philosophy of art is distinguished from the empirical-historical approach to the arts that is content with classifying works of art under general concepts. The task of the *intellectual intuition* of the philosopher is to present these ideas in a *constellation*, as distinct from the objects of empirical intuition addressed by the theoretician of art. Ideas are as irreducible to the conceptual logic of subsumption as the presentation of the absolute in intellectual intuition is to the theoretical representation of particulars. Ideas as truth, in their highest mode of being, are at one with absolute beauty. Absolute beauty is none other than 'the truth of ideas': it radiates like rays emanating from a 'constellation'. Schelling writes:

> Philosophy, which concerns itself only with ideas, must present only the general laws of phenomenal appearance as regards the empirical side of art, and must present these only in the form of ideas, for forms of art are the essential forms of things as they are in the archetypes. Hence, to the extent that these can be comprehended universally and from the perspective of the universe in and for itself, their presentation is a necessary part of the philosophy of art . . . philosophy of art in the larger sense is the presentation of the absolute world in the form of art. Only theory concerns itself directly with the particular or with a goal, and only according to theory can a project be executed empirically . . . that which the philosophy must recognize and

present in it is of a higher sort, and is one and the same with absolute beauty: the truth of ideas. (Schelling 1989: 7)

The metaphor of the *constellation* is indispensable to understanding the early Schelling. Taking this metaphor from the theory of physics that Plato propounds in *Timaeus*, in his philosophy of art Schelling transforms the theory of ideas as essential forms into a theory of potencies: absolute beauty is 'the truth of ideas' which must be displayed in a constellation (Schelling 1984). This vocation of the Schellingian philosopher is thus distinguished from the goal of the art theoretician. In the philosopher's presentation of ideas and in the display of their absolute beauty works of art appear as universalities without losing their singularity. This philosophical task is wholly different from that of the theoretician, who violently subsumes singularity into particularity and then places it under the generality of the concept, repressing and de-facing the elemental singularity of the phenomenon. From this logic of theoretical subsumption, which is the thetic operation of the cognitive intellect, the metaphysical 'violence of the concept' is inseparable. Intellectual intuition is here not the dark night in which 'all cows are black' (Hegel 1998: 9); it is rather a non-composite and *non-descript* disclosure of phenomena in their irreducible singularity *holding*-together with the essentiated universality. It is *nondescript* because it simultaneity constitutes their irreducible *dieresis*: 'insofar as this intuition cannot be compared to a universal geometrical figure but is particular to each soul like a perception of light in each eye, it is here a merely individual revelation; however, in this individuality there is also a universal revelation, just as light is for the empirical senses' (Schelling 1989: 15).

Far from subsuming the singularity of the phenomenon under the *logos* of the concept, Schelling's Platonism rather attempts to salvage phenomena from their reduction to attributes, predicates and numbers. Essences of phenomena are neither facts nor concepts but their truth. As un-subsumable and un-subsuming archetypes, ideas are potencies or potentialities of the absolute, forms of determination in which the absolute appears as *singular-universal*. Such an idea of truth cannot be thought within the categorical-cognitive-predicative structure of judgement. The question concerning the 'essence' of art, with which is Schelling grappling here, cannot be posed within the metaphysics of thetic positing. The universality of ideas is to be distinguished from the 'universality' of genus/species, since it is not achieved in the conceptual manner of subsumption. The harmony of these ideas, which Schelling compares with a constellation of celestial bodies, is here expressed in the image of a *happiness* unimpaired by the violence of cognitive enclosures.[1] Each potency in its unique, singular and un-subsumable mode is at once the singular reflection of the absolute as a whole; each exhibits, in its own manner, its own time in conjunction with eternity, its mortality with immortality, its limitation with the immeasurable. In their irreducible singularities, ideas are super-numeric: they can neither be measured by numbers, determined by attributes, nor assigned to any denomination by with given predicates of a subject. 'For just this reason', writes Schelling,

> all number or determination by number is suspended. The particular [singular] thing in absoluteness is not determined by number, for if one reflects upon the particular within it, it is itself the absolute whole and possesses nothing outside of or external to itself. If one reflects upon the universal, it is in absolute unity with all other things. Accordingly, only it itself subsumes or comprehends unity and multiplicity within itself, though it is itself not capable of being determined by these concepts. (Schelling 1989: 34)

Life is the *nondescript* singularity: it bears the other trait, the trait of *withdrawal* from the violent 'maximising thrust of the universal'. As such, it remains apart from 'the hegemonic fantasm' of the Concept (Schürmann 2003). The absolute operates here un-suffocated by the plethora of attributes, numbers and predicates. The freedom that ideas enjoy in this state of *blessedness* also constitutes the very enigma of life: 'life is found only within particularity [singularity]' (Schelling 1989: 36–7). Unlike the violence of theoretical cognition that subordinates singularity to an empty generality, it is the task of philosophical-intellectual intuition to redeem singularities from their reduction and totalisation into the logic of objects (of cognition). Such a redemption from the violence of cognition makes possible their participation in the divine excess that releases them to the unconditional blessedness or absolute beatitude. As singulars, 'they nonetheless enjoy the blessedness of the absolute, and vice versa (to strive toward blessedness = to strive as a particular [singular] to partake of absoluteness)' (39).

Blessedness or beatitude is the state of being released from the thetic grasp of the law, absolved from the nomothetic operation of the concept. Art, philosophy and religion are three modes of partaking in this unconditional beatitude; they are the three modes of absolute beatitude which is the highest possibility of existence for us. Absolute beatitude is an eschatological event: an *arrival* in excess of all measurement, of all predications and judgements, of all qualifying attributes of a cognitive object. Appearing as *harmony*, as in the harmony of celestial bodies, attaining beatitude is the task of the philosophical contemplation and presentation of the truth in which phenomena redeem themselves. Such blessedness is an unsaturated gift coming from an eschatological excess which is that of eternity over time.[2] To participate in this possibility, philosophy must assume the task of mortification, of releasing the soul of phenomena from its enclosure in their brute empirical existence. The truth of the phenomenon, which is nothing other than absolute beauty, must be released, through mortification, from its subsumption to the *nomos* of the concept. In other words, the attributes, predicates and numbers by which the work of subsumption is made possible must undergo mortification so that the unconditional may be presented *as* unconditional. Far from wounding the phenomenon with the violence of subsumption, this work of mortification redeems it and thereby enables it to participate in the radiance of absolute beatitude. In philosophical contemplation, the phenomenon *phenomenalises* itself; that is, in truth, the phenomenon is given *to* itself; it *lets* the phenomenon *be* as it is, in its existing without 'why', released from the regime of constituted phenomenality.

Despite his infamous restlessness, which inhabits and un-works all his attempts to constitute a definitive 'system' (so I would like to argue), Schelling remains singularly *attuned* to the fundamental philosophical task of his life that he articulates early on in this series of lectures on the philosophy of art. This task consists of releasing the eschatological potentiality of the unconditional from all possible enclosures of the immanence of conditional self-presence. This, in turn, demands from us a work of mortification to operate on attributes and predicates and numbers (*kenosis*) so that the truth and beauty of phenomena present themselves in their *unsaturated excess*, now freed from these normative enclosures and referents that constitute them into 'objects' of rational cognition. This is this enigma of redemption: the glory of the phenomenon is at one with *kenosis*.

Allegory of the invisible

The philosophy of art lectures begin with a historical presentation of two successive conceptions of the relation of infinite and finite, the universal and the singular, the unconditional and conditioned. Instead of conceiving various works of art from different historical periods under common, generalising concepts, Schelling presents a historical construction of the content of art. The content of art is said to be 'mythological', the meaning of which Schelling will deduce in the course of his investigation. Thus the Greek mode of presentation is understood to be symbolic (a synthesis of the schematic and the allegorical),[3] a realist mythology in which the synthesis of finite and infinite is achieved in such a way that the finite counts in itself without being subsumed in the infinite. In the symbolic representation of realist mythology, the wedding of the infinite and finite is presented as their *simultaneity*, as in a constellation of celestial bodies where the infinite radiates in each finite body. This space of *simultaneity* in which each symbol is unique and singular at the same time is the *space* of nature. This symbolic world of nature can be said to exist without history in the sense that it has not yet fallen into time (which is a succession of potencies). Necessity is felt here as the *fate* that Greek tragedies represent symbolically on the stage. These ideas are nothing other than the archetypes with which mythology is 'properly' concerned with as its content.[4] In this sense, mythology is the content of Greek works of art (and of philosophy) as such. Nature here is the tragic stage where the individual is not yet experienced as separated from the collective, the finite is not yet felt apart from the infinite, 'where the highest morality lies in the recognition of the boundaries and limitations to which human beings are subject' (Schelling 1989: 55). The simultaneity of beings belonging-together as archetypes enables us conceive philosophical polytheism as the proper possibility of Greek mythology. The rebellion of the finite against the infinite conjures up fate, but since the finite is not just to be annihilated for the sake of the infinite, this rebellion marks the very heroic virtues and sublimity of the tragic people of Greece.

The decay of this mythological content brought to an end the epoch of Greek antiquity. Born in the ruins of the tragic stage of Greek nature, Christianity brings into the stage of existence not nature but history, not mythology but allegory, not the infinite at one with the finite but the infinite *removed* to a transcendence without measure: 'mythology concludes as soon as allegory begins' (Schelling 1989: 48). Schelling cites the fall of the Roman Empire as the most remarkable moment of this rupture, between the decay of the mythological world and the birth of the allegorical. The decadence of the Roman Empire brought dissatisfaction with the immanence of mythic existence. The infinite is now no longer experienced as immanent within the well-rounded sphere of mythic nature but is removed to an unattainable beyond of nature. The immanence of mythic continuity, where figures of the divine immediately manifest themselves on the stage of nature, is no longer felt to be sufficient, and is replaced by a succession of historical epochs that partially disclose a God otherwise hidden from nature. The absconding infinite renders impossible the satisfaction of the human spirit in the immanent mode of mythic existence: Schelling marks this moment as the birth of modernity. The modern man, dissatisfied with any earthly consolations, now wrests himself away, almost violently, from taking any satisfaction in the laws of the earthly and in the fruits of its soil.

> The modern world begins when man wrests himself loose from nature. Since he does not yet have a new home, however, he feels abandoned. Wherever such a feeling comes over an entire group, that group turns either voluntarily

> or compelled by an inner urge to the ideal world in order to find a home. Such a feeling had come over the world when Christianity arose. Greece's beauty was gone; Rome, which had collected all the world's splendour into itself, lay crushed under its own massive weight. The complete saturation and satisfaction of all objective needs naturally generated boredom and an inclination toward the element of the ideal . . . the universal feeling that a new world must come, since the old one was no longer able to continue, lay like sultry air over the entire world at that time, an atmosphere like that announcing a great movement in nature. (Schelling 1989: 59–60)

The birth of history renders nature non-autochthonous, bereft of any inherent meaning and beauty. No longer fate but *providence* is now experienced in this tragic stage of history.[5] Uprooted from mythic immanence, and exposed to an immeasurable boundlessness on all sides, man himself becomes the separated being, *spaced* between nature and history, time and eternity, individual and the collective, finite and the infinite. In this condition of worldlessness and homelessness, the infinite can be presented not as simultaneous with the finite but only as succession, as an utterly transient manifestation, like the flickering of a light appearing against an immense abyss of darkness, only to be held fast momentarily, only to let the finite go the next instance. While the infinite has now the absconded to an indeterminate and un-localisable place (a 'non-place'), the finite too has lost its inherent meaningfulness and inner validity. Deprived of both the infinite and the finite, the *abandoned* man looks for the unity of being, now sundered apart, in an eschatological future. Schelling conceives this eschatological future in terms of a mythology: not that of the mythic immanence whose glory is now past, but a mythology *to come*. The loss of archetypes, marking the decay of the Greek mythology (for, properly speaking, mythology is Greek), now opens up, for the first time, the birth of *religion*. Strictly speaking then, Schelling does not understand the tragic world of Greek mythology to have religion at all, for religion is a historical phenomenon incommensurable with the mythic context of Greek consciousness. *Religion is rather a negation and replacement of mythology.* Homelessness or world-alienation is the Gnostic idea here, which tirelessly *unbinds* man from the cages of the worldly *nomos*. Religion, writes Schelling,

> necessarily assumes the character of a revealed religion and is for that reason historical at its very foundation. Greek religion, as a poetic religion living through the collectively itself, had no need of a historical foundation, as little as does nature, which is always open. The manifestations and figures of the gods here were eternal. In Christianity, on the other hand, the divine was only a fleeting appearance and had to be held fast in this appearance. (Schelling 1989: 69)

In the tragic-mythic unity of beings, nature is *always already* open. In this Open of nature, divine manifestations are an eternal and enduring presence. Nature is a landscape of blazing clarity where the gods appear in their pure immanence. By contrast, in the tragic-religious absolute *disunion* of the infinite and the finite, nature is *withdrawn* as a *mystery*. The opening of the finite to the infinite can now only be conceived as that which 'falls into time and accordingly from history'. 'For this reason Christianity in its innermost spirit and highest sense is historical. Every particular moment of time is a revelation of a particular side of God, and in each he is absolute. What Greek religion possessed as simultaneity, Christianity possesses as succession even if the time of separation of appearances and with it of form has not yet come' (Schelling 1989: 63).

Schelling, then, conceives religion as the historical phenomenon par excellence. The concept of *revelation* presupposes, as a philosophical necessity, not the mythic context of continuity but the historical *disjunction* between the phenomenal realm and the 'wholly other', freed from the laws of the profane order. With revelation as its intrinsic principle, religion disrupts the serenity of the mythic immanence and introduces into the world the abyss of an absolute caesura between infinite and finite, collective and individual, nature and history, transcendence and immanence. The synthesis of infinite and finite, now no longer available as archetypes as they were in the mythic context of nature, makes symbolic representation impossible. Thus the displacement of the mythic context by the *absolute disunion of religion* has its counterpart in the artistic modes of representation: the symbolic representation of archetypes is displaced by the allegorical mode of representation. While mythology is the symbolism of the finite, which in itself is at one with the infinite, *religion is an allegory of the infinite*. In such an allegorical mode of representation, the finite is emptied of its inherent signification and the infinite is removed to an inaccessible transcendence beyond nature. On the stage of history, the infinite or the divine may appear only in its utter weakness, like Christ dying an ignoble death on the cross. Like the flickering light against an immense, unfathomable darkness, the logic of the manifestation of the divine in the profane order does not follow the determinate order of necessity, as does the determinate order of mythic immanence marked by fate. Released from fate, the divine arrival becomes the incalculable event par excellence; with it, the earthly *nomos* is invalidated and de-legitimated. Schelling's metaphor here is that of the sudden appearance of a comet, as a transient apparition in a desolate landscape. Its incalculable apparition sets the *worldlessness* of Christianity in remarkable contrast to the metaphor of the eternal harmony of the planets, which is the symbolic-mythic space of Greek blessedness:

> The ancients are the planets of the world of art, limited to a few individuals who are simultaneously the collective and who nonetheless even in the highest freedom of movement remove themselves the least from their identity with that collective. Taken as a group themselves, these planet analogies are also characterized by definite subtypes. Those with the most depth are the rhythmic ones. Those more distant – where the mass structures itself as a totality, where everything positions itself concentrically in rings and moons around the center, like the petals of a blossom – are the dramatic ones. Boundless space belongs to the comets. When they appear, they come directly from infinite space, and though they well may draw near to the sun, just as certainly do they also distance themselves from it again. (Schelling 1989: 73–4)

In this metaphor of the comet Schelling presents an allegory of the infinite which is the phenomenon *absconditus* par excellence. Even the appearance of Christ on the stage of history does not make the world any more 'homely' for fallen mankind. Here the meaning of the infinite is not presented as an enduring and eternal presence fixed in its mythic blessedness, but as a transiency that must be wrested at opportune, incalculable moments as soon as it appears momentarily against a boundless darkness of non-being. Thinking in the manner of a Pauline eschatology in which the Gnosticism of early Christianity was still resonating, Schelling presents these moments as *turns of time* (*Kairos*). The infinite reveals itself at these turnings of time, that is, without being exhaustively determined by the determinate logic of historical Reason. Religion, for Schelling, is none other than this *Kairos*-allegory of revelation. In the same way that the law of the comet's appearance can't be subsumed under the homogeneous logic of conceptual-historical Reason, so the allegory of the infinite can't be grasped on the basis of the symbolic representation of archetypes. Religion thus exceeds both the mythic context of a nature ruled by the law of eternal recurrence of the Same, and that of historical Reason which presents the historical order itself as under the law of the quantitative and homogeneous process of Reason's self-becoming.

This last point is of crucial importance for us. Schelling's eschatological deconstruction sets itself against the immanent order of mythic immanence as well as against the historical Reason that was consolidating itself in his own time. Religion is neither 'natural' nor simply 'historical' (at least in the sense determined by the historical Reason of the nineteenth century). The new sense of religion given to us by Schelling is 'eschatological', which means it is *historical* too, but in a wholly other sense. Religion, in this new sense, is the non-originary, non-autarchic and non-sovereign opening to the infinite; it is the incessant and exuberant opening to an *excess* beyond all enclosures of the mythic immanence, and beyond the self-sufficiency of the laws of the earth. Far from sinking its teeth into the *nomos* of the earthly, and thereby finding consolation in a self-satisfaction with what already exists, religion opens itself to an eschatological arrival which disjoins us from what already exists in the profane realm of world-domination. Thus the allegory of religion, in itself indeterminate of meaning and emptied of all inherent self-foundation, is the very opening up of meaning, now no longer exhausted in the language of judgement and predication. It is this irreducible anguish of disjointure, this absolute suffering of disunion, and this utter desolation of a caesura, that Schelling calls 'religion': 're'-ligion not as a re-binding to the *nomos* of the earthly, but as an eschatological un-binding, an *antinomic* releasing to a *future* mythology yet to arrive. At the very heart of the mythic unity of being, religion opens up an abyss of exodus wherein the divine can present itself only as *absconding*. The uncoupling of religion from the mythic immanence introduces a disruption, a *separation* or a caesura within the realm of Christianity itself. Unlike in the Greek symbolic order, which needs no historical foundation and in which 'religion' is inseparable from the state, in Christianity 'there is a separate history of religion and of the Church' (Schelling 1989: 69). Christianity for Schelling, in its very spirit and promise and from its very inception, is a religion of the *separation* and *partitioning* of beings. By virtue of being given in such an indelible wound or caesura, it is *set apart* from politics, as if religion and politics each has a history of its own distinct from the other, separated by an irreducible abyss of meaning, by an empty space of tragic time.

The question of the miracle here is particularly revealing. The occurrence of a miracle, like the appearance of the comet, is only possible in Christianity and not in the mythic context of nature. This is because the occurrence of a miracle presupposes the possibility of an absolute and incalculable disunion from the law of the earth, the dismemberment of the infinite from the finite: 'Christianity, which is possible only within absolute disunion, is at its very inception already founded on miracles. A miracle is an absolute viewed from the empirical perspective, an absolute occurring within the finite realm without for that reason having any relationship to time' (Schelling 1989: 69). Religion as such, and Christianity in particular, would mean, for Schelling, none other than this instance of *setting apart*. This fundamental *cision* (*Scheidung*), this irreducible *distance*, must release the eschatological potentiality of the future from the foundation of the world. Such eschatological potentiality constantly opens the closures of history to a future mythology yet to arrive. In Schellingian terms, Christianity is to be understood in this verbal resonance of the infinitive 'to'. Eschatology, which is the principle of religion in a fundamental sense, is absolutely incommensurable with the mythic world of immanence. Eschatological suffering, in so far as the world as it exists is perceived to be insufficient, understands the potencies or powers of the world claiming sovereignty to be insufficient, being transient and devoid of any inherent signification and validity. Even though the Church is the only symbolic body within Christianity that bears the character of a public manifestation, even it can't claim an absolute obligation from us, in so far as the reason of its very being is separate from that of the State.

In the *antinomic* eschatological schema of Schellingian thought, religion manifests in the world as an *inoperation* of political sovereignty that already exists. When the sting of this inoperation is taken away from religion, it becomes not only just like all the other powers that manifest themselves in the profane realm, but also their very foundation. In more than one place Schelling asks us to beware the dangers that arise from acts of political legitimisation based on a theological foundation. Even Christianity as it exists, in so far as it exists as non-absolute, can only be for him a transition (in its verbal infinitive 'to') to a future mythology. Such a final destiny of mankind demands, however, that we pass through the entire eschatological passage of history to a fulfilment (*pleroma*) always *to come*, an arrival which is not grasped in the self-generating concept of Reason, as in Hegel, but is intimated in the prophetic waiting for the *pleroma* to burst onto the stage of history.

Breaking away

It is of singular importance that in Schelling's eschatology the ethical is always thought to be irreducible to the political. As 'a directive for beatific life' (Schelling 2010: 8), *ethics is seen to be surplus to politics*, if the political is to be understood as the realm of conditioned negotiations and pragmatic engagements with the sovereign powers of the world. The ethical here is understood neither in terms of the Kantian regulative-formal principle of moral law nor in terms of the Hegelian notion of the absolute concept, but as the exuberance of a life opening to the unconditional *eschaton* of beatitude. According to this Platonic schema ('the Good beyond being'), beatitude – which is the unconditional principle at one with truth – can't be attained by the powers of the world-historical order. The Kantian mere-formal regulative principle of the moral law appears to Schelling to be an empty experience bereft of the historical and linguistic constituents of our exuberant existence. Similarly, the Hegelian dialectical philosophy, in its reduction of 'the riddle of existence' to the webs of the conceptual order, works like a legitimacy-seeking political order which, with its system of law, attempts to reduce life to a mere function of the State. By contrast, Schelling thinks *life* itself eschatologically, as oriented to the absolute beatitude which must be released both from the cages of the *nomos* of world-domination and from its petrification in the formal order of an inherently empty experience. The ethical here is not just part of a composite existence that can be added and subtracted at will, but is rather the very apex, the summit of life, which is a *non-composite* and *non-descript* singular-whole. Life, as a whole, must orient itself toward this absolute beatitude, toward this nameless Good; its plenitude consists in its excess over the mere life or bare life that *nomos* grasps. The true 'toward-ness' of life, life in its entirety, must follow a path to beatitude whose logic is absolutely heterogeneous to the law of calculable economy (of politics); such a logic of the ethical is unthinkable in the categorical mode of rational cognition.

In his 1804 *Philosophy and Religion*, Schelling tentatively works toward an expression of such a metaphysics of life. *Life is not a composite*; it is neither a product nor a result of the unification of opposites (subjective and objective), nor an object of rational cognition attained through negative descriptions. The *singularity* of such a life, which is simultaneously universal, is non-descript, indemonstrable and unexplainable, for 'only a composite can be known through description' (Schelling 2010: 15). Only *intellectual intuition* can open itself to the indemonstrable disclosure of the non-composite absolute. Life, being finite, is an eschatological reflection in its weakest form; it is radiance, an expression of a splendour whose source it cannot grasp by the nomothetic operation of the human intellect. That is why, for Schelling, tragedy is the supreme artistic 'expression'. The germ of Schelling's future Hegel-critique can already be seen here, even before Hegel's critique of Schelling has itself appeared. For the intellectual intuition of life as a whole, the categorical-cognitive and negative descriptions of the absolute are never final. This is because such negative descriptions must already presuppose an affirmation before all the negativity of description, demonstration and production. One cannot miss in the following lines, clearly inspired by Meister Eckhart and Plato, the fact that the future Hegelian critique is already anticipated by Schelling:

> For as the essence of God consists of absolute, solely unmediated reality, so the nature of the soul consists in cognition that is one with the real, ergo with God; hence it is also the intention of philosophy in relation to man not to add anything but to remove from him, as thoroughly as possible, the accidentals that the body, the world of appearances, and the sensate life have added and to lead him back to the originary state. Furthermore, all instruction in philosophy that precedes this cognition can only be negative; it shows the nullity of all finite opposites and leads the soul indirectly to the perception of the infinite. Once there, it is no longer in need of those makeshift devises of negative descriptions of absoluteness and sets itself free from them. (Schelling 2010: 15)

The metaphysics of life expresses itself in such an indemonstrable excess of affirmation: it is a *Yes* before every yes, a *before* that can't be traced back apophantically as if to an origin, a radiance unattainable in syllogistic forms of rational cognition.[6] It is as if an abyss *sets apart* the unconditional affirmation of beatitude from all possible negative descriptions that want to return regressively to the 'originary state'. A dialectic that returns to the same at the end of its process through the self-cancellation of negation (of which Hegel's speculative dialectic is the best example), cannot return to this immemorial radiance that bestows on us the gift of beatitude. Between the ethical orientation of life to the absolute beatitude (which is to be unconditionally affirmed) and the systematic order achieved through the negative work of the concept there lies a *breaking away*. If Hegel understands the state as one of the highest expressions or 'one of the figures of the negative' (Wirth 2003: 22), the ethical demand of the unconditional finds no satisfaction in the happiness that man attains in the profane order of the political. Schelling, thus, perceives the state not as a glorifying figure of the absolute but as that which belongs to the realm of apostasy (*Abfall*), even in its highest expression as a mere symptom of the fundamental disjunction or the Fall from the absolute.

What Schelling calls here, after Eckhart and Plato, 'the originary state', where the like is recognised by the like,[7] is never an 'origin' in the mythic-immanent sense. There is no homogeneous, continuous line along which one can trace back, in a retrogressive manner, to the point of a mythic origin lying at the very beginning (which, retrogressively, is the end) of that line. 'The originary state' is rather to be understood as an eschatological arrival from the extremity of the future that disrupts the immanence of any mythic origin. 'The originary state' is an immemorial past *to come* from an eschatological future, precisely by *breaking away* from the mythic immanence of a creationism as well as from the logic of emanation and continuum, as if a re-turn to the originary is only possible on the basis of a fundamental experience of *distance* or *apartness* from any origin at all. Eschatology, in this sense, cannot be understood mythically but only as the fundamental opening of *re-ligion*, a religion that re-turns to the *originary* without returning to the *origin*; wherein the originary *breaks away* from the origin, and is yet to be disclosed in the extremity of a time *to come*. The 'originary' is without 'origin': such is the meaning of the *eschaton* and of religion; it opens up a 'to' in the irreducible verbal resonance of the infinitive.

Schelling's 1804 essay is a remarkable document. Perhaps it is his first attempt at a renewal of metaphysics that seriously incorporates the idea of a *falling away* or a *breaking away* (*Abfall*), an idea that will find such intensity of expression in his 1809 treatise on human freedom. Schelling scholars rightly point out here the influence of Jacob Böhme. What is fascinating in this context is Schelling's deduction of the problem of the political on the basis of this metaphysical framework of *breaking away*, a framework that enables him to think of the political as the realm that cannot claim the legitimacy of its sovereignty. Religion, in its non-autochthony and non-autarchy, abandons us to abandonment where the very gift of being arrives to us: this gift is prior to all the political-legal projections of man, 'before' all programmatic calculability of human knowledge, 'before' all conditioned negotiations of world-political questions. If the essential content of this discourse called 'philosophy' must be understood as none other than 'the eternal birth of all things and their relationship to God' (Schelling 2010: 8), then philosophy (as metaphysics) must account, without recourse to blind faith or irrational premonitions of any type, for this birth 'of all things'. Metaphysics must account the potencies or potentialities of all things. Metaphysics as such is a discourse of potentiality. First worked out in his *Philosophy of Nature*, Schelling presents here the theory of potencies that must be able to give an account of how *difference*, the essential condition of all finite, phenomenal modes of being, erupts out of the Absolute (which Schelling at that time understood as the absolute principle of identity).

The dominant metaphysics of the Occident explains the event of the eruption of difference and consequently the birth of the phenomenal world on the model of emanation and creation. The phenomenal world of difference is grasped as a gradual decrement from the light of the origin, the progressive darkening and opaqueness of being to the point at which the clarity of the origin is submerged in the abyss of non-being, and this non-being in turn is determined to be matter. The dominant metaphysical image of the Occident is that of continuity: a homogeneous, quantitative, progressively downward line connects the clarity of the origin with the most debased and the most abject phenomenon called evil. It is in the Neo-Platonic conception of emanation that this dominant metaphysics of continuity finds its definitive expression. It is thus onto-theo-logically constituted: God as the ground of beings, as the sovereign origin of all phenomenality, as the Absolute concept that includes within it the entire history the concept's self-becoming (as in Hegel), is conceived as 'the sovereign referent' that arranges all phenomena in the mythic context of the law. From Plotinus to Hegel, including Leibniz, this framework of continuity has remained the sovereign metaphysical framework, the ultimate ontological horizon in the West. Religion is understood as 're-ligion': binding back to the mythic origin. Religion in its revolutionary potentiality and eschatological energy is replaced with a theology of creation or a theodicy of history. Such a theodicy, founded upon the notions of creation and emanation, is pantheism in its most fulfilled expression. The divine is claimed to be embodied, even if in a privative manner, in the profane realm of the world-historical politics. The unjustifiable violence and evil of that politics can here be justified as a necessary privation of the Good. Evil appears as a mere attenuated variation of the universal march of history whose continuity is constantly being filled up with events falling as into an empty scale of time. The historical Reason of nineteenth-century Europe, arising out of and against Enlightenment, ends up as an apologist for what exists, since what already exists appears inevitable and necessary, given the continuity of the line that necessarily connects the clarity of the origin and the fulfilment of it at its end.

Schelling's 1804 essay can now be seen, retrospectively, as one of the first decisive interruptions of this history, one that opens Occidental metaphysics to a wholly new inauguration of thinking, anticipating Marx, Kierkegaard and Nietzsche. With it the history of the Occidental metaphysics itself momentarily comes to a caesura. By introducing the revolutionary potentiality of eschatological thinking into philosophical discourse, and thereby breaking away from the creation-theology of Pantheism and the theodicy of historical Reason, Schelling's theory of potencies opens itself to the thought of radical finitude. In this essay, Schelling undertakes to deconstruct the dominant metaphysics by posing the unthought and scandalous question of the possibility and actuality of radical evil. If radical evil cannot be seen to have derived directly from God (which would make him the originator of evil), its possibility and actuality exposes us to an aporia which the traditional metaphysics cannot dissolve. The possibility of radical evil presupposes a radical disjunction or discontinuity, a fundamental breaking or falling away in the very nexus of beings: an idea unthinkable in the philosophy of emanation. For radical evil to be possible, or even for the phenomenal order to be possible at all, the abyss of separation or distance must occur between the Absolute and the finite-phenomenal order. An immeasurable distance, an *interval* breaking the circle of mythic immanence, undoes all pantheistic attempts at constructing an analogy or continuity between the divine and the profane order. As Schelling writes:

> [I]n the absolute world there are no confines anywhere, and just as God can only bring forth the real-per-se and absolute, so any ensuing effulgence is again absolute and can itself only bring forth something akin to it. There can be no continuous passage into the exact opposite, the absolute privation of all reality, nor can the finite arise from the infinite by decrements. (Schelling 2010: 24)

The idea of continuity can't explain the birth of the phenomenal world. It is only conceivable as a falling or breaking away from the Absolute 'by means of a leap':

> If philosophy were able to derive the origin of the actual world in a positive manner from the Absolute, then the Absolute would have its positive cause in the same; however, in God resides only the cause of the ideas, and only those produce other ideas. There is no positive effect coming out of the Absolute that creates a conduit or bridge between the infinite and finite. Furthermore: philosophy has only a negative relation to phenomenal objects; since it demonstrates less the truth of their being than their non-being, how could it therefore ascribe to them a positive relationship to God? The absolute is the only actual; the finite world, by contrast, is not real. Its cause, therefore, cannot lie in an impartation of reality from the Absolute to the finite world or its substrate; it can only lie in a *remove*, in a *falling away* from the Absolute. (Schelling 2010: 26)

'Remove' or 'falling away' (*Abfall*) is the fundamental eschatological principle here. Reading Plato against the dominant understanding of the Neo-Platonic idea of emanation and against the creation theology of Christianity, Schelling conceives of a *remove*, a *distance* or an immemorial *falling away* that must *space open* an abyss (*Abgrund*) in order for the phenomenal world to take birth. What would this abyssal space be if not the abyss of freedom? The birth of the world arises in this abyss of freedom whose essence is a non-being.[8] It is this non-being, this finite self-hood of freedom, separated from the Absolute in its self-dependence, that *potentiates* the world (therefore, the Absolute in-itself is not directly connected with the worldly potencies). The actuality of the world, however, lies in the *falling away* itself. With this, Schelling's eschatology turns creation-theology inside out. The ground, the cause, the foundation of the phenomenal world can't now be traced back to the Absolute directly but only to the abyss of a freedom that is the counter-image of the Absolute. Like Meister Eckhart's Godhead beyond even God, the Schellingian Absolute too can't even be called a principle, an *arché*, a sovereign cause, or an original foundation of the phenomenal order. This Absolute is not even potentiality but *actuality without potentiality*, a *non-arché*, a non-sovereign Good before the distinction that comes to be with the fall of man, the distinction between good and evil.

The idea of the soul that Schelling adopts here is the Gnostic-Cabbalistic principle of *Pneuma*. It is the remainder of that divine *spark* that is left over in the fallen world, the remnant of a light that is now imprisoned in the cages of the law. It is the acosmic, 'ahistorical', spectral Gnostic principle which must be released from the cages of the world-historical order of earthly sovereignties. The soul here is the other principle, otherwise than a 'principle': worldless, independent of time, a dim reflection of the absolute. Rather than bearing the positive knowledge of the phenomenal order, it rather bears witness to the non-being of all that is earthly and of all that is instituted by the fragile powers of the mortal. This eschatological

Pneuma, by virtue of its discontinuous relation to the *nomos* of the world, does not have its equivalence in the external, conditioned relationships of worldly existence. The absolute breaking away from the Absolute undoes all attempts to embody the divine in the domain of world-historical politics on the basis of analogy. 'No fine thing can directly originate from the Absolute or be traced back to it', Schelling says, 'whereby the cause of the finite world is expressed as an absolute breaking away from the infinite world' (Schelling 2010: 29).

Schelling, therefore, does not see the possibility of partaking in the gift of the absolute beatitude in a direct mode. The influence of Meister Eckhart here is unmistakable again: partaking in the gift of beatitude demands an *indirection* – a path without path, a *wandering* – which demands the mortification of all egotism and the releasement of *Pneuma* from its imprisonment in the *nomos* of the worldly-sensate life. If the fundamental presupposition of pantheism is the idea that the phenomenal worldly order has an inherent, positive being of its own, then Schelling's understanding of his own philosophy, which is based upon an irreducible *separation*, would not allow pantheism as an appropriate designation for that philosophy (Schelling 2010: 37–8). The inescapable remainder of *the rift*, or *the cleft*, opened in the very opening of the world to itself, will forever haunt any theologico-political totalisation of our existence. Rather than closing the abyss here by the force of the worldly powers of sovereignty, Schelling thinks a path of *indirection*, that is, the *intensification of separation as the very opening to absolute beatitude*. What it calls forth from us is an infinite task of mortification or renunciation of the world-historical claim to sovereignty. Beatitude is the event of eschatological surprise: it arrives in the abyss of the *distance*, a distance that spaces open the wound where the gift becomes a manifestation, phenomenality, a revelation, a matter of faith that sees the invisible and un-sees the visible. This event of the unconditional is also a violence; not that to which we must succumb 'like single bodies succumb to gravity' (Schelling 2010: 43), but more like those blessed celestial bodies where the polarity of two paths – egress and return, centrifugal and centripetal – coincide, not just accidentally but in an essential manner. The metaphor of the celestial body once again enables Schelling to conceive the blessedness of this mode of being wherein polarity of two paths coincide:[9]

> Just as an idea – and its reflection, the celestial body – absorbs its center, identity, and at once resides within it, and vice-versa, so also the soul; it's inclination toward the center, to be one with God, is morality. This would only be a negative difference, were it not for the fact that the resumption of finitude into infinitude is also a passage of the infinite into the finite, e.g. a complete being-within-itself of the latter. Thus morality and beatitude

> are but two different sides of the same oneness; in no need of being complemented by the other, each is absolute and comprehends the other. The originary image of being-one which is that of both truth and beauty is God. (Schelling 2010: 43)

Nature is 'the image of God's beatitude' (44). In the eschatological conception of history, the coincidence of freedom and necessity is the equivalent of the celestial body in the realm of nature. In the realm of the ethical, it is to be understood as the coincidence of truth and beauty, virtue and beatitude.[10] This co-incidence of the opposites – day and night, arriving and passing, mortality and immortality, holy mourning and absolute beatitude – is the highest task of existence, and the work of art, as much as philosophy and religion, 'expresses' it without having to master it, or appropriate it in cognition.

As primarily ethical, where the ethical is understood as 'direction to a beatific life' (Schelling 2010: 8), religion is conceived by Schelling as that which can only have *an indirect* relation to the order of the political. Even in its highest moral order, the state cannot be seen as an embodiment of the divine. Distinguishing within religion itself its esoteric and exoteric dimensions, its secret mystery cult and its public-external form, religion can only have the meaning of *secrecy*. The *secret* of the *sacred* is the forever secret, the secret that does not pass over into the visibility of public mortality, into the visibility of the visible church, or of the legal-profane order of conditioned politics:

> God, however, as identity of the highest order, remains above all reality and eternally has merely an indirect relationship. If then in the higher moral order the State represents a *second nature*, then the divine can never have anything other than an indirect relationship to it; never can it bear any real relationship to it, and religion, if it seeks to preserve itself in unscathed pure ideality, can therefore never exist – even in the most perfect State – other than esoterically in the form of *mystery cults*. (Schelling 2010: 51)

Withdrawn from all public and private manifestation, religion doesn't have its home in the significance of world-historical manifestation. Neither public nor private, neither external nor mere interiority, religion is *secret* in an essential sense: secrecy as withdrawal from the general order of the world-political manifestation, a withdrawal of the immemorial from the linguistic registrar of judgement and signification, a withdrawal from the order wherein phenomenality gets subsumed under the *nomothetic* principle of worldly hegemonies. In Schellingian eschatology, the triumphal order of the world-historical politics is stripped of the final significance: the 'last disclosure' (Schelling 2010: 55), which will reconcile 'the falling away from the Absolute' and transform this negativity into an unconditional affirmation, would rather exhibit the nullity of all such triumphalism of world-historical politics. History is predicated upon freedom and not vice versa: 'thus, religion, having a purely moral effect, is kept from the danger of mixing with the real, the sensate, or from laying claims to external dominion and violence, which would be contrary to its nature. Philosophy, on the other hand, and those enamoured with it, the naturally initiated, remain eternally allied with religion' (55).

Ontology of separation

In his 1810 private lectures at Stuttgart, Schelling further intensifies and concretises his earlier conception of caesura or separation. The influence of Jacob Böhme, already manifest in his *Freedom* essay, passes through these lectures and finds its most profound and creative expression in Schelling's incomplete *The Ages of the World*. The notion of 'transition' from essence to existence and from potentiality into actuality is grasped here, in the manner of Böhme, not on the basis of the principle of continuity and emanation but as the most fundamental crisis of a 'caesura' (*Scheidung*) that enables revelation (*Offenbarung*) to break through as divine life. This *setting apart* of *transition* is less a cancellation of identity than the *doubling* (*Doublirung*) of essence that rends asunder the polar principles of the divine being (and so of the mortal being). What Being (*Seyn*) is to being (*das Seyende*), the ground is to existence: the former, being mere ground, serves as the non-being to the latter while still having a being of its own, an independent life or self-hood of its own.[11] In fact, it is this non-being that is the principle of self-hood, the principle of finitude and negativity. In contrast to the *Logic* of Hegel (who does not distinguish non-being from nothingness), Schelling distinguishes this principle of non-being (which Being – *Seyn* – is) from 'nothingness'. The latter cannot be said to be the principle of freedom, for only as the non-being of freedom can there be finitude, self-hood, personality and actuality. A philosophy of freedom like Schelling's can't begin with the concept of nothingness that passes into being and vice versa[12] but only with non-being as the potentiality of being (*das Seyende*). That is why there always remains a residue of non-being, an 'irreducible remainder', a remnant of darkness, even when it is actualised and elevated into the light of being (*das Seyende*). The eternal remnant of non-being, as the very condition of possibility of life, refuses the Hegelian *Aufhebung* into the Absolute concept: it remains un-sublated, as something like an eternal remnant, eternally outside 'being' and outside the thinkable.

Against both the Neo-Platonic conception of emanation and the

Hegelian pantheistic theodicy of history, Schelling's eschatology makes this 'principle' of *separation* the very condition of existence and actuality, of life and revelation. God contracts, limits, withdraws, restricts or descends himself by virtue of his absolute freedom,[13] bringing into being the absolute crisis of *separation* between principles, expelling (without thereby extinguishing) the principle of self-hood into the dark, abyssal foundation of being.[14] *Difference*, opened by this crisis of *separation* and by the *partitioning* of powers, is the non-axiological difference, not difference grasped as a succession of conceptual categories, as in Hegel, but difference as a *holding-together* (*Zusammenhang*) of the powers conceived in their 'simultaneity'.[15] Such difference is not a mere attenuated variation of identity but difference *as* difference (and not a representation of difference). Only in this non-axiological difference can the phenomenal realm of the world and the mortal still have a relative independence of being apart from God.[16] Gilles Deleuze rightly perceives in this Schellingian ontology of separation a decisive attempt to think difference *as* difference irreducible to the representation of difference (Deleuze 1994: 190–1). Life can only be found in this *apartness* opened by the abyss of *difference*, in this *partitioning* of powers, in this *parting away* of ground and existence. Such life, actualised and exuberant, and not a mere logical category, can only exist as a *bond* or *jointure* among beings: God, man and nature, in which man is the intermediary link, the point of transition between God and nature (see Heidegger 1985).

Man appears in such an ontological nexus of beings as the condition of the *contiguity* of beings, a contiguity that is *always already* opened in the abyss of discontinuity emerging from the night of indifference. As the 'transition' (which is in fact a 'rupture') from God to nature, man is simultaneously *removed, separated, parted* from both God and nature. In other words, an essential *disjointure* must always already operate as a possibility in the very *jointure* and continuity that runs from God to nature through the historical passage of man in this world. In this drama of redemption occurring on the stage of history, the place, or rather non-place, of man is the crucial *hinge*. As the hinge that may open as well as close beings toward redemption, that makes possible both the contiguity and discontinuity and the jointure and disjointure of beings, man must *duplicate* the very *crisis* of *separation* of principles in himself on the basis of his freedom, a finite freedom that is borrowed from the absolute freedom of God. Like God, he, too, must *separate* in his own finite realm the dark, unconscious principle from the ideal principle of light in order to constantly elevate the expelled principle into the light of revelation. Such an ontology of separation is at the same time ontology of *strife*, grounded in the groundless (*Abgrund*) freedom. As the fundamental law of opposition and strife constitutes the very life of the divine, so the same opposition and strife rules within the finite life of the mortal. The contiguity of beings, arising out of the fundamental *cision* of principles, cannot therefore be a homogeneous line of progressive succession. Released from the logic of 'progressivity' (Deleuze 1994: 191) – the image of thought that understands difference on the basis of the identical – the jointure of beings can be disjoined (see Heidegger 1985), the nexus can be broken, the bond can undergo displacement, and the contiguity of beings can be disrupted, since it arises out of the groundless freedom. Man as the linkage in this contiguity of beings can also be the very condition of their discontinuity when there occurs an inversion of principles in him, when non-being in its incessant hunger for being attempts to assume the place of being (*das Seyende*). Evil is thereby let loose on the spiritual stage of history, and the passage of communication and continuity among beings undergoes a *clotting* (*Stockung*) or inhibition (*Hemmung*), affecting the entire connection of man with God and nature. Cut off from man, through his own fault, and from partaking of divine life, nature now no longer sees in man her redemptive possibility. She suffers the most unspeakable of diseases. Man too, finding no way to relate to God and nature, suffers the most violent disease of spirit. The disease in nature finds its echo in the radical evil occurring on the stage of history. They reflect each other as in a mirror. The melancholy of man, which is the deepest aspect of his being, finds its attunement with the profound melancholy of nature, as in a musical instrument where a touch of one string reverberates in all the other strings.

> The most obscure and thus the deepest aspect of human nature is that of nostalgia [*Sehnsucht*], which is the inner gravity of the temperament, so to speak; in its most profound manifestation it appears as melancholy [*Schwermuth*]. It is by means of the latter that man feels a sympathetic relation to nature. What is most profound in nature is also melancholy; for it, too, mourns lost good, and likewise such an indestructible melancholy inheres in all forms of life because all life is founded upon something independent from itself. (Schelling 1994a: 230)

The metaphysics of life that Schelling constructs here is founded upon the principle of *separation* or *cision*. The separation of principles, the cision of existence from the essence that is its ground, the relative independence of non-being (as Being in relation to itself) from being (*das Seyende*), and also, most importantly, the relative independence of man from God and nature: such *separation* is the very condition of possibility of all life, not only of the finite life of man and nature but even of the divine life as well. It is on the basis of *separation* that revelation occurs on the stage of history, opening thereby the entire spiritual realm of the historical to a future redemption *to come* which is the eschatological possibility not only for man but for the entire finite world of existence.

It has often been alleged that Schelling has an anthropomorphic idea of God. However, a deeper understanding of the Schellingian notion of man discloses the paradoxical character of the place of man in the jointure of being. The privileged place of man, privileged in so far as he alone is the site though which redemption passes, is at once a non-place, the place of danger arising out of his demonic freedom, *an empty measure* in which alone the measureless measure of the *eschaton* must take place. As the in-between link between the divine life and nature, man is at the same time the one in whom extremities meet: the extremity of an immemorial past and the future redemption coming from the other extremity of time; God on one hand, and nature, on the other; the melancholy of nature and the absolute beatitude in God. The place of man, this *in-between*, is thus an *Atopos* opened by that abyss of separation on the basis of which alone is there communication among beings. Yet, this non-place that sets man *apart* from God and nature alike, while calling both toward him, is the very *taking place* of death as well as life, of disease as well as blissfulness, of poison as well as redemption, of violence as well as its *coming* redemption. This eschatological drama of redemption presupposes a being (namely, man) whose privilege consists in its possibility of being an empty measure through which the measure of existence becomes possible. It appears as if man can only take his privileged part in this eschatological drama of redemption as a non-sovereign, non-autochthonous and non-autarchic being. *This necessity of non-sovereignty is the most fundamental principle of the Schellingian political eschatology.*

Already in 1809 essay on human freedom, Schelling understands this *non-place* where *the taking place* of revelation occurs as the groundless freedom of man. This borrowed freedom is gifted by God. Heidegger rightly perceives here Schelling's most important contribution to philosophy: existence is grasped as *event* (*Ereignis*), unthought and unthinkable in the traditional metaphysics of the West. Schelling effectively releases the *eventive* character of a finite existence from the predicative-judgemental-categorical structures of Occidental ontology. As a non-sovereign and finite being (finite because of his non-sovereignty), man becomes open to the *coming* of redemption from an extremity of time; he is that *historical* existence whose *historicity* consists in an eschatological *breaking open* to the divine and nature alike. If the *eschaton* is the fundamental principle of religion, then the sense of religion must be none other than the *breaking open* of the mythic immanence of autochthony and autarchy. This instance, far from being the concluding moment of the progressive historical becoming of the Occidental metaphysics, is the instantaneous apparition of a lightning flash against the dark abyss of the identical: what the lightning flash discloses, momentarily, is that possibility of redemption which man must seize without violence. At this moment metaphysics must take *the turn* (*Kehre*) toward that which it cannot grasp: the eschatological event of redemption, the surprise of the future, the wound of Love. It is as though metaphysics itself must turn against itself at the very instance of its fulfilment, bringing thereby the most unthinkable caesura into the innermost ground of philosophy. At this moment (so intimately tied up with the advent of Schelling) philosophy comes to itself again as a caesural, finite and non-sovereign thinking.

Metaphysics and politics

The political stakes of Schelling's eschatology must be derived from his metaphysics of separation, and we see Schelling himself drawing out those stakes in the concluding part of his Stuttgart lecture of 1810. The argument is as follows:

By the fault of man – who is the link, hinge and point of jointure – the contiguity among beings is disjoined. Nature has lost its unity and its place in the contiguity of beings in the same measure that man too has lost his natural unity with God and nature. Since man is granted a freedom on the basis of which he can create a new unity, he now creates a second natural unity 'superimposed on the first' (Schelling 1994a: 227). It is a paradoxical unity in that it is both 'artificial' (being a second nature) and 'natural', in so far as it is 'subject to the fate of all organic life, namely to bloom, to ripen, eventually to age, and finally to die' (227); 'spiritual' (since it is created out of human freedom) and yet 'material' (since it shares with materiality its imperfection). This artificial-natural, spiritual-material unity, this poor supplement of the lost unity and violent imposition of a second nature, is none other than the modern state. 'The natural unity', writes Schelling, 'this second nature, superimposed on the first, to which man must necessarily take recourse, is the *state*; and to put it bluntly, the state is a consequence of the curse that has been placed on humanity. Because man no longer has God for his unity, he must submit to a material unity' (227).

The state bears the mark of the degradation and the fragility of man rather than the plenitude of his natural 'goodness'. Like the fallen man, the existence of the modern state – in its innermost constitution – is also precarious and merely provisional. The modern state, then, is transient, bereft of sovereignty and of the unconditional legitimacy of its being. Hence the constant necessity felt by the state to legitimise its *raison d'être* by invoking a 'moral setting'[17] that it lacks, and by invoking the instance of exception, now becoming the norm of the state, in order to elicit absolute obligation from its citizens. The state of exception, whether invoked in the name of morality or in the name of a constant waging of war, becomes the *raison d'état*. The state acts like the principle of non-being which, due to its eternal lack of being, constantly feels a malicious hunger to attain being (*das Seyende*). If, according to Schelling, the latter is the very condition of the actualisation of radical evil and not a mere potentiality, then we can say that radical evil is not a mere accidental result of the existence of the state but somehow belongs to its very constitution. The violence of the state and of the world-historical politics at large have to do with this aporetic foundation of the state. This aporia of the state is the very aporia of radical evil. Like the principle of non-being – whose insatiable hunger for the attainment of being intensifies the more it falls below being (this is why it is *radically* evil), thereby increasing its devouring power – the instance of exception both works and un-works for the state. At work here is the principle of non-being (which is the very principle of its un-working) which now and then turns into the worst form of despotism: human freedom, through which the human is given the gift of partaking in the divine beatitude, turns demonic due to its abuse by man. While the principle of non-being is the very ground of being, this principle – when it wants to appropriate being for itself – turns against mankind, becoming dangerous and demonic. The violence of the worldly institutions – the state and the Church – has its metaphysical essence in this devouring malice of non-being.

Schelling here takes up three events or discourses of his own time – namely, the French Revolution, the Kantian concept of freedom and Fichte's 'closed Trade system' – which have each attempted to 'demonstrate how unity could possibly be reconciled with the existence of free beings; that is, the possibility of the state would, properly speaking, be but the condition for the highest possible freedom of the individuals' (Schelling 1994a: 227). All such attempts are destined to fail; as mere human institution, fragile and precarious it is, the state – when it is made purely an end in itself – turns out to be merely an apology for the existing order of world-historical politics. 'Hence it is quite natural', Schelling concludes, 'that the end of this period during which people have been talking of nothing but freedom, the most consequent minds, in their pursuit of the idea of a perfect state, would have arrived at the worst kind of despotism' (227).

Therefore, the insufficiency and precarious character of the state, instituted by the impoverished and insufficient action of fallen man in order to supplement a lost unity, demands a second attempt to re-establish a lost unity similar to the original one. But this time it is undertaken by God himself. This is 'revelation', which occurs in several stages until God himself must appear on the stage of history as man. Christ here is the mediator between God and man, in the way that man himself was the mediating link between God and nature before the link was broken by man's own fault. Christ is now the passage from nature to God; his ignoble dying on the Cross is the abyss of suffering that must pass through nature to God so as to redeem all of creation. The Church, then, is the immediate consequence of the second revelation. Schelling's account of the origin of both the Church and the state here is deduced from his metaphysical framework of separation, conceived as an absolute event of *breaking away* or a fall. If the event of breaking or falling away (*Abfall*) was not there in the very jointure of beings as a potentiality, then neither the state nor the Church would ever have come into being. Then the possibility and actuality of evil could only have been a mere privation, a mere attenuated decrement emanating from the light of the Good. Schelling draws immense political consequences from the metaphysics of emanation. The theodicy of history – by denying the potentiality and actuality of radical evil and minimising its terror into a necessary privation of the Good (which is the determinate *telos* of a necessary historical process) – ends up justifying the violence of world-historical politics in the name of a future which is indefinitely postponed; or, it ends up glorifying the historical existence of the modern state as one of the figures of the absolute spirit that progressively masters the powers of the irrational in the institutional ground of Reason. The violence of historical Reason would then be justified. A century later, Benjamin transforms this Schellingian critique of historical Reason into a messianic deconstruction of that 'homogeneous empty time' in which the past suffering of the vanquished and the oppressed is justified in the name of a quantitative, progressive approximation to a fulfilment that is deferred to a future that is never to arrive.

The politico-theological import of the Schellingian eschatology must be measured against such a legitimising theodicy of an empty historical process. The Church is not immune from Schellingian attack in so far as – instead of remaining opposed to the powers of the world as it should be according to its spirit – it enters into alliance with the earthly sovereignties. Instead of remaining withdrawn from the external, violent unity instituted by those sovereignties, the Church now becomes the very theological foundation of world-historical conquest. The result is a 'one-dimensional humanity'. The healthy separation of principles and domains in *belonging-together* – external unity from internal, non-being as mere foundation of being (*das Seyende*), the theological from the political – is collapsed into the unspeakable terror of universal domination and 'political tyranny':

> In surveying more recent history, which with good reason, is said to begin with the arrival of Christianity in Europe, we note that humanity had to

> pass through two stages in its attempt to discover or produce a unity; first that of producing an internal unity through the Church, which had to fail because the Church simultaneously sought to become the external unity and eventually attempted to produce external unity by means of the state. Only with the demise of hierarchical [systems] has the state attained this importance, and it is manifest that the pressure of political tyranny has increased ever since in exact proportion to the belief that an inner unity seemed dispensable; indeed it is bound to increase to a maximum intensity until, perhaps, upon the collapse of these one-dimensional attempts humanity will discover the right way. (Schelling 1994a: 229)

With the assumption of external unity, the Church acts exactly like the modern state, and in this way they can collaborate in the triumphal project of world-historical conquest. If that is so, then the sense of religion must not be exhausted in the axiomatics of world-historical institutions like the Church. If the *eschaton* is the fundamental sense of religion, and it implies separation, then this separation must inscribe itself, not so much between the Church and the state, but between religion and the political. Only then can the one-dimensional attempts of humanity be overcome.

Schelling conceives of 'philosophical religion' as this overcoming of one-dimensional humanity. Both the Church and the state are one-dimensional: the first because it has forgotten the very spirit and promise of its existence, and thus comes to be allied with the state; the second, because the state in its very existence as a legitimising institution cannot but be one-dimensional. Radical evil is also essentially one-dimensional: it displaces the nexus of the twofold powers and, in a one-sided manner, totalises everything under the power of its non-being. Religion, on the other hand, is an overcoming of all such one-dimensional attempts in the name of the true unity that is an eschatological potentiality. But this religion can only be understood as a *religion to come*, a future possibility, bound up with the messianic-apocalyptic redemption of mankind. This philosophical-religious concept of true unity or universality has an intrinsic relation to the advent, to the event of arrival, to the *coming* future, which is not the future that grows, ripens and passes away like the state, but the future always *to come*, a future of redemption for the whole of mankind. This universality of philosophical reason is implied in the very idea of philosophy and religion. Schelling's idea of a philosophical religion always *to come* is thus not the religion that already exists in alliance with the world-historical powers, but a *promised religion*, the religion of promise and hope:

> Whatever the ultimate goal may turn out to be, this much is certain, namely, that true unity can be attained only *via* the path of religion; only the supreme and most diverse culture of religious knowledge will enable

> humanity, if not to abolish the state outright, then at least to ensure that the state will progressively divest itself of the blind force that governs it, and to transfigure this force into intelligence. It is not that the Church ought to dominate the state or vice-versa, but that the state ought to cultivate the religious principles within itself and that the community of all peoples ought to be founded on religious convictions that, themselves, ought to become universal. (Schelling 1994a: 229)

This hope is an eschatological one: it demands dissatisfaction with all the possible one-dimensional attempts to which human history now bears witness. It is a hope, then, for the un-hoped for, contrary to the programmatic and calculable politics of the profane, secular world-order. Schelling hereby anticipates the Kierkegaardian eschatological critique of Christianity by separating religion from the political in such a way that religion itself can't be completely conflated with the Church, to the extent that it has given up its true, inner unity for the sake of an external unity. The worldly religion has forgotten its task, that is: the necessity of withdrawing from all world-historical triumphalism. Wherever is there triumph, religion is absent.

To understand the immense ethico-political consequences of Schelling's political eschatology, it is not enough to view him solely against the socio-historical-philosophical background of the early nineteenth century. It is true that such consequences can't be separated from Schelling's timely confrontations with the spirit of his age: with the secularising tendency of the Enlightenment that gave rise to the modern state; with the totalising theodicy of historical Reason that found such an overpowering expression in Hegel's grand system; and with the religious fanaticism implicit in thinkers like Jacobi, etc. It is also true that Schelling's timely eschatological critique of both the state and the Church alike prepared the way for Marx's atheistic eschatological critique of religion and the state and Kierkegaard's existential-theological critique of Christianity and the state. The more interesting question today, however, is how to renew this infinite critique of historical Reason when it has assumed a more sophisticated and complex totalisation in the 'democratic' neo-liberal societies of the contemporary world-historical order. If such a renewal is an inescapable task today, then Schelling's political eschatology, with its insistence on a messianic-eschatological promise and hope, seems indispensable. The renewal of Schellingian thinking, whether one takes one side (atheistic eschatology/messianism) or the other (theological eschatology/messianism), must learn one important lesson from the history of the reception of Schelling's thought: that the task of philosophy and religion – or more appropriately, of 'philosophical religion' – is to conceive of a deconstructive strategy for the delegitimation of the sovereignty of all worldly powers, whether those of the state or the Church, in such a manner that, through an intensification of difference, the promise of a future will be kept open, a future always *to come*.

Notes

1. Again one can see here the proximity of Benjamin with Schelling. Like Schelling – who understands potencies as stars where each such celestial body, in its own singular manner, reflects the entire universal and where each potency is, in its very finitude, a reflection of the infinite – Benjamin also conceives every idea as a sun, 'related to other ideas just as suns are related to each other. The harmonious relationship between such essences is what constitutes truth' (Benjamin 1998: 37). Apart from the influence of Plato on both Schelling and Benjamin, it is Leibniz's idea of monadology – Leibniz who thinks truth musically, that is, truth as 'harmony' – that decisively influenced them.
2. For Schelling, the eschatological arrival of eternity, truly conceived, is not to be understood as a mere endlessness of time, time that is prolonged to an endless duration, a homogeneous endless empty infinite. He rather conceives – like Benjamin later – the eternity of beatitude as 'timeless' and thus as 'ahistorical': 'the soul is not eternal because its duration is without beginning or end but rather because it has no relationship to time at all. Therefore it cannot be called immortal in a sense that would include an individual continuity. Since this could not be conceived of independent of finitude and the body, immortality would only be continued mortality and an ongoing imprisonment of the soul rather than a liberation' (Schelling 2010: 47). Between eternity and time, immortality and finitude, there is a discontinuity, a caesura and a rupture that can't be bridged by a continuous movement of a homogeneous time endlessly extended to the infinite. Both Benjamin and Rosenzweig, each on his own way, understand the idea of discontinuity and interruption in a messianic manner. Schelling's eschatology is thus founded upon the idea of discontinuity and interruption between what exists as finite and what is to come from an extremity of the future.
3. While in the schematic mode of representation the particular is intuited through the universal, in the allegorical mode of representation the universal is intuited through the particular. The synthesis of schematic and allegorical is the symbolic mode of representation. In a strict sense, according to Schelling, mythology can be understood only symbolically and in that sense only Greek art is symbolic: 'mythology as such and every poetic rendering of it in particular is to be comprehended neither schematically nor allegorically, but rather symbolically' (Schelling 1989: 48).
4. Archetypes or ideas – which are the contents of mythology – are the individuated absolute. Schelling also calls them potencies. He deduces the idea of mythology in the following manner: 'The absolute is absolutely one; viewed absolutely in particular forms, however, such that the absolute is thereby not suspended this one = idea. The same holds true for art. It, too, views or intuits primal beauty only in ideas as particular forms, each of which, however, is divine and absolute for itself. Whereas philosophy intuits these ideas as they are *in themselves*, art intuits them *objectively* . . . the universal symbolism or universal *representation* of the *ideas* as real is thus given in mythology' (Schelling 1989: 17).
5. Schelling writes: 'All of ancient history can be viewed as the tragic period of history. Fate, too, is a form of providence, except that it is intuited within the real, just as providence is fate intuited in the ideal. Eternal necessity reveals itself during the time of identity with it as nature. This was the case with the Greeks. After the fall from nature it reveals itself in bitter and violent blows as fate. One can escape fate only in one way: by throwing oneself into the arms of providence . . . The old gods lost their power, the

oracles and celebrations fell silent, and a bottomless abyss full of a wild admixture of all the elements of the past world appeared to open itself up before mankind. Above this dark abyss the only sign of peace and of a balance of forces seems to be the cross, a kind of rainbow of a second flood' (Schelling 1989: 61).
6. Schelling offers here three forms of reflective cognition: categorical, hypothetical and disjunctive (Schelling 1989: 12–15).
7. 'All philosophizing begins', writes Schelling, 'with the idea of the Absolute come alive. That which is true can only be recognized in truth; that which is evident, in evidence' (Schelling 2010: 15).
8. Schelling here distinguishes his concept of *non-being* from *nothingness*.
9. Similarly Schelling writes in *Bruno*: 'In the heavenly bodies, the element whereby things separate themselves and distance themselves from the image of identity is not divorced from the element whereby they are assimilated into the infinite concept, and they are not split up into contending forces. Instead their elements are harmoniously yoked, and just as they alone are truly immortal, so these heavenly beings alone enjoy the blessed condition of reality as a whole, even in the state of separated existence . . . you should therefore think of the planets' course of motion as something perfectly whole and simple, not a composite of forces, but an absolute identity thereof. One of the factors of this identity [centripetal force] causes a thing to inhere within the identity of all things; it is commonly called gravity. The other is [centrifugal force] which causes a thing to reside in itself; we commonly view it as the opposite of gravity. But these are absolutely equivalent forms of the identity that constitutes the planet's motion; both are the same totality, one thing in fact' (Schelling 1984: 169).
10. Schelling compares the whole eschatology of history as an epic with two parts: 'History is an epic composed in the mind of God. It has two main parts: one depicting mankind's egress from its center to its furthest point of displacement; the other, its return. The former is, as it were, history's *Iliad*; the latter, its *Odyssey*. In the one, the direction is centrifugal; in the latter it becomes centripetal. In this way, the grand purpose of the phenomenal world reveals itself in history. The ideas, the spirits, must fall away from the center and insert themselves into the particularity of nature, the general realm of the falling away, so that afterward, and as particularities, they may return to indifference and, reconciled with it, may be able to abide in it without disturbing it' (Schelling 2010: 44–5).
11. Of non-being as the foundation of the being (*das Seyende*) of God, Schelling writes: 'This is indeed a non-being in that it originally relates to Him merely as the foundation, as that which He Himself is not, or as that which exists merely as the basis for that which truly is. And yet it is also a being in and of itself' (Schelling 1994a: 209).
12. See 'The Doctrine of Being' of Hegel's *Logic* (1975).
13. This act of contraction in God can only be understood as the decision of God arising out of his absolute freedom. Thus Schelling writes: 'This act of restriction or descent on the part of God is spontaneous. Hence the explanation of the world has no other ground than the freedom of God. Only God Himself can break with the absolute identity of His essence and thereby can create the space for a revelation' (Schelling 1994a: 204).
14. Of this primordial separation, Schelling writes: 'Hence, once God has separated Himself internally, He has separated Himself *qua* being from his Being . . . whoever does not separate himself from his Being considers this *Being* essential rather than his inner superior, and more truthful essence. Likewise, if God were to remain as immersed in his Being, there would be no life, no growth. Hence, He separates Himself from his being precisely because it is merely a tool for Him' (Schelling 1994a: 209).
15. Schelling conceives this simultaneity of difference in the following manner: 'God posits Himself as the first power, *as* something unconscious; however, he cannot concentrate His self into the Real without expanding as the Ideal, that is, He cannot posit Himself as the Real, as an *object*, without positing Himself *simultaneously* as a subject;

and both of these constitute *one Act* of absolute simultaneity; with His actual concentration into the Real, God also posits His expansion as the Ideal' (Schelling 1994a: 207).

16. '[Non] being relates to God as the flower relates to the sun. Although the flower emanates from the dark earth only through the efficacy of the sun and is transformed by light, there nevertheless remains always something whose very root exists independently of this [flower]. If the relation of man to God was not of this kind he would not have any freedom with respect to God and would be but a ray of sunlight or a spark of fire' (Schelling 1994a: 224).

17. Schelling says: 'The state, even if it is being governed in a rational manner, knows well that its material power alone cannot effect anything and that it must invoke higher and spiritual motives. These, however, lie beyond its domain and cannot be controlled by the state, even though the latter boasts with being able to create a moral setting, thereby arrogating to itself a power equal to nature. A free spirit, however, will never consider such a natural unity sufficient, and a higher talisman is required; consequently, any unity that originates in the state remains inevitably precarious and provisional' (Schelling 1994a: 227).

Chapter 6

The Tragic Dissonance

Integrative law of the speculative

We know that a certain dominant determination of the tragic constitutes the philosophical thinking that we now refer to as 'dialectical-speculative'. Such thinking does not remain satisfied with merely tracing the dissolution and corruption of all that is called 'actuality', but discovers therein a logic of being capable of converting the nothing into being, the negative into the positive. For such a logic, nothing essentially 'human' must be lost to dissolution and corruption, unless by default the speculative voyage of the negative fails to arrive at its destination. That destination is the *pleroma* of a complete recuperation, of a full retrieval of self-presence which is almost lost and yet is always regained. The dialectical operation, at least in its manifest desire, would then mean nothing other than the desire of self-presence through conversion of the negative into the positive. The speculative voyage is tragic in the sense that it must undergo generation and corruption, dereliction and dissolution precisely in order to restitute itself as Subject. Is there any other name or *nomos* (law) than 'tragic' to designate this process whereby the restitution of the Spirit is achieved by undergoing an absolute agony of finitude? The 'tragic' here would signify nothing other than the integrative law of a speculative restitution of the Subject. Such a tragic-speculative Subject institutes itself as the 'sovereign referent' of the hegemonic discourse that would constrain our thinking and existing – a discourse that does not tolerate any radical other outside the integrative law of dialectical opposition and subsumption.

With a certain reservation we may perhaps say that this economy of the law also constitutes the thought-structure of what we call 'theological'.

This is so, provided that we undertake here to open the theological to its innermost other, its intimate neighbour, *the holy*. *The holy* is the *differend* which is unbearable to theological-speculative thought. In its eschatological intensity, and as incommensurable with any 'sovereign referent', it tears apart the fundamental ground of the world. It is in this sense that we speak here of a 'speculative-theological' desire, despite the infinitely complicated relation between speculative thought and theology whereby one inseparably conjures up the other, while, all the time, insisting on a *difference* never to be bridged by a simple operation of negativity or positivity. Let me call it, evoking Heidegger (2002), the 'onto-theological' structure of a thought or discourse from which a fundamental co-relation of *pain* and *logos* (Heidegger 1998: 291–322), and hence a certain *tragic* determination of metaphysics, is inseparable. This tragic co-relation would be thought by Heidegger as an instance of the epochal closure of metaphysics and of another inauguration in a leap beyond metaphysics. This is not the only way that Heidegger opens up the passage of undergoing the tragic experience (*Er-fahrung*) in order to *hint* or *beckon* toward an eruption that may occur at the closure of metaphysics. Hence there is no closure pure and simple without a simultaneous opening toward the *Abgrund* into which we must *leap*. It is a *hinting* or *beckoning* (in the Heideggerian sense of *Wink*) toward the occurrence of the possibility of an 'other' thinking. From *Contributions to Philosophy* onwards, Heidegger comes to think this occurrence with the name of *Ereignis* (the event of appropriation). The *Ereignis* is 'tragic' but in an entirely different mode, in a heterogeneous linguistic register that has remained unthought and unthinkable within metaphysics. In other words, the name *Ereignis*, in its agonal double-bind of appropriation-expropriation, would *beckon* toward an unthought *tragic*, heterogeneous to the speculative investment of metaphysics. Here it is not merely the discourse called 'Idealism' that is put into question, but the destiny of Occidental metaphysics *as such* in its fundamental gathering. There is thus, for Heidegger, *another* tragic thought than this 'speculative-theological' investment of metaphysics, a tragic thought that has to do with the destitution of a dominant metaphysics in order to open it up toward an inauguration *to come*. It is this other thought of the tragic that we propose to think with the help of Schelling.

Tragic caesura

As we remarked above, at the heart of speculative thought lies a logic of the law which is also 'theological', the desire for the *pleroma* of *finding* oneself as found, *touching* oneself as touched in the intimacy of self-presence. Since this 'finding oneself' is a movement or a process, a voyage, it must undergo a *passage* of inevitable loss, of a dereliction and dissolution. The *pleroma* of *logos* must not remain uncontaminated by the violence of pain. Since it must undergo the agony of finitude precisely in order to restitute itself, the speculative desire cannot remain untouched by pain. As Georges Bataille has shown in his unique analysis of the Hegelian discourse, the *logos* of metaphysics is a tragic theatrical representation of the speculative which paradoxically amounts to nothing less than a 'farce' or a 'comedy'. In his justly famous analysis Bataille discovers a certain logic of the 'tragic' (and thereby the 'comic') at work whose foundation is provided by the rituals of sacrifice (Bataille 1997: 279–95). In Bataille's analysis it emerges that in this tragic desire, wherein the *logos* is immersed without definitively being lost, speculative thought arrives at a comic default. What remains unbearable for the Hegelian speculative discourse is the sovereign *pleroma* itself, which is un-economical and irreducible to the concept because it suspends itself at the very instant of its advent. The advent of the *pleroma* without reservation is an unbearable excess that deprives the speculative Subject of its status as the 'sovereign referent'. At stake here is nothing less than the foundational possibility of a speculative thought, or rather, of its failure, wherein onto-theological metaphysics founders, having reached its fulfilment (*Vollendung*).

It is the merit of Philippe Lacoue-Labarthe's justly famous essay entitled 'The Caesura of the Speculative' (1989: 208–35) to have demonstrated the following:

1. That what is at stake in such a determination of the 'tragic' is not so much or not merely the tragic as a mere particular or specific treatment of a dramatic genre called 'tragedy' within an aesthetic discourse that exists alongside other discourses such as 'logic', 'ethics', 'politics' and 'metaphysics'. At stake here is rather the 'thought structure', the foundational possibility of the 'speculative' as such in its 'onto-theological' constitution. The question of the tragic is now inseparably connected with the structural condition of (im)possibility of the 'speculative' as such, with the structural condition of the opening or closure (opening and closure at the same time) of metaphysics in its instance of fulfilment (*Vollendung*). In the tragic determination of the speculative, 'onto-theologically' constituted metaphysics reaches its uttermost achievement and thereby confronts the instance of its default, its failure to fulfil the demand that the tragic itself imposes in its wake. This default manifests, most painfully and tragically, as an *epochal dissonance*, an *eccentric* opening and closure, an 'empty measure of time' (Fóti 2006) breaking into in the Hölderlinian tragic 'theatre'. What Lacoue-Labarthe shows, then, in his analysis of that tragic theatre is nothing other than the momentary default of metaphysics suddenly

breaking into the discursive continuum of the historical as an *epochal break*, which he calls a 'caesura'.

2. That this eruption of the tragic-speculative is not limited merely to a specific and unique discourse called 'German Idealism' at the onset of nineteenth century but has to do with the essentially *sacrificial* foundation of Occidental metaphysics per se.[1] We know from Bataille's celebrated analysis that the 'tragic', at least in its dominant discursive appropriation, is constituted on such a sacrificial foundation. For Lacoue-Labarthe, as for Heidegger, its 'poetic' articulation is given in the most elaborate and systematic manner in Aristotelian *cathartic* poetics. What is at stake for Lacoue-Labarthe here is not merely the constitutive possibility of 'Idealism' but the destiny or default of a metaphysics whose foundation is provided by a sacrificial determination of the tragic. This constitutive possibility of the speculative also carries its potential momentary advent of 'caesuras' by an 'ineluctable' logic of the 'always already' that refuses the ground of the concept. Lacoue-Labarthe's name for such a logic is *desistance*.

Such caesuras mark the momentary breaking-in of the *other* tragic thought that remains potentially in the speculative-sacrificial determination of the tragic: it remains an excess over the latter as an uncontainable surplus, as an eccentric path, as an infidelity to the origin, withdrawn from the immanence of self-presence. Despite agreeing with Peter Szondi's analysis of tragic thought on many points, it is at this point that Lacoue-Labarthe departs from him – the point at which Lacoue-Labarthe perceives the tragic thought of Schelling and Hegel to be inseparable from the sacrificial foundation of a metaphysics whose 'philosophical' articulation is provided in the Aristotelian *cathartic* logic of tragedy.[2] In his well-known *Essay on the Tragic*, Szondi says:

> Since Aristotle, there has been a poetics of tragedy. Only since Schelling has there been a philosophy of the tragic. Composed as an instruction in writing drama, Aristotle's text strives to determine the elements of tragic art; its object is tragedy, not the idea of tragedy. Even when it goes beyond the concrete work of art and inquires into the origin and effect of tragedy, the *Poetics* remains empirical in its theory of the soul . . . the philosophy of the tragic rises like an island above Aristotle's powerful and monumental sphere of influence, one that knows neither national nor epochal borders. Begun by Schelling in a thoroughly non-programmatic fashion, the philosophy of the tragic runs through the Idealist and post-Idealist periods, always assuming a new form. (Szondi 2002: 1)

For Lacoue-Labarthe it is the Hölderlinian tragic thought that introduces caesuras into the speculative constitution of metaphysics, thereby stepping beyond, even if momentarily, the Aristotelian poetics of tragedy. This instance of the caesural occurrence brings into play, in a movement of 'regression', that which already haunts Plato 'under the name of mimesis and against which Plato fights with all of his philosophical determination until he finds a way of arresting it and fixing its concept' (Lacoue-Labarthe 1989: 227). The agonal play of *mimesis* is unpresentable and un-representable within the patience of the concept, as that which haunts the philosophical dream of mytho-poetic self-presence. It introduces an indiscernible fault line into the touch *touching* itself, into the poetological restitution of the Subject as 'sovereign referent'. It is the 'other' tragic dissonance without *Aufhebung* and without dialectical resolution, destabilising and destituting the speculative model of the tragic in advance, *always already*, even 'before' it comes into being. This other tragic dissonance, this destituting non-dialectical caesura of the speculative, this destabilising 'always already' of *difference*, desists the speculative. Not being founded upon the self-presence of *logos*, the tragic pain of mimesis desists the gathering act of the Subject in the intimacy of its work. For Lacoue-Labarthe, Hölderlin's *Grundstimmung* of mourning is this tragic pain which is irreducible to the speculative pain of the auto-engendering Subject of work. This other tragic pain is *worklessness*, a dispersal that resists any *cathartic* unification into the self-presence of the self-same. It is the tragic agony without *nomos* (law), without *principium* or *arché*, deprived of its sovereign referentiality. Such an agonal phenomenology of the tragic *singularises* each one of us in turn by exposing us to the undeniable, though invariably denied, manifestation of mortality *as* mortality.

The speculative Schelling?

How, then, is Schelling's philosophical problematisation of the tragic to be understood in this context? At the most manifest level, it is unproblematic and self-evident enough. Schelling is generally considered to be the initiator of a distinct philosophy of the tragic which is inseparably bound up with the emergence of the speculative-dialectical thought called 'German Idealism' at the end of eighteenth century. This philosophy of the tragic is to be distinguished from the 'poetics of tragedy'. The philosophy of the tragic is to determine to a great extent the course of the ('post-Idealist') philosophies to come, even if these philosophies will turn away from the foundational questions of Idealism in a fundamental manner, as is the case with Nietzsche and Kierkegaard. In sum, this is the argument Szondi puts forward in his *Essay on the Tragic*. According to this understanding, the position of Schelling in relation to the constitutive possibility of the speculative-dialectical discourse, in the context of Idealist investment of the tragic, is not very complicated. We must mark here that it is the very early Schelling that Szondi is concerned with. He does not take into account the fact that Schelling comes back once again to the problem of art, if not so much to the tragic, in his 1807 Munich lecture *On the Relationship of the Plastic Arts to Nature*.

According to Szondi's view just mentioned above, Schelling's tragic philosophy, far from radically destabilising or interrupting the speculative, is in fact the moment at which the speculative is instituted on a new foundation. This founding moment of the speculative has to be 'aesthetic', and more specifically, 'tragic'. From this perspective it is possible to argue that Schelling's philosophy can conveniently be seen, at least regarding the question of the deployment of the tragic, as the inaugural moment in the Hegelian dialectical determination of the tragic wherein the speculative thought-structure receives its most consummate articulation. This argument determines the Schellingian thought of the tragic as a consolidation of the law of the speculative rather than its destitution. The argument can be supported through textual analysis by showing that Schelling, unlike Hölderlin, never took the problematic of the tragic too seriously, given that his meditation on it as a problematic is limited to his early career, and that it almost disappears from his works soon after. One can thus argue that, although initiating the speculative model of tragedy, he will soon abandon this problematic in order to deal with the most idiosyncratic and eccentric questions of philosophy, such as the questions of evil, of mythology and of revelation, thereby inspiring later denunciation from the likes of Friedrich Engels who dismissed him as an 'obscurantist'. It is thus claimed that Schelling's philosophy of the tragic is nothing other than an initial formulation of the speculative-dialectical mechanism itself: the conversion of nothing into being, the work of *Aufhebung* and its hidden foundation on the rituals of sacrifice (where sacrifice does not go in vain but serves a 'meaning' and hence is rightly an 'investment'), the dialectical reduction of difference to the 'identity of identity and difference', and the tragic restitution of the Subject as the 'sovereign referent' of the epochal condition of modernity.

Despite his disagreement with Szondi on the question whether the philosophy of the tragic can indeed be separated from the sacrificial, ritualistic foundation of tragedy on the one hand, and, on the other, from the *cathartic* schema of dialectical resolution in terms of tragic effects, Lacoue-Labarthe does not contest the 'incontestable' place of the tragic in Schelling's thought as the institutive moment of his subsequent consolidation of the dialectical-speculative discourse. Schelling has remained understood as the constitutive moment of the speculative discourse of Idealism, a moment of inauguration that is to reach its consummation Hegel and its destitution in Hölderlin. It is the merit of Jean-François Courtine (1993: 157–76) and later Jason Wirth's (2003) pioneering efforts to have shown us, or to rather to have hinted at, in the Heideggerian manner of *Wink*, the other agonal tragic thought at work in the Schellingian discourse as a whole in its fundamental tonality. This manifestation of the agonal tragic is not just limited to the Schellingian meditation on the philosophy of art alone. Rather it infinitely contests the speculative form from within that form itself in such a manner as to expose us to that immeasurable excess of all forms, and of form as such. The mortal may participate in this divine excess only on the basis of undertaking a process of mortification of the will and of egotism, by taking the eccentric path of *über etwas hinaus* (going beyond by going through it), by an *indirection* or a detour of *Wink*. Since this participation cannot be thought as the *telos* of a dialectical process to be achieved by the labour of the concept, the immeasurable arrival arrives without destiny. It is what sends destiny to the mortal in advance (Wirth 2003: 131–53).

Here, in close proximity with Hölderlin's other tragic thought, a moment occurs in Schelling's work where a destitution of the speculative always already takes place, a moment which, henceforth assuming ever new names and ever new ways of beckoning, leads Schelling later to bring dissolution to the speculative from within its fundamental ground. It is enigmatic and paradoxical that this instance of arrival occurs at the moment of the birth of speculative theory itself, right at the moment of its consolidation and intensification. The tragic, thus, has never ceased to haunt the speculative from within its ground, even though the name 'tragic' itself disappears, at least in its manifest form, from Schelling's later works. This unthinkable tragic agony has *always already* been unworking the speculative from within, leading ultimately to its destitution it in a decisive manner, a destitution that at once introduces a caesura into the foundational ground of metaphysics in a manner never to be bridged again. Even though the name or the word itself disappears from the Schellingian discourse from the middle of his career, the tragic remains (un)working within that discourse under other names, each time newly minted and soon abandoned. Hence the *protean* nature of the Schellingian discourse, wherein each name is a substitution for what thought is incapable of naming but which it must always name with a renewed passion. For Schelling, 'philo-sophia' is the name for this *protean* passion of naming the unnameable, and a bearing witness to the ultimate failure of all nomination, denomination and *nomos*.

Schelling's thought thus shows the extreme difficulty of confronting what is truly tragic, that is to say, the unthinkable excess of all being, that which is the remainder of all thought, and which thereby can't be incorporated into the integrative work of law without suspending that law from within. Hence the necessity for Schelling constantly to renew the path of his thinking: philosophy becomes a finite thinking, withdrawing itself from the self-satisfaction of completion which the system imposes upon it, like an unnamed and unnameable categorical imperative. This withdrawal or errancy at work in Schelling from the inception of his philosophical career exercises an attraction upon his thinking like that toward a death which is undeniable and which *singularises* itself each time at each moment of its constitution. Schelling's energy of thought and protean passion is constantly solicited by death or madness, by an essential peril of being, though regulated each time anew. His is, thus, a philosophy of death, where death, instead of signifying a cessation of life and thinking occurring at the end of its possibility, rather opens thinking to the *taking place* of the unconditional which defines the tragic condition of the mortals *as* mortals. It is so because such a path of thinking, by an ineluctable law of necessity which is also its freedom, must follow the eccentric path of going through to go beyond, the *über etwas hinaus* wherein the immeasurable, the inscrutable abyss of freedom, the groundless exuberance of being, the generosity of the anarchic, is furtively glimpsed in the manner of a momentary co-incidence of opposites. In his great *System of Transcendental Idealism*, Schelling names this momentary co-incidence in the Leibnizian manner as a 'pre-established harmony'. Such coincidence is like an eternity of the transient that suspends the sacrificial foundation of the tragic-speculative thought structure. Even though occurring momentarily and in an incalculable manner, there now takes place the other tragic agony that does not follow the dialectical logic of conversion, negation and preservation into the higher speculative truth of self-presence and the tragic restitution of the Subject as the 'sovereign referent' of modernity.

This is the other divine mourning, never attained by means of the law of sacrifice. Here the speculative is at default, failing to invest itself through the sacrifice of a scapegoat, in order to recuperate the *pleroma* of its self-presence. The divine mourning, on the other hand, is the desert of an *abandonment* of all possession, of mastery and of appropriation. This other tragic agony is that of the mortal pulled apart or disjoined by the simultaneous claims of *singularisation* and universalisation,[3] which yet, in the desert of *abandonment*, suddenly coincide as the 'monstrous harmony' of freedom and necessity. The 'pre-established' harmony here is never pre-established in the determinate manner of the concept but in an 'absolute' sense, in excess of a causal connection between conditioned entities. Such tragic agony lacks the patience of dialectical resolution, of *Aufhebung* in the concept, of the conversion of the negative into the positive. The tragic *interrupts* the system by working and unworking within it at the same time, disjoining while joining the jointure of system at the same instance.

It is in this sense possible to say that the tragic is the innermost attunement, the *Grundstimmung*, of Schellingian thinking. At the beginning of his career, the tragic beckons toward that which is yet *to* come and yet which is *always already* there in his thought. Here the tragic always already beckons to the abyss of destitution at work at the moment of its institution, at the founding moment of the philosophical thinking called 'Idealism'. This is precisely because such thinking claims to think that which can't be thought without being exposed to the abyss of a tragic *belonging*-together of the highest discordance of freedom and necessity. This *belonging*-together of freedom and necessity is also their undeniable *discordance*, where freedom is absolutely in an agonal *polemos* with an absolute necessity. Like the sacred fire of Heraclites, it holds together life and death in equal measure and, when it manifests itself *as* itself, strikes us with mortality, like the fire-struck Semele suddenly exposed to the divine excess which is destructive to mortals. One can only participate in it by releasing one's egotism and claims to self-mastery to an infinite abandonment. Therein the tragic pain touches mortals with an infinite, divine mournfulness. The tragic figure of Oedipus is here no longer the one who embodies an acute speculative self-consciousness, a representative figure of the speculative-tragic embodying the integrative law of the cathartic dialectic. He is now the other Oedipus, withdrawn into the *singular* and *singularised* by mortality: the mournful Oedipus, renouncing the work of law and giving himself up to the wilderness of *abandonment*, to the non-condition of seeing without seeing. This monstrous Oedipus, blinded by an excessive vision and abandoned in the desert of the world, is not a 'figure' at all; above all, he is not the figure of the Subject, the speculative-specular Subject of onto-theological metaphysics. He is rather the other 'one', deprived of all the predicates that constitute the subject *as* Subject: the singular and solitary one, exposed to a mortality that does not in turn convert itself into the positive, the one who is *apart*, departing from all that constitutes the law of the city. Uprooted from all inhabitation and all denomination, this Oedipus is the errancy of law inside out.

The question here is: how could such an Oedipus occur at all in Schelling's tragic thought, given the supposedly 'incontestable' evidence that his early thought is modelled on the integrative logic of the speculative-dialectical thought structure that is, after all, 'onto-theologically' constituted? Is it possible to think the tragic outside of the model of the integrative logic of the speculative law, to think an agony that is not necessarily the intimate gathering of the speculative Subject, a tragic dissonance that does not have to be integrated into the vicious re-circulation of guilt and punishment?

Is it possible to think the tragic without the specular law of restitution, as irreducible to the integrating function of the law as such? If yes, then the idea of the tragic here should be able to release, beyond the vicious re-circulation of guilt and punishment, of fate and atonement, that which withdraws from all integration, in the manner of the *always already*, effecting a destitution of the law without assuming the dialectical resolution of opposites. These are difficult questions, and yet precisely therefore the questions that must now be asked, with the help of Schelling's tragic thought.

Blind Oedipus

Commentators on Schelling's philosophy of tragedy almost unanimously agree that he takes Oedipus to be the tragic figure par excellence. Oedipus is also the prime example for the Aristotelian cathartic poetics. This coincidence is not supposed to be fortuitous or accidental. Lacoue-Labarthe's reading of Schelling dwells on this coincidence, from which he infers the sacrificial, ritualistic, homeopathic or cathartic foundation of Schellingian tragic thought. Passing anonymously through Schelling's philosophy of the tragic, according to this dominant 'incontestable' interpretation, Oedipus bears the name of the Subject, the tragic-speculative restitution of the sovereign *principium*, the 'sovereign referent' of the *nomos* of metaphysics in its onto-theological constitution. The pathos of modern metaphysics, so we are told, is the Oedipal pathos of the Subject. The tragic poetics of this metaphysics is that of the diremption of the Subject through a necessary *apostasy* (*Abfall*) of suffering in order to reconfigure itself. It thereby wins immortality for itself at the very moment of succumbing to mortal punishment for the wrong which it unwittingly inflicts. Through the tragic pathos of guilt, suffering and punishment, the sovereign *nomos* of metaphysics de-configures and re-configures itself as the integrative law of tragic violence.

Who can contest this 'incontestable' proximity of Schellingian tragic thought to this work of the law of tragic violence? Does not the 'figure' of Oedipus provide the 'incontestable' evidence that what is at stake here is nothing other than the sacrificial foundation of tragic law itself? To answer that, it will be necessary to undertake an investigation, not only of what is at stake in Schelling's philosophy of the tragic, but of art as such. We should thereby be able to show how 'philosophy', thanks to its proximity to the poetic, enters into a constellation that marks the onto-theological foundation of metaphysics with an indelible fragility, with an inexorable insufficiency which will ultimately destitute the self-founding speculative thought from within, opening it up to caesuras unbridgeable through any conceivable cathartic process. The tragic will thus ultimately leave philosophy deprived of its 'sovereign referent'.

Has philosophy ever been able to dissociate itself, in its very condition of possibility, from this constitutive weakness, from such a destituting fragility, if not in intention then at least in the fundamental task that it gives itself, in the desire in which it moves, in the law by which it abides, in all the proliferating predicates in which it describes itself and knows itself to be itself? Would not the unnameable fragility of philosophy be that which will have made it a necessary task, to be renewed and given up again, precisely to be destituted so that we are kept open to that which is without law and without sovereignty, the un-predicative singular and the non-descript other time disjoined from itself? What other discourse is there, replacing whatever we call by the name 'philosophy', to envisage the tragic task of destituting the speculative of its 'sovereign referents'? Is not philosophy in itself, even when it does not explicitly call itself by the name 'tragic', *always already* tragic in its structural opening of itself to itself, where this very opening would be inseparable from an unspeakable *difference* always escaping the language of philosophy? An unheard of difference, an unthinkable caesura, irreducible to dialectical oppositions and sublation into the integrative fold of the law, may have already made philosophy 'tragic' and Oedipus blind, the Oedipus who sees now more lucidly than ever before this tragic coincidence of agonal difference.[4] Such is the blind Oedipus, wandering in the desert of the unthinkable – singular, apart, lonely.

Our task now is to show how this Oedipus finds himself at the threshold where destitution of the 'sovereign referent' takes place at the very moment of its institution, where the absolute is momentarily glimpsed as an incalculable passing, in a sudden co-incidence of the incommensurable, like a flickering light in the desert of abandonment at the limit of representation. In this glimpse or blink of an eye (*Augenblick* literally means 'blink of an eye'), there arrives at the scene of a tragic representation that immeasurable excess, exceeding all power of representation, that Schelling calls 'sublime'. The deployment of the tragic, at the very moment of its speculative investment, turns out to be the 'site' where something otherwise than the speculative return of presence takes place. The tragic here turns out to be the *spacing* of a sublime excess, giving us the world in intuition and withdrawing from the concept: a gift immeasurable and exuberant, which is the gift of the world itself.

But after such a detour, it is time to read Schelling himself.

Monstrous jointure of opposites

In what discursive context does Schelling deploy the tragic figure of Oedipus? Readers familiar with his works will know that Schelling first raises the problematic of the tragic in his 1795 epistolary essay called *Philosophical Letters on Dogmatism and Criticism*. It is the work of a twenty-year-old student. The importance and significance of its epistolary form has already been well commented upon (see Courtine 1993; Wirth 2003). What is attempted here is something different: to lay bare the fundamental philosophical context in which the question of the tragic, and consequently the 'figure' of Oedipus, emerge, and to hint at the *taking place* of a tragic *agonal difference* that is irreducible to the investment of speculative thought: *the taking place of the immeasurable, the de-figuring excess of the other*.

The task that Schelling sets himself in this essay is to think, in a fundamental manner, the agonal *belonging*-together of freedom and necessity, death and life, mortality and natality, finitude and the infinite. A careful reading of the Schelling's oeuvre in its entirety will reveal, despite the ever changing pathways of his thinking, that such a *belonging*-together is the fundamental trait of his thought as a whole. If what we are here calling the 'tragic' is nothing other than the unbearable agony of a difference *belonging*-together, whose discordant being-together is the undeniable truth, denied each time, then perhaps one can say that the tragic is the fundamental tonality of Schellingian thought. This is true despite the fact that the words 'tragic' and 'tragedy' virtually disappear from his work soon after 1804. One might say that the tragic is the *rhythmus* of the Schellingian music as such. And we know from both Emile Benveniste (1973) and Philippe Lacoue-Labarthe (1989), the sense of the word *rhythmus* is inseparable from caesuras, from intervals or interruptions, from a cision or moment of *cutting off* irreducible to the thought of a continuity whose image is that of the flow of a river.[5]

The tragic is the *rhythmus* of difference. Difference is an agonal *rhythmus*. One can say that the *rhythmus* is in itself *agonal*, and hence is tragic. What is 'expressed' in it is the agony of the disparate in its most tragic copulation: between the immeasurable, the excessive, the inexorable necessity on the one hand, and the equally undeniable 'nay' saying of a freedom, *rising each time in its very falling*, always in infinite contestation with the former. The *rhythmus* opens up a *space of play* between them, an *opening* or *spacing* of strife and agony, of mortification and immortality, without subsuming one to the other under a common denominator which will totalise their *belonging*-together in a universal unity. The *rhythmus* is the undecidable limit, the undecidable as limit (or the limit as undecidable), that holds together the disparate whose *belonging*-together can only be a momentary co-incidence, a sudden passing of the Absolute without remainder. Unlike the Hegelian deployment of the concept of limit, the limit here signifies less a determinate negation constitutive of the objectivity of the 'object' of knowledge than a *differentiation* that becomes indiscernible in the sudden eruption of an incalculable coincidence.

What Schelling attempts to think in this work, as also in all his other works under new names and on ever new pathways of thinking, is nothing other than this tragic *rhythmus* of freedom *and* necessity which in the aesthetic field is glimpsed in *aesthetic intuition* (best exemplified in tragedy as a poetic genre), and in philosophy as *intellectual intuition* (at least according to the early Schelling). While tragedy is the privileged site of the glimpse into the momentary passing of the absolute within the aesthetic field, the same agonal manifestation of the absolute is momentarily glimpsed in intellectual intuition in the philosophical *astonishment* at the generosity of an exuberant being, the un-representable excess of all that is thinkable under the sovereign law of the concept. Each in its singular manner is singularly *tragic* in its fundamental trait, and each in its own manner refuses to be integrated into the speculative mediation of *Aufhebung*. In his *System of Transcendental Idealism* of 1800, written five years after the *Philosophical Letters* and four years before his lectures on the *Philosophy of Art*, art is considered to be of paramount concern to the philosopher.[6] Schelling thinks of art as the privileged 'site' of disclosure, as the *spacing* of the 'everlasting revelation' of that 'supreme event' of the unexpected and un-expectable 'absolute concurrence' of what is in absolute *polemos*. Surprisingly, he calls this disclosure *phenomenon*, an utterly 'unaccountable', 'incomprehensible' and yet undeniable *taking place* of the unconditional *event*, eliciting from us astonishment (Schelling 1978: 223): the *taking place* of the infinite in the finite itself before and in excess of all predication, before and beyond the cognitive categorical grasp of entities. Both aesthetic intuition and intellectual intuition allow us a glimpse into this *taking place* of the unconditional, where the Absolute momentarily and unexpectedly *gleams* through as that which makes all *phenomenality* possible in advance, is a disclosure not of entities in the predicative-categorical manner of the subject-predicate co-relation (which sensory intuition discloses), but of the 'inapparent' itself. Being in excess of all denomination and withdrawing from the simple oppositions of the empirical and the ideal, both aesthetic intuition and intellectual intuition – each in its own manner – disclose for us the agonal *belonging*-together in the tragic *verbality* of *showing*. In that sense, the disclosure of art as such is a tragic disclosure, a *tragic phenomenology* of the unexpected event of a concurrence of the opposites.

Such an agonal manifestation of the opposites occurs at the limit of all representation, as an indiscernible *passing*, where this instance of occurring can only be, at the same time, the highest *partitioning of being*, an instantaneous occurrence without being fused into the synthetic mediation of the absolute concept. The question of the tragic thus occurs in the *Philosophical Letters on Dogmatism and Criticism* in the philosophical context of a discussion of freedom and necessity. The tragic *belonging*-together is denied, being un-representable to thought, when one form of thinking makes exclusive claims over the other, thereby elevating one particular claim into the status of an exclusive, universal and sovereign presence-at-hand. The result is what Schürmann (2003) calls 'tragic denial': not the denial of *this* or *that* but the denial of the tragic itself in its agonal manifestation of *belonging*-together without a common denomination. Schelling's essay traces this tragic denial, this reduction of the agonal coincidence of the opposites, through various philosophical systems, with special reference to the systems prevalent in his own time, namely, dogmatism and criticism.

The first letter of the *Philosophical Letters* begins with a critique of dogmatism for surrendering the living, irreducible, agonal strife of the mortal against the immeasurable to a 'quiet abandonment of oneself to the absolute object' (Schelling 1980: 157). The greatness of the sublime, which is the tragic par excellence, is here denied or is subsumed under the posited 'sovereign referent' of the moral God who is now supposed to fulfil his legislative function of guaranteeing the unity of the world. This is so in so far as the 'very ground' of the sublime consists in this 'struggle against the immeasurable' (157). In this quiet denial of the tragic strife, the moral God acts as the *nomothetic* (legislative) referent of the world. With this subsumption of God to a legislative function, as nothing other than the guarantor of a moral world-order, there arises 'ethics', that philosophical discipline of practical reason concerned with distinguishing the morally good from the morally bad. Schelling here subjects to a deconstructive reading the Kantian (or better, Kant-inspired) thetic positing of a 'sovereign referent' called 'the idea of a moral God', whose empty place – precisely by virtue of the emptiness of its 'site' – supports the legislative order of universal morality and the inexorable insistence of necessity. It thereby denies the other claim of the singular with its equal insistence of freedom in its forever 'nay' saying, its refusal to surrender to the immeasurable without the sublimity of strife.

Thus in this first letter itself Schelling reveals the aporia inherent in the dogmatist's insistence on 'practical reason' alone while all the time presupposing precisely that which it claims to exclude, namely, the work of 'theoretical reason'. The dogmatist's insistence is based upon a false claim of independence from 'theoretical reason', upon a denial of the tragic *jointure* of freedom and necessity. Schelling thus interrogates his interlocutor:

> For what *you* think when you speak of a merely *practical assumption*, frankly I cannot see. Your phrase cannot mean more than the acceptance of something as true. And that, like any other acceptance of a truth, is theoretical in form; in its foundation or matter, however, it is practical. Yet, it is precisely your complaint that theoretical reason is too narrow, too restricted, for an absolute causality. If so, from where can it receive the theoretical justification for accepting as true that assumption for which, as you say, your practical reason has given the ground; from where a new form broad enough for an absolute causality? (Schelling 1980: 159)

If the possibility of the 'sovereign referent' of the moral law is based upon the un-binding of practical reason from theoretical reason, then the institutive functionality of this moral God is *always already* haunted by the other insistence, contaminating in advance practical reason's quiet abandonment into the 'arms of the world' (Schelling 1980: 157). Each time the moral law seeks to formulate itself – and it must be formulated in language so as to elicit from us a normative obligation – it ineluctably assumes the form of a theoretical statement. This means that the reduction of the actuality of the divine to the legislative functionary of humanity, and to the guarantor of the unity of the world, is haunted by an irreducible, undeniable claim of the singular. And this haunting of the singular in turn will always return, like an ever recurring spectre, to the pure practical order of moral-objective necessity. The generous *actuality* of the divine, who is always this singular, refuses to be restricted to the function of being the administrator of the world. The divine refuses to align himself with the dogmatic legitimisation and legislative domestication of the world on a theological foundation. In excess of this nexus of moral-legislative functions, God is here not the 'sovereign referent' but rather the eternal foreigner, the eternal remainder of every moral distinction between good and bad, the irreducible groundless ground of the world.

Thus the dogmatists' attempt to elicit from us a normative obligation to their moral-legislative order ('surrender to the arms of the world without struggle!'), on the basis of their reduction of God to the guarantor of their world, ends up in a tragic denial of the sublime coincidence of the agonal difference between freedom and necessity. This is so in so far as the actuality of God itself refuses such denial. Being in excess of all predicates of the world and, as the irreducible remainder, the divine is an infinite *withdrawal* from the *potentia* (powers) that manifest themselves in the profane order of the world. Later in his fascinating 1810 private lecture at Stuttgart, Schelling meditates on this actuality of God as an unthinkable excess of generosity that never belongs to potentiality, and who as such cannot even be thought as 'being' but is over or beyond being (*Überseyn*). The moment this actuality of God is acknowledged, the dogmatist cannot begin with the thetic positing of the pure order of moral necessity, and at that very moment our obligation to the legislative ordering of the world also ceases. Therefore, dogmatism begins neither with pure practical thetic positing in its empty universality, nor with theoretical reason alone, but with existence (*Dasein*) itself. Such dogmatism must acknowledge the exuberance of the world whose unity is not guaranteed by a mere conceptual God, deprived of his generous actuality of *Dasein*. The other insistence contaminates, in advance, the dogmatic legitimising order of the moral law in such a way that the tragic agony of freedom and necessity itself remains inexorable. Despite the minimising operation in which dogmatism reduces the agonal manifestation of difference by eliciting our quiet surrender to the empty, formal order of universal necessity, this irreducible tragic strife of freedom and necessity remains operative all the while, albeit denied each time. The attempt to minimise the tragic strife between freedom and necessity does not really resolve the agony, because such 'quiet abandonment' into the arms of the world bears witness to the exuberance of the divine, whose *actuality* remains irreducible to the unity of the world. For Schelling, the divine in its singular ecstasy of existence is this extra-world of moral postulates, and this excess deprives the moral law of its ultimate character in each turn of the world.

The dogmatic insistence on the universal power of necessity hides from itself its innermost anxiety – an anxiety that accompanies any discourse of morality that would align itself with the legislative act of a norm-positing operation. It is the anxiety in the face of the immeasurable, the inexorable and the agonal. Its quick surrender into the 'arms of the world' forecloses the sublimity of the tragic-agonal manifestation of phenomena. In this 'tragic denial', the sovereignty of the legislative order restitutes itself. The sublime tragic strife is now reduced to a representable phenomenon within the given unified world present-at-hand whose unity is determined to be guaranteed by the moral God. The subject now subjects itself to the universal law of necessity that is applicable to all, to the order of generality where particulars are bound under the obligation to the *koinon* (common). It abandons itself to a quiet resignation, and gives up the nobility and sublimity of saying 'no' out of its groundless freedom. Schelling sees this conjunction of 'ethics' *and* 'legality' to be constitutive of the matrix of the juridico-political administration of the world. This ordering of the world legitimises the claim of the universal as an immeasurable 'objective' necessity, an anarchic power which now strikes the subject as 'fate' or 'destiny'. It comes with the terror of an imperative, with the power of command:

'surrender quietly to necessity, otherwise you are guilty of a crime and the fate of law (and the law of fate) will befall you inevitably'. Fate-struck, the singular is subsumed as a particular under a 'common' law which is supposed to expiate the crime by punishment. The law of this *nomothetic-tragic* that bases itself upon a logic of equivalences between the crime and punishment (the punishment must be equivalent to the magnitude of the crime committed) is now understood to have a significance beyond the aesthetic in the domains of the 'ethical' and the 'legal'.

Schelling sees in this dogmatic installation of the universal as objective necessity a unilateral act of subsumption by means of which the power of the law asserts itself. Schürmann calls this unilateral act of subsumption 'natality': the pure power of the institution and subsumption of mortality within the universality of the law. It is the power that institutes, through the violence of thetic positing, an order of totality where 'all' will find 'quiet abandonment' and their sense of being alive. The other attraction, that of mortality as impoverishment, and consequently the tragic-agonal matrix, is denied. There now arises the illusion, given by the *nomos* of necessity, of a pure life of founding and positing, of a quiet abandonment untouched by de-positing, destituting, unworking mortality. Here the power of the law renews itself by constantly equalising crime and punishment, in the work of fate that judges one guilty of a crime and in the same gesture punishes for this crime. The juridico-political nexus that dogmatism propagates, the nexus between the 'ethical' and the 'legal', constitutes itself by a fiction, by mysticism, by a fable or a deception. It invents the logic of an economy between the supposed crime and its punishment in order to minimise the agonal coincidence of freedom and necessity. It does this by one-sidedly emphasising an immeasurable necessity to which one must succumb, without sublimity, without struggle, without saying 'no'. As a reward for our succumbing in quiet resignation, dogmatism offers us the cheap prize, not of life as such, but of the feeling of merely being alive.[7] Thus the agonal coincidence of freedom and necessity exceeds that order wherein the logic of equivalences – of crime and punishment, between fate and guilt – legitimises the legal order.

This fable, this fiction of the juridico-political, is necessary for legitimising the dogmatist's restitution of a hegemonic sovereignty. The particular, having bought the illusion of pure life at the cost of sublimity, is now satisfied with the sovereign repose of life and prefers to 'abandon himself to the youthful world' rather than affirming a freedom that singularises him in a tragic struggle to the death:

> While the spectacle of the struggle presents man at the climax of his self-assertion, the quiet vision of that rest on the contrary finds him at the climax

of simply being alive; he abandons himself to the youthful world in order to quench his thirst for life and existence as such. To be, to be! is the cry that resounds within him; he would rather fall into the arms of the world than into the arms of death. (Schelling 1980: 157)

The law strikes the one who seeks life, who knows life in no other way than 'simply being alive'. This 'simply being alive' – what Benjamin calls 'mere life' (1986: 297) – is only possible when the tragic agonal *belonging-together* of life and death is already uncoupled by the violent act of the law. The dogmatic system, according to Schelling, achieves this by uncoupling practical reason from theoretical reason. Death is now deprived of its *eventive* character of jointure that inwardly constitutes and deconstitutes 'life' in a primordial manner. As a result, the one who is 'simply being alive' will never live a life of true greatness. The life of the one who is 'simply being alive' is only the site of the law, which neutralises the greatness, the sublimity and the tragic agony of life by condemning particular beings to a petrified life, a *life without life*. By uncoupling the agonal difference of life and death it thinks the one against the other, or one at a time, as the 'merely alive' or as the 'lifeless'. Against this, Schelling dreams of a tragic thought that would join the opposites in their very discordance: 'man ought to be neither lifeless nor merely alive. His activity is necessarily intent upon objects, but with equal necessity it returns into itself. The latter distinguishes him from the merely living being, the former from the lifeless' (Schelling 1980: 185). Because the law of fate strikes in equal measure both the lifeless and the merely alive without expiation, only when life appears as tragic does it radically open itself to a mode of being in which it is freed from the cages of the law and from the vicious circle of guilt and fate.

In a similar way, in the positing of a moral God, the exuberant and generous life of the divine is emptied out with a view to turning it into a 'sovereign referent' at the service of an objective juridico-moral order. The elevation of the figure of God into the universal guardian of the world-order at once deprives the life of the divine of its exuberance. The universal order of an objective, immeasurable necessity remains insufficient to measure the life of the divine, whose tragic sublimity consists of an *irreducible non-coincidence of life with mere law*. As a result, existence itself, as the site of the agonal *belonging*-together of freedom and necessity, *un-works* in advance any attempt to make the law at one with the will.

This last point is important for Schelling. The aporia of the law's relation to the will destitutes in advance the dogmatic attempt to think the world and life under the denomination of a representable world-unity and to think the singular as mere particular subsumable in the objective necessity of a juridico-moral order. There is something excessive about the 'will' that renders its conformity to the law, in 'quiet abandonment', impossible. One of Schelling's greatest contributions to philosophy lies here: *to think the will as irreducible to the choices exercised by a Subject*. Schelling interrogates his interlocutor once again:

> How can you be convinced that the will of that being is in conformity with this law? The shortest reply would be to say that that being is itself the creator of the moral law. However, this is against the spirit and the letter of your philosophy. Or, is this moral law simply to exist, as independent of any will? That puts us in the domain of fatalism. For a law that cannot be explained by anything that might exist independently of that law, a law that dominates the greatest power as well as the smallest – such a law has no sanction other than that of necessity. (Schelling 1980: 159–60)

If the conformism of will with the moral law is the grounding presupposition of the dogmatist's position, then dogmatism is *always already* self-refuted by this very grounding presupposition. This is because such a presupposition can present itself only as an unavoidable aporia of law. What is it that escapes, if not freedom itself, the other irresistible claim of mortality, the forever 'nay' saying of the singular, the destituting-undoing work of death, the desert and the solitude of the mortal?

In his 1800 *System of Transcendental Idealism* Schelling describes the co-relation of aesthetic intuition and intellectual intuition in the following terms: aesthetic intuition is intellectual intuition objectified. The aesthetic and intellectual intuition of the inward principle of beauty is the momentary coincidence of two opposite principles in *polemos*. The dogmatist's positing of a moral God at the service of the moral law forecloses the very possibility of such a glimpse into the momentary eruption of an agonal coincidence. With the idea of a moral God as the guardian of the moral order, the agonal manifestation of the world is taken away. The world now becomes a representable unity wherein the law presents itself in a sovereign manner, giving us the consolation of a quiet repose in the arms of the world. In such an order, everyone finds 'life' in the arms of the All. Such a life, subsumable to the law, is that of 'merely being alive'. It is pantheism in a simple sense, where the divine, as moral source, finds embodiment in the universal-objective order of history, now made absolute, deified and irresistible.

Schelling's deconstruction of the one-sided claims of the supposedly universal dogmatist position shows that the tragic is to be thought otherwise than in such a pantheistic theodicy of history. What is at stake here is other than the speculative Subject or the speculative object. *The apparition of the absolute in such an instantaneous coincidence of freedom and necessity is tragic because it marks the most painful intensification of a difference un-subsumable under the law of one-sided unity.* Such an instantaneous coincidence marks an abyss of a caesura that will render impossible the embodiment of the *theos* on the immanent plane of profane history. The tragic here turns out to be the most agonal de-legitimation of each and every hegemonic assertion of earthly sovereignty. For Schelling, as for Hölderlin, such a caesura presents itself in the most intense form of tragic presentation. We must now show how such hegemonic assertions of the power of the law deny the sublimity of the tragic caesura which, as caesural, makes possible the monstrous coincidence of freedom and necessity.

Mysticism of law and tragic denial

The criticism of the dogmatic order of the juridico-political will be incomplete if it remains satisfied with merely showing that the uncoupling of practical reason from theoretical reason is unachievable. The criticism that reveals the indemonstrability of a constituted order of moral law remains trapped in the aporia of the law itself. This is because such a mode of criticism, like dogmatism, remains one-sided in so far as it accepts the subject-object reduction of existence (*Dasein*) to either an object of knowledge or an idea of a moral postulate. Whether in dogmatism or in criticism, *existence as existence* does not appear in its true sublimity and tragic nobility, that is, in its irreducibility to the alternate determination of existence either as 'lifeless' or as 'merely being alive'. Schelling here tacitly distinguishes the singularity of existence in all its exuberance from the subject-object opposition between 'merely being alive' and the 'lifeless'. Where the tragic must manifest itself in its true sublimity, it must appear as *existence*, which is irreducibly singular, irreducible to the conceptual determination of theoretical reason and to the moral determination of it as subsumable under the universal, merely formal law of the objective. Only when criticism occurs at the level of *existence*, and itself assumes the task of existence in all its exuberance, can it reach a fruitful confrontation with dogmatism. Here dogmatism itself is elevated from a mere dogmatising tendency. Only then does it become possible for criticism to confront the mysticism of the law on a new basis. Schelling's juxtaposition of dogmatism and criticism is thus not posed at the merely theoretical level but as an *existential* confrontation with the tragic strife of freedom and necessity.

The maximising positing of the universal, objective power of necessity is, paradoxically, also a certain *ecstasy* of mysticism (*Schwärmerei*). There is, thus, an intriguing connection of the law with mysticism. The law mystifies, dupes and subsumes the particular under the universal form of necessity by injecting daily doses of sedatives, of false utopian dreams of a 'youthful world' of quietude. It is against this mysticism of the law that

Schelling poses the ontological problematic of the tragic relation of man to the world. Hence the problematic of the tragic can only be understood against the background of the highest ontological question, namely, the question regarding the 'riddle of the world': 'the question of how the absolute could come out of itself and oppose to itself a world?' (Schelling 1980: 173–4). Schelling's tragic thought responds to this highest ontological problematic in a manner that un-works the mysticism of the law and thereby beckons us, in a momentary glimpse, to the passing of the unconditional which is the sudden coincidence of the agonal strife of necessity and freedom.

This 'riddle of the world' is the meeting point for the *polemos* between the dogmatist and the critical philosopher: it is here that they clash with each together, and here that they (must) remain apart. It is here that the possibility of a true contestation with the mysticism of the law arises in a primordial ontological manner, in the mode of the question: how can the absolute or the unconditional at all be seen in relation to the world? In the text under discussion here, Schelling juxtaposes two responses to the above question: on the one hand, the dogmatic-pantheistic response that understands the divine on the basis of the world, and thereby legitimises in advance a certain theodicy of history; on the other hand, the equally one-sided response of criticism which asserts the unconditionality of an inscrutable freedom without necessity, on the basis of a forever rebellious 'nay' saying. In both responses Schelling perceives a twofold danger at work, accompanied by the 'tragic denial': on the one hand the danger of the legitimisation of an objective world-order on a theological foundation, where the mysticism of the law unleashes its horror; on the other hand the danger of a demonic freedom lacking the sober prose of justice. In a double reading, Schelling asks us not to give up the tragic double-bind of freedom and necessity, but to attend to the dangers arising from tragic denial:

> If it were really the destiny of our race to be tormented by the terrors of an invisible world, would it not be easier to tremble at the faintest notion of freedom, cowed by the superior power of that world, instead of going down fighting . . . The man who would obtain his existence in the supersensuous world by begging, will become the tormentor of humanity in this world, raging against himself and others. Power in this world will compensate him for the humiliation in that. Waking up from the delights of that world, he returns into this one to make it a hell. (Schelling 1980: 194)

Freedom, freed from its own necessity, turns demonic.[8] There is an arbitrariness that belongs to freedom as its inherent ontological possibility, hence the necessity, given by freedom to itself out of its *Abgrund*, of that justice which alone will make the demonic freedom bearable to us. Here

Schelling truly fights on many fronts against more than one adversary. One must constantly resist the reduction of existence to 'merely being alive', against the mysticism of the law that subsumes particulars (already no longer singular) under the empty, formal universality of objective necessity; on the other hand, one must also constantly regulate the danger of a demonic freedom that constantly threatens to degenerate into the most terrifying arbitrariness. The very source of life, when it seeks to actualise itself without regulation and without the measure of justice, turns against life itself and becomes the most devouring fire.

The question here cannot be that of a simple opposition or choice between dogmatism and criticism; it is rather one of thinking their ground in the unconditional *belonging*-together of freedom and necessity in the irreducibility of their strife. The tragic task of thinking and existing does not have to choose between the two, but has to think another task, the unconditional task of welcoming the incommensurable *difference* at play in the un-thinkable coincidence that *sets them apart* at the same time.

The enthusiasm of Spinoza

One of the profoundest insights that German Idealism has bequeathed to subsequent thinking, an insight whose initial articulation appears in this essay by Schelling, is that an unmediated access to the absolute is not only impossible but undesirable in itself, being destructive to the life of mortal. While it can be the very source of life when approached with the sober measure of justice, it turns demonic when it is approached in an unmediated manner, thereby unleashing the most unthinkable evil on the profane order. It is this measure of justice that, for Schelling, is exemplified by poetic works, most specifically Greek tragedy. Greek tragedy presents for us, within the limits of aesthetic representation, a measured and regulated participation in the unconditional which, precisely through this presentation never reaching closure, exposes us to that which is in excess of all representation. The question here is one of a regulated participation, by virtue of a sobriety given in the aesthetic mode of presentation, with the infinite, with the sublime and with the immeasurable excess, failing which either the 'horrors of ecstasy' (Schelling 1980: 189) are let loose or 'the terrors of the objective world' befall us.[9] But this is also the risk, the wager, that Greek tragedy assumes, for the limit is never fixed once and for all, and may at any incalculable moment be lifted, exposing us to the abyss without measure. In this risk lies the courage of the Greek people. It is in this that their sublimity consists: in refusing any quiet abandonment into the arms of the objective necessity of the universal power.

From this insight Schelling develops the possibility of a tragic thought that will come to constitute the fundamental attunement of his entire existence and philosophy. Later, his friends Hölderlin and Hegel, in their different ways and with their singular linguistic and existential gestures, will develop this tragic insight and make it their own. Readers of Hölderlin will know that we are here not very far from his tragic insistence on poetic measure, on the soberness of justice, on the cultivation of the formative drive so as not to fall into the demonic excess of the fiery passion. The tragic glimpse into the unconditional can proceed only by indirection, being exposed to an excess which is unbearable to finite beings, even to the grand tragic heroes of Greek tragedies. It is this excess that tragedy bears witness to by passing through the limit of aesthetic representation and opening to the un-representable and immeasurable event in the manner of a tragic double-bind: we must cultivate, which means we must regulate, what presents itself to us as the *agonal*. The entire deception that the mysticism of the law seduces us into is rooted in the belief in an unmediated access to the measureless divine excess. It is a deception that seduces even the noble and the great, for it promises them (though vainly) that they will thereby achieve the profoundest and highest existence, that is, unity with the divine excess, the attainment of an absolute beatitude in its unity with the absolute morality, achieved in a synthesis of their own existence with the absolute and with the world. They thereby forget that such a synthesis can only, at its best, be an infinite task, which does not present itself as a pure, unmediated participation in the absolute present-at-hand. Only as mediated through the sobriety of form and poetic measure does it allow us a glimpse into the passing of the unconditional which erupts incalculably and unforeseeably in the midst of existence.

It was this deception that led even a great philosopher like Spinoza to a certain mysticism of the law. At this point, with this reference to Spinoza, the Schellingian deconstructive reading reaches its utmost intensity. Since for Spinoza the task of participating in the divine excess cannot begin with a transition from the infinite to the finite, it can only be understood as a tendency of the finite toward the infinite, 'a perpetual striving to lose itself in the non-finite':

> In demanding that the subject lose itself in the absolute, [Spinoza] had demanded implicitly the identity of the subjective with the absolute causality. He had decided, practically, that the finite world is but a modification of the infinite; finite causality is merely a modification of infinite causality.
>
> That demand was to be fulfilled, not by the subject's own causality, but by a foreign causality in the subject. In other words, the demand was this: Annihilate yourself through absolute causality! Be absolutely passive towards absolute causality! (Schelling 1980: 178–9)

'Annihilate yourself through absolute causality!' – a far more profounder imperative than the dogmatising version: 'Quietly abandon yourself into arms of the world!' This is the ultimate fantastication of all mysticism, including the mysticism of the law. The 'sovereign referent' of all hegemony is this ultimate fantasy, the intellectual intuition eliciting obligation from us in the form of a moral demand: 'Annihilate yourself by submitting to the objective, ineluctable necessity without a struggle, without the sublimity of a tragic freedom. *The mysticism of the law denies the tragic by refusing the sober measure of justice.* Schelling, thus, addresses his interlocutor: 'here, my friend, we have the principle of all eccentric fantasy (*Schwärmerei*). Whenever such fantastication becomes a system, it arises from nothing but the objective intellectual intuition, from the fact that one would take the intuition of oneself for an intuition of an object outside of oneself, the intuition of the inner intellectual world for an intuition of a supersensuous world outside of oneself' (Schelling 1980: 182). In such fantastication, lacking a resistance in the objective, intuition never returns to itself: an abyss of intuition opens up, subsuming all singularity into particulars determined beforehand as mere modifications of the universal. The eternity of this abyss is not the eternity that suddenly erupts as the tragic temporality of the instantaneous breaking through of the absolute, but the abyss of eternity as a mere expansion without limit of a poetic form, without the measure of justice, without the determination of a halt, where everything that is singular is annihilated in a fantasmatic space of empty universality. Here, as Hegel says, is the absolute night in which all cows are black.

Against this eternity conceived as mere expansion, which is supposedly achieved in the mysticism of annihilation, against this eternity of the one embodying itself as omnipresent in the pantheistic mysticism of history whereby the coincidence of opposites is immediately reduced or annulled, Schelling evokes the tragic occurrence of eternity breaking through in an instance when freedom and necessity come to coincide with each other. While such a coincidence is the *telos* even of dogmatic mysticism, the tragic is denied the moment the unconditional is seen as a self-presence present-at-hand. What the dogmatic mysticism of the law cannot tolerate, what remains unthinkable for such *Schwärmerei*, is the agonal manifestation of freedom and necessity in their coincidence wherein alone lies the sublimity of their strife. Hence, the tragic agonal opening of freedom to necessity and vice versa is immediately subsumed under an 'ethical' universality in nexus with the legislative thetic positing, emphasising one over the other but never their irreducible agonal strife. The result is either a fanaticism close to a mysticism of sorts, or the arbitrariness of a demonic freedom. In either case, the tragic agonal coincidence of freedom and necessity remains unbearable. The irreducible and highest task of existence itself, that of thinking together freedom and necessity as the unconditional occurrence of the event, remains withdrawn from both. Thereby this task, *as* infinite, loses its task-character and is immediately included in the integrative fold of the law present-at-hand. The 'ethical' and 'legislative' nexus is in this manner protected from the unbearable agony of the tragic. The unbearable character of tragedy makes philosophy itself abandon itself 'to all the horrors of ecstasy (*Schwärmerei*)' (Schelling 1980: 189), to the fantastication of the ethical and legislative nexus, to the arbitrariness of a demonic freedom which one does not know how to regulate. In either case, what remains unthinkable is freedom in its unconditional manifestation coinciding with the highest manifestation of necessity. Not being able to bear this contradiction in coupling, mortals take shelter in hypostatising 'one' over the 'other' (the subject over the object or vice versa) to such a degree that the horrors of evil break through on earth and the unregulated violence of power is unleashed.

This is why Schelling does not, strictly speaking, support one system over the other, criticism or dogmatism. The moment one system is considered to be the only system possible, the ethico-legislative fantastication takes place, and the potentiality of its violence is immediately present before us. Long before Hegel formulated his system, the following remark by Schelling already alerts us to the danger that lies in this desire of the system and prefigures the eventual Schellingian deconstruction of the Hegelian onto-theological constitution of metaphysics:

> The genuine philosopher has never felt himself to be greater than when he has beheld an infinity of knowledge. The whole sublimity of his science has consisted in just this, that it would never be complete. He would become unbearable to himself the moment he came to believe that he had completed his system. That very moment he would cease to be *creator* and would be degraded to an instrument of his own creature. How much more unbearable he would find the thought if somebody else should want to force such fetters on him. (Schelling 1980: 172)

This remark belongs to the very essay that is considered to be the first articulation of the tragic-speculative matrix constitutive of the movement of German Idealism. An attentive reading of Schelling reveals that his tragic thought has already departed from the integrative logic of speculative thought at the very moment of its institution. At this instituting moment, the tragic presents itself as the instance of its destitution. Therefore the tragic task of philosophical *presentation* (*Darstellung*) can only be an infinite one. It is the infinite presentation of destitution, opening to an excess that does not present itself as present-at-hand. One can say here, with Lacoue-Labarthe, that the tragic is the 'desistance' of the speculative. The legislative, the *nomothetic* desire of speculative fantastication, is momentarily disrupted, delegitimised, *deferred* and *differed* by the caesura opened up by the tragic. The tragic as the infinite task, never realised in the immanence of self-presence, desists the *Schwärmerei* of all conditioned politics and totalising ethics. In Schellingian tragic thought one can hear the resonance of that sober measure of justice that must invigilate, almost like an insomniac, to ensure that the irresistible power of the law, with its objective drive of thetic positing, does not end up assuming the name of justice without remainder. Without the measure of justice, the power of violence is immediately legitimised, and the annihilation of oneself in the supposed name of objective necessity is immediately sanctioned. The mystic is enthusiastic in annihilating himself because he treats the intellectual intuition that takes place in the open site of freedom and necessity as taking place in the absolute object itself, the infinite, the 'there'. This 'there' is the exceptional site of the opening of the law, which encloses us in turn in the pure ecstasy and madness of annihilation. The deeper ground of Spinoza's mysticism lies here.

The Schellingian tragic task is thus an infinite task of existence, beyond the 'capacity' or 'power' of the mortal subject. It must rather occur as an event beyond the subject-object matrix of speculative metaphysics, an event which incalculably manifests itself as passing through form to go beyond form, as a paradoxical excess, indemonstrable either in the propositional form of theoretical reason or in the moral postulates of an empty universality. It strikes existence itself *as* existence in its utter nakedness, exposing the ground of the naked being to the sublimity of an inexorable strife.

Unbearable agony

How could Greek reason bear the contradictions of Greek tragedy? This is the question Schelling asks in the last letter of his *Philosophical Letters on Dogmatism and Criticism*. The passage deserves to be quoted in full:

> A mortal, destined by fate to become a malefactor and himself fighting *against* this fate, is nevertheless appallingly punished for the crime, although it was the deed of destiny! The ground of this contradiction, that which made this contradiction bearable, lay deeper than one would seek it. It lay in the context between human freedom and the power of the objective world in which the mortal must succumb *necessarily*, if that power is absolutely superior, if it is fate. And yet he must be *punished* for succumbing because he did not succumb *without a struggle*. That the malefactor who succumbed

under the power of fate was punished, this tragic fate was the recognition of human freedom; it was the *honor* due to freedom. Greek tragedy honoured human freedom, letting its hero *fight* against the superior power of fate. In order not to go beyond the limits of art, the tragedy had to let him succumb. Nevertheless, in order to make restitution for this humiliation of human freedom extorted by art, it had to let him *atone* even for the crime committed by fate. As long as he is still *free*, he holds out against the power of destiny. As soon as he succumbs he ceases to be free. Succumbing, he still accuses fate for the loss of his freedom. Even Greek tragedy could not reconcile freedom and failure. Only a being *deprived* of freedom could succumb under fate. It was a *sublime* thought, to suffer punishment willingly even for an inevitable crime, and so to prove one's freedom by the very loss of this freedom, and to go down with the declaration of free will. (Schelling 1980: 192–3)

This is one of the most cited paragraphs in the Schellingian oeuvre, and it is most often cited to support the view that Schelling is here describing the tragic matrix of speculative thought. According to this view, it is incontestable that Schelling here offers the first speculative-cathartic determination of the tragic (inheriting thereby the Aristotelian legacy of a poetological metaphysics of tragedy), or the first tragic determination of the speculative logic: the conversion of the negative into the positive through the representation of a dialectical contradiction to be resolved by synthesis. The task for us here is to show that, at this institutive moment of the speculative, the tragic has already introduced a fissure that will remain open throughout Schelling's works, tearing the fabric of his thought in the most painful manner. The wound of a painful *rhythmus* will, henceforth, never cease to haunt, like a spectre, the Schellingian music to come. This wounding *rhythmus* is the event of speech in the mode of the declaration of a refusal, a refusal that singularises the tragic hero at the very instance of his death. This singular event of language, so bound up with mortality *as* mortality, escapes the speculative logic of *Aufhebung*. As a result, the Schellingian speculative system could never achieve completion. It is as if the more his thinking struggles with the inexorable pain of its fissure, the more it must abandon the *nomothetic* desire of systematic completion. That fissure occurs precisely at that moment when the declaration of free will transforms the language of the law into *an event of declaring*. This happens at the instance of death – the death of Oedipus which singularises him, and thus releases him from the bond of the law.

The tragic hero here does not sacrifice himself in order to be reconciled, voluntarily, with the *nomothetic* order of the law, nor does he constitute himself as a sovereign exceptional being, as the Subject that returns to itself as a master of free will. Here both the situation and the response to it take place in a different context to that of the mysticism of the law.

The tragic hero is atoned, not in the sense of being reconciled with the objective order of necessity in the form of fate, but rather in the sense that he *declares at all*, even at the last moment of his existence, the event of language that affirms a freedom to say 'no'. It is this *declaring* itself, this event of *uttering* itself (even when one is silent), that *singularises* him at this indiscernible instance of the *taking place* of death. The tragic hero Oedipus is *singularised* by his mortality, and duly abandons the juridico-legislative nexus of the world. 'The riddle of the world' is here neither minimised nor made bearable by the event of declaring in the mode of a refusal, but is rather intensified to the utmost instance of an occurrence in which the life of the tragic being touches death. At this indiscernible moment, he is neither a particular subsumable under the universal order of the law nor is he assuming the name of universality himself as the 'sovereign referent'. He loses his entitative, attributive, predicative modes of being in the world and is exposed to the event of being breaking in on him as this singular being through whom the language of declaration *passes* as an event. Here free will is not something that belongs to the tragic hero as a property; it is that through which the singular being occurs to Oedipus as event.

Precisely at this indiscernible instance where his life touches death, Oedipus is exposed to the truth that the necessity of freedom is freedom's ownmost necessity itself. This is why he does not succumb without a struggle, for the arrival of this tragic truth does not lie so much in a victory for him or in a victory for fate, but is rather this adamant event of *declaring* itself, exceeding the predicative structure of the world. To declare this truth, one does not have to succumb; to declare it is not to be reconciled to the law as an external necessity imposed as fate. 'As soon as he succumbs he ceases to be free. Succumbing, he still accuses fate for the loss of his freedom. *Even Greek tragedy could not reconcile freedom and failure*' (Schelling 1980: 192–3, italics mine). The instance of atonement releases the tragic being from the vicious guilt-context of the law,[10] the law that incorporates and denominates each one of us as a 'criminal'. The recognition that the necessity of freedom is its own necessity out of its groundless ground is the unconditional, sublime gift of releasement. But this is not a merely negative result. It occurs out of the originary affirmation of the absolute beatitude. The arrival of beatitude passes through that desert wherein all the predicates of the law, all the normative referents, undergo *kenosis*. The coincidence of freedom and necessity is not the subsumption of particulars under the cathartic law of *Aufhebung* but remains agonal for as long as the *declaring* resounds.

What Schelling attempts to do here is think the tragic coincidence of agonal opposites without following the logic of subsumption. Oedipus rejects even the reward or consolation of happiness. Abandoned to the desert of the world, he is not even rewarded with atonement as a consolation. For him, the gift of tragic knowledge lies in the fact that he declares his refusal *at all*. This refusal is the instance of *kenosis* that empties out the predicates of the law. Or better, the *kenosis* is this instance itself, this instance of the *taking place* of mortality that singularises Oedipus as outside the law. It manifests itself as the mortality to Oedipus.[11] Here Oedipus is not a Subject assuming his freedom on the basis of a capacity to declare his non-subjugation to the objective necessity of the law. He is rather this *instance* itself, the instance of an agonal coincidence of freedom and necessity. By virtue of this, Oedipus is *Dasein*, an *existence*, neither mere practical reason nor theoretical reason, neither object nor subject, but existence as *ex-sistence*: the instance of excess, the generosity of actuality or exuberant being, which is also the utter impoverishment and nakedness of a tragic confrontation that empties out the given predicates of the world. This instance of mortality and mortification releases Oedipus from the originary guilt-context of fate and opens him to the desert of that beatitude with which virtue unites itself.

This is why Schelling's Oedipus rejects happiness. He leaves behind the realm of profane happiness to enter into the severity of the desert wherein alone absolute beatitude coincides with virtue. This virtue is not the morality that forms a nexus with the legislative desire of the political, just as the absolute beatitude of the desert is not the happiness realised in the conditional realm of pragmatic politics. Influenced by Meister Eckhart's notion of *Gelazenheit*, Schelling affirms here the mortification of all egoism and abandons even the claims of happiness and morality. Here is the profoundest moment in his tragic thought:

> Morality itself cannot be the highest, it can be only an approximation of the absolute state, only a striving for absolute freedom which no longer departs from any law, yet which also does not know any law but the unalterable, eternal law of its own essence. If it is to be thought of as morally possible, happiness can be thought of only as an approximation to a beatitude which no longer differs from morality and which therefore can no longer be a *reward* of virtue. As long as we still believe in a rewarding happiness we also presuppose that happiness and morality, sensuality and reason are conflicting principles. But we *ought* not to do this. That conflict ought to cease, absolutely.
>
> Happiness is a state of passivity: the happier we are, the more passive we keep ourselves toward the objective world. The freer we become, and the more closely we approach reasonableness, the less we need happiness, that is, a beatitude which we owe not to ourselves but to luck. The purer our concepts of happiness become, and the more we gradually separate from them whatever is contributed by exterior objects and by sense gratification, the more closely happiness approaches morality and ceases to be happiness. (Schelling 1980: 183)

This beautiful passage demands our careful attention. Beatitude in the true sense of the term is not a reward for virtue. It is neither to be called 'happiness' nor can it be the consolation or consolidation of the law. The absolute beatitude is rather the absolute desolation bereft of all consolation, the instance of the event breaking into mortality and touching the highest intensity of life. The desert of singularity wherein the absolute may arrive incalculably is this monstrous juxtaposition of what *belongs-together*. This *coming* together of the opposites does not allow itself to be thought in terms of a higher unity of dialectical synthesis, as the *Aufhebung* of their opposition, but is the instance of death *taking place*. Their coming together is death itself, which does not in turn convert itself into the third, the synthesising positivity of the Subject. The tragic being, abandoned to the desert of the absolute beatitude, must therefore reject the ecstasy of the mysticism of the law with horror. It must abandon all the rewards of the law, all the consolations of happiness, every consolation by means of which one quietly abandons oneself into the arms of the world. In the desert of abandonment, one must abandon even God.

The instance of death

In his 1804 lecture on the *Philosophy of Art*, written almost a decade after the *Philosophical Letters*, Schelling returns to these questions once again. Taking the example of Niobe, whom he takes to be the archetype of sculpture, Schelling now treats this juxtaposition of the opposites and their coming together as the very characteristic of life in its true profundity and greatness:

> All life is based on the joining of something infinite in itself with something finite, and life as such appears only in the juxtaposition or opposition of these two. Wherever its highest or absolute unity is, we also find, viewed relatively, death, and yet for just that reason also the highest degree of life. Since it is indeed the task of sculpture to portray that highest unity, then the absolute life of which it shows reflections already appears in and for itself – also compared with the appearance itself – as death. In Niobe, however, art itself has uttered this mystery by portraying the highest beauty in death. Furthermore it allows that *particular* peace – the one inhering only within the divine nature itself and completely unattainable to mortals – to be gained in death itself, as if to suggest that the transition to the highest life of beauty, at least as far as that which is mortal is concerned, must appear as death. (Schelling 1989: 197–8)

The highest intensity of life is not attained by Niobe out of her capacity or potential for being 'human' or being 'Subject', whereby the subject would return to itself as itself. Niobe is not a master of the originary agonal difference. The occurrence of the highest intensity of life is rather the gift of death, an impossible gift in excess of all the possibilities and capabilities of mortals. This gift *joins* itself to life like an excess which, while potentially there all along, does not occur everywhere and at all times. Only at the utmost intensification of time, which is also the highest intensification of difference *as* difference, does the excessive gift occur incalculably. It is the highest task of art through aesthetic intuition, and of philosophical thinking through intellectual intuition, to *beckon* toward this indifference that is the coming together of agonal differences in their apartness.

Hegel's remark on Schelling in his *Phenomenology of Spirit* is therefore misguided: indifference is not the dark night in which all cows are black. Schellingian indifference is not an absence of difference; nor is it a dialectical subsumption of differences within the unity of synthesis. What Schelling here attempts to think is rather the unconditional *coming together*, the *jointure*, of agonal differences that is mortality, and to think the excessive gift of an absolute beatitude without the consolidation of the law. This gift cannot be thought within any system except as the *event of existence*, as *Dasein* in its innermost finitude. *Dasein* itself is nothing other than this tragic-agonal *jointure* of infinite and finite, life and death, eternity and time. This *jointure* is haunted by its fundamental dissonance, by a tragic discordance that arrives like death arrives to life. In his later readings of both Schelling and Anaximander, Heidegger (1985, 1980a) attempts to think this jointure in terms of *Ereignis*, the event of appropriation at the limit of Occidental metaphysics. He thus understands this *Ereignis* as the *tragic* manifestation of an agonal difference, as a *belonging*-together that gives itself by way of withdrawal in each of its epochal manifestations. Here, Being *that* gives itself is a giving; or rather, it gives nothing other than itself. Being giving itself to us and *coming* to us as *presencing* is *Ereignis*, the event that brings together concealment and unconcealment in their discordance. The early Schelling thinks the *jointure* of freedom and necessity in their highest discordance as an unconditional event that erupts and passes away. Being in excess of the concept and its categorical grasp, this unconditional arising and passing of coincidence can only be thought as a tautology of intuition. The early Schelling names this non-empirical intuition as intellectual intuition: *intuition intuiting* itself, intuition *giving* itself to itself. Such is the tautology of absolute freedom. At the highest instance of its manifestation, freedom gives itself the law which, as otherwise than 'this' or 'that' law, is *the law without law*, the law that does not found the ethico-legislative nexus and does not give itself up to the mysticism of surrender. The inscrutable groundlessness of freedom itself coinciding with the highest necessity is a tautology. Before it all predication ceases because it comes before all predicates, as an actuality without potentiality.

Such a tragic thought is the infinite task of thinking that we call philosophy. That it is a *task* and not an achievement or accomplishment already discloses the finitude of all thinking. Finitude de-links us in advance (while linking us all the while) from our obligations to the constituted order of the law. This de-linking or un-binding in respect of the law is the highest task of thinking freedom. Freedom is understood here not just in the negative and privative sense as *freedom from*, but in a sense that is far more 'originary' (without 'origin'): as the structural opening of the world *as such*. It is as if an agonal difference, the strife of the discordant, the infinite contestation of the formless from within form, without dialectical resolution, makes possible in advance all (de)phenomenalisation as such. Speaking in the name of *Aletheia*, the later Heidegger will think such a paradoxical phenomenology in its primordial and true sense as the 'phenomenology of the inapparent' (Heidegger 2003b: 79–80). In this primordial sense, phenomenology is essentially tragic. Such a tragic dissonance would mean, then, nothing other than the event of *phenomenalising* itself. The inapparent here is not a speculative potentiality passing over, while being sublated or converted into what is called 'being' or 'actuality', but that which, while passing over, does not *phenomenalise* itself without leaving a remainder, without a withdrawal from all constituted phenomenality. It thereby shelters the event of *phenomenality* from the constituted order of what has already manifested itself as present-at-hand. The inapparent freedom, in excess over the integrative law of the manifest-constituted order, gives us the gift of *phenomenality* as such. By de-linking us from the integrative violence of the manifest law, it leaves or rather abandons the law, without subsuming us, in the manner of an obligation or sacrifice, in the constituted order of politics. The event of freedom is the appropriating-expropriating agony of *phenomenality* on the basis of which alone can there be any 'politics' or 'ethics' at all. If the task of thinking is 'to linger on the conditions in which one is living', 'provided that the essential fragility of the sovereign referents becomes evident to it' (Schürmann 2003: 3), then Schelling's tragic philosophy remains for us an indispensable moment in the conversation to come – that we might linger on the conditions in which we live, without the consolations that the 'sovereign referent' of the world would provide.

Notes

1. On the question of sacrifice in relation to the metaphysical ground of community, see Jean-Luc Nancy's important essay on Bataille, 'The Unsacrificeable' (2003: 51–77).
2. Lacoue-Labarthe writes: 'My ambition is simply to show that the so-called philosophy of the tragic remains in reality (though certainly in a subjacent manner) a theory of the tragic effect (thus presupposing the *Poetics* of Aristotle), and that it is *only* the persistent silence which this philosophy maintains in regard to its affiliation that allows it to set itself up, over and above the Aristotelian mimetology and theory of catharsis, as the finally unveiled truth of the "tragic phenomenon"' (Lacoue-Labarthe 1989: 215).
3. Thus 'Antigone ends up broken, not exactly by disparate laws but – as we shall see – *singularized under one law, through a withdrawal toward the other*. The tragic condition inserts one into a constituted phenomenality, and yet wrenches one from this through an undeniable (but hubristically denied) allegiance to an other' (Schürmann 2003: 3–4).
4. Heidegger writes of this Oedipus, quoting Hölderlin: 'In his poem "In Lieblicher Bläue Blühet . . .", Hölderlin wrote keen-sightedly, "perhaps King Oedipus has an eye too many". This eye too many is the fundamental condition for all great questioning and knowledge and also their only metaphysical ground' (Heidegger 1999: 107).
5. Similarly Heidegger writes of rhythm, 'Rhythm, *rhusmos*, does not mean flux and flowing, but rather form. Rhythm is what is at rest, what forms the movement of dance and song and thus lets it rest within itself. Rhythm bestows rest' (Heidegger 1982: 149).
6. 'If aesthetic intuition is merely transcendental intuition become objective, it is self-evident that art is at once the only true and eternal organ and document of philosophy, which ever and again continues to speak to us of what philosophy cannot depict in external form, namely, the unconscious element in acting and producing, and its original identity with the conscious. Art is paramount to the philosopher, precisely because it opens to him, as it were, the holy of holies, where burns in eternal and original unity, as if in a single flame, that which in nature and history is rent asunder, and in life and action, no less than in thought, must forever fly apart' (Schelling 1978: 231).
7. Walter Benjamin's following remark illuminates this problem with a peculiar intensity here: 'mythical violence is bloody power over mere life for its own sake' (Benjamin 1986: 297).
8. In his 1797 essay called 'Treatise Explicatory of the Idealism in the Science of Knowledge', Schelling writes: 'Everything about man has the character of freedom. Fundamentally, man is a being that inanimate nature has released from its guardianship and thereby entrusted to the fortunes of his own (internally conflicting) forces. His fundamental continuity is one of *danger*, forever recurring and forever to be mastered anew, a danger that man seeks by his own impulse and from which he saves himself anew' (Schelling 1994a: 94).
9. 'As long as man remains in the realm of nature he is *master* of nature, in the most proper sense of the word, just as he can be *master* of himself. He assigns to the objective world its definite limits beyond which it may not go. In *representing* the object to himself, in giving it form and consistency, he masters it. He has nothing to fear, for he himself has set limits to it. But as soon as he does away with these limits, as soon as the object is no longer representable, that is, as soon as he himself has strayed beyond the limit of representation, he finds himself lost. The terrors of the objective world befall him. He has done away with its bounds: how shall he now subdue it? He can no longer give distinct form to the boundless object. It is indistinctly present to his mind. Where shall he bind it, where seize it, where put limits to its excessive power?' (Schelling 1980: 193).
10. In his essay 'Fate and Character', Benjamin writes: 'Law condemns, not to punishment but to guilt. Fate is the guilt context of the living' (Benjamin 1986: 308).

11. Quoting Hölderlin, the same lines that Heidegger quotes, Schürmann says: 'the excess of a nocturnal knowledge in daylight, which defined the tragic hero (Oedipus, blinded, "has perhaps an eye too many . . . to live is death, and death is also a life") has become our own excess. We owe it to the *Kenosis*, to the emptying out of normative representations' (Schürmann 2003: 4).

Bibliography

Adorno, Theodor (1987) *Negative Dialectics*, trans. E. B. Ashton, New York: Continuum.
Angelus Silesius (1986) *Cherubinic Wanderer*, trans. Maria Shrady, Mahwah, NJ: Paulist Press.
Balthasar, Hans Urs von (1992) *The Theology of Karl Barth*, trans. Edward T. Oakes, San Francisco: Ignatius Press.
Barth, Karl (1975) *Church Dogmatics, I/1*, Edinburgh: T & T Clark.
Bataille, Georges (1997) 'Hegel, Death and Sacrifice' in *The Bataille Reader*, ed. Fred Botting and Scott Wilson, Oxford: Blackwell Publishers, pp. 279–95.
Benjamin, Walter (1998) *The Origin of the German Tragic Drama*, trans. John Osborne, New York: Verso.
Benjamin, Walter (1986) *Reflections*, ed. Peter Demetz, New York: Schocken Press.
Benjamin, Walter (1985) 'Theses on the Philosophy of History' in *Illuminations*, ed. with an Introduction by Hannah Arendt, trans. Harry Zohn, New York: Schocken Books, pp. 245–55.
Bensussan, Gérard (2007) *Marx le Sortant*, Paris: Hermann.
Bensussan, Gérard (2006) 'Mythe et Commencement: Heidegger, Schelling' in *Heidegger: La Danger et la Promesse*, ed. Gérard Bensussan and Joseph Cohen, Paris: Klime, pp. 323–42.
Benveniste, Emile (1973) *Problems in General Linguistics*, trans. Mary Elizabeth Meek, Coral Gables: University of Miami Press.
Bloch, Ernst (2009) *Atheism in Christianity: The Religion of the Exodus and the Kingdom*, trans. Peter Thomson, London: Verso.
Bloch, Ernst (2000) *The Spirit of Utopia*, trans. Anthony Nassar, Stanford: Stanford University Press.
Bloch, Ernst (1995) *The Principle of Hope*, vol. 1, trans. Neville Plaice, Stephen Plaice and Paul Knight, Cambridge, MA: MIT Press.
Blumenberg, Hans (1985) *The Legitimacy of the Modern Age*, trans. Robert Wallace, Cambridge, MA: The MIT Press.
Breton, Stanislas (2011) *A Radical Philosophy of Saint Paul*, trans. Joseph N. Ballan with an Introduction by Ward Blanton, New York: Columbia University Press.
Brown, Robert F. (1977) *The Later Philosophy of Schelling: The Influence of Böhme in the Works of 1809–1815*, London: Associated University Press.
Cattin, Emmanuel (2012) *Sérénité: Eckhart, Schelling, Heidegger*, Paris: Vrin.

Chrétien, Jean-Louis (2002) *The Unforgettable and the Unhoped For*, trans. J. Bloechl, New York: Fordham University Press.
Courtine, Jean-François (1993/1988) 'Tragedy and Sublimity: The Speculative Interpretation of *Oedipus Rex* on the Threshold of German Idealism' in *Of the Sublime: Presence in Question*, trans. Jeffrey S. Librett, Albany: State University of New York Press, pp. 157–76.
Courtine, Jean-François (1974) 'Schelling et l'achèvement de la métaphysique de la subjecti(vi)té', *Les Études Philosophique*, 4, pp. 147–70.
Deleuze, Gilles (1994) *Difference and Repetition*, trans. Paul Patton, London: The Athlone Press.
Derrida, Jacques (2006) *Politics of Friendship*, trans. George Collins, London and New York: Verso.
Derrida, Jacques (2002) 'Force of Law: The Mystical Foundation of Authority' in *Acts of Religion*, ed. Gil Anidjar, New York and London: Routledge, pp. 228–98.
Derrida, Jacques (1998) *Archive Fever: A Freudian Impression*, trans. Eric Prenowitz, Chicago: University of Chicago Press.
Derrida, Jacques (1996) 'By Force of Mourning', trans. Pascale Ann Brault and Michael Naas, *Critical Inquiry*, vol. 22, no. 2, pp. 171–92.
Derrida, Jacques (1995) *On the Name*, trans. David Wood, John P. Leavey and Ian McLeod, Stanford: Stanford University Press.
Derrida, Jacques (1994) *Of Grammatology*, trans. Gayatri Spivak, Delhi: Motilal Banarasidass, Indian Edition.
Derrida, Jacques (1980) 'Violence and Metaphysics' in *Writing and Difference*, trans. Alan Bass, London: Routledge Classics, pp. 97–192.
Engels, Frederick (1841) 'Schelling on Hegel' in *Telegraph fur Deutschland*, Nos. 207/208; online source: http://marxists.architexturez.net/archive/marx/works/1841/anti-schelling (accessed 6 August 2014).
Frank, Manfred (1975) *Der Unendliche Mangel an Sein: Schellings Hegelkritik und die Anfange der Marxschen Dialektik*, Frankfurt: Suhrkamp.
Fóti, Veronique (2006) *Epochal Discordance: Hölderlin's Philosophy of Tragedy*, Albany: State University of New York Press.
Habermas, Jürgen (2004) 'Dialectical Idealism in Transition to Materialism: Schelling's Idea of a Contraction of God and its Consequences for the Philosophy of History' in *The New Schelling*, ed. Judith Norman and Alistair Welchman, London and New York: Bloomsbury Academic, pp. 43–89.
Habermas, Jürgen (1985) 'Ernst Bloch: A Marxist Schelling' in *Philosophical-Political Profiles*, trans. Frederick G. Lawrence, Cambridge, MA and London, pp. 61–78.
Habermas, Jürgen (1954) *Das Absolute und das Geschichte: Von der Zwiespältigkeit in Schellings Denken*, Bonn University, PhD dissertation.
Hegel, G. W. F. (1998) *Phenomenology of Spirit*, trans. A. V. Miller, Delhi: Motilal Benarasidass, Indian edition.
Hegel, G. W. F. (1975) *Logic*, trans. William Wallace with a Foreword by J. N. Findley, Oxford: Clarendon Press.
Hegel, G. W. F. (1900) *Lectures on the Philosophy of History*, trans. J. Sibree, London: G. Bells & Sons.
Heidegger, Martin (2014) *Hölderlin's Hymns "Germania' and 'The Rhine'*, trans. William McNeill and Julia Ireland, Bloomington: Indiana University Press.
Heidegger, Martin (2003a) *The End of Philosophy*, trans. Joan Stambaugh, Chicago: University of Chicago Press.
Heidegger, Martin (2003b) *Four Seminars*, trans. Andrew Mitchell and Francois Raffoul, Bloomington: Indiana University Press.
Heidegger, Martin (2002) *Identity and Difference*, trans. Joan Stambaugh, Chicago: University of Chicago Press.

Heidegger, Martin (2001) 'The Origin of the Work of Art' in *Poetry, Language, Thought*, trans. Albert Hofstadter, New York: Harper Collins, pp. 15–86.
Heidegger, Martin (1999) *An Introduction to Metaphysics*, trans. Ralph Manheim, Delhi: Motilal Benarasidass, Indian edition.
Heidegger, Martin (1998) 'On the Question of Being' in *Pathmarks*, ed. William McNeill, Cambridge: Cambridge University Press, pp. 291–322.
Heidegger, Martin (1996) *The Principle of Reason*, trans. Reginald Lily, Bloomington and Indianapolis: Indiana University Press.
Heidegger, Martin (1995) *Aristotle's Metaphysics Θ 1–3: On the Essence and Actuality of Force*, trans. Walter Brogan and Peter Warneck, Bloomington and Indianapolis: Indiana University Press.
Heidegger, Martin (1985) *Schelling's Treatise on the Essence of Human Freedom*, trans. Joan Stambaugh, Athens: Ohio University Press.
Heidegger, Martin (1982) *On the Way to Language*, trans. Peter D. Hertz, New York: Harper Collins.
Heidegger, Martin (1980a) 'Der Spruch des Anaximander' in *Holzwege*, Frankfurt am Main: Vittoria Klostermann.
Heidegger, Martin (1980b, 'Hölderlins Hymnen "Germanien" und "Der Rhein"' in *Gesamtausgabe*, vol. 39, Frankfurt: Vittorio Klostermann.
Heidegger, Martin (1977) *The Question Concerning Technology and Other Essays*, trans. William Lovitt, New York: Harper & Row Publishers.
Heidegger, Martin (1962) *Being and Time*, trans. J. Macquarrie and E. Robinson, New York: Harper & Row.
Hölderlin, Friedrich (1998) *Selected Poems and Fragments*, trans. M. Hamburger, Penguin Classics.
Hölderlin, Friedrich (1988a) 'Judgment and Being' in *Essays and Letters on Theory*, trans. Thomas Pfau, Albany: State University of New York Press, pp. 37–8.
Hölderlin, Friedrich (1988b) 'Becoming in Dissolution' in *Essays and Letters on Theory*, trans. Thomas Pfau, Albany: State University of New York Press, pp. 96–100.
Hölderlin, Friedrich (1966) *Poems and Fragments*, trans. Michael Hamburger, London: Routledge and Kegan Paul.
Hühn, Lore (2014) 'A Philosophical Dialogue Between Heidegger and Schelling', trans. David Carus, *Comparative and Continental Philosophy*, vol. 6, no. 1, pp. 16–34.
Husserl, Edmund (1954) *Die Krisis der Europaeischen Wissenschaften und die Traszendentale Phaenomenologie*, The Hague: Martinus Nijhoff.
Johnson, Keith L. (2010) *Karl Barth and the Analogia Entis*, London and New York: T & T Clark.
Kant, Immanuel (1993) *Critique of Pure Reason*, ed. Vasilis Politis, London: Everyman Library.
Kierkegaard, Søren (2004) *Training in Christianity*, trans. Walter Lowrie, New York: Vintage Books.
Kierkegaard, Søren (1968) *Attack upon Christendom*, trans. Walter Lowrie, Princeton: Princeton University Press.
Kierkegaard, Søren (1957) *The Concept of Dread*, trans. Walter Lowie, Princeton: Princeton University Press.
Lacoue-Labarthe, Philippe (1989) 'The Caesura of the Speculative' in *Typography*, ed. Christopher Fynsk, London and Cambridge, MA: Harvard University Press, pp. 208–35.
Lévinas, Emmanuel (1969) *Totality and Infinity*, trans. Alphonso Lingis, Pittsburgh: Duquesne University Press.
Löwith, Karl (1991) *From Hegel to Nietzsche: The Revolution in Nineteenth-Century Thought*, trans. David E. Green, New York: Columbia University Press.
Löwith, Karl (1957) *The Meaning of History: The Theological Implication of the Philosophy of History*, Chicago: Chicago University Press.

McGrath, Sean (2012) *The Dark Ground of Spirit: Schelling and the Unconscious*, New York: Routledge.
Nancy, Jean-Luc (2003) 'The Unsacrificeable' in *A Finite Thinking*, trans. Simon Sparks, Stanford: Stanford University Press, pp. 51–77.
Nancy, Jean-Luc (1993a) *The Birth to Presence*, trans. Brian Holmes et al., Stanford: Stanford University Press.
Nancy, Jean-Luc (1993b) *The Experience of Freedom*, trans. B. McDonald, Stanford: Stanford University Press.
Nancy, Jean-Luc (1991) *The Inoperative Community*, ed. Peter Connor, Minneapolis: University of Minnesota Press.
Nietzsche, Friedrich (2005) *The Anti-Christ, Ecce Homo, Twilight of the Idols, and Other Writings*, trans. Judith Norman, Cambridge: Cambridge University Press.
Nietzsche, Friedrich (1997, 'On the Uses and Disadvantages of History for Life' in *Untimely Meditations*, trans. R. J. Hollingdale, Cambridge: Cambridge University Press, pp. 57–124.
Peterson, Erik (2011) *Monotheism as a Political Problem: A Contribution to the History of Political Theology in the Roman Empire in Theological Tractates*, trans. Michael J. Hollerich, Stanford: Stanford University Press, pp. 68–105.
Przywara, Erich (2013) *Analogia Entis: Metaphysics: Original Structure and Universal Rhythm*, trans. John R. Betz and David Bentley Hart, Cambridge, MA: Wm. B. Eerdmans.
Rosenzweig, Franz (2004) *The Star of Redemption*, trans. Barbara E. Galli, Madison: Wisconsin University Press.
Rosenzweig, Franz (2000) 'The New Thinking' in *Philosophical and Theological Writings*, trans. Paul W. Franks and Michael Morgan, (Indianapolis and Cambridge: Hackett.
Schelling, F. W. J. von (2010) *Philosophy and Religion*, trans. Klaus Ottmann, Putnam: Spring Publications.
Schelling, F. W. J. von (2007a) *The Grounding of Positive Philosophy*, trans. Bruce Matthews, Albany: State University of New York Press.
Schelling, F. W. J. von (2007b) *Historical-Critical Introduction to the Philosophy of Mythology*, trans. Mason Richey and Markus Zisselsberger, Albany: State University of New York Press.
Schelling, F. W. J. von (2002) *Clara: or, On Nature's Connection to the Spirit World*, trans. Fiona Steinkamp, Albany: State University of New York Press.
Schelling, F. W. J. von (2000) *The Ages of the World*, trans. Jason Wirth, Albany: State University of New York Press.
Schelling, F. W. J. von (1994a) *Idealism and the Endgame of Theory*, trans. Thomas Pfau, Albany: State University of New York Press.
Schelling, F. W. J. von (1994b) *On The History of Modern Philosophy*, trans. Andrew Bowie, Cambridge: Cambridge University Press.
Schelling, F. W. J. von (1992) *Philosophical Inquiries into the Nature of Human Freedom*, trans. James Guttmann, La Salle: Open Court.
Schelling, F. W. J. von (1990) 'On the Source of the Eternal Truths', trans. Edward A. Beach, *The Owl of Minerva*, vol. 22, no. 1, pp. 55–67.
Schelling, F. W. J. von (1989) *The Philosophy of Art*, trans. Douglas W. Stott, Minneapolis: University of Minnesota Press.
Schelling, F. W. J. von (1984) *Bruno, or On the Natural and the Divine Principle of Things*, trans. Michael G. Vater, Albany: State University of New York Press.
Schelling, F. W. J. von (1980) 'Philosophical Letters on Dogmatism and Criticism' in *The Unconditional in Human Knowledge: Four Early Essays*, trans. Fritz Marti, Associated University Press, pp. 156–218.
Schelling, F. W. J. von (1978) *System of Transcendental Idealism*, trans. Peter Heath, Charlottesville: University Press of Virginia.
Schelling, F. W. J. von (1975) 'Brief über den Tod Carolines vom 2. Oktober, 1809',

ed. Johann Ludwig Döderlein, *Kleine kommentierte Texte I*, Stuttgart-Bad Constantt: Fromann-Holzboog.
Schelling, F. W. J. von, *Philosophie der Offenbarung*, from Paulus Nachschrift, trans. Michael Vater, unpublished.
Schelling, F. W. J. von (1856–61) *Sämtliche Werke*, ed. K. F. A. Schelling, Stuttgart: J. G. Cotta'scher Verlag.
Schmitt, Carl (2008) *Political Theology II: The Myth of the Closure of any Political Theology*, trans. Michael Hoelzl and Graham Ward, Cambridge: Polity Press.
Schmitt, Carl (2005) *Political Theology: Four Chapters on the Concept of Sovereignty*, trans. George Schwab with foreword by Tracy B. Strong, Chicago: Chicago University Press.
Schmitt, Carl (1996) *Roman Catholicism and Political Form*, trans. G. L. Ulmen, New York: Greenwood Press.
Scholem, Gershom (1995) *Major Trends in Jewish Mysticism*, Foreword by Robert Alter, New York: Schocken Books.
Schürmann, Reiner (1978) *Meister Eckhart: Mystic and Philosopher*, Bloomington: Indiana University Press.
Schürmann, Reiner (2003) *Broken Hegemonies*, trans. Reginald Lilly, Bloomington: Indiana University Press.
Schürmann, Reiner (1986) *Heidegger on Being and Acting: From Principles to Anarchy*, trans. Christine-Marie Gros, Bloomington: Indiana University Press.
Steinkamp, Fiona (2002) 'General Introduction' to F. W. J. von Schelling, *Clara*, Albany: State University of New York Press, pp. vii–xxxviii.
Steinkamp, Fiona (2005) 'Eternity and Time: Lévinas Returns to Schelling' in *Schelling Now: Contemporary Readings*, ed. Jason Wirth, Indiana and Bloomington: Indiana University Press, pp. 207–22.
Szondi, Peter (2002) *An Essay on the Tragic*, trans. Paul Fleming, Stanford: Stanford University Press.
Taubes, Jacob (2013) *To Carl Schmitt: Letters and Reflections*, trans. Keith Tribe, with an Introduction by Mike Grimshaw, New York: Columbia University Press.
Taubes, Jacob (2010) *From Cult to Culture: Fragments toward a Critique of Historical Reason*, ed. Charlotte Elisheva Fonrobert, Stanford: Stanford University Press.
Taubes, Jacob (2009) *Occidental Eschatology*, trans. David Ratmoko, Stanford: Stanford University Press.
Taubes, Jacob (2003) *The Political Theology of Paul*, trans. Dana Hollander, Stanford: University Press.
Tillich, Paul (1975a) *The Construction of the History of Religion in Schelling's Positive Philosophy: Its Presuppositions and Principles*, London: Associated University Press.
Tillich, Paul (1975b) *Mysticism and Guilt Consciousness in Schelling's Philosophical Development*, London: Bucknell University Press.
Wirth, Jason (2003) *The Conspiracy of Life: Meditations on Schelling and His Time*, Albany: State University of New York Press.
Wirth, Jason (2000) 'Translator's Introduction' in *The Ages of the World*, Albany: State University of New York Press, pp. vii–xxxii.

Name Index

Adorno, Theodor, 158
Anaximander, 241
Anselm, 84
Aristotle, 14, 43, 47, 50–8, 69, 102, 123

Baader, Franz, 100, 141, 169
Balthasar, Hans Urs von, 130
Barth, Karl, 130
Bataille, Georges, 213
Benjamin, Walter, 23, 37, 54, 93–4, 109, 115–16, 118, 120, 133, 142–3, 145–7, 169, 178
Bensussan, Gérard, 8, 11, 25
Benveniste, Emile, 222
Blanchot, Maurice, 13
Bloch, Ernst, 19, 23, 28–9, 31, 60–1, 87, 93, 139
Böhme, Jacob, 20–1, 34, 54, 80, 83, 100, 113, 139, 141, 194, 199
Breton, Stanislas, 88

Cattin, Emmanuel, 14
Chrétien, Jean-Louis, 168
Cortés, Donoso, 92
Courtine, Jean-François, 217

de Bonald, 92
de Maistre, 92
Deleuze, Gilles, 22, 200–1
Derrida, Jacques, 63
Descartes, René, 64–8, 84

Eckhart, Meister, 14, 21, 24, 26, 34, 49, 54, 116, 138, 149–54, 192–3, 196, 197, 239
Engels, Friedrich, 216

Fichte, J. G., 108
Fóti, Veronique, 213
Frank, Manfred, 28

Habermas, Jürgen, 23, 28
Hamann, Johann Georg, 16, 139, 141
Hegel, G. W. F., 5–7, 10, 16, 18, 19, 22, 24, 30–4, 37, 41, 43, 47, 53, 56, 58–60, 63–6, 68–70, 73–5, 78, 80, 83–4, 87, 91–8, 104, 108, 111–12, 119, 138, 144, 172–3, 179, 191, 194, 199, 200, 216, 233–5
Heidegger, Martin, 3–5, 7–8, 12–13, 24–7, 32, 46, 48, 56, 59, 77, 86, 144, 147, 160–1, 166, 170, 177–8, 201, 214, 241–2
Heraclitus, 49
Hölderlin, Friedrich, 8–9, 15, 24, 26, 35, 38, 42, 101, 103, 144, 160, 169, 213–14, 216–17, 230, 233
Hühn, Lore, 25
Husserl, Edmund, 99

Jacobi, Friedrich Heinrich, 16–18, 44, 62–3, 105, 107–8, 207
Johnson, Keith, 130

Kant, Immanuel, 16, 30, 33, 43, 64, 77, 85, 87, 98, 100, 108, 174, 179

Kierkegaard, Søren, 16–17, 19–20, 22–4, 27–8, 31, 36–7, 56, 64–5, 74, 77, 87, 91, 94, 98, 118, 123, 139, 195, 207, 215

Lacoue-Labarthe, Philippe, 213, 236
Leibniz, G. W., 84
Lévinas, Emmanuel, 21
Löwith, Karl, 64, 90, 95–6

McGrath, Sean, 29
Marx, Karl, 11, 19, 20, 22–4, 31, 64–5, 74, 195, 207

Nancy, Jean-Luc, 161
Nietzsche, Friedrich, 9, 14, 20, 24–5, 29, 96, 105, 134, 195, 215

Oedipus, 219, 221–2, 237–9

Peterson, Erik, 130
Plato, 49–50, 136, 183, 192–3
Plotinus, 194
Plutarch, 102, 123
Przywara, Erich, 130

Rosenzweig, Franz, 27, 28, 31, 37, 94, 139, 141, 165

St Paul, 115
Schelling, F. W. J. von, 5, 7, 8–39, 41–50, 52–6, 58–63, 63–6, 68–74, 76–7, 79, 81–6, 93–4, 97–112, 114–16, 118–20, 123, 126, 135–44, 146–50, 152–4, 160–1, 165–74, 176–8, 180–90, 192–203, 206–7, 218, 232–9, 241
Schmitt, Carl, 30, 90–3, 133
Scholem, Gershom, 22
Schürmann, Reiner, 1–5, 8–9, 13–15, 17, 30, 32, 34, 48, 149, 153–4, 224, 227
Silesius, Angelus, 149–50
Socrates, 43, 49–50
Spinoza, Baruch, 18, 233, 236
Szondi, Peter, 216

Taubes, Jacob, 23, 61, 90, 92–3
Tillich, Paul, 28

Voltaire, 90

Wirth, Jason, 217

Subject Index

abandonment, 4, 7, 11–12, 14, 26, 60, 116, 135–6, 218
Abfall, 18, 167
Abgrund, 46, 48, 109, 126, 153–4, 168
   of freedom, 72, 80
   Absolute, 18, 21, 194–7
   beatitude, 198, 202, 238–40
   blessedness of the, 184
   concept, 118, 199
      freedom, 200
      Spirit, 66
Absonderung, 118
abyss, 196
   of freedom, 94
Achtung, 179
actuality, 3, 6, 10, 12, 26–7, 42, 59, 61, 63, 67, 74, 94, 98, 110, 168, 175–8, 181, 199, 211, 225–6
   absolute *prius* of, 80
   divine, 71
   immemorial, 78
   marks kenosis, 49
   without potentiality, 4–6, 8, 10, 14–15, 20–1, 25–6, 29, 34, 36–7, 45–7, 49, 52–4, 58–60, 63, 86, 100, 104, 111, 196
actus, 51–2
Adamic naming, 178
aesthetic intuition, 223, 229
aesthetic objects, 182
anamnesis, 99
an-arché, 4, 17, 24, 30, 76
antinomianism, 93
antinomic eschatological schema, 191
antinomic releasing, 190
apartness, 193
apostasy, 18, 95
arché, 1–3, 6–8, 14, 17, 21, 27, 29–30, 35, 43, 46, 48, 52, 54–6, 67, 72, 76–7, 79, 86, 92, 94, 102, 108–9, 132, 196, 215
   of God functions, 68
   originary, 105–6
   violence, 65
archetypes, 186, 188–9
astonishment, 49, 223
atheism, 62, 74, 139
attunement, 15
Aufhebung, 24, 76, 100–1, 124, 215, 240
   cathartic law of, 238
   dialectical movement of, 64
   speculative mediation of, 223
Augenblick, 86
Ausgang, 11, 24, 27
autarchic, 6, 52, 132–3
autochthony, 52
   autochthonic, 6, 132–3
   autochthonous foundation, 166
   autochthony and autarchy, 38, 105, 150, 202

beatific life, 147, 154
beatitude, 37–8, 46, 60, 139, 174, 177, 184, 193, 197
   eschaton of, 191
beauty, 115–16, 182–3, 185

SUBJECT INDEX

beginning, 2, 7, 25, 62, 70, 133, 135
   immemorial, 84
   of judgement, 58
   of nature, beginningless, 119
Begriff, 132
being, 3, 46–9, 51–2, 58, 62–3, 68–9, 84, 91, 104, 106, 108, 113, 114–15, 117, 132, 139, 163, 166, 177, 182, 199–201, 241
   above, 110
   actuality, 15
   being-in-God, 169
   beyond being, 24, 50, 77, 85, 92
   blind being, 73
   double traits of, 35
   dunamis of, 97
   exuberance of, 72, 75
   human, 159
   infinite capacity of, 65
   infinite potentiality of, 78
   jointure of, 202
   negative determination of, 80
   non-potentiality of, 7
   phenomenal modes of, 194
   as potency, 111
beings, 8, 67, 175
   arché of, 21
   contiguity of, 141, 144–5, 201, 203
   jointure and disjointure of, 200–1
   nexus of, 22
   ontological nexus of, 200
   tragic-mythic unity of, 188
   univocity of, 26
belonging, 160, 222
belonging together, 1–2, 4–5, 35–6, 42, 45, 47, 56, 167–8, 170, 175, 186, 205, 219, 223, 240–1
   of freedom, 232
   tragic, 224
   tragic agonal, 228
Bio, 159, 162
blessedness, 184
   blessed life, 124
breaking
   absolute event of, 205
   away, 194
   through, 98

caesura, 8, 9–12, 24, 26–7, 35–6, 44, 46, 86, 161, 188, 199, 203, 214, 221, 230
   of the speculative, 101
catharsis, 219, 221
celestial bodies, 183–4, 197–8
Christendom, 27, 65
Christianity, 23, 57, 81, 87, 95–6, 188, 190–1, 207
   Christian deconstruction, 19
   Christian eschatological deconstruction, 74
   Christian speculative mystic, 14
   Christian theological hegemony, 79
   Creation theology of, 196
   Gnosticism of early, 189
Church, 18–19, 23–4, 136, 191, 204–7
cision, 190, 201
clotting, 201
cognitive, 182–3
concept, 5, 70, 76, 84, 183–5
   dialectical movement of the, 137
   labour of the, 99
   sovereign law of the, 223
consciousness, 103, 121–2
constellation, 182–3
continuity, 188
   and emanation, 199
contradiction, 100–2, 107, 112, 123
   dialectical other of, 103
   ecstatic, 104
cosmic potency and logos, 82
creation, 141
   creationism, 193
   and emanation, 194
   nexus of, 177

darkness, 70, 116, 187–9, 199–200
Dasein, 48
death, 13, 136, 148, 227, 238
   instance of, 237, 240
   living, 150
   and mourning, 143
   philosophy of, 218
decision, 9–10, 33–4, 36, 59, 91, 101, 106–18, 126, 161–2
deconstruction, 1, 17
destiny, 46, 134
   destinal, 32
   destination, 211
destitution, 15, 44, 221
   and dissolution, 19
destruction and annihilation, 176
dialectic, 5–6, 18, 72, 76, 120
   agonal structure, 96
   immanent movement, 25
   knowledge, 137
   mediation, 18, 22
   movement, 6, 69

dialectic (*cont.*)
　opposition, 124: and subsumption, 211
　resolution, 218, 242: cathartic schema of, 216
　speculative, 6, 44, 216
différance, 66, 94
difference, 9, 22, 59, 102, 161, 165, 200, 212, 221–2, 236
　as difference, 56, 76, 86–7
　differentiating forces, 167
　differentiation, 74, 223
　eschatological intensification of the, 92
　eschatological principle of, 61
　qualitative, 108
différend, 1–2, 5, 10, 13, 16, 18, 35, 56, 101
　tragic, 36, 38, 46, 58, 100
disappropriation, 164
discontinuity, 20, 23, 31, 172, 201
discordance, tragic, 25
discourse, 5, 213
disfigured, 161
dis-installed, 160
disinvestment, 93
disjoined, 160, 200
disjunction, 106, 193
dissolution, 19, 211
distance, 20, 22, 33, 50, 104–5, 119, 193, 196
diversion, 166
divine, 15, 21–2, 123, 141, 174, 198
　being, 199
　de-cision, 22
　excess, 12, 138
　freedom, 108, 111, 113–14, 118, 120, 122, 125, 181
　as holy, 27
　im-potentia, 126
　justice, 17
　life, 104, 124, 199, 201: and nature, 202
　lordship, 57
　Love, 147
　monarchy, 54
　or mortal, 102
　mourning, 15, 147, 154
　nature, 109, 110, 115, 117, 202
　power, 119
　violence, 87
dogmatism, 224, 226, 230
　and criticism, 18, 224
　dogmatic mysticism, 234

dominion and violence, 199
duality, 124, 153
　in unity and unity in duality, 126
dunamis, 32, 95
dynámei ón, 52

ecstasy, 25, 160
　contradiction, 102, 105–6
　of eternity, 8
　of reason, 28
egotism, 197, 217
emanation, philosophical system of, 106
empiricism, 73, 78
　empirical-historical approach, 182
energéia ón, 52
energy and power, 172
Enlightenment, 16, 195
epochal, 19, 22, 30, 32
　breaks, 93, 168, 173, 214
　closure, 2, 10, 25–6, 31, 39, 41–2, 48
Ereignis, 25, 46
eschatological, 32, 59, 82, 95, 97, 138, 190, 195
　Augenblick, 87
　Christian deconstruction, 27
　energeia, 64
　energy, 31, 194
　excess, 184
　index, 122
　messianic, 125; suspension of potentiality, 71
　moment, 86; *nunc stans*, 120
eschatology, 8, 17, 30, 32, 39, 92, 95, 190
　Political, 20
　scandal of, 15
　without sovereignty, 92
eschaton, 4, 7, 15, 18, 29, 32, 34, 36, 46, 48, 59, 85, 90, 97–8, 121–2, 206
eternity, 106, 120–1, 123, 184, 234
　eternal past, 168
　eternal return, 111
ethics, 141
　ethical, 192, 198
　ethical and legislative nexus, 235
　ethical rights, 163
　and legality, 226
event, 7, 9, 13, 20, 22, 27, 29, 32, 36, 46, 63, 70, 79, 102, 106, 161, 163, 165
　of cutting, 71; and decision, 78, 102; of un-pre-thinkable decision, 109
　of the future anterior, 5
　messianic, 98
　of time, 59

SUBJECT INDEX | 255

evil, 18, 96, 124, 162, 164, 175, 194–5
  actuality of, 108
  and good, 162, 174
  possibility and actuality of, 205
  possibility of, 175–6
  potential, 113
  radical, 148, 162, 201
  terrible melancholy of, 181
exception without sovereignty, 30
excess, 160
existence, 27, 43, 48, 163–4, 168, 198
  and actuality, 200
  and freedom, 78
exodus, traditional eschatological idea of, 28

falling away, 196
fanatical mysticism, 100
fantasm, 9, 17, 27, 69
  categorical, 48, 65; without, 52
  fantastication, 234
fate and guilt, 227
  fatalism and nihilism, 62
  fateless, 46, 134
finitude, 78, 177, 242
  finite and the infinite, 187
  and mortality, 164
  and negativity, 175, 199
force, 124, 159, 167, 170, 174–5
fragility, 1, 11, 17, 23, 36
freedom, 5, 18, 21, 24, 26, 31, 35, 42, 44, 46, 57, 60–1, 70, 77–8, 82–4, 94–5, 97–8, 102, 106, 108–10, 114, 117, 119–21, 126, 148, 158–62, 163–5, 168–70, 179–80, 184, 196, 218
  anarchy of, 32, 73
  divine, 108
  exuberant energy of, 67
  gentle, 108, 114, 124
  groundless, 22, 68, 162, 200–1, 226
  human, 72
  and the law, 82, 116
  and necessity, 35, 38, 42, 109, 224, 227, 230, 234–6, 238: belonging-together of, 222, 228; tragic jointure of, 225
  non-being of, 199
  philosophical problematic of, 158
  philosophy of, 35, 199
  tragic rhythmus of, 223

Geist, 30
Gelassenheit, 4, 12, 14, 116, 239

German Idealism, 14, 19, 35, 214, 232, 235
gift, 25–6, 36, 58–9, 144, 173, 178, 184, 197, 204, 238
  of beatitude, 193, 197
  of being, 154
  divine, 139
  of freedom, 148
Gnosticism, 54, 60–1, 102, 109
  atheistic interruption, 28
  Kabbalistic mode, 21
God, 14, 17, 20–1, 48–9, 52–6, 62, 66–71, 80, 83–4, 86–7, 98, 101–2, 104, 107–9, 110–11, 113–14, 119, 136, 152–4, 169, 171–2, 179–80, 196, 200–5
  as actuality, 117
  moral, 226
Godhead, 14, 22, 54, 104, 107–8, 110, 113, 119, 138, 150, 152–4, 196
Good, 50
  and evil, 58, 161, 196
Greek antiquity, 186
Greek blessedness, symbolic-mythic space of, 188
Greek conception of history, 90
Greek mythology, 186–7
Greek (Occidental) thought, 51
Greek philosopher, 14
Greek religion, 188
Greek symbolic order, 190
Greek tragedy, 186, 232–3, 236
ground and existence, 105
Grundstimmung, 219
guilt and punishment, 220

happiness, 179, 239
harmony, 71, 136, 184
having-being, 112
hegemony, 1–4, 17, 48, 54, 68, 78–9, 133, 211
  hegemonic fantasm, 9–10, 13–14, 16, 27, 49, 55, 57–8, 101, 148, 184
  hegemonic order, 6, 18
  hegemonic sovereignty, 227
  modern, 64–6, 133
hepoménos ón, 52–3
hiatus, 161
historical, 7, 29, 64, 77, 169, 202
  deconstruction, 63
  Reason, 195: totalising theodicy of, 207; violence of, 36, 205

history, 8, 18, 22, 32, 37–8, 41, 43, 58–9,
    61, 76, 95–6, 98, 123, 163, 173,
    176, 187, 189, 199, 201
  Christian theological pattern of, 138
  dunamis of, 28
  eschatological, 93, 94, 97, 198
  Hegelian account of, 172–3
  historico-political, 169–70, 176–7
  messianic event of, 86
  nineteenth-century philosophy of, 34
  order of profane, 74
  pantheistic, 92, 104, 234
  and politics, 179, 180: secret password
    of, 178
  speculative-dialectical philosophy of, 91
  sublime event of, 82, 85
  theological notion of, 90
holding-together, 183, 200
holy, 4, 7, 26, 31, 37, 48, 61, 118, 138
human, 144–6, 154, 186
  freedom, 147, 169, 193, 202–4
  humanity, 163, 203, 206, 225
  intellect, 192
  knowledge, 194
  rights, 179
hylikôs ón, 52
Hypokeimenon, 167–8, 170

Idealism, 101, 103, 132, 140, 215–16,
    219
  contradiction of, 107
  dialectical method of, 99: dialectic, 118,
    123, 140
  Idealist bureaucrats, 101
  Idealist metaphysics, 45, 140
  speculative, 44, 97, 160
identity, 36, 101, 194, 199–200, 202
  principle of, 2, 160, 165, 167, 172
immanence, 6, 75–6, 79,190
immemorial, 103, 134, 166, 170
immortality, 184
infinite, 185–6, 188–9, 241
intellectual intuition, 182, 192, 223, 229,
    234, 241
intelligibility, 103
intensification, 118
interiority, 198
interruption, 26, 59, 106
invisible, 197
irrational, 119, 152

jointure, 241
  hinge and point of, 203

Judeo-Christian thought, 90
Judgement, 55, 121, 137, 160, 168, 174,
    183–4
  language of, 73, 178, 190
  and signification, 198
justice, 17–18, 95, 158, 163–4, 231–4
  eschatological, 93, 96

Kairos-allegory of revelation, 189
kenosis, 4, 6, 15, 32, 34, 36, 49, 60, 85,
    93, 110, 114, 136, 148, 185, 238–9
  kenotic eschatology, 93
Kingdom of God, 95
knowledge, 9, 49, 135–6, 138
  tragic, 239
koinon, 59, 226

language, 10–11, 25, 78, 141, 145, 178,
    180, 221, 237–8
  fantasmatic, 43
  of judgement, 58
  of man, pure naming, 169
  paradisiacal, 170
  promise of, 139
law, 3, 7, 12, 26–7, 37, 46, 55, 59, 80, 82,
    93, 99–101, 103, 109, 114, 116–17,
    120–1, 125–6, 136, 138–40, 149,
    159, 218, 221, 230, 240
  cages of the, 31, 45, 93, 110, 149, 228
  of the earth, 153, 189
  eternal return of the, 111
  and fate, 36, 227
  hegemonic fantasms of the, 68
  and justice, 159
  of Koinon, 2
  lawful, 73, 152
  lawless, 73, 109
  legality, 73
  legitimacy, 23, 30, 38, 73
  manifest law, integrative violence of
    the, 242
  messianic suspension of the, 61
  metaphysical violence of the, 113
  mysticism of, 230–1, 237
  mythic, 60, 67, 73, 114, 117, 134
  of violence, 124, 133, 141, 220
  of the worldly legitimate, 119
life, 54, 68–9, 74, 102, 104, 107, 113–15,
    116–17, 124, 133–4, 148, 152, 159,
    162, 170–1, 180, 184–5, 192–3,
    199–201, 228
light, ideal principle of, 200
lightning flash, 8–9

logos, 27, 215
love, 47, 55, 57–8, 73, 114, 116, 118, 124–5, 147, 164, 175

madness, 124, 218
manifestation, 11, 43, 197–8
materiality, 139
mè ón, 52
mechanical physics, 141
mediation, 16,
    dialectical, 83, 91
melancholy, 146, 177–9, 181
messianic
    fulfilment, 138, 164
    futurity, 80
    instances, 118
    intensity, 97
    justice, 164–5
    Kingdom, 18
    paradox, 98
    promise, 178
    redemption, 137
messianism, 39, 92
metaphysics, 4–5, 7–11, 20, 24–5, 29–30, 34–5, 43, 47–8, 73, 76–7, 85, 105, 135–6, 154, 165, 192, 203, 217, 212
    deconstruction of the, 9
    end of, 132
    epochal closure of, 29, 77
    history of, 41–2
    logos of, 213
    metaphysical, 11, 94, 118, 159: empiricism, 16, 63, 77–8, 79, 81–2; violence, 6, 66, 100, 122, 147
    metaphysician, 152
    onto-theological constitution of, 70
    and politic, 203
Might and Violence, 108
modernity, 3, 15–16, 23, 30–1, 39, 67–8, 73, 77, 92, 126, 134
    discourse of, 82, 90
    epochal, 36, 82: condition of, 1–2, 30, 216; epochal principle of, 17, 72
    eschatological deconstruction of, 28
    hegemonic fantasm of, 100
    hegemonikon of, 3–4, 78, 133
    liberal-humanist pathos of, 30
    modern epoch, 73
    modern state, 18, 203: dialectical account of the, 34
    secularising project of, 62–3
    sovereign referent of, 218

momentarily, 187
    momentary manner, 8
monarchy, 54
    divine, 37
monothetic, 52
morality, 186, 204, 224, 233
    moral effect, 199
    moral law, 17, 191, 225–6
    moral order, 198
    rational law of, 82
mortal, 15, 22, 104, 107, 141, 145, 174, 176–7, 179, 218, 232
    mortality, 3, 13, 20, 36, 45, 48, 148–50, 164, 184, 219, 227, 239–41: of existence, 46; and immortality, 198; and natality, 42
    mortification, 116, 184–5
mourning, 15, 23, 143, 145
movement and event, 171
mysticism, 230
    mystical authority, fantasm of, 79
    mysticism, legitimising authority of, 79
myth, 33
    mythical movement, 80
    mythology, 186
mythic, 16, 61, 133
    auto-poetic, 120
    constitution, 16
    continuity, 186
    continuum, 68, 95
    existence, 186
    foundation, 7, 34, 80, 87, 162
    immanence, 36, 61, 187, 188
    of the law, 100, 124
    law of the eternal return, 117
    law of nature, 82, 186
    process, 79
    violence, 55, 61
    vitality, 112

naming-language, 145
natality and mortality, 2
natural animal, 163
nature, 111, 116, 118, 120–2, 154, 169, 186, 189–90, 198, 203
    attunement of, 146
    blind necessity of, 113
    and history, 15, 187–8
    melancholy of, 23, 201–2
    mystical violence of, 122
necessarily, 10, 66, 79
    progressive, 68

necessary, 75, 77
  ideals of Reason, 17
necessity, 17–18, 26, 44, 95, 105, 226, 234
  and freedom, 42, 231
  mythic law of, 80
  objective, 232: order of, 238
  rational-logical order of, 31
  rational-logical principle of, 36
negative, 192
  negative and positive philosophy, 44, 47
  philosophy, 47, 50–1, 57
  political theology, 110
  power of, 135
Neo-Platonic, 20, 194
  of emanation, 196, 199
  metaphysical discourse, 77
  Neo-Platonic model, 54
  nihilism, 108
nomos, 6, 17, 23, 29, 37–8, 54, 60–1, 68, 83, 85–6, 114–16, 136, 153, 185, 192, 197
  earthly, 138, 188, 190
  of the world, 21
nomothetic, 52. 86
  arché, 54
  and monothetic principle, 63, 68, 198
  tragic, 227
nunc stans, 121

obsession, 111
Occident, 194
Occidental
  eschatology, 61
  history, 5, 52
  metaphysics, 1–3, 5, 9, 14, 19, 24, 35, 38, 63, 195, 202, 212, 214, 241
  ontology, 47, 202
  philosophy, 28
ontological difference, 161
onto-theological, 135, 213
  discourse, 154
  foundation, 84
  metaphysics, 122–3, 213
oúk ón, 52–3
outside, 110, 126

pain and logos, 212
Pantheism, 18, 71, 105, 194–5, 197
  pantheistic-immanent metaphysics, 91
passé, 94, 158
  figure, 33
phenomenon, 5, 185, 189

phenomena, tragic-agonal manifestation of, 226
phenomenal order, 196
phenomenal realm, 188
phenomenality, 1-3, 5, 13, 76, 139, 194, 197: event of, 242; gift of, 242
phenomenology, 2, 3
Philosophy, 8, 20, 32, 58, 64, 81, 199
  investigation, 41
  negative, 41, 45, 47, 52, 85–6, 123: and positive, 11–12, 29, 35, 64
  philosopher, 150, 231
  philo-sophia, 81
  philosophical discourse, 8, 43, 195
  philosophical-intellectual intuition, 184
  polytheism, 186
  religion, 82, 87, 100
  system, 13
  thinking, 105, 136, 138, 211
Phusis, 28–9
positive, 37, 41, 42, 45, 47–8, 51–2, 63, 77, 86, 94, 97–8
  and religion, 38, 184, 198, 207
physics, theory of, 183
Platonism, 49, 105, 183
  Platonic, 21, 49, 51, 60
pleroma, 96
  of *logos*, 213
Pneuma, 21, 30, 111, 115, 196
  eschatological, 196
  pneumatic principle, 115
polemos, raging, 109
polis, 6, 177–8
political, 93–4, 158–9, 162–3, 169, 193–4
  hegemonies, 33, 152
  ontology, 34, 159
  sovereignty, inoperation of, 191
  theological critique of violence, 122
  theology, 39, 61, 110: without hegemony, 109
  topos of the, 163
politico-legal necessity, 104
politico-theological consequence, 106, 110
politics, 28, 159, 163, 179, 198
  and an ethics, 177
  and totalising ethics, 236
possibility, 162–4, 169, 179–80
  eschatological, 201
potency, 110–11, 113–14, 124
potentia, 51

SUBJECT INDEX | 259

potentiality, 3–6, 9, 26–7, 46, 48, 50–2, 54–5, 57–8, 61, 63, 66, 69–72, 75, 77, 111, 161–2, 172, 175–6, 226, 242
power, 27, 46, 73, 140, 163, 200
principium, 215
principles, 102, 201, 205
promise and hope, 206
prótos ón, 52–3
provisionality, eschatological, 61

quantitative, 194
quid sit, 73, 75
quod sit, 73

radical, 103, 163, 173–4, 176, 180
    breaks, 59
    deconstruction, 159
    discontinuity, 58, 60, 168
    disjunction, 20, 107
    evil, 20, 72, 108, 162–5, 169, 173, 178–9, 181, 205–6: actualisation of, 204; actuality of, 22; possibility and actuality of, 195
    exteriority, 29, 43, 72
    finitude, 195
    political theology, 61, 92–3
    transformation, 60–1
rationalism, 78, 80
    rational cognition, 192–3
    rational movement, 68
    rational religion, 82, 85, 100
    rational-ethical necessity, 109
real, 74
realist mythology, 185
Realist philosophy, 140
reality, 74
Reason, 13, 17–19, 23, 28, 31, 33, 35, 61–3, 65–7, 71–2, 74–81, 84, 84–7, 98–100, 103–6, 109, 112, 119, 141, 149, 152, 189
    birth of historical, 95
    dialectical, 101: cunning of, 1; principle of, 139
    ecstatic, 102: and alive, 124; past of, 122
    grounding arché of, 48
    hegemonic fantasm of, 42
    historical, 27, 29, 94
    maximising violence of, 26
    of modernity, historical, 90
    political, 93
    secular historical, 96
redemption, 59, 141, 164, 203

religion, 13–16, 23–4, 33–4, 38, 93, 109, 138–9, 188–90, 193–4, 198–9, 202, 206–7
    eschatological deconstruction of, 23
    eschatological sting of, 68
    future of, 18
    religious, 56, 82, 91, 138, 207
Revelation, 16, 37, 79, 141, 188, 197
    and mythology, 33
    and Reason, 42
rhythm, 95, 237
rights, 91, 159, 163
rotatory movement, 118

sacred, 198
secularisation, 90–1
    project, 73, 90–2
    secular world-history, 84
    secular world-order, 207
self-hood, 180, 199–200
sense and essence, 180
separation, 10, 12, 15, 22, 50, 59, 118, 138, 190, 199–202, 205–6
singularity, 2, 13, 20, 26–7, 48, 55–7, 183–4, 192, 215, 218
    divine, 54
    of existence, 27
    infinite, 76
    and universality, 18
soul, 184
sovereignty, 10, 13–15, 17, 21, 24, 30, 34, 36–9, 42, 51, 54–5, 57, 71–2, 91–2, 104, 109–10, 125–6, 135, 154, 197, 220–1
    destitution of, 12
    earthly, 37, 174
    political theology of, 96
    worldly, 95
space, 74, 196
    spacing, 64, 74, 177
speculative, 168, 212–13, 216–17
    dialectical, 123, 215, 219: Idealism, 38; logic, 64; mediation, 59; ontology, 97
    Idealism, 122
    self-consciousness, 219
spirit, 38, 60, 96, 171, 180
    of dialectics, 87
    eschatology of, 83
    and promise, 206
    spiritual, truly, 150
    spirituality, 63
    violent disease of, 201

subject, 2, 7, 9–10, 17, 25, 39, 64–5, 67–8, 78, 94, 133, 162–3, 173, 184, 219
  metaphysical, 168
  purely rational, 140
  of rights, 163–4
  subjectification, 6
  Subjectum, 167, 170
sublation, 73
subsumption, 183, 185
suppositum, 64, 67
Surrealism, 61
system, 35, 43
systole and diastole, 113

telos, 28, 32, 36, 49, 51–2, 60, 66, 68–70, 72, 75–6, 95–7, 118, 120–1, 205, 234
theodicy, 30
theology
  theological, 92: foundation, 5; mystical foundation, 63; speculative thought, 212
  theologico-political consequences, 62
  theologoumenon, 31
theoretical cognition, violence of, 184
theoretician, 183
theosophical empiricism, 80
time, 121, 123–4
  and eternity, 125, 187
  and event, 59
  futurity, 42, 161, 165
  historical, 27
  temporalising, 26
  temporality, nexus of, 173
tonality, fundamental, 217
totality, 1, 36, 43, 53–4, 57, 72, 170, 174, 176
  hegemonic fantasm of, 76
  totalisation, 73, 76, 158, 184
  totalising: malice, 175; manner, 180; order, 141; system, 140
  totalitarianism, 180–1
tragedy, 213
tragic
  agonal jointure, 241
  agony, 25
  denial, 230
  deployment of the, 216
  fate, 23
  interrupts, 218
  phenomenology, 224
  singularly, 223

speculative thought structure, 218
struggle, 227
transcendence, 30, 47, 54, 58, 63, 96, 98
  and immanence, 188
  infinite, 35
truth, 10, 185, 198

unbedingt, 168
unconsciousness, 107–8, 122
unground, 78, 167, 174
universal, 25, 174
  history, 27
  and the singular, 185
  universality, 206, 238
  world-historical politics, 37, 121, 126
  world-history, 30, 59, 91
un-pre-thinkable, 6, 10–12, 46, 53, 92, 106, 117, 126, 168, 171, 180
  decision, 118
  event, 120

value, 139, 141
  economy of, 136
violence, 6, 9–10, 13, 104, 113, 116, 121, 133, 136, 183–4, 203
  the concept of, 27, 99, 137, 140
  creative, 8–9
  and evil, 195
  and injustice, 32
  the law of, 26
  metaphysical, 66: foundation of, 133
  mythic foundation of, 134
  and power, 54, 101, 236
  state power of, 23
  visible, 197–8
Vorhandenheit, 48

wonder, 49
world, 93, 190
  nomos of, 56, 192
  world-historical, 206: foundation, 38; hegemonic regimes, 10; hegemonies, 31, 33, 76, 139; movement, 32, 59, 64, 84, 92, 96; negotiations, 28; order, 22, 191, 196, 207; politics, 18, 22–3, 32, 36, 38, 76, 87, 93–4, 100, 120–1, 137, 143, 149, 195, 198, 204; powers, 23, 38; process, 125; Reason, 6, 60; regimes, 62; situation, 33; stage, 33; triumph, 32; triumphalism, 207
  world-history, 29, 31, 34, 83
  worlding of the world, 178

world-language, 147
worldlessness and homelessness, 187
worldly: cognition, 80; existence, 197; institutions, violence of the, 204; order, 15, 93; politics, 23; power, 18, 37; sensate life, 197; truth, 15; values, 10; world, 136
world-nihilism, politics of, 93
world-order, 17, 68, 96, 153, 171: legitimising principle of the, 152
world-political manifestation, 198
world-political questions, 194
world politics, 17
world-revolution, 33

Zoë, 159, 162
Zoë and *Bio*
    Aristotelian distinction between, 171
    distinction or indistinction between, 163
Zuhandenheit, 48
Zusammenhang, 167, 172–3
Zusammenhang of forces, 170

EU representative:
Easy Access System Europe
Mustamäe tee 50, 10621 Tallinn, Estonia
Gpsr.requests@easproject.com

www.ingramcontent.com/pod-product-compliance
Lightning Source LLC
Chambersburg PA
CBHW061709300426
44115CB00014B/2621